From Garum to Mole

From Garum to Mole

Sauces and Identity in the Western World

Edited by

ANDREW DONNELLY

BETH M. FORREST

DEIRDRE MURPHY

OXFORD
UNIVERSITY PRESS

OXFORD
UNIVERSITY PRESS

Oxford University Press is a department of the University of Oxford.
It furthers the University's objective of excellence in research, scholarship,
and education by publishing worldwide. Oxford is a registered trade mark of
Oxford University Press in the UK and in certain other countries.

Published in the United States of America by Oxford University Press
198 Madison Avenue, New York, NY 10016, United States of America.

CIP data is on file at the Library of Congress.

ISBN 9780190622091 (hbk)
ISBN 9780190622107 (pbk)

DOI: 10.1093/9780190622138.001.0001

Printed by Marquis Book Printing, Canada

The manufacturer's authorized representative in the EU for product safety is
Oxford University Press España S.A. of Parque Empresarial San Fernando de Henares,
Avenida de Castilla, 2 – 28830 Madrid (www.oup.es/en or product.safety@oup.com).
OUP España S.A. also acts as importer into Spain of products made by the manufacturer.

Andrew dedicates this book to Katie, for everything.

Beth dedicates this book to Edward Angelo DiGiovanni, with whom she shared a deep love of talking about food, cooking, and eating. The dinner table is not the same without him. Also, she dedicates it to Jane and Ludwig "Viggy" James, both of whom always loved the sauce far more than the rest of their food.

Deirdre dedicates this book to Sean, who has been here for so much of this, even if he didn't know it.

Contents

Acknowledgments

WE WOULD LIKE TO thank the authors who contributed to this volume for their patience and persistence throughout this epically long project, one that has endured a global pandemic, the rise and fall of online teaching, a temporary obsession with bread-baking, job changes, and the birth of multiple children.

Thanks most of all to Susan Ferber, our editor at Oxford University Press, for her enthusiasm, expertise, and for her incredible eye for detail. We also appreciate her understanding that sometimes the sauce takes extra time to simmer.

Foreword

MAKING THE LITTLE SHOE

Ana Roš

I DON'T THINK WE can talk about sauce unless we first discuss the Italian *fare la scarpetta*, or the idea that sauce is too precious, too important to be wasted—so much so that one must use a piece of bread to wipe up every last bit of sauce before the meal can be deemed finished. With roots in the reality that food was not to be wasted during a time when food was scarce, *scarpetta* is now one of the highest compliments a chef can receive. This concept does not just stop at the border. It is every bit apparent on Slovenia tables, where you see heaps of fresh cut bread always at the ready and plates smothered in velvety sauce. Our sauces are the product of thoughtful ingredients and usually hours of stewing. They are so full of character and flavor that we often choose to serve our main dishes in bowls instead of plates. This allows us to spoon every delicious bit of sauce into us before we (of course) use a little bit of bread to get the last drop!

I wanted to pay homage to the idea that a main course can be enjoyed with a spoon and a bit of bread instead of a fork and knife. For this, we served a main dish of rabbit smothered in a version of rich Mexican mole with roasted vegetables, local bean salad, and fried herbs.

Slovenian Mole (serves 6)

Ingredients:

10 kg rabbit bones
1 carrot
1 yellow onion
½ kg green celery
200 g whiskey

2 each cinnamon stick
3 each star anise
7 each clove
5 each long pepper
5 each green cardamom
3 each dried red chili pepper
50 g dark unsweetened chocolate

Procedure:

1. Roast the rabbit bones in the oven (200 degrees Celsius) for 18 minutes or until the bones are a deep golden brown.
2. Wash and rough chop the carrots, onions, and celery. Heat a large stock pot until hot. Add a drop of vegetable oil and quickly sauté the vegetables. Add just 6 kg of the roasted rabbit bones straight from the oven and deglaze the pot with the whiskey. Fill the stock pot with enough water to cover the bones.
3. Bring the water to a boil and reduce to simmer for 8 hours, skimming off any scum that floats to the top.
4. Strain the stock.
5. Heat another stock pot and add the remaining 4 kg of rabbit bones, searing until they are warmed through and just start to create a fond at the bottom of the pot.
6. Pour the stock over the roasted rabbit bones and reduce rapidly by half.
7. Strain out the bones and add all the spices, reduce until it has a consistency of a nappe.
8. Strain the spices and whisk in the dark chocolate.

I hope it suits you.

All the best!

Ana Roš is chef and restaurateur of Hiša Franko, 3-star Michelin restaurant in Kobarid, Slovenia. Hiša Franko has been listed as one of the World's Best Restaurants since 2018. Roš, author of *Ana Roš: Sun and Rain*, was named the 2017 World's Best Female Chef and was featured in season two of Netflix's *Chef's Table*.

Contributors

Meredith E. Abarca is Professor of Latino/a Literature and Food Studies at the University of Texas at El Paso. She is author of *Voices in the Kitchen: Views of Food and the World from Working-Class Mexican and Mexican American Women* and co-editor of *Rethinking Chicana/o Literature Through Food* and *Latin@'s Presence in the Food Industry*, and has published articles in *Food and Foodways*; *The Sociological Review*; *Food Pedagogies*; and *The Routledge Companion to Latino/a Literature*. Dr. Abarca sits on the editorial board of *Food, Culture & Society* and was the book review editor of *Food & Foodways*.

Joshua Abrams is the Past President of the Association for Theatre in Higher Education, and was recently Deputy Director Academic at the Hong Kong Academy for Performing Arts and Dean of the Royal Central School of Speech and Drama, University of London. He is the co-editor of the "On Taste" issue of *Performance Research*, and his publications have appeared in a range of books and journals, including *Theatre Topics*, *Performance Research*, *TDR*, *PAJ*, and many others. He is currently the Chief Experience Officer for the award-winning Yardley Brothers Craft Brewery in Hong Kong.

Melitta Weiss Adamson is Professor of German and Comparative Literature at the University of Western Ontario, Canada. She is an expert in medieval cookbooks and dietetics, has published numerous articles on the subject, and is the author of the books *Medieval Dietetics: Food and Drink in 'Regimen Sanitatis' Literature from 800 to 1400*; *Daz buoch von guoter spise (The Book of Good Food): A Study, Edition, and English Translation of the Oldest German Cookbook*; and *Food in Medieval Times*. She is also the editor of two volumes of essays: *Food in the Middle Ages* and *Regional Cuisines of Medieval Europe*, and co-editor with

Francine Segan of the two-volume encyclopedia *Entertaining from Ancient Rome to the Super Bowl*.

Amy Bentley is Professor in the Department of Nutrition and Food Studies at New York University. A historian with interests in the social, historical, and cultural contexts of food, her work focuses on the meanings and uses of food in the twentieth/twenty-first century United States. She is author of the award-winning *Inventing Baby Food: Taste, Health, and the Industrialization of the American Diet* (2014), and co-editor of *Practicing Food Studies* (2024). Current research includes a history of food in US hospitals, the role of flavor in human and planetary health, the cultural contexts of food waste, and an assessment of how historians write about food.

Maureen Costura is Professor of Liberal Arts and Applied Food Studies at the Culinary Institute of America. She has authored "Access to First Choice Foods and Settlement Failure at French Azilum" in *Archaeological Perspectives on the French in the New World* and co-author of "Eating in the Time of the Dead: Farming, Foraging, and Food Insecurity in Zombie Cinema," in *Food in Memory & Imagination: Space, Place, and Taste*. She holds a PhD in Anthropology and was the Excavation Director at French Azilum, Pennsylvania State Historic Site, in Towanda, PA.

Jonathan Deutsch is Professor of Culinary Arts and Food Science at Drexel University. He is co-editor of *Gastropolis: Food and Culture in New York City* and co-author of *Food Studies: An Introduction to Research Methods*; *Culinary Improvisation*; *Jewish American Food Culture*; and *Barbecue: A Global History*, among others. A classically trained chef, Dr. Deutsch also runs the Food Lab at Drexel, where students focus on product development and innovative solutions to solve food issues to promote the health of people, planet, and economies.

Andrew Donnelly is Assistant Professor of History at Texas Tech University. A historian and archaeologist, he has recently published articles on the phenomenology of the Roman meal, Roman and late antique foodways, and the dietary habits of sailors based on evidence from several late antique Mediterranean shipwrecks.

Beth M. Forrest is Professor of Liberal Arts and Applied Food Studies at the Culinary Institute of America. She is co-editor of *Food in Memory & Imagination: Space, Place, and Taste* and of a special issue on chocolate for *Food & Foodways*. She has authored and co-authored several articles that appear in *Routledge International Handbook of Food Studies*; *Global Food History*; and *Food, Culture & Society*. She has also contributed to *Gastronomica* and *The SAGE Encyclopedia of Food Issues*, among others. Dr. Forrest is the former president of the Association for the Study of Food and Society.

Paul Freedman is Chester D. Tripp Professor of History at Yale University. With a background in medieval social history, Dr. Freedman is author of *Out of the East: Spices and the Medieval Imagination*, co-editor of *Food in Time and Place*, and editor of *Food: The History of Taste* (winner of an International Association of Culinary Professionals Book Award). More recently, his books include *Why Food Matters*; *America Cuisine and How it Got this Way*; and *Ten Restaurants That Changed America*. His article, "Women and Restaurants in the Nineteenth-Century United States" in the *Journal of Social History* won the Belasco Prize for Scholarly Articles from the Association for the Study of Food and Society.

India Aurora Mandelkern is a historian and writer. She is the author of *Electric Moons: A Social History of Street Lighting in Los Angeles*, *Wilshire Subway: The Making of the D Line Subway Extension*, and has contributed to many publications. She occasionally moonlights as a sommelier and is writing a book about wine.

Deirdre Murphy is a Professor of Liberal Arts and Applied Food Studies at the Culinary Institute of America. Her work has appeared in *Working-Class Notes*; *XCP: A Journal of Cross-Cultural Poetics*; *Literature Resource Center*; *Perspectives on History*; *Common-Place: A Common Place, an Uncommon Voice;* and *Transformations: The Journal of Inclusive Scholarship and Pedagogy*, for which she has also served as a guest editor. She has also co-authored "Food and the Senses" for the *Routledge International Handbook of Food Studies*.

Fabio Parasecoli is Professor of Food Studies at New York University. He is author of *Al Dente: A History of Food in Italy*; *Knowing Where It Comes From: Labeling Traditional Foods to Compete in a Global Market*; *Food*; and *Gastronativism: Food, Identity, Politics,* in addition to several articles and book chapters. He is also co-author of *The Pierogi Problem: Cosmopolitan Appetites and the Reinvention of Polish Food* and co-editor of the six-volume *Cultural History of Food*.

Jeffrey M. Pilcher is Professor of Food Studies in the Department of Physical and Environmental Sciences at the University of Toronto, Scarborough. He is author of *Hopped Up: How Travel, Trade, and Taste Made Beer a Global Commodity*; *Planet Taco: A Global History of Mexican Food*; *¡Que vivan los tamales! Food and the Making of Mexican Identity*; *Food in World History*; and *The Sausage Rebellion: Public Health, Private Enterprise, and Meat in Mexico City*. He edited the *Oxford Handbook of Food History* and the four-volume anthology *Food History: Critical and Primary Sources*. He is also founding editor of the journal *Global Food History*.

Emmanuelle Raga, PhD, is currently a chef and sommelier in the South of France. She is a former scientific collaborator at the Université Libre de Bruxelles. Her publications include "Romans and Barbarians at the Table: Banquets and Food as Tools of Distinction according to Sidonius Apollinaris (Fifth-Century Gaul)" in *Inclusion and Exclusion in Mediterranean Christianities, 400–800* and "The Impact of Christian Ideology on the Notions of Diet, Nutrition and Health" in *The Routledge Handbook of Diet and Nutrition in the Roman World*. She has also served as secretary of the IEHCA journal *Food and History*.

Lyra Spang, PhD, is an anthropologist and owner of Taste Belize Tours, a culinary and cultural tour company based in Placencia Village, Belize. She is author of *Bite Yu Finga! Innovating Belizean Culture*; "The Corn-Coconut Divide: Taste and the Cultural Politics of Gastronationalism in Belize" in *The Cultural Politics of Food, Taste, and Identity: A Global Perspective*; "Paradise on a Bun" in the *Indiana Food Review*; "Fruits and Culture: A Preliminary Examination of Food-for-Sex Metaphors in English-Language Caribbean Music" in *Folklore Forum*; and "Chasing the Mango: Food as Sexual Metaphor in Belizean Pop Culture" in *Appetite*. She was a recipient of an Institute for International Education Research Award (Fulbright Hayes) and can husk a coconut in twenty seconds.

Joey Williams is Senior Lecturer of Classics and Letters and the Associate Director of the Center for Mediterranean Archaeology and History at the University of Oklahoma. He directs archaeological projects in Portugal and Italy with research focusing on colonial landscapes,

Roman material culture, and the communication of power. His publications include "Amphorae at the Origins of Lusitania: Transport Pottery from Western Hispania Ulterior in Alto Alentejo" in *Lusitanian Amphorae: Production and Distribution* and *The Archaelology of Roman Surveillance in the Central Alentejo, Portugal.*

Introduction

WHAT IS SAUCE? "IT IS SAUCE"

Andrew Donnelly, Beth M. Forrest, and Deirdre Murphy

IN 2014, ON a trip to Ljubljana, Slovenia, Beth (one of the editors) was having dinner at a restaurant that specialized in seafood. The menu featured a large selection of Adriatic fish and crustaceans to which one could add, for an additional €0.50, a side of "sauce." When she asked her waiter what the "sauce" was, he simply responded, "It is sauce." He then went back to work, confident that he had answered the question. "Oh, of course," she would love to have replied, "sauce. Right. How silly of me. . . ." But, as it quickly became apparent, the lack of explanation or description was not the problem. Rather, a deeper lack of familiarity with the regional cuisine was. She had to go ahead and order the enigmatic sauce, if for no other reason than to figure out what it was. As she would soon discover, it was a simple combination of olive oil, parsley, and garlic. She later learned that this was frequently called *tržaška omaka*, or "sauce of the Trieste region," named after a city less than sixty miles away.

When Beth returned to Slovenia the following year, she found herself reading the same nondescript offering of "sauce" on yet another menu, this time in the seaside town of Piran. After finding out it was the exact same mixture of ingredients, she mentioned to the waiter at this restaurant that, in broader circles, this item was referred to as "Trieste sauce." She asked if he knew whether anyone there ever called it that. His response was succinct and revealing: "but it is our sauce, so why would we call it anything more than 'sauce'?"

Each waiter felt this sauce was *their* sauce. But how can this one sauce, made from the exact same ingredients, be both ubiquitous yet so connected to each server's local identity? There are few cuisines around the world from which sauce is absent. And yet, its widespread and varied presence across time, place, and repast is not always formally defined, as these meals and conversations with the people who served them attest. Sauces are not staples.

They are neither filling, sturdy carbohydrates, nor are they critical proteins. They are not crucial to one's survival. Nor, despite the casual intimacy with which they might go un-named or only vaguely named, are they only half-considered or barely recognized add-ons to even the most anemic side salad. Sauces are intrinsic to the meals with which they are served and intimately tied to the culture from which they come. The popularity and ubiquity of Trieste sauce—named after a city in Italy, not Slovenia—serves as a reminder of empires long fallen and traditions and foodways far older than present-day lines on a map. Sauces define regions and communities by their taste and ingredients and serve as markers of local identities, national congruence, and diasporic cultures.

This Slovenian-inspired curiosity about how sauces have shaped meals and, in turn, identities led to this book. The experiences in Ljubljana and Piran are mirrored in countless others: Chicagoans' love of mustard on hot dogs (but never ketchup!); the British fondness for HP Sauce on a bacon butty; the hot and chili sauces increasingly present on the tables of friends who might be seen as "thrill seekers."[1] The chapters in this collection—addressing sauces as varied as mole, sriracha, and Roman garum—each explore the relationship between sauces and the cultures who made and ate them, and how these liquids helped shape the identities of their manufacturers and consumers. Sauces, via their consumption and rejection, create bonds between peoples, as well as ways of distinguishing outsiders. They are a vehicle for understanding a very specific sort of identity, one based on the community built by people who season their foods similarly and use these sauces to provide flavor and moisture to food, and to evoke emotions by those who eat them and those who reject them.

Sauce has been a critical part of several important works on food and identity, although it was not always the primary foodstuff examined. One of the earliest publications to turn to sauce is Elizabeth and Paul Rozin's article "Culinary Themes and Variations" (1981), which identified flavor principles, or "the distinctive seasoning combinations which characterize many cuisines."[2] The practice of seasoning food with a recurring, predictable combination of flavors (which includes olive oil, lemon, and oregano in Greece and chili-based sauces in Mexico) removes the fear of the unfamiliar or unknown and provides pleasure through the familiar that is also "associated with satiety and the appropriate social context," which, in turn, is repeated over generations.[3] They also note that contemporary understanding of the term "curry" was inextricably bound to an understanding of sauced foods.

In that same decade, anthropologist Paul Stoller and sociologist Cheryl Olkes's experience while doing fieldwork among the Songhay people in the Tillabéri region of Niger revealed that sauce—including a memorable experience with *fukko hoy*, which was made from a local plant—communicates wealth, status, aesthetics, and emotions.[4] Sociologist Stephen Mennell expanded on the study of relationship between sauce and identity in *All Manners of Food: Eating and Taste in England and France from the Middle Ages to the Present*.[5] Mennell noted that English and French aristocratic cuisines, quite similar during the Middle Ages, developed in diverse directions in the sixteenth to eighteenth centuries. These divergences, which stemmed from different religious and political institutions in both countries, impacted foodways across the globe and elevated the importance of food—including the liberal use of sauces in France and the outright rejection of sauce in England—in defining aristocracy and social classes in general. Our book seeks to continue this conversation by offering fifteen case studies that focus on sauce and identity collectively.

To begin with, what do we mean by "sauce"? Our approach is ecumenical. Here the less traditional—ketchup and olive oil—sit along with standard staples, such as tomato sauces and ragout. Defining the term "sauce" is a harder task than it might at first seem. As Gary Allen notes in his 2019 volume *Sauces Reconsidered*, "Everyone knows the answer, right? It's that fluid substance we pour onto our food to make it taste better."[6] But, as Allen agrees, this is not enough of an answer. One person's definition of what that fluid substance is might differ from another's. And this, in turn, might differ from the definition of someone living a continent away or who lived a millennium ago. Cultural definitions of sauce matter just as much as physical properties. In this we seek to move—as the author of the final chapter of this book, Jonathan Deutch, encourages us—away from a classical French understanding of sauces, which are often associated with Georges Auguste Escoffier, whose cooking and writing at the turn of the twentieth century revolutionized restaurants and food culture.[7]

This focus on Escoffier and others, such as Marie-Antoine Carême, has had a significant impact. Though sauces, as you will read here, significantly predate Escoffier, his tremendous influence on the cooking world means that when one thinks of sauces, one often thinks not only of French sauces but also that a liquid *is* a sauce based on how closely it hews to the examples he popularized. But there are competing views on how one should view sauce, even from Escoffier's own era. Consider, for example, pioneering scientist

J. L. W. Thudichum, who in his 1895 book *Cookery, Its Art and Practice*, described sauce in the following manner:

> Solid varieties of food, soluble only by digestion, are not rarely dry in substance, or unattractive in taste, or insufficiently or too strongly flavoured. To make such dry food moister, to lubricate it and thus aid in its use, to increase the attractiveness of the taste by additions of flavours and juxtaposition of contrast, to hide or mask excessive flavours, certain liquid additions have been invented which pass by the name of sauces.[8]

Here something else is focused on, namely physical properties. Sauces here are liquids first and foremost. But they also are thought to improve food, adding a new and varied sensory experience to a meal. Thudichum, known for his work in biochemistry, may be an obscure source to use in a volume on food. But his scientific description of sauces has been important in shaping our own thoughts on defining the term.

One of the most recent and best books on sauce, Maryann Tebben's *Sauces: A Global History*, offers a broad, thematically organized account of the topic, beginning with the historical origins of sauce and then turning to condiment sauces, French sauces, gravies (for meat and pasta), "odd" sauces, and sauces that vary according to nationality. In Tebben's view, sauces do not depend on specific ingredients, though they must have more than one. Rather, sauces have core attributes: namely, they are liquids, are applied to a dish to enhance its flavor, are refined preparations (and not raw materials), and are complementary.[9] Thus "elemental ingredients," such as "syrups, spice pastes, oils, vinegar and even salt," are not sauces to Tebben.[10]

In a work on identity across a vast geographic landscape and chronology, a definition that focuses solely on specific physical properties is not sufficient, as it might ignore what some cultures have identified as sauces—thus, this book's inclusive approach. As Allen notes, a problem with creating a taxonomy of sauce is that a specific definition of what constitutes a sauce can easily leave out things that are, to some, sauces.[11] Consider, for example, foams. Would a foam served at Alinea in Chicago or El Bulli have been considered a sauce to someone like Escoffier or Carême, the nineteenth-century French chef whose work helped define the *haute cuisine* that gave us so many of our sauces? What about salt? Few now would consider salt to be a sauce, but to read the *Deipnosophistae* ("The Dinner Philosophers"), the late second/early third-century CE work by the Greek writer Athenaeus, is to see salt referred to with a word that can mean, alternatively, relish, tidbits, and, indeed, sauce. What about ketchup? Is it a sauce? Or a condiment? Is a condiment a sauce? We see the words as synonymous, following the lead of Andrew Smith, who uses them interchangeably in *Pure Ketchup: A History of America's National Condiment*.[12] After all, Australians call ketchup "tomato sauce." But what about a single ingredient? Can a single ingredient, such as maple syrup, be considered a sauce? Tebben argues that a sauce must be composed of multiple ingredients and would thus exclude it. But if this single ingredient is used as a sauce, to us, it is a sauce.

Context, as is so often the case, is everything. We believe that recognition of the familiarly understood methods of creation, consumption, and perception of sauce within a culture is as, or perhaps more, important than classifying all that sauce's acceptable physical characteristics. We agree with Thudichum here, choosing to examine liquids that add flavor and contrasting texture to food. This liquid nature is part of our definition: sauces here are liquids that are manipulated or processed and added to food and do not lose their identity once added. Indeed, in many cases, they are what give identity to the dish itself. Thus, there are chapters on mole, béchamel, sauce Ti-Malice, and Italian tomato-based sauces. We have also deliberately included foods less traditionally seen as sauces, such as maple syrup, olive oil, and even human sweat. Sauces, as Emmanuelle Raga reminds us in this volume, are liquids—from salsa to ragout to fish paste—that produced an emotional experience for the consumers who added them to their food and were understood as sauces by the people who ate them. These emotions include pleasure, fear, and disgust. This emotional experience imparts an identity to the food being prepared. It also helps define the identity of the consumer. What is essential is that the liquids were, to the people who used them, most definitely sauces, whether or not that definition still holds in modern kitchens or modern imaginations. As one of our authors reminds us, a simple drop of oil, within a particular set of circumstances, counted as a sauce for early monks in the remote Egyptian desert.

There is significant thematic overlap across our chapters, both in terms of how sauces were defined by cultures and also how they were used. Sauce was a tangible representation of moral reckoning on the tables of early Christian monks in Egypt, for members of the back-to-the-land movement in the 1970s in the United States, and to Europeans in seventeenth-century Saint-Domingue, the latter of whom tied morality—specifically corruption—to the sauces of the colonized. The relationship between tradition and exploring new frontiers in sauce-making is explored in chapters on French cuisine and modern cooking pedagogy. Chapters on sriracha and ancient Roman garum allow for analysis of the importance of containers used for the storage and transportation of sauce and the relationship between specific containers, the display of those containers, and the status that such a display awards the user. Though the peoples in this book are separated by vast chronological and geographic gulfs, these chapters together indicate how sauces are central to the formation, display, and maintenance of their identities.

Families, ethnic groups, and political identities in Europe and North and Central America are central in this volume, in part a function of our expertise. This grouping also allows for cultural commonalities to be discussed more cohesively than a broader, pan-global volume might. Though Asia, Africa, and South America can all be found here, they are on the periphery of our investigation. They deserve books produced by scholars who specialize in those areas. Indeed, the history of sauces and identities can fill several volumes.

This volume is divided into four parts, each of which concentrates on an aspect of sauce and identity. Part One is broadest in scope, with chapters that look at the history of sauce across large time periods and make arguments relating to periodization and the changing understanding of the norms of sauces. French sauces feature prominently. Though this prominence is challenged in later chapters, they must be part of any conversation about the development of sauces in Europe and beyond. Melitta Weiss Adamson in Chapter 1 provides the historical foundation with a sweeping overview of European sauces and their ingredients. Adamson moves from the Roman text of Apicius in roughly the first or second century CE through the later Middle Ages. Her chapter draws out the complex relationship between food for pleasure's sake and medical advice on what is best for the body. In this wide-reaching chapter, Adamson challenges the long-held idea that food that was perceived as healthy also must be bland, tasteless fare. Instead, by focusing on the sauces in which foods were served, she identifies a strong connection between the medicinal value of food and its tastiness.

Paul Freedman builds upon this in Chapter 2 in his discussion of a revolution of "taste" in the French canon of sauces. In the medieval period, the sauce provided the actual flavor of a dish, while the protein portion of a meal was a passive medium. This would change in the seventeenth century, when a preference for simplistic flavors eclipsed highly complicated sauces produced by an amalgamation of flavors. Freedman extends this analysis through the moral aesthetics of the Enlightenment, and then moves on to the development of "restaurants," the aesthetics of Carême, and the *nouvelle cuisine* of the 1960s, which—again—rejected earlier sauces in favor of lighter fare, though this time inspired by Asian cuisine. Freedman ends by examining the ambiguous state of French sauces in light of the chemist Hervé This's work with molecular gastronomy.

Part Two of this book considers the relationship between sauces and the self, with chapters that show how sauces have played roles in defining or reflecting aspects of identity of the cultures that used them. Joey Williams discusses the production and use of Roman garum, or fish sauce, in Chapter 3. He links the production of garum at the Iberian site of Troia to the manufacture of a particular type of ceramic transport vessel, called an amphora, from the nearby area of Lusitania. These amphoras (and, thus, garum) appeared in the inland Alantejo region of Portugal in the first century BCE, which was a neighbor of Rome but not yet under its rule. This area is dry, with few rivers to transport goods, making the purchase of garum (in amphoras) a particularly conspicuous form of consumption. That garum could have been transported in other containers that were easier to manage suggests that garum amphoras had value in and of themselves, and indicates either an arrival of new people longing for food from home, or that the local population felt that the visible consumption of Roman-style foods added a certain tangible status in their own domain.

Chapter 4, by Emmanuelle Raga, was of fundamental importance for establishing our definition of sauce. It, too, examines status and sauce, specifically the connection between sauces, pleasure, and self-denial at the end of the Roman Empire under the growing influence of Christianity. Raga notes that many of the elites who embraced Christianity had to reconcile their affluent and sumptuous dietary habits with the ascetic impulses of this new religion. Sauce played an important role in the communal, convivial meals that were a requirement of both monastic and Roman aristocratic identity, but to very different ends. To certain members of the Christian community, sauces were seen as sensual, decadent, and linked to worldly delights. They were, thus, to be situationally rejected. This created tension for certain aristocrats for whom communal meals reinforced power, as well as for hungry members of monastic communities.

Fabio Parasecoli, in Chapter 5, focuses on sauces and nation-building via the businessman and writer Pellegrino Artusi, who played a pivotal role in the development of a nascent Italian cuisine at the end of the nineteenth century. Artusi's 1891 cookbook, *Science in the Kitchen and the Art of Eating Well*, featured many sauces, including tomato-based ones, and their semantics reflected the diversity and fragmentation of Italian traditions. By creating a canon of sauces, Artusi helped unite the bourgeoisie and promote the very existence of the new Italian nation-state, one that created a common culture based on a shared cuisine.

The desire to use sauce to create community is examined on a more local level in Chapter 6 by Deirdre Murphy, who writes on the connection between maple syrup and the back-to-the-land movement in the 1970s of the United States. Industrial syrup, sickly-sweet and made in factories, came to represent the corruption of cities and the vacuity of consumerism that back-to-the-landers rejected. The often laborious, time-intensive processes of tapping maple trees and making real maple syrup from their sap were activities that reflected the aspirations of those in the movement to create a new and more "purely" lived existence for themselves. As they defined it, this was one free from the pollutions and false promises of mainstream society, and rooted in a communion with nature. Murphy shows how making and consuming their own small-batch, uncorrupted maple syrup came to stand as an emblem for all that they dreamed of accomplishing: lives defined by the rhythms of nature in which working hard and independently could bring the reward of sweet pleasure at the table.

Lyra Spang opens Chapter 7, "*Bixa orellana* in Belize: Flavoring Postcolonial Cuisine," by connecting nation-making and the creation of a unique national sauce. Post-colonial Belizean history has been deeply marked by the intertwining of a range of Central American and Caribbean cultures. Sauce became a unifying force for the evolution of a particularly Belizean cuisine. The author focuses on sauces that take as their central ingredient *Bixa orellana*, or annatto, which is native to Central America. *Bixa orellana*'s ubiquity in Belizean sauces reveals the development and characteristics of national identity from the colonial era up to the present.

The complex factors that led to the rise and growing popularity of sriracha are examined by Joshua Abrams in Chapter 8, the final chapter of this section. Abrams considers not just the flavor of this sauce, but other elements of its aesthetic appeal, including its distinctive bottle and creative packaging. Reasons for the growth of this sauce include the personal experiences of the Huy Fong version and its creator David Tran; the perception of Asian food and identity and the United States; the arrival of this semi-imagined Asian foodstuff into the melting pot of southern California at a very specific time; and its championing by food critic and writer Jonathan Gold and a local foodie movement that gradually expanded to the rest of the United States. Abrams concludes by analyzing the recent challenges that Tran's sauce company has experienced in its transition from being a modish and new product to an established brand.

Part Three focuses on how certain cultures have used foodways, specifically sauces, to define and represent the characteristics of an "other." In Chapter 9, India Mandelkern investigates the appearance of ragout in seventeenth-century England. She argues that the "rhetoric surrounding ragouts animated deep-seated questions about . . . the human sense of taste, and its impact on the body and social relations. . . . Understood as a thick, rich, highly seasoned sauce . . . and imported from abroad, ragouts raised latent anxieties about appetite and desire." Mandelkern relies on a range of sources, from medical texts to satires, to draw attention to the many ways in which English authors interpreted the use of French ragouts in English society. These sauces, according to these authors, not only made the English lose their ability to taste, but also made them lose their ability to reason. In the end, ragout became the symbol for all things foreign, decadent, and corrupting.

In Chapter 10, Maureen Costura uses sauce to examine another example of food as corrupting force, this time in the complex racial structures present on the island of Saint Domingue (now Haiti) in the late eighteenth century. Europeans who arrived here were exposed to a variety of foods made from chili peppers, including a number of vinegar-based sauces. These foods were seen as one of many causes of "colonial degeneracy," or the devolution in status as well as racial and cultural purity that Europeans believed would occur as a result of their exposure to a variety of indigenous influences.

In Chapter 11, on nineteenth-century Spain, Beth Forrest also examines the relationship between sauce and cultural decay, specifically by investigating the language used by English and American travelers to describe olive oil and olive-oil based dishes. While Spanish olives were prized in this period, almost all discussions by outsiders of Spain's olive oil focused on its foul taste and rancidity. Charges of rancidity, Forrest notes, were part of a broader critique of a European power that had recently lost its empire. In this context, the perception of rancidity was interpreted as a metaphor for the decay of Spanish morality and work ethic, proof not only of the decline of the empire but also why it happened.

Chapter 12, the last chapter in Part Three, by Amy Bentley, investigates the political controversies of ketchup in the modern United States. Bentley introduces readers to the rise of ketchup as "the United States' most ubiquitous condiment" throughout the twentieth century and explains how it came to be firmly and popularly associated with American cuisine. She then turns to the role of this sauce in the "Ketchup as a Vegetable" political debate of 1981, where school lunchrooms became battlegrounds where disagreements over federal spending were fought and the foods served, including sauces, were used to define political opponents in the early years of the Reagan administration.

Part Four features chapters that offer new parameters for researching, teaching, and making sauces. Meredith Abarca, in Chapter 13, draws on Barbadian writer Austin Clarke's 1999 culinary memoir, *Pig Tails 'n' Breadfruit*, to examine the profoundly physical and sensual side of sauce-making. To Clarke, the very physicality of sauce-making transmits and preserves individual, family, and collective memories in Barbadian culture. The chef's body is an essential and intimate part of the process, to the extent that the very salt he or she produces becomes one of the intrinsic components of the sauce. For Abarca, this physicality links cultural culinary genealogies, so that "contemporary cooks are united with the original inventors" of any given dish. Ultimately, for Abarca, sauce "bridges historical lineage through both preparation and consumption."

In Chapter 14, Jeffrey Pilcher also looks at historical lineage, here employing digital methods of network analysis to outline a taste profile of mole. He argues that flavor profiles of this complex sauce must be understood as they relate to Mexican political and cultural history. He sees three historic interpretations of mole: late colonial, Porfirian, and contemporary. By contextualizing the nature of mole, Pilcher suggests that it changed in response to outside cultural and political pressures. Charting recipes, or "distant[ly] reading" them, he argues, allows the scholar to better understand the contours of historical change through its literature.

Jonathan Deutsch, in Chapter 15, concludes this book with an assessment of how sauces are taught at culinary schools in the United States. Deutsch's chapter is both a warning and a corrective. He identifies and then cautions against a dogmatic adherence to classical training of sauces in contemporary culinary education, which he finds in the excessive celebration of and adherence to Georges Auguste Escoffier's work, particularly his towering *Le Guide culinaire*. Moreover, Deutsch finds that even Escoffier's categorization of sauces, though appearing to be elegantly structured, is far from precise. As such, Deutsch advocates for a more practical, experiential, and inclusive approach to teaching in secondary and post-secondary culinary programs, one that evolves alongside restaurant kitchens and guests.

Each chapter contains a story or stories about the diverse ways in which sauces can be used to understand the people who made and consumed them.

Sauces bear and meld complex flavors and are a hallmark of the identities of those who create and consume meals. They give pleasure to the consumer. As all the contributors demonstrate, sauce and sauce-making are intrinsically, sensually, and often pleasurably attached to identity and culture. Consequently, sauces both define food and contain stories. In keeping with this awareness, we have included recipes for many of the sauces discussed in this volume at the conclusion of each chapter. If we have learned anything, it is that saucing the meals we serve can be a profound way of engaging with others. These recipes then, are an invitation to engage with the ideas presented here—and also, we hope, to eat well.

Tržaška omaka or "Trieste Sauce"
Recipe by Beth Forrest, 2023

Ingredients:

½ cup chopped parsley
2–4 garlic cloves, minced
¼ tsp salt
Good quality olive oil

Method:
Mix the parsley, garlic, and salt in a small bowl. Add enough oil to smother the mixture. Serve with grilled fish, seafood, or vegetables, along with fresh lemon wedges.

Notes

1. Paul Rozin, Lori Ebert, and Jonathan Schull, "Some Like it Hot: A Temporal Analysis of Hedonic Responses to Chili Pepper," *Appetite* 3 (1982): 13–22.
2. Elizabeth Rozin and Paul Rozin, "Culinary Themes and Variations," *Natural History* 90 (1981), 6.
3. Ibid., 11.
4. Paul Stoller, *The Taste of Ethnographic Things: The Senses in Anthropology* (Philadelphia: University of Pennsylvania Press, 1989).
5. Stephen Mennell, *All Manners of Food: Eating and Taste in England and France from the Middle Ages to the Present*, 2nd ed. (Urbana-Champaign: University of Illinois Press, 1996).
6. Gary Allen, *Sauces Reconsidered: Après Escoffier* (Lanham, MD: Rowman & Littlefield, 2019) 1.
7. Georges Auguste Escoffier, *Le Guide culinaire* (New York: John Wiley and Sons, [1903] 2011).

8. John Louis William Thudichum, *Cookery, Its Art and Practice: The History, Science and Practical Import of the Art of Cookery, with a Dictionary of Culinary Terms* (London: Frederick Warne & Co., 1895), 223–224.
9. Maryann Tebben, *Sauces: A Global History* (London: Reaktion Books 2014), 13.
10. Ibid.
11. Allen, *Sauces Reconsidered*, 2.
12. Andrew Smith, *Pure Ketchup: A History of America's National Condiment with Recipes* (Columbia: University of South Carolina Press, 2011).

Selected Bibliography

Allen, Gary. *Sauces Reconsidered: Après Escoffier*. Lanham, MD: Rowman & Littlefield, 2019.

Rozin, Elizabeth, and Paul Rozin. "Culinary Themes and Variations." *Natural History* 90 (1981): 6–14.

Tebben, Maryann. *Sauces: A Global History*. London: Reaktion Books, 2014.

Andrew Donnelly, Beth M. Forrest, and Deirdre Murphy, *Introduction: What is Sauce? "It is Sauce"* In: *From Garum to Mole: Sauces and Identity in the Western World*. Edited by: Andrew Donnelly, Beth M. Forrest, and Deirdre Murphy, Oxford University Press. © Oxford University Press 2026. DOI: 10.1093/9780190622138.001.0001

PART ONE

Histories of Sauce

1

Sauces and Condiments in the Middle Ages

Melitta Weiss Adamson

WHEN THE FIRST medieval cookbook manuscripts appeared in Europe around 1300 CE, sauces and condiments were already an integral part of the recipe collections. Far from being an invention of the late Middle Ages, sauces had by then enjoyed a long tradition in European cookery. That no cookbooks have come down to us from much of the Middle Ages does not mean that recipes were not recorded. It was the medical community that took an early interest in food in general, and sauces in particular. Physicians identified a handful of standard sauces thought to be beneficial as appetite stimulants or aids to digestion and included them in medical manuscripts as early as the twelfth century. One physician, Magninus Mediolanensis, later even wrote a detailed sauce-book in which he discussed a variety of foods and their appropriate sauces from a medical perspective. Given this close connection between food and medicine, medieval physicians played a central role not only in the early transmission of culinary recipes but also in the genesis of the late-medieval cookbook. By the end of the Middle Ages, with the genre fully established, the number of standard sauces had been substantially augmented with ever more elaborate creations. The resulting plethora of sweet-sour sauces had much in common with the Roman tradition of sauce-making and signaled the emergence of a new gourmand culture and the ultimate separation of medicine and cookery in early modern Europe.

From Fine Dining in Imperial Rome to Healthy Nutrition in Merovingian Gaul

A look at ancient sources shows that Europe's love affair with sauces and condiments goes back thousands of years. Complex sauces with a myriad of strong seasonings were the hallmark of Greco-Roman cuisine, so much so that at the very beginning of Greek culinary writing, in the fourth century BCE, Archestratus was already criticizing this habit, advocating instead for natural flavors with minimal seasoning.[1] But the trend continued, as the recipes in *De re coquinaria* (The Art of Cooking), the only extant cookbook of the ancient world, illustrate. This book was attributed to the gourmand Apicius, who was also credited with a book on sauces, aptly titled *De condituris*.[2] The majority of the over 450 recipes in *De re coquinaria* are for sauces. Dozens of seasonings and spices were used and mixed with a variety of fruits and liquids, including dates, honey, wine, olive oil, and the fermented fish sauce known as *garum* or *liquamen*, and thickened with starch, eggs, crumbled bread, or dough.[3] Such sweet-sour sauces accompanied meat, fish, and seafood, but also vegetables and on occasion mushrooms, eggs, or cheese.

In the Apicius cookbook, gourmandise clearly wins out over any considerations of health and well-being.[4] Although *De re coquinaria* was copied in parchment codices, presumably in Tours and Fulda, in the ninth century, and excerpts of it by Vinidarius in the eighth century, it took until the end of the thirteenth century for the first medieval European cookbooks to appear.[5] One of the oldest texts containing culinary recipes was *De observatione ciborum* (On the Observance of Foods), a dietetic letter written in the early sixth century by Byzantine physician Anthimus for Theuderic, king of the Franks.[6] The letter begins with general guidelines on nutrition, ranging from the effects of food on the body and the amount and proportion of food and drink to the preparation and variety of food. Anthimus invokes the Ancients in his call for moderation, and he strongly recommends cooking food. He then discusses individual foodstuffs in this order: bread, meat, eggs, mushrooms, fish, vegetables, legumes, milk, butter, cheese, wheat flour, and fruit, with a brief section on beer, mead, vermouth, and *ptisanes* (a beverage made from barley soaked in water), inserted into the meat section.[7] The recipes Anthimus provides are mainly for meat dishes, vegetables, and legumes.

Garum, or *liquamen*, the dominant condiment in Greco-Roman cookery, is almost completely missing from the dishes, despite dating not long after the fall of Rome.[8] *Liquamen* is only mentioned once negatively, in the recommendation that pure salt, and not *liquamen*, be used to dip pork in, and *garum* also only once, in diluted form.[9] One reason for the absence of the fish sauce may be the fact that Anthimus apparently tried to tailor his dietetic advice to the food customs of the Franks, as evidenced in his discussion of the Frankish love for bacon.[10] Sauces are not discussed separately by Anthimus. Vegetables and legumes are usually prepared with salt and oil, to which water, wine, vinegar, and occasionally coriander, mint, or Syrian sumac are added.

Anthimus uses the term *iuscellum* for the broths in which the various meat dishes are to be prepared and for which he provides recipes.[11] The most elaborate of these is for beef. The meat is cooked in water and vinegar, then leek, pennyroyal, celery, or fennel are added, followed by honey and the mixture of ground pepper, costmary, spikenard, cloves, and where available honey, must (unfermented grape juice), or reduced sweet wine. For young hare he recommends a sweet broth with pepper, a small amount of cloves, ginger, costmary, and the stem or leaf of spikenard. Peacock should be prepared in a honey and pepper broth.

The Earliest Collections of Sauce Recipes in Medieval Europe

In its dietetic advice, if not in its recipes, the letter by Anthimus is rooted in Greco-Roman medicine. It does not bear the stamp of the Arab reception of ancient medicine, as do the writings initially disseminated throughout Europe via the medical school of Salerno, be it the medical works translated by Constantinus Africanus, known as the *Corpus Constantinum*, or the European books of simple and compound drugs and the regimens of health the *Corpus* inspired. One of the early works originating in Salerno, the oldest medical school in medieval Europe, was the *Circa instans*, a drug manual that contains a number of references to sauces and actual sauce recipes. A search of the new edition and translation of the *Circa instans* by Konrad Goehl yields a number of references to sauces referred to as *salsa* or *salsamentum*: under garlic, cinnamon, cumin, caraway, mint, parsley, sage, and zedoary. Under vinegar is found a *salsamentum dicitur Pictaviensium* (A Sauce from Poitou) whose ingredients are sage, parsley, pepper, mint, and vinegar.[12] A recently discovered collection of sauce recipes similar to the recipes in the *Circa instans* was recorded within a parchment codex in Durham, England, at approximately the same time, between 1150 and 1175. Inserted in a list of medical recipes is a section entitled *Incipiunt diuersa genera pictauensium salsamentorum* (Here begin various types of Poitou sauces).[13] What follows are ten recipes for sauces and condiments to accompany meat, fish, and fowl, two general guidelines on seasoning, and a recipe for a ginger confection. The first sauce is for sausage, whose list of ingredients—parsley, sage, vinegar, pepper, and garlic—is reminiscent of the Poitou sauce in the *Circa instans*. Pepper, garlic, and vinegar are the basis for most of the sauces, to which one or two other seasonings, such as parsley, coriander, or sage, may be added. Only the recipe for ram is more elaborate. With ten ingredients it is comparable to the complex sauce recipes in Apicius.

The long-held view that dietetic recipes eventually became culinary recipes has recently been challenged by the French food historian Bruno Laurioux. According to him, culinary recipes were incorporated into medical texts in the Middle Ages and their dietetic qualities subsequently added.[14] Examining the context in which the sauces in the *Circa instans* are mentioned, it is usually to stimulate appetite or aid digestion. This has been argued as also the case for the Durham recipes. Poitou was famous for its gastronomy, in particular its sauces, which, according to this theory, were medical because they were gastronomical—in other words, tasty.[15] Not surprisingly, a Poitou sauce called *la poitevine* also found its way into all extant manuscripts of the famous French cookbook of the Middle Ages, *Le Viandier* (The Provisioner) by Taillevent,[16] including the earliest known version from Valais, Switzerland, which predates the birth of Taillevent by a decade. The sauce is more elaborate than the Durham version, calling for ginger, cloves, grains of paradise, burnt toast, roasted chicken liver, verjuice or wine and verjuice, and grease from the roast, and is recommended for fowl. Only the fifteenth-century version from the Vatican contains the advice to serve it in winter, which the editor of the *Viandier* attributes to the sauce's humoral qualities.[17] This might indicate that the Poitou sauce was only later "medicalized." The appearance of a *poitevine* in the *Viandier* manuscripts may go back to actual culinary practice handed down by cooks, but the spread of the Poitou sauce's fame in Italy, Germany, and beyond is more likely due to its inclusion in drug manuals such as the *Circa instans*.[18] The sauce was included without the Poitou assignation as the only recipe in the popular thirteenth-century *Regimen sanitatis Salernitanum* (The Salernitan Regimen of Health).[19] Complete with medical information and reference to Poitou, the sauce was also incorporated around 1300 in a Latin cookbook compilation in northern Italy, probably Padua, which is now lost but whose early fifteenth-century Bavarian translation has survived.[20]

Also lost is a manuscript that may well have been the earliest medieval European cookbook, whose "original," according to the food historian Constance Hieatt, could go as far back as the twelfth century.[21] Judging from the extant manuscripts of the *Libellus de arte coquinaria* (Little Book on the Art of Cookery) written in Danish, Icelandic, and Low German, the small collection of some thirty-five recipes circulated in northern Europe from the late thirteenth to the fifteenth centuries. The *Urtext* (archetype) of the collection of recipes was likely in Low German, but the recipes themselves are clearly of southern European provenance: five nut recipes, four of them for almond preparations such as almond oil and almond milk, are followed by ten sauce recipes (reminiscent of the ten sauce recipes in the Durham manuscript), four milk recipes, a pasty of deer marrow, and fifteen chicken recipes. The oldest extant manuscript comes from Copenhagen, and as in the Durham collection, the Danish recipes are part of a medical codex, in this case consisting of an herbal rooted in the tradition of the School of Salerno, a lapidary, and the cookbook.[22] Since the early nineteenth century they have been associated with the physician Henrik Harpestræng, also known as Henricus Dracus, who "studied and practiced medicine in Orleans, France, in 1181, and subsequently became physician to the Danish king."[23] If the connection to Henrik Harpestræng is correct, then the little cookbook, which was probably originally in Latin given the Latin recipe titles that have survived in some manuscripts, points back to twelfth-century Orleans—a place not too far from Poitou—with a physician yet again playing a key role in the transmission of a collection with a strong focus on sauces.

Overall, the sauces in the *Libellus*, referred to in the Latin titles as *salsum*, are more detailed than those in the Durham collection. Most of them provide relative quantities for the ingredients and information on how long a given sauce will keep, ranging from less than a day for a green sauce made with garlic to half a year for *sauce cameline* (camel-colored sauce), a standard sauce "for lords" in late-medieval cookbooks.[24] It is with this aristocratic sauce, containing cloves, nutmeg, cardamom, pepper, cinnamon, ginger, toasted bread, and vinegar, that the sauce section in the cookbook opens. The second recipe informs the reader that this sauce is good for venison, goose, and duck and preserves the meat for up to three weeks. What follows are two mustard recipes, one a basic mustard seed, honey, and vinegar mixture, and the other with anise and cinnamon added, which apparently extends the "best before" date from forty days to three months. The collection continues with two simple and cheap sauces, one using the dripping of a roasted fish mixed with vinegar for a "Hunter Style" preparation, and the other a sauce of "minimal cost" (*minimi valoris*) prepared from onions, parsley, broth, and vinegar. The sauces with the closest resemblance to the Durham recipes are the sauce for small fish and green sauce. Aside from the similar title, the ingredients in the *Libellus* for the small fish sauce are the three core ingredients in the Durham sauces (pepper, garlic, and vinegar), here complemented with salt. The Durham sauce for small fish by comparison lists coriander, pepper, and garlic as ingredients. The two green sauces in the *Libellus* that conclude the sauce section and call for mint, parsley, cinnamon, pepper, vinegar, and thyme, sage, parsley, cinnamon, and vinegar, respectively, differ only slightly from the first one of the Poitou sauces in the Durham codex, and the Poitou sauce in the

Circa instans. Sandwiched between the two green sauces in the *Libellus* is another simple sauce for fresh meat made from garlic, unripe grapes, and salt. Cinnamon is the exciting "new" sauce ingredient, featuring prominently in the *Libellus* recipes, and valued no doubt for its exclusivity but also for its presumed preservative qualities. By comparison, cinnamon plays no role in the Durham sauces, and is only mentioned once, in the last recipe for a ginger confection that was a well-known recipe in the medical works associated with the School of Salerno in the twelfth century, from the *Circa instans* to the *Liber graduum* (Book of Degrees) of Constantinus Africanus, and the *Antodotarium Nicolai* (Pharmacopoeia of Nicolaus).[25]

Arab Dietetics and the Beginnings of European School Medicine

The interest of physicians in foodstuffs and dishes was not a new phenomenon in the Middle Ages. Galen, for instance, the famous Greek physician and philosopher of the second century CE who practiced in Rome, wrote books on simple and compound drugs, but also a description of the nutritional qualities of foodstuffs.[26] A comparison of Galen's lists of drugs and foodstuffs brings to light an area of overlap. Included in both categories are such herbs and spices, fruits, and vegetables as marjoram, dill, mint, caraway, cinnamon, saffron, fennel, poppy seed, mustard, squash, cucumber, wheat, barley, lentils, apricots, citrons, onions, and garlic. In the Arabic reception of Galen's work, the connection between foodstuffs and drugs is even closer. Haly Abbas, the tenth-century Baghdad physician of Persian descent, distinguishes between remedies, poisons, remedial foods, and pure foods.[27] While Galen restricts assigning levels of intensity (*gradus*) of the humoral qualities hot, cold, wet, and dry to his simple and compound drugs, Haly Abbas extends it to foodstuffs. The trend continues with Avicenna in the early eleventh century, who abandons the separation between foodstuffs and drugs and discusses both together in Books II of his *Canon medicinae* (Canon of Medicine). His contemporary Ibn Butlan, in his *Tacuinum sanitatis* (Tables of Health), applies *gradus* information to all foodstuffs, be they remedial or pure foods. Ibn Jazla, who like Haly Abbas and Avicenna, practiced at the famous ʿAdudi Hospital in Baghdad in the second half of the eleventh century, epitomizes this move away from heavy drugs to dietetics. As a first resort, he recommends "dietetic measures, baths, and the right diet, and only then simple drugs."[28] Consequently, his pharmacopoeia of over two thousand entries combines foodstuffs and dishes with simple and compound drugs, and was mined by Europeans in the thirteenth century for culinary recipes.[29]

As Ibn Jazla's medical approach illustrates, food was only one aspect of a person's lifestyle that was to be attended to for the maintenance of health as well as healing. Not surprisingly, it was in the Middle East that the *regimen sanitatis* (regimen of health) as a distinct genre of medical writing was developed. This used humoral theory as its theoretical foundation and the six non-natural causes of sickness and health as its ordering principle.[30] These causes were air, exercise and rest, food and drink, sleep and waking, repletion and excretion, and the passions and emotions, all of which needed to be properly managed, with moderation as the guiding principle. As one of the primary means to maintain or regain a balance of the humors in the body, diet was of central importance, and the food and drink chapter was the most extensive in the regimens of health. With the regimen in the *Liber pantegni* or *Liber regius* (Royal Book) by Haly Abbas in the translation of Constantinus Africanus, Salerno had one of the most beautifully structured texts at its disposal. In addition to the general regimen for healthy (male) adults, and one under the aspect of habit, Haly Abbas provides a number of special regimens, including a *Regimen omnium etatum*, a regimen for all ages, from pregnancy and childhood to adulthood and old age, as well as a regimen for convalescents and one for plague sufferers.[31] In Latin translation, the Arab regimens were eagerly adopted by the newly established European medical schools and physicians in their practice, with their own individual compilations from the school texts and translations into the vernacular soon to follow. The regimen for healthy adults in the *Liber pantegni* contains five recipes for legumes and other plant foods, four of which ask for *obsomogarum*, an ingredient whose meaning is unclear.[32] In the German version of the regimen that is part of the *Breslauer Arzneibuch* (Breslau Pharmacopoeia), the recipes are not identical, and any reference to *obsomogarum* has disappeared.[33] This is a first indication that the Arab regimen recipes were either adjusted or replaced altogether by Europeans adopting them.

The European Regimen sanitatis

The number of recipes inserted in regimen literature rose dramatically when the French town of Montpellier became the new center of medical learning. Among the texts that came across the Pyrenees to southern France from Toledo, Spain, were the Latin translations of Rhazes's *Liber de medicina ad*

Almansorem (Book about Medicine for Almansor) and Avicenna's *Canon medicinae*, produced by Gerard de Cremona in the thirteenth century. In addition, the *Regimen sanitatis* by the physician and poet Avenzoar was translated into Latin at Montpellier by Prophatius Judaeus around 1300. This intense interest in dietetics led to two of the first regimens compiled in Europe by Montpellier professors Bernard de Gordon and Arnald de Villanova in 1308.[34] Arnald's *Regimen sanitatis ad inclitum dominum regem Aragonum* (Regimen of Health for the Illustrious Lord, the King of Aragon), which turned out to be the more popular, integrates an amazing eighteen recipes in the dietetic list of foodstuffs ranging from dishes for grains, legumes, fruits and vegetables, to cheese, pies, and sauces.[35] Many of the recipes contain almonds, often in the form of almond oil or almond milk. The interest in cookery at the medical school in the early fourteenth century is also illustrated by the fact that the famous Montpellier surgeon Henri de Mondeville copied several of the earliest extant recipe collections, the two northern French cookbooks known as *Tractatus* (Treatise) and *Enseignemenz* (Education) and the oldest Italian cookbook, the *Liber de coquina* (The Book of Cookery), in a parchment codex in the same time period, between 1304 and 1314.[36]

For his regimen Arnald drew heavily on the *Liber de medicina ad Almansorem*, but he largely edited out the Arabic terms for foodstuffs and dishes that had made it into the Latin translation and replaced them with European culinary content. The frequent mention of almond milk and a chapter on sauces and condiments, entitled "*De saporibus et condimentis*," are two of the most obvious substitutions. While Arab cuisine certainly used almonds, almond milk rarely appears in the recipes but became the hallmark of medieval courtly cookery in Christian Europe. Even as early as the late twelfth century, it was used in recipes for the sick contained in the *Summula de preparatione ciborum et potuum infirmorum* (A Little Summary on the Preparation of Food and Drink for the Sick) by the Salerno physician Petrus Musandinus.[37] With their long tradition in Europe, sauces continued to play an important role in the Middle Ages. In fact, as the Italian scholar Massimo Montanari points out, they were "one of the foundations (an absolute *must*) of medieval cooking."[38] By contrast, they were not as central to Arab cuisine at the time. A recipe for the green sauce encountered in the early European sources was borrowed by the Spanish Arabs and eventually found its way into the thirteenth-century Hispano-Arab cookbook *Fiḍalat al-Khiwān* by Ibn Razīn al-Tujībī. The author comments that such sauces were used by Christians with roasted and boiled meat or fish, and describes the sauce as "...one of their most venerable foods by virtue of its innate heat."[39] According to food historian Charles Perry, not just the sauces but also the term *ṣalṣ*, used for them in the late-medieval Arab cookbooks, were borrowed by the Arabs.[40]

The chapter on sauces in Arnald's regimen contains a number of recipes, including sauces and spice powders in which almonds figure prominently.[41] Since the regimen was written for the king of Aragon who suffered from hemorrhoids, the chapter begins with warnings against very strong sauces such as pepper sauces (*piperatas*) and garlic sauces (*alliatas*), as well as pungent sauces such as mustard (*sinapi*) and rocket (*eruca*). He provides a recipe for how to make rocket sauce, commonly found in Catalan and Italian cookbooks, more suitable for his patient.[42] Arnald also advises that honey is to be replaced with sugar, and confections and sauces containing pepper, a large amount of ginger, galingale, nutmeg, cloves, and saffron are to be avoided. He then provides a recipe for a spice powder with exact quantities and consisting of the whitest ginger, coriander boiled in vinegar, cardamom, behen nut, ivory shaving, cloves, saffron, and cinnamon, which is to be mixed with ground almonds, and a moderate amount of vinegar or verjuice, which can also be used for pies. Arnald goes on to caution about too much acidity being added to pies from pomegranate, lime, lemon, or orange juice, which can be offset by almonds or almond milk. Citrus fruits are to be used only when completely ripe. Pomegranate juice from the previous year is said to be weaker than fresh juice. When it comes to roasted birds, a sauce from wine, a lot of rose water, and a moderate amount of salt is recommended. For roasted four-legged animals, salt and rocket sauce or green sauce are listed. For his *salsamentum viride* or green sauce, he has kept the cinnamon from the *Libellus* but replaced pepper with almonds, which would have made it less pungent, yet another concession to his patient. He ends the chapter with general advice for roasted meat and fish to be seasoned with cinnamon, almonds, and vinegar, and ginger to be added in winter. Arnald ultimately devised various ways to make his dishes suitable for the king of Aragon and his medical condition by toning down the sharpness of the European sauces.

There are indications that a now lost dietetic text with many recipes circulated in the south of France in the early fourteenth century from which regimen authors excerpted a variety of dishes, including sauces. One of them was the German physician Konrad von Eichstätt who was likely educated at Montpellier, and used Avicenna's *Canon* and Rhazes's *Liber de medicina ad Almansorem* as his main sources, which he complemented with material from Averroës's *Colliget* (General Medicine).[43] The other was fellow German physician Arnold von Bamberg, who studied at Bologna but wrote his regimen not far from Montpellier, in Malausanne, outside Avignon.[44] The recipes in the list of foodstuffs of Konrad's regimen are focused mainly on meat and fish, and most of them are for sauces. Chapter 4 deals with the meat of non-flying animals and ends with the five standard medieval sauces: a white sauce made from ground almonds, sugar, wheat flour, and vinegar, for which he provides exact quantities; a green sauce made from parsley, mint, salt, spice powder, and vinegar; a *cameline* sauce referred to simply as "another sauce," *alia salsa*, made from cinnamon, sugar, and vinegar; the best pepper sauce, *optima piperata*, made from ginger, cinnamon, cloves, mace, pepper, vinegar, bread, and saffron; and finally, a good garlic sauce, *bonam alleatam*, made by adding crushed garlic to the white sauce.[45] Konrad's fish recipes don't refer specifically to sauces, just the medium in which the fish are to be prepared: vinegar and spices, water or wine and salt, or jelly.[46]

Arnold von Bamberg, who drew on the same dietetic source text for the recipes as Konrad, but included many more (namely forty recipes in his regimen), uses a chapter on spice powders as a preamble for his sauce chapter.[47] All three spice powders listed give exact measurements, and the second, a mixture of fennel seed and long pepper, is supposedly good against wind, for digestion, and for improved vision. The first spice powder contains fourteen ingredients (ginger, saffron, cardamom, galingale, licorice, cloves, long pepper, mace, nutmeg, melegeta pepper, cubeb, zedoary, spikenard, and cinnamon), and the third one thirteen (cinnamon, ginger, cardamom, cloves, nutmeg, malabathrum, cubeb, galingale, licorice, long pepper, fennel seed, clary sage [salvia sclarea], and sugar). The sauces Arnold provides in the following chapter are essentially the white, green, *cameline*, and garlic sauce found in Konrad.[48] Only the pepper sauce has been replaced by a new sauce, a *Salsa rubea* or red sauce, consisting of grapes, cooked egg yolk, one of the spice powders he mentioned in the previous chapter, and the juice of *amarillarum*(?) or red vinegar. Since the two French cookbooks, the *Tractatus* and *Enseignemenz*, and the Italian *Liber de coquina* were known in Montpellier at the time Arnald, Konrad, and Arnold compiled their regimens, it is worth comparing the sauces in the cookbooks with the sauces in the regimens. While the *Enseignemenz* does not deal with sauces, the *Tractatus* praises the green and *cameline* sauce as the best and then lists their recipes, followed by two mustard sauces.[49] All five sauces of Konrad's regimen are contained in the Italian cookbook *Liber de coquina*, where they follow a sauce for roasts made from basil, pepper, and verjuice or citrus juice, and a sauce for pasta made from onions, spices, and grated cheese. They appear in this order: garlic sauce, pepper sauce, white sauce, *cameline* sauce, and green sauce.[50] While their ingredients vary somewhat from the regimen recipes, they nevertheless demonstrate that Konrad had correctly identified the key sauces that by the early fourteenth century had also made it into an Italian cookbook.

The Physician Magninus Mediolanensis and His Little Sauce-Book

The exact measurements in some of the spice powder and sauce recipes in the regimen literature, which are more typical of drug manuals, as well as Arnald's modifications of the recipes for a patient suffering from hemorrhoids, point to the close connection between cooking and medicine and illustrate to what extent cookery by the early 1300s had become medicalized and turned into a science. This trend reached new heights in the 1330s with the *Opusculum de saporibus et condimentis* (Little Work on Sauces and Condiments) by the Italian physician Magninus Mediolanensis.[51] Originally from Milan, Magninus taught at the University of Paris from 1326 to 1336, from 1331 on as professor of medicine.[52] He later served as one of the medical astrologers at the Visconti court, and died around 1368.[53] From 1331 to 1333 he was also physician to Andrea Ghini de' Malpighi, Bishop of Arras, and it is to him that he dedicated an extensive *Regimen sanitatis*, which went through six printed editions before 1500 alone.[54] The regimen in the 1504 edition contains a discussion of sauces entitled *De condimentis et saporibus* (On Condiments and Sauces). In the 1505 edition of the regimen, a more detailed sauce chapter appears that was not only closer to the original version by Magninus but also closer to the *Opusculum de saporibus* and helps to establish him as the author of both texts.[55] What remains unclear, however, is whether the *Opusculum de saporibus* was written prior to the sauce chapter in the regimen or whether it is a later elaboration of the same.

The *Regimen sanitatis* versions of the sauce chapter begin by praising sauces in the preparation of dishes for their role in making food more delectable and consequently more digestible, and continue with a discussion of the use of salt, lard, oil, and butter in cooking, in particular with regard to vegetables and legumes. This may hint at a reason why vegetables and legumes are not covered in the *Opusculum*, which focuses on the more exclusive foodstuffs (meat, fish, and seafood) and their appropriate sauces and condiments. The comment "as the cooks of the lords know" (*ut sciunt coci dominorum*) is a clear indication who the target audience for the *Regimen* was, presumably the same as for the *Opusculum*. The sauce chapters then make the observation the

Opusculum opens with, namely that "the pleasures of sauces were invented by gluttons more for the sake of delight than of health" (*SAPORUM delectamenta propter voluptatem magis quam propter sanitatem a gulosis fuerunt primitus adinventa*).[56] As appetite stimulants, sauces can do more harm than good, however, as Magninus points out, in that they lead people to overeat. In addition, they turn rotten food more palatable so they make people eat what should not be consumed. As something more akin to drugs than nourishment, sauces should be consumed sparingly by those in good health, deployed as a corrective for unhealthy foods, or as a means to stimulate appetite and aid digestion. The author then provides four general guidelines regarding sauces, the first two dealing with the nature and consumption of sauces depending on whether they are closer to medicine or to food. The third guideline concerns modifications in the use of spices and seasonings in summer and winter, and the fourth the connection between the humoral qualities of foods and the role of sauces to achieve a humoral balance.

Following the general introduction in the *Opusculum*, Magninus provides detailed information on individual dishes and the appropriate sauces. Instead of arranging the information according to sauces, he starts with a type of meat, fish, or seafood, age of the animal, and its preparation (boiled, roasted, fried, baked), and gives seasoning options for summer (e.g., verjuice, citrus juice) and winter (vinegar, wine, hot spices). He occasionally mentions sweet and strong spice powders, usually in connection with pies, but does not provide any recipes for them. This is in contrast to the sauces, for which he normally does include the recipes, and sometimes even gives quantities for ingredients. When arranged by sauce type rather than animal, the core sauces that emerge are very similar to the sauces encountered earlier in Arnald de Villanova, Konrad von Eichstätt, Arnold von Bamberg, and the Italian *Liber de coquina*. Green sauce tops the list with six references and a recipe that provides quantities. It is followed by four occurrences each of mustard sauce, rocket sauce, and *cameline* sauce, for which Magninus offers two different recipes, one with quantities. Less clear-cut is the distinction between white sauces and white garlic sauces. Five sauces are classified as "white," and of these, three also contain garlic. Two more are referred to as *alleata*, garlic sauce, one of which also deemed "white." When it comes to pepper sauces, they are all boiled sauces, with two referred to as black pepper sauces, and two as pepper-saffron sauces. Jellies appear twice for fish, and mentioned one time each are a saffron sauce, an onion sauce called *cinefium*, a sauce with no name, and a wine sauce.[57]

Of the twenty-eight sections in the *Opusculum*, the first thirteen deal with four-legged animals, poultry, and wild fowl, and the rest with fish and seafood. Boiling is the method specified for the initial five types of meat, ranging from castrated veal, goat, and kid to beef. Beginning with pork, the preparation of the meat becomes more varied and includes roasting, pies and pasties, and frying. Roasting, the clear favorite, is recommended for most meats from rabbit and pullet, dove, partridge, pigeon, and quail to duck and goose, and baking in pastry an occasional second choice. Only once in this segment is boiling mentioned for birds, namely for capons and pheasants. From waterfowl Magninus turns to a general discussion of fish, which is followed by entries on porpoise, sturgeon, lamprey, moray, eel, salmon, trout, whiting, red mullet, gurnard, lobster, tench, carp, small carp and other small fish, and concludes with oysters. For fish and seafood, boiling, roasting, baking, frying, and encasing in jelly are all mentioned, with boiling perhaps slightly more popular than the other methods. Two examples serve to illustrate Magninus's method of matching a specific type of meat with the appropriate cooking method and sauce. For beef, with its humoral qualities cold and dry, he recommends boiling to add warmth and moisture, and serving it with either a boiled pepper-saffron sauce, a rocket sauce, or a boiled white garlic sauce. The warming qualities of ingredients in all three sauces would have imparted further warmth, and the boiling of the first and third sauce would have provided some extra moisture to the boiled meat.[58] For lobster, with its humoral qualities tending toward the cold and moist, like most fish and seafood, the sauce to be used is green sauce, which would have had a warming and drying effect.[59]

The Sauces in Late Medieval Cookbooks

The sauces Magninus employed for his scientific method were well known in Europe when the *Opusculum* was written, and the cooks for wealthy families presumably followed the dietetic advice of Magninus and the other physicians at least some of the time, if not on a daily basis.[60] The sauce repertoire expanded in the fourteenth and fifteenth centuries, judging from the cookbook literature that was coming into its own during that time. One of the popular new sauces that appears in French cookbooks beginning around 1300 but is not mentioned in the *Opusculum* is *jance*.[61] Several versions of *jance* are contained in the *Viandier* of Taillvent, for instance, which divides the sauces in two categories, unboiled and boiled sauces. In the first category are *cameline* sauce, *cameline* garlic sauce, white garlic sauce, green garlic sauce, fresh herring garlic sauce, an unnamed almond garlic sauce, a green sauce, and a sauce to preserve fish. The boiled sauces include Robert's Beard Sauce, a yellow pepper sauce, black pepper sauce, cow's milk *jance*, garlic *jance*, ginger *jance*, a Poitevin Sauce, and a list of necessary sauce ingredients.[62] The sauces and condiments in the oldest German cookbook, *Daz buoch von guoter spise* (The Book of Good Food), from around 1350, all appear in the first half of the cookbook, and none in the second half, which was copied from another source.[63] In seasonings, liquid bases, and thickeners, the cookbooks by and large follow the conventions of the earlier medical and culinary literature. Not adopted, however, were the names of the standard sauces used elsewhere in Europe, such as *cameline* or *jance*.

One of the new features in the late fourteenth and fifteenth centuries, reminiscent of Roman sauces, was the use of diverse fresh or dried fruit in sauce-making. The famous Italian cook Maestro Martino, for instance, in his *Libro de Arte Coquinaria* (The Art of Cooking) presents in the third chapter, entitled "How to make every type of sauce," twenty-three sauce recipes, several of which use fruit as an ingredient, ranging from raisins and dried prunes to red grapes, mulberries, black cherries, and cornel cherries.[64] In her last book, noted food historian Constance Hieatt provides a representative example from each of the different culinary recipes from medieval Britain. Of the thirty-seven sauces, twenty-five specify the meat they are to accompany. Of these, fifteen are recommended for domestic and wild fowl, four for fish, three for pork, two for beef, and one for veal.[65] The preponderance of birds may explain why liver, gizzard, and entrails figure prominently as sauce thickeners. An interesting feature of the English recipes is the use of ale in sauces, while verjuice, so ubiquitous on the continent, and must (unfermented grape juice) play a negligible role. In addition to the all-important almonds, pine nuts also occur in some recipes from England.

From the early examples included in medical texts of the twelfth century to the fifteenth-century aristocratic cookbooks, sauces of the Middle Ages evolved from herbs and spices combined with vinegar or wine to more complex preparations while retaining their character as non-emulsified lean sauces. The age of emulsified sauces had not yet arrived. The *garum* or *liquamen* of the Romans was replaced by salt in the medieval recipes, and the seasonings the *Viandier* recommends that cooks have on hand are as extensive as those of the Romans. In the French cookbook they include ginger, cinnamon, cloves, grain of paradise, long pepper, round pepper, cassia buds, saffron, nutmeg, bay leaves, galingale, mace, cumin, sugar, almonds, garlic, onions, shallots, and for color or tart taste parsley, herb bennet, sorrel, vine leaves or vine shoots, currants, and green wheat in winter. In the *Viandier* the preferred liquids for sauces are white wine, verjuice, vinegar, water, greasy broth, cow's milk, and almond milk.[66] Breadcrumbs, ground nuts, cooked liver, gizzards, hard-boiled egg yolks, and occasionally flour are the typical late-medieval thickeners. Pounding ingredients in a mortar and straining sauces through a sieve-cloth ensured their smooth consistency. These complex sweet-sour sauces at the end of the Middle Ages were actually not too dissimilar from their Roman ancestors. They paved the way for the emergence of a new gourmand culture and the gradual separation of cookery and medicine in early modern Europe.

Cameline and Poivre Noir Sauces[67]

The Viandier of Taillevent, fourteenth century

Cameline. To make cameline sauce, grind ginger, a great deal of cinnamon, cloves, grains of paradise, mace and, if you wish, long pepper; strain bread that has been moistened in vinegar, strain everything together and salt as necessary.

Poivre noir. Black pepper sauce. Grind ginger, round pepper, and burnt toast, infuse this in vinegar (var.: and a little verjuice) and boil it.

Notes

1. Christopher Grocock and Sally Grainger, *Apicius: A Critical Edition with an Introduction and an English Translation of the Latin Recipe Text Apicius, with Illustrations by Dan Shadrake* (Devon: Prospect Books 2006), 8.
2. Ilaria Gozzini Giacosa, *A Taste of Ancient Rome*, trans. Anna Herklotz (Chicago: University of Chicago Press, 1992), 26.
3. For the list of typical seasonings in Roman sauces, see ibid., 27.
4. Grocock and Grainger, *Apicius*, list only five references to health, though see Raga, Chapter 4 in this volume, for more on this topic.
5. For a description of the Apicius manuscripts and stemma, see Grocock and Grainger, *Apicius*, 116–120.
6. Eduard Liechtenhan, *Anthimi De observatione ciborum: ad Theodoricum regem Francorum epistula* (Berlin: Akademie-Verlag, 1963). For an English translation, see Mark Grant, ed. and trans., *Anthimus: De observatione ciborum/On the Observance of Foods* (Devon: Prospect Books, 1996).
7. Liechtenhan's German translations of the drinks are *Bier*, *Met*, *Wermut*, and *Ptisanen*. Grant translates them as "beer," "mead," "spiced mead," and "barley soup." See Liechtenhan, *Anthimi*, 39; Grant, *Anthimus*, 57.

8. See Williams, Chapter 3 in this volume.
9. *et si durioris fuerint, quando manducantur, melius est, sich tamen, ut in sale puro intingantur. nam liquamen ex omni parte prohibimus; et in egrogario in gauata conponatur quomodo monticlos.* Liechtenhan, *Anthimi*, 7, 16.
10. For *liquamen*, see Liechtenhan, *Anthimi*, 8. In Section 34, Anthimus mentions *egrogarium*, which Liechtenhan translates as "Fischbrei," and Grant as "diluted fish sauce"; see Grant, *Anthimus*, 63. For a discussion of the Anthimus letter, see Melitta Weiss Adamson, *Medieval Dietetics: Food and Drink in Regimen Sanitatis Literature from 800 to 1400* (Frankfurt am Main: Peter Lang, 1995), 31–37; and specifically of meat, see Liliane Plouvier, "L'Alimentation carnée au Haut Moyen Âge d'après le De observatione ciborum d'Anthime et les Excerpta de Vinidarius," *Revue belge de philologie et d'histoire* 80, no. 4 (2002): 1357–1369.
11. See *iusculum*, translated as "broth" or "soup" in P. G. W. Glare, ed. *Oxford Latin Dictionary* (Oxford: Oxford University Press, 1982). The diminutive form *iuscellum* used by Anthimus is translated as "gravy, gelatine" in Alexander Souter, *A Glossary of Later Latin to 600 A.D.* (Oxford: Clarendon Press, 1949). Only once, in Section 65 on beans, Anthimus uses the term *conditura* as an alternative to broth, oil, or salt, but he provides no recipe. See Liechtenhan, *Anthimi*, 24, who translates it as *Gewürzsauce*, and Grant, *Anthimus*, 73, as "seasoning."
12. Konrad Goehl, ed. and trans., *Das 'Circa instans': Die erste große Drogenkunde des Abendlandes* (Berlin: Deutscher Wissenschafts-Verlag, 2015, Ms. 674).
13. Faith Wallis discovered the sauce recipes in the Durham codex now housed in Sidney Sussex College, Cambridge, MS 51, fols. 39r–v. I wish to thank her for sending me a copy of the manuscript pages, and the article Giles E. M. Gasper and Faith Wallis, "*Salsamenta pictavensium*: Gastronomy and Medicine in Twelfth-Century England," *The English Historical Review* 131 (2016): 1353–1385.
14. Bruno Laurioux, "Cuisine et médecine au Moyen Âge: Alliées ou ennemies?" *Cahiers de recherches médiévales et humanists: Journal of Medieval and Humanistic Studies* 13 (2006): 223–238.
15. Gasper and Wallis, "*Salsamenta pictavensium*."
16. See Freedman, Chapter 2 in this volume.
17. Terence Scully, ed., *The Viandier of Taillevent: An Edition of All Extant Manuscripts* (Ottawa: University of Ottawa Press, 1988), 90f. For the recipe of this boiled sauce in the *Viandier*, see Recipe 169 in ibid., 229f.
18. German scribes appear to have been confused by the assignation *pictaviensium*. In the Erlangen manuscript of the drug manual it is spelled *pictavientium*, the Breslau manuscript *pictacensium*, the Vienna manuscript *pictavensium*, and the Leipzig manuscript *pictamense*. See the edition by Hans Wölfel, "Das Arzneidrogenbuch Circa Instans in einer Fassung des XIII. Jahrhunderts aus der Universitätsbibliothek Erlangen: Text und Kommentar als Beitrag zur Pflanzen- und Drogenkunde des Mittelalters" (PhD diss., Friedrich-Wilhelms-Universität Berlin, 1939), 15 and 124, note 155, and "Allium" in Goehl, *Das 'Circa instans'*.

19. *Salvia, serpillum, piper, allia, sal, petrosillum, / Si bene condantur et aceto confiteantur, / Ex his fit salsa, si non sit regula falsa.* See Salvatore de Renzi, ed., *Collectio Salernitana*, vol. 1. (Naples: Filiatre-Sebezio, 1852), 454.
20. *Ain grùn Sals pictamensium*, see Munich, Bayerische Staatsbibliothek, Cgm 415, fol. 53r.
21. Rudolf Grewe and Constance B. Hieatt, eds., *Libellus de arte coquinaria: An Early Northern Cookery Book* (Tempe: Arizona Center for Medieval and Renaissance Studies Press, 2001), 1.
22. Ibid., 4–8.
23. Ibid., 5.
24. Ibid., 84f.
25. Gasper and Wallis, "*Salsamenta pictavensium*."
26. Mark Grant, trans., *Galen on Food and Diet* (London: Routledge, 2000).
27. Melitta Weiss Adamson, *Food in Medieval Times* (Westport, CT: Greenwood Press, 2004), 207f.
28. Melitta Weiss Adamson, "Ibn Ǧazla auf dem Weg nach Bayern," in *Wissen über Grenzen. Arabisches Wissen und lateinisches Mittelalter* (Miscellanea Mediaevalia, vol. 33), ed. Andreas Speer and Lydia Wegener (Berlin and New York: Walter de Gruyter, 2006), 360.
29. For Ibn Jazla's recipes in his pharmacopoeia, their Latin and German translation, see Ylva Schwinghammer et al., *Speisen auf Reisen: Das frühneuhochdeutsche Púch von den chósten und seine Wurzeln im lateinischen Liber de ferculis und im arabischen Minhāj al-bayān in synoptischer Edition mit Übersetzung und überlieferungskritischem Kommentar* (Graz: Unipress, 2019).
30. Adamson, *Medieval Dietetics*, 9.
31. Wolfram Schmitt, "Theorie der Gesundheit und 'Regimen sanitatis' im Mittelalter" (Medizinische Habilitation, University of Heidelberg, 1973), 94f.
32. Adamson, *Medieval Dietetics*, 47f.
33. Ibid., 107.
34. Melitta Weiss Adamson, "Bernard de Gordon and Arnald de Villanova: A Tale of Two Regimes," in *Eine Topographie historischer Gleichzeitigkeit* (Miscellanea Mediaevalia, vol. 35), ed. Andreas Speer and David Wirmer (Berlin and New York: Walter de Gruyter, 2010), 419–435.
35. Adamson, *Medieval Dietetics*, 114–116.
36. Paris, BN Cod. Lat. 7131. For an edition of the *Tractatus* and *Liber de çoquina*, see Marianne Mulon, ed., *Deux traités inédits d'art culinaire medieval* (Paris: Bibliothèque nationale, 1971), 380–395, 396–420. For the *Liber de coquina*, see also the study and edition by Anna Martellotti, *I ricettari di Federico II. Dal "Meridionale" al "Liber de coquina"* (Florence: Olschki, 2005). For an edition of the *Enseignemenz*, see Carole Lambert, "Trois réceptaires culinaires médiévaux: Les 'Enseignemenz,' les 'Doctrine,' et le 'Modus.' Édition critique et glossaire détaillé" (PhD diss., Université de Montréal, 1989), 87–111.

37. Grewe and Hieatt, *Libellus de arte coquinaria*, 3, 10f, 23; Bruno Laurioux, "La cuisine des médecins à la fin du Moyen Âge," in *Maladies, médecines, et sociétés: Approaches historiques pour le present*, ed. François-Olivier Touati, vol. 2: *Actes du VIe Colloque d'Histoire au Présent* (Paris: L'Harmattan et Histoire au Présent, 1993), 136–148; Charles Perry, "Isfidhabāj, Blancmanger, and No Almonds," *Petits Propos Culinaires* 31 (1989): 25–28.
38. Massimo Montanari, *Medieval Tastes: Food, Cooking, and the Table*, trans. Beth Archer Brombert (New York: Columbia University Press, 2015), 9.
39. See Grewe and Hieatt, *Libellus de arte coquinaria*, 91; For the English translation of the recipe in the *Fiḍālat al-Khiwān fī Ṭayyibāt al-Ṭaʿām wa ʾl-Alwān*, see Nawal Nasrallah, *Fiḍālat al-khiwān fī ṭayyibāt al-ṭaʿām wa-al-alwān = Best of Delectable Foods and Dishes from al-Andalus and al-Maghrib: A Cookbook by Thirteenth-Century Andalusi Scholar Ibn Razīn al-Tujībī (1227–1293)* (Leiden and Boston: Brill, 2021), 213f.
40. Charles Perry, "The Ṣalṣ of the Infidels," *Petits Propos Culinaires* 26 (1987): 55–59. A thirteenth-century Syrian cookbook contains a section of eleven *ṣalṣ* recipes, see Perry, ed. and trans., *Scents and Flavors: A Syrian Cookbook* (New York: New York University Press, 2017), 230–235, and a fourteenth-century cookbook from Cairo contains a section of fifteen *ṣalṣ* recipes; see Nawal Nasrallah, trans., *Treasure Trove of Benefits and Variety at the Table: A Fourteenth-Century Egyptian Cookbook* (Leiden and Boston: Brill, 2018), 315–322. Five *ṣalṣ* recipes are also contained in the *Kitāb Waṣf al-aṭʿima al-muʿtāda*, an expanded version of the thirteenth-century al-Baghdādī cookbook; see Charles Perry, "The Description of Familiar Foods," in *Medieval Arab Cookery*, ed. Maxime Rodinson, A. J. Arberry, and Charles Perry (Totnes: Prospect Books, 2001), 388–390, 392f.
41. Luis García-Ballester, Juan Antonio Paniagua, and Michael McVaugh, eds., *Arnaldi de Villanova Opera medica omnia 10, pt 1: Regimen sanitatis ad regem Aragonum* (Barcelona: Universidad de Barcelona, 1996), 460–462.
42. See *eruga*, rocket sauce, in Carole Lambert, "Medieval France: The South," in *Regional Cuisines of Medieval Europe*, ed. Melitta Weiss Adamson (New York and London: Routledge, 2002), 70.
43. See Adamson, *Medieval Dietetics*, 142–149. For a detailed analysis of Konrad's regimen, see Christa Hagenmeyer, *Das Regimen Sanitatis Konrads von Eichstätt: Quellen—Texte—Wirkungsgeschichte*, Sudhoffs Archiv Beihefte 35 (Stuttgart: Franz Steiner Verlag, 1995), 11–62.
44. Adamson, *Medieval Dietetics*, 150–160. For the proof of a common source used by Konrad and Arnold, see Hagenmeyer, *Das Regimen Sanitatis Konrads von Eichstätt*, 46–53.
45. Ibid., 98f.
46. Ibid., 100f.
47. For the edition of Arnold's regimen, see Karin Figala, "Mainfränkische Zeitgenossen Ortolfs von Baierland: Ein Beitrag zum frühesten Gesundheitswesen in den

Bistümern Würzburg und Bamberg" (Pharm. diss, University of Munich, 1969), 160–190. The spice powders are contained on ibid., 178f.

48. Ibid., 179f.
49. Mulon, *Deux traités inédits d'art culinaire medieval*, 394f.
50. Ibid., 410.
51. Lynn Thorndike, "A Medieval Sauce-Book" *Speculum* 9 (1934): 183–190. For a detailed study of the sauce-book, see Terence Scully, "The Opusculum de Saporibus of Magninus Mediolanensis," *Medium Aevum* 54 (1985): 178–207.
52. Thorndike, "A Medieval Sauce-Book," 183f; Schmitt, "Theorie der Gesundheit und 'Regimen sanitatis' im Mittelalter," 16; Scully "The Opusculum de Saporibus of Magninus Mediolanensis," 178; Adamson, *Medieval Dietetics*, 121; For a study of his life and works, see Caroline Proctor, "Perfecting Prevention: The Medical Writings of Maino de Maineri (d.c. 1368)" (PhD diss., University of St. Andrews, 2006).
53. Thorndike, "A Medieval Sauce-Book,"183f; Proctor, "Perfecting Prevention," 5.
54. In a 1504 edition from Lyons it is included in the works of Arnald de Villanova, but doubts about Magninus's authorship have since been dismissed.
55. See Adamson, *Medieval Dietetics*, 127f., based on the incunabulum-edition of Maynus de Mayneriis, *Regimen sanitatis* (Lyons: François Fradin, c. 1505). Scully, "The Opusculum de Saporibus of Magninus Mediolanensis," 178f., compares the edition of the sauce chapter in the Thorndike edition with the fifteenth-century manuscript version of the *Regimen sanitatis* in Vatican Library, MS Palatine 1331, ff. 228r–302v, in which it also forms a more detailed Chapter 20.
56. Thorndike, "A Medieval Sauce-Book," 186.
57. The numbers after the sauces refer to the sections in Thorndike adhered to by Scully, "The Opusculum de Saporibus of Magninus Mediolanensis," *Salsa viridis* 1, 7, 19, 22, 25, 27; *sinapium* 1 (*dulce*), 6, 7, 27 (*dulce*); *eruca* 1, 4, 6, 7; *salsa camellina* 8, 17, 23, 26; *brodium album* 2, *salsa alba* 19; *sapor albus* 17, 19, 22; *alleata alba* 5; *alleata* 12; *piperata nigra* 13, 15; *piperata crocea* 4, 20; *gelatina* 16, 18; *sapor croceus* 28; *cinefium* 2; sauce with no name 18; *salsa conveniens est vinum* 23.
58. Thorndike, "A Medieval Sauce-Book," sections 4, 5; discussed in Scully, "The Opusculum de Saporibus of Magninus Mediolanensis," 185f.
59. Thorndike, "A Medieval Sauce-Book," section 25.
60. See Laurioux, "Cuisine et médecine au Moyen Âge," esp. 225f.
61. Scully, *The Viandier of Taillevent*, recipes 36, 98, 106, 126, 145, 166, 167, 168; Terence Scully, *Du fait de cuisine / On Cookery of Master Chiquart (1420)* (Tempe: Arizona Center for Medieval and Renaissance Studies Press, 2010), recipes 43, 46, 58.
62. Scully, *The Viandier of Taillevent*, recipes 155–170. A *cameline* sauce and marjoram sauce are added in one of the *Viandier* manuscripts and counted as recipes 171 and 172 in Scully. The *Viandier* does not give a recipe for Robert's Beard Sauce, but according to a recipe from another source it was an onion sauce, see recipe 163 in ibid., 226.

63. Melitta Weiss Adamson, *Daz buoch von guoter spise (The Book of Good Food): A Study, Edition, and English Translation of the Oldest German Cookbook* (Krems, Austria: Medium Aevum Quotidianum, 2000), recipes 16, 21, 26, 30, 31, 32, 32a, 33, 34, 35, 41, 42, 48, 49, 50, 51.
64. Maestro Martino of Como, *The Art of Cooking: The First Modern Cookery Book, with Fifty Modernized Recipes by Stefania Barzini*, ed. Luigi Ballerini and trans. Jeremy Parzen (Berkeley: University of California Press, 2005), 76–79.
65. Constance B. Hieatt, trans., *The Culinary Recipes of Medieval England* (Devon: Prospect Books, 2013), 147–155).
66. Scully, *The Viandier of Taillevent*, recipe 170.
67. Scully, *The Viandier of Taillevent*, recipe 155 and 165.

Selected Bibliography

Adamson, Melitta Weiss. *Medieval Dietetics: Food and Drink in Regimen Sanitatis Literature from 800 to 1400*. Frankfurt am Main: Peter Lang, 1995.

Adamson, Melitta Weiss. *Food in Medieval Times*. Westport, CT: Greenwood Press, 2004.

Grewe, Rudolf, and Constance B. Hieatt, eds. *Libellus de arte coquinaria: An Early Northern Cookery Book*. Tempe: Arizona Center for Medieval and Renaissance Studies Press, 2001.

Hieatt, Constance B., trans. *The Culinary Recipes of Medieval England*. Devon: Prospect Books, 2013.

Montanari, Massimo. *Medieval Tastes: Food, Cooking, and the Table*. Translated by Beth Archer Brombert. New York: Columbia University Press, 2015.

Perry, Charles, ed. and trans. *Scents and Flavors: A Syrian Cookbook*. New York: New York University Press, 2017.

Scully, Terence, ed. *The Viandier of Taillevent: An Edition of All Extant Manuscripts*. Ottawa: University of Ottawa Press, 1988.

Melitta Weiss Adamson, *Sauces and Condiments in the Middle Ages* In: *From Garum to Mole: Sauces and Identity in the Western World*. Edited by: Andrew Donnelly, Beth M. Forrest, and Deirdre Murphy, Oxford University Press.
 DOI: 10.1093/9780190622138.003.0001

2

Sauces

THE BASIS FOR CLASSIC FRENCH CUISINE

Paul Freedman

FRENCH CUISINE DEFINED the international standards of refined dining from the seventeenth century until just recently. A significant aspect of culinary history since 1980s has been the end of French domination, not necessarily a decline in absolute terms, but in France's control over what constitutes prestige. Deference to French models has been replaced by a variety of trends—molecular, Asian-fusion, farm-to-table, new Nordic—none of which have captured the authority France enjoyed for so long. A chapter devoted to French sauces is, in some sense, a survey of the evolution of French cuisine because, both within and outside France, sauces were the essence, so to speak, of its culinary identity.

In a book about sauces, Louis Diat, a celebrated French chef who made his career at New York's Ritz Carlton, asked, rhetorically, "who ever heard of a good French chef who was not first a good *saucier*?"[1] At the beginning of the twentieth century, Auguste Escoffier (1846–1935), who authored the century's most influential French cookbook, asserted, "Sauces represent the fundamental element of cuisine. They have created and maintained the universal dominance of French cuisine."[2] Popularizers of French cuisine also emphasized the centrality of sauces not just for the mastering of technique, but for the aesthetic appeal of French cooking. In *Mastering the Art of French Cooking*, Julia Child pointed to sauces as "the splendor and glory of French cooking."[3] Even those who opposed or made fun of the export of French tastes paid particular attention to sauces. In 1761, the English review *Connoisseur* noted that, because the cook at White's (a prestigious club) was French, he would presumably soon "oblige the world by a treatise on the art and mystery of sauces."[4] Two years earlier, Tobias Smollet in the *Critical Review* attacked English chef William Verral, an advocate of French cookery, as bewitched by the "pernicious slops, sauces and kickshaws of the French."[5]

Medieval Sauces

The importance of sauces antedates the seventeenth-century "revolution in taste" that constitutes the French invention of modern cuisine.[6] The first cookbook to have survived from between the early sixth century and 1200 is a recently discovered group of ten sauce recipes forming part of a twelfth-century manuscript composed at Durham Cathedral Priory, now at the Sidney Sussex College Library in Cambridge. The sub-section of a group of medical preparations in the manuscript is entitled *Salsamenta pictavenisia*, "Sauces from Poitou."[7] It features sauces to be served with meat and fowl, flavored with garlic, mustard, pepper, and parsley, so they are not as highly inflected with tropical spices on the order of ginger, cinnamon, or cloves as later medieval examples would be.

It is sometimes assumed that France established the standards for medieval cookery as well as modern, and indeed the chef from the Middle Ages best known to posterity is Taillevent (c. 1310–1395), who was so prized by King Charles V of France that he was ennobled and given an admittedly somewhat derisive coat of arms, three marmites or stew pots. Taillevent was credited with the authorship of the *Viandier*, a widely diffused cookbook that he may have revised, but whose original form antedated his career.[8] Notwithstanding the distinction of this French chef, medieval cuisine was international in the sense that no single nation exerted the kind of sway that France enjoyed in the modern period.

There were a number of regional differences among ingredients and sauces in Europe, some based on climate and environment and others on more purely culinary opinion. Thus, citrus fruit and eggplant were more common in southern Europe, particularly Spain. Olive oil was more important in Mediterranean littoral countries, where olive trees can be grown, than in northern Europe, where pork fat and secondarily butter were used as cooking media. In medieval Europe, olive oil was a necessity everywhere during Lent when animal products were forbidden, so there was a substantial trade in olive oil to serve the north. A further cultural dimension to fat choices is the popularity of duck fat in southwestern France, not explicable simply because of supply. Also purely matters of taste, unrelated to external conditions, are the greater popularity of ginger and sugar in England than in Italy, and the enthusiasm for grains of paradise in France, a spice much less favored elsewhere.[9]

Even with regional variations, there were consistent patterns to medieval culinary preferences: the importance of spices; the use of sugar across the menu so that there was little distinction between sweet and savory; the prestige of meat and contempt for vegetables and dairy products; recipes adapted to cycles of fasting mandated by the church calendar; ostentation, illusion, and color. Medieval cuisine adored artifice and, in a world in which all chickens were free range and no produce was genetically modified, cooks expressed very little sentiment in favor of simplicity or of enhancing the inherent flavor of the core ingredient of a dish. Rather, sauces partook of the medieval love of complexity. They were conceived as a separate and supreme culinary art, not as an outgrowth or distillate of the primary meat or fish they were ornamenting or enhancing. Sauces were generally made without reference to the meat they were going to be served with. In a group of twenty-three sauces, the author of the recipe section of the *Ménagier de Paris*, a late-fourteenth-century household miscellany, calls for carp broth as the basis for a sauce to accompany that fish and capon fat drippings for a quick capon sauce, but otherwise the preparations have nothing to do with the meat or fish juices.[10] This is in clear contrast to the principles that would become the basis for modern French cuisine. It was a mark of the new French repertoire of the seventeenth century that cooked meat juice was concentrated and used with the appropriate meat dish. Medieval sauces were much less reliant on what was extracted from the principal meat or fish dish they accompanied. Making a sauce might start with cooking meat pieces or broth. The *Llibre de Sent Soví* has a meat sauce that could be served with a variety of dishes, and a *salsa salvatgina*, game sauce, that was intended only to accompany roast crane, and the cook is instructed not to use crane or other birds in preparing the sauce.[11] Generally, however, the compatibility of a sauce was judged by attributed health properties—balancing the properties of hot, cold, moist, and dry—not an aesthetic sense of relation.

Medieval sauces were not designed to bring out or intensify the flavor of what they were served with, but rather constituted in themselves the principal taste for which the meat or fish was a passive medium. In this sense, medieval cuisine was what scholar Massimo Montanari calls a "synthetic" cuisine, one in which the goal is to create a layering or spectrum of flavors, rather than an "analytic" cuisine in which distinctions among flavors (sweet, salty, bitter, sour, spicy) as well as dishes themselves (meat, starch, vegetable) are clearly demarcated.[12] Synthetic cuisines are familiar in the modern world, although European and American foods have based themselves on an analytic aesthetic. Mexican and Indian dishes are established on synthetic principles. The complexity of flavors is more important than emphasizing the basic ingredient, and sauces such as mole or vindaloo have their identity apart from specific meats or fish.

Medieval sauces were thought to have humoral properties that balanced out those of the meats they complemented. Most spices were regarded as hot and dry to varying degrees and therefore appropriate in sauce form to counteract the attributed properties of meat and fish. How important medical considerations were in the actual cooking and planning of meals is debatable. Certain famous stories about great men ignoring dietary advice and paying the consequences suggest that, then as now, medical warnings could be solicited and yet ignored. King Henry I of England died within a week of defying his doctor's orders to stay away from lampreys that, although highly prized, were dangerously cold and wet. A black pepper sauce or a multi-spiced galantine (aspic) offered ways of tempering the negative humoral nature of lampreys, along with cooking procedures that began with drowning the lampreys in red wine.[13] Melons were thought to be almost indigestible and likely to rot in the stomach, yet Renaissance Italy was swept by an irresistible passion for eating them. Doctors recommended avoiding them but allowed that accompanying them with something salty, such as caviar or prosciutto, might work to mitigate their danger.

Medical teaching and taste preferences assigned particular sauces to certain kinds of dishes. Thus, *cameline* sauce, whose name comes from its camel-brown color and whose most important spice was cinnamon, was thought to go with veal, chicken, mutton, and salmon. Goose, however, should be served with pepper or garlic sauce. The very popular *poivrade* sauce combined pepper with vinegar or verjuice and was thickened with breadcrumbs. Sauces that were humorally nearly neutral, such as *jance* made with ginger, were the most versatile, but considered not sufficiently powerful for some kinds of meat.[14]

Medieval sauces were predominantly spiced and strongly flavored with acidic tastes such as vinegar, citrus juice, verjuice, or mustard. At the same time, sugar or honey could be added to provide a sweet-and-sour effect. Garlic was sometimes used for additional bite.[15] Sauces were thickened with breadcrumbs (usually toasted) or almonds or liver, but emerged thin by modern standards. Butter and flour were never used, and so richness and glossy thickness were not attributes of the medieval sauces. *Jance*, *poivrade*, *cameline*, green sauces, and garlic sauces were major categories, and there were many variations on these themes, not only by different chefs operating in different parts of Europe, but also within the same cookbook, thus the *Viandier* has three *jance* recipes.[16] Medieval chefs developed a number of cold sauces, as well. While medieval sauces tended to disappear in modern French cooking, certain cold types such as *ravigote* or *gribiche* retain the sharp, vinegar taste of their medieval predecessors, even if they have dropped the oriental spices.

Sauces and the Invention of Modern French Cuisine

In contrast to art and architecture, the Renaissance (which roughly coincides with the sixteenth century in northern Europe) was not dramatically distinct in its culinary style from that of the Middle Ages.[17] The crucial change would have to await the era of Louis XIV (reigned 1643–1715). Beginning in the seventeenth century and first clearly demonstrated by La Varenne's *Le cuisinier françois* of 1651, French chefs and food theorists created a new set of culinary principles that broke with medieval precedent and would serve as the model for modern *haute cuisine*.[18] The movement presented itself as a reform. Very much in the manner that a religious or political reform program conceives its mission as eliminating corrupt excrescences and returning to virtuous practices of the past, the French culinary reformers advocated nature and classical restraint as guides to cooking. A major characteristic of all culinary reforms, which includes two *nouvelle cuisine* waves in French history and the American farm-to-table cooking style, is to exalt the natural taste of primary ingredients and to condemn over-elaboration as being used to distract from the use of poor-quality ingredients. Nicolas Bonnefons, cookbook author and valet at the court of Louis XIV, in 1656 declared that "cabbage soup should taste of cabbage, leeks of leeks, turnips of turnips."[19] Behind what seems at first glance a banal truism is a radical declaration that focuses attention on the taste of even humble vegetables and implies that their preparation must bring out, rather than cover, that taste. This is a move away from the synthetic aesthetic of the Middle Ages, which emphasized transformation and a multiplicity of flavors, toward an analytic approach in which the intensity and apparent simplicity of flavor triumphs over complex multiplicity of tastes.

As is also the case with reforms and revolutions, the early militants are not always radical enough for their successors. The unknown author who signed himself "L. S. R.," author of *L'Art de bien traiter* published in 1671, denounced La Varenne for not sufficiently embracing the purity and delicacy of the new French cuisine and for his attachment to the "villainous tastes of the Arabs." Specifically, La Varenne was taken to task for dishes on the order of frogs' legs with saffron or turkey with raspberries. Two prominent sins, according to new orthodoxy, were the use of exotic spices and of sweet ingredients outside of dessert.[20]

If the denunciations of the culinary reformers targeted medieval sauces, their program by no means did away with sauces as such, but rather substituted a radically different aesthetic in which sauces were crucial. The sauces developed in the late seventeenth and early eighteenth centuries are the basis of modern French cuisine. The new theory and practice of sauces proceeded from guiding principles of intensification rather than harmonizing contradictory tastes. Notions of complementarity focused less on medical theories of humoral balance and more on whichever meat or fish the sauce was accompanying. The flavor of beef or chicken was enhanced by a sauce made from its juices, which by means of boiling it down resulted in concentrated stocks and essences, thus distilling the nature and flavor of the primary ingredient. Complementing a sauce of this kind was not spice, with the exception of pepper, but rather herbs, mushrooms, truffles, and other flavorful products of European woodlands and gardens. The sauce became thicker and glossier than its medieval antecedent, and its flavor was rich rather than sharp. Butter mixed with flour (*roux*) was a way of achieving this kind of texture and taste. Where the *Viandier* had virtually no sauces in which butter was an ingredient, L. S. R. called for butter in 80 percent of his sauce recipes. This principle extends to modern French cookery—the grand eminence of mid-century restaurant cuisine, Fernand Point, laid down a golden rule: "Butter, Always Butter!"[21] In Anthony Bourdain's *Kitchen Confidential*, the term for finishing a sauce with butter (*monter au beurre*) is a kind of battle cry.[22] Lots of butter is why "my sauce tastes richer, creamier and mellower than yours," he boasted. Eugénie Brazier, in her 1977 cookbook, *La Mere Brazier: The Mother of Modern French Cooking*, includes as her final chapter of recipes, "Les Beurres et les sauces" as well. In fact, of the thirty-five recipes included in the chapter, only seven do not use butter as an ingredient.

Such taste and texture were not the goal of La Varenne or Bonnefons, most of whose recipes involve no sauce other than the natural juices of the meat being cooked.[23] In this sense, L. S. R.'s critique notwithstanding, they were the more radical innovators, because their successors elaborated sauces even more esoteric than the medieval preparations until rebellions in the eighteenth century attacked the richness of the now classic sauces. The early pioneers' reliance on the liquid given off by the meat itself in cooking intensified flavor in a manner that became the hallmark and purpose of the modern French sauce. The essence of the primary ingredient would be distilled from the flesh, which would fall away in a process that had as its intellectual origins the practices of alchemy. In that semi-science, the search for spiritually powerful formulae used distillation to create a rarified spirit (*quintessence*) from which the corporeal elements had been discarded.[24] The word *quintessence* is used in both alchemical and cooking treatises of the early modern era.

In terms of practical cooking, this focus on distillation meant that sauces were boiled down and reconstituted by means of additional liquids and complementary flavorings. The resulting concentrates were known as *jus* and *coulis*. The codifier of this important step in the development of French sauces was François Massialot, author of *Le Cuisinier roïal et bourgeois* (1691) and *Nouvelle instruction pour les confitures* (1692). These two encyclopedic works were authoritative for several decades during which time French sauces started to define high-status cuisine internationally.

Massialot identified three categories of *jus* appropriate for fowl, meat, and fish. Roasted poultry was pounded and the juices that it gave off when strained and skimmed of grease had a smoky flavor in addition to the taste of the browned meat. Beef, mutton, or veal slices, slowly cooked in an earthenware pot covered with dough, produced a light but intense *jus*, thickened only by the gelatinous content of the meat. *Jus de poisson* was produced by pressing cooked fish, much as with poultry *jus*, but in this case freshwater fish (especially carp or tench) were sautéed in butter, dusted with flour, browned further, moistened with court bouillon and herbs, and then strained and pressed. Massaliot's *coulis* (unrelated to the contemporary idea of the coulis as a light purée) was based on *jus*, but it used mashed meat, fish, vegetables, or even almonds (for fast days) and had a grainy texture.[25] The combination of *jus* and the pounded solids was strained through a sieve. The *coulis* exemplified the same "ethos" of intensification but was more complex than the simple *jus*.

The *jus* or *coulis* could be stored and then added to soups, ragouts, and sauces as needed. Rather than the sauce being made all at once, the new idea was to have a reserve or sauce base (*fonds*). In Massialot the *jus* or *coulis* was a sauce in itself or a finishing agent. In the later elaboration of French sauces, it was the starting point for creating hundreds of different recipes. Already in Massialot there was a degree of complexity following from the use of sauce fundamentals. *Jus* or *coulis* thickened with a *roux* (flour bonded with butter) produced a ragout; using egg yolks and/or cream as thickening agents produced a fricassee. Preparations such as *civet*, *daube*, *estoufade*, and *hachis* were techniques built on *jus* and *coulis* foundations.

What began as a radical simplification and defense of what was called a "delicacy" and the taste of the primary ingredients became almost comically elaborate throughout the eighteenth century. England, where the French style gained fervid adherents among elite chefs and diners, was also a site of resistance to the fashion in sauces because of their imputed complexity, both in terms of preparation and taste—the same accusations that had been leveled at the medieval recipes. Writing to Horace Mann in 1749, Horace Walpole described a forthcoming series of banquets at Cambridge University for which cooks had been working for ten days in advance, "distilling essences of every living creature, and massacring and confounding all the species that Noah and Moses took such pains to preserve and distinguish."[26] An article in *The Connoisseur* in 1757 expressed shock at the expense of boiling down meat into ragouts: "We have a cargo of hams every year from Westphalia, only to extract the Essence of them for our soups; and we kill a brace of bucks every week, to make a coulis of the haunches."[27]

Massialot presented twenty-three different kinds of *coulis*, but the French sauces produced and codified in the eighteenth and nineteenth centuries reduced the number of *coulis* recipes and directed them toward preparation of foundation or "mother sauces" that were the base of further elaboration. Already in L. S. R.'s cookbook, a *coulis universel* anticipates the *sauce espagnole* that was the basis for French brown sauces. This sauce, made with brown roux, an essence of beef or veal, tomatoes, mushrooms, and a mirepoix, was used to prepare brown or meat sauces such as Bigarade (an orange sauce), Bordelaise (red wine sauce), or Chasseur (with mushrooms, wine, and tomato sauce). *Allemande* and *velouté* were the bases for white sauces (for example, Villeroy, which has ham and truffle essence); Hollandaise was the base for acidified butter and egg-yolk sauces (such as Béarnaise). This all seems complicated and indeed requires a considerable amount of time, knowledge, and skill, but lends itself to systemization in professional kitchens. The basic sauces form the trunk of a prolific tree with many subsidiary branches. Preparation does not have to be all at once but is rather the product of prepared mixtures and a large but defined range of additional ingredients.[28]

The First Nouvelle Cuisine

Beginning in the 1730s, a reaction against the complexity of sauces reaffirmed the virtues of simplicity, not merely as an aesthetic idea of authentic flavors, but linked to a morality of natural health and a disdain for pretension. Jean-Jacques Rousseau, the foremost philosopher of nature and opponent of social artificiality and inequality, fervently advocated a rustic, even vegetarian simplicity. The mainstream of French culinary opinion, however, went only part of the way toward this renunciatory extreme. What from 1742 was called *nouvelle cuisine* rejected artifice and over-elaboration, but not elegance. Its chief advocates, François Menon and François Marin, described their cuisine as simple, refined, hygienic (*propre*), and, in Enlightenment fashion, scientific.

In fact, the same principles of reduction and distillation as before were employed, but the ideal was bouillon rather than a heavy rich sauce of the *espagnole* type. The prologue to Marin's *Les dons de Comus* (1742) described modern sauces as inspired by a species of chemistry: "The science of the cook consists today of deconstructing foods, turning them into quintessence, of taking their nourishing and light juices and blending them so that none dominate the others." The ingredients were expensive and the process could be quite complex, but the bouillon or, as the strongest, most concentrated bouillon was termed, *restaurant*, was supposed to restore (*restaurer*) health damaged by over-complex gastronomy and bring about a kind of moral reform of the sort that today might be associated with gluten-free or at least a "sauce-on-the-side" concern for the self.[29]

Bouillon could be served as a healthful consommé or used to create sauces. The ideal in Marin's *Les Dons de Comus* was to reduce the cooking liquid from meats or sautéed ingredients and add small amounts of concentrated bouillon. *Sauce à l'ivoire* was made by sautéing sliced onions with chopped veal, ham, and salt pork, seasoned with herbs and garlic, and then adding champagne and reducing. The result was then thickened slightly with consommé.[30] But this consommé might require all manner of expensive ingredients (partridge and veal, for example), hours of simmering, skimming, and tending, and so it amounted to an expensive and refined form of simplicity, about as close to real rusticity as the mock dairy at Petit Trianon.

Despite the manifesto of the *nouvelle cuisine* and frequent calls for reform in manners and outlook as regards dining, there is more continuity than rupture in the history of French cuisine in its formative period. This is visible in the proliferation of sauces, which might vary more than the seventeenth-century basics, but which reproduced the ethos of distillation and intensity. The major innovation was institutional: the development of the restaurant as a place where one had a substantial choice of dishes, times when a diner could be served, and fellow eaters with whom one would dine. The emphasis on such options distinguished restaurants from inns, take-out establishments, *traiteurs*, taverns, and the like. In the nineteenth century, the restaurant would define *haute cuisine*.

"Classic" French Cuisine and the Second Nouvelle Cuisine

The next great codifier of the French food style was Marie-Antonin Carême (1784–1833), a master of what sociologist Priscilla Parkhurst Ferguson has called "systematic simplicity." Carême explicated what was already implicit in the variations on foundational sauces. Here was another great chef who presented himself and was regarded as a simplifier but whose work today seems immense, encyclopedic, and complex. Some of his own rhetorical flourishes served to fight battles that were already won, against highly spiced sauces, for example. The cult of naturalness was exalted by Carême's followers, such as the Anglo-Irish noblewoman Lady Morgan, who praised a dinner of Carême's for the absence of vulgar spices or relishes and the presentation of the meat with its natural aroma and every vegetable with its proper verdure. Taste, according to Lady Morgan, was a proper aesthetic balance in accord with a notion of a civilized rather than riotous form of culinary pleasure.[31]

Carême invented, or at least popularized, many aspects of what was regarded for over 150 years as classic French cuisine: vols-au-vents, soufflés, herb mixtures (*bouquet garni*). He also invented sauces, all of which were founded on four classic formulae: espagnole (thickened dark stock with tomato), velouté (thickened stock), béchamel (thickened milk), and allemande (thickened egg and acid emulsions).[32]

Carême presented 358 sauces in volume four of *L'art de la cuisine française au dix-neuvième siècle* (1845), many of them his own inventions, but all traceable to the foundational sauces, and a few other preparations such as mayonnaise. He gave many of the sauces the names of notable, mostly French personages: sauces Colbert, Molière, Victor Hugo. Others were named after places in France. Some of these, such as Périgord, Provence, or Normandie, evoke particular flavorings (truffles, garlic with tomatoes, and cream, respectively), but others have no identifiable link to ingredients (*sauce française, parisienne*). Moreover, many sauces that bear place names are deceptive. Thus, *sauce Bénévent* is not named after the Italian city of Benevento but after one of Carême's employers, Prince Talleyrand, who bore the title "Prince of Benevento." Better known today is béarnaise sauce, whose ingredients have nothing to do with the Pyrenean region of Béarn but was rather a tribute to King Henry IV, who was prince of Béarn before becoming the first king of the Bourbon dynasty at the end of the wars of religion.

The fact that many sauces, including the basic espagnole and allemande, seem to indicate foreign origins was not, according to Carême, any sort of indication of French deficiency. He was contemptuous of M. Marin, author of *Brévaire du gastronome*, who had protested against these foreign appellations. In a prologue to *Le Cuisinier parisien* (1828), Carême dismissed the notion that such names were an insult to France or that they indicated some sort of dependence on external inspiration. Their origins may have been in Spain or Germany, Carême acknowledged, but France so changed and perfected them that it was merely French generosity rather than logical attribution that preserved the geographical name. France had made sauce allemande "as unctuous and as smooth as it is perfect"—it did not arrive in that condition.[33]

Carême was employed by kings, princes, and men of great wealth: the English Prince Regent, the future George IV, who equipped him with a still-extant kitchen at the Mughal-revival palace at Brighton; Prince Talleyrand, the greatest diplomat of the early nineteenth century; and Baron James Meyer Rothschild. He even had an offer from the czar of Russia, which he did not accept. But the setting for the future regulations and innovations regarding sauces was not to be palaces but restaurants, created for the haute bourgeoisie. Mornay sauce (béchamel with egg and grated cheese) was invented by Joseph Voiron, chef of the restaurant Durand (named after his son); Choron (béarnaise with tomatoes) was the creation of the restaurant Voisin.[34]

Auguste Escoffier defined French cuisine in the late nineteenth and early twentieth centuries. In many respects he continued the path established by Carême, but unlike his predecessor, Escoffier spent his career as a chef in grand hotel restaurants, moving from the National in Lucerne to the Savoy and then the Carlton in London.[35] Escoffier's lasting contribution to French cuisine was the organization of the restaurant kitchen into five *parties*, and it is a mark of the importance of sauces that the head chef's second-in-command in this system was the *saucier*. The sauces in Escoffier's *Guide culinaire*, first edition (1903), were summarized in the *Répertoire de la cuisine*, which explicitly claims to be a handy reference work and summary for the cuisine of Escoffier. The great chef kept the principle of foundational "mother" sauces defined by Carême but added tomato sauce as one of the building blocks and emphasized the use of aromatic stocks (*fumet*) that did not always directly derive from the now fourfold *fonds*: espagnole, velouté, béchamel (incorporating allemande), and tomato. Escoffier confirmed the status of sauce espagnole as the leading member of the "*Grandes sauces de base.*"[36]

Under Escoffier's direction, French sauces were not only classified but amounted to a set of rules, an extensive set of options, but nevertheless, despite the effusion of possibilities, a repertoire based on a few fundamental principles: distillations and concentrations of flavor, butter and flour, and a range of additional flavors that did not, however, include tropical aromatic spices or other products.

Depending on one's point of view and historical position, the Belle Époque and the first two-thirds of the twentieth century mark the efflorescence of French cuisine, or its gradual calcification into a form of culinary obscurantism and, once more, neglect of basic ingredients. The reformers of the 1970s were the advocates of what was called *la nouvelle cuisine*, similar in its manifestos to the demands of the first *nouvelle cuisine* of the mid-eighteenth century. Once again, this program advocated sweeping away of conventional practices. Once again, sauces came in for particularly withering criticism for their heaviness, lack of freshness, and their distraction from what they were supposed to complement rather than cover up. Guidebook writers and food experts Henri Gault and Christian Millau in 1973 came up with the "Ten Commandments of Nouvelle Cuisine," of whose prohibitions the one most clearly relevant to sauces was "Thou shall eliminate brown and white sauces," a frontal attack on the edifice built up by Carême and Escoffier. Other commandments echoed or repeated the demands made in previous cycles of culinary reform: "Thou shalt not overcook; Thou shalt use fresh, quality products; Thou shalt lighten thy menu."[37]

Gault and Millau specified what they called *les horreurs de la cuisine* that they wanted to eliminate, practices such as excessive reliance on farmed fish and on herbes de Provence and the use of skimpy amounts of canned or jarred truffles, but key to their program was to change the sauces hitherto regarded as the glory of French cuisine. No more recycled espagnole base, and in general "away with rich sauces that have murdered too many livers and concealed so much tasteless fish." This was repeated by French chemist Hervé This, whose work in molecular gastronomy has led to him calling traditional sauces "the gourmand's poison," leading to a cycle of gout and dieting.[38]

What was truly new about *nouvelle cuisine* of the late 1960s and the 1970s was not so much its opposition to sauces and exaltation of primary products as the notion of innovation, a plan to break with the past and not merely reform it. Although Gault and Millau warned, "Thou shall not be systematically modernistic," they also advocated inventiveness and new techniques. The great chef was becoming not just a uniquely skilled artisan working within a tradition, but rather something closer to an artist, whose creativity was not limited by a set of rules established in the past. The actual sauces recommended might be lighter versions of tradition—*jus* reduced and emulsified with small amounts of butter or cream (but no flour). But *nouvelle cuisine* sauces tended to branch out in two contradictory directions: a *cuisine minceur* (more or less a "spa cuisine"), whose most famous exponent was Michel Guérard, who banned cream, butter, and egg yolks, and promoted an eclectic, Asian-inflected tendency that added such flavors as vanilla, mango, and kiwi. Alain Senderens developed "Salmon Shizuo or the Return of Japan" with soy sauce, although finished with butter.[39] Both schools came in for a degree of satire and criticism for preciousness, affectation, strangeness, and expense, not matched by heartiness or subtlety.[40] They share a "back to basics" aesthetic and indeed anticipate the current emphasis on the quality of basic ingredients and avoidance of artificial distractions characteristic of American culinary reformers and the pioneering work of Alice Waters and other chefs both inspired by France and intent on creating a particularly American sense of seasonality and locale. On the other hand, the polemical agenda of *nouvelle cuisine* invited ridicule and gave rise to an anxiety about the future of French traditions that has not abated in the intervening decades.

The current state of French cuisine is hotly debated, as clearly the nation has lost the hegemony over international high-end taste that it enjoyed from the late seventeenth century to the late twentieth. The fact that the French government recently found it necessary to campaign for "the French gastronomic meal" in the UNESCO Intangible World Heritage list indicates a desire for validation and corresponding lack of confidence that is shocking given centuries of unchallenged supremacy that preceded this grudging designation. (Grudging because France had asked for French cuisine *tout court* to be given the status as a World Heritage item. Other countries objected, asserting that their cuisines were equal to that of France. The compromise was that the entire French meal, including wine, the table setting, and the service rituals, would be sufficiently distinctive.)

The emergence of Catalonia and the Basque Country as sites of a culinary avant-garde was well established by the beginning of the twenty-first century. What was commonly called "molecular gastronomy" pushed away the preeminence of France. American authorities such as Arthur Lubow, in a *New York Times Magazine* article in 2003, proclaimed that the torch of culinary leadership had passed from France to Spain. Soon Denmark, Japan, and Peru would either be anointed or at least identified as "hot" in the increasingly global and fast-moving competition.

Yet, despite frequent and reiterated pronouncements of the eclipse of France and its cuisine, despite the scanty representation of France in the annual San Pellegrino rankings of the world's (supposedly) greatest restaurants, there are signs of life in contemporary France cuisine. The current reform or restructuring of French dining is not as centered on sauces as was the case with culinary upheavals of the past, although the leading exponent of molecular cuisine in France, Hervé This, has categorized the 351 (by his count) classic French sauces into 14 physio-chemical types. Molecular gastronomy has had the effect of expanding the definition of sauces and blurring the border between sauce as accompaniment and overall transformation of flavors and textures. In addition to the creativity of the latest scientific renewal of cuisine, such trends as the expansion of global influences, re-emphasis on regional, local, and high-quality products, and rediscovery of basic ingredients such as bread, small-scale restaurants ("*bistronomiques*") all either incorporate a tradition of French sauces, expand on it, or are less reliant on sauces for what defines French cuisine.

Sauce Espagnole

From Auguste Escoffier, *Ma cuisine* (Paris 1934, 13–14)

To obtain a liter of Brown Sauce, prepare 100 grams of roux as indicated earlier and cook it until it is just ready. Remove the pot from the fire and let the roux cool for a few moments. Then mix it with a liter of brown sauce-base (*fonds*), whisking in whipped egg-whites so as to obtain a smooth, glossy texture without lumps. Bring sauce to a boil, continuing to stir with a whisk or spatula. Keep it at a slow and regular boil, putting it at the side of the fire.

Add to the sauce a mirepoix prepared in this way: 30 grams of lard chopped into small dice; 30 grams of onion; 50 grams of carrots, diced; a sprig of thyme; a small bay leaf and several parsley stems.

Melt the lard in a saucepan with 30 grams of butter, add the prepared vegetables and herbs and brown them lightly.

Continue boiling the sauce for three hours, adding a few deciliters of cold brown sauce-base from time to time to facilitate skimming the fat from the sauce. The frequency of skimming will depend on the degree to which the sauce-base has been saturated with the meat juices used in its preparation.

Once arriving at the desired stage, pour the sauce through a fine-meshed strainer into a terrine, pressing lightly on the mirepoix, and swirl it until it has cooled almost completely. Keep in reserve.

The finished sauce is prepared the next day with the addition of tomatoes and more brown sauce-base, cooking for another hour, if a starch roux is used or several hours for a flour roux.

Notes

1. Louis Diat, *Sauces, French and Famous* (New York and Toronto: Rinehart, 1948), ix.
2. Auguste Escoffier, *Le Guide culinaire* (Paris, 1993), 4, as quoted in Maryann Tebben, *Sauces: A Global History* (London: Reaktion Books, 2014), 49, 56.
3. Tebben, *Sauces*, 49, 56.
4. Mr. Town, *The Connoisseur*, Vol. 1 (London: R. Baldwin), 110.
5. T. Sarah Peterson, *Acquired Taste: The French Origins of Modern Cooking* (Ithaca, NY, and London: Cornell University Press, 1994), 206, 208.

6. Susan Pinkard, *A Revolution in Taste: The Rise of French Cuisine* (Cambridge: Cambridge University Press, 2008), 3–50.
7. Giles Gasper and Faith Wallis, "*Salsamenta pictavensia*: Gastronomy and Medicine in Twelfth Century England," *English Historical Review* 131, no. 553 (2016): 1353–1385.
8. Terrence Scully, *The Viandier of Taillevent: An Edition of All Extant Manuscripts* (Ottowa: University of Ottowa Press, 1988).
9. Bruno Laurioux, "De l'usage des épices dans l'alimentation medieval," *Médiévales* 5, no. 15–31 (1983): 18; Melitta Weiss Adamson, ed., *Regional Cuisines of Medieval Europe* (New York and London: Routledge, 2002).
10. Gina Greco and Christine Rose, trans., *The Good Wife's Guide (Le Ménagier de Paris): A Medieval Household Book* (Ithaca, NY: Cornell University Press, 2009), 321–325.
11. Joan Santanach, ed., and Robin Vogelzang, trans., *Llibre de Sent Soví*, 1324 (Rochester, NY: Barcino-Tamesis), 190.
12. Massimo Montanari and Beth Archer, trans., *Medieval Tastes: Food, Cooking, and the Table* (New York: Columbia University Press, 2012), 10–11.
13. Terrence Scully, *The Art of Cookery in the Middle Ages* (Woodbridge and Suffolk: Boydell Press, 1995), 45; Scully, *The Viandier of Taillevent: An Edition of All Extant Manuscripts*, 130–133; Jean-Étienne Surlève-Bazeille, *Le Livre de la Lamproie* (Bordeaux: Éditions Confluences, 2007), 122–128.
14. D. Eleanor Scully and Terence Scully, *Early French Cookery: Sources, History, Original Recipes, and Modern Adaptations* (Ann Arbor: University of Michigan Press, 2002), 113.
15. Pinkard, *A Revolution in Taste*, 22.
16. Scully, *The Viandier of Taillevent*, 228–229. Jance sauce used ground almonds as a base.
17. Ken Albala, *Eating Right in the Renaissance* (Berkeley: University of California Press, 2002).
18. Pinkard, *A Revolution in Taste*; Françoise Sabban and Silvano Serventi, *La gastronomie au Grand Siécle: 100 recettes de France et de L'Italie* (Paris: Stock, 1998).
19. Alberto Capatti and Massimo Montanari, *Italian Cuisine: A Cultural History* (New York: Columbia University Press, 2003), 86.
20. Priscilla Parkhurst Ferguson, *Accounting for Taste: The Triumph of French Cuisine* (Chicago and London: University of Chicago Press, 2004).
21. Jean-Robert Pitte and Jody Gladding, trans., *French Gastronomy: The History and Geography of a Passion* (New York: Columbia University Press, 2002), 94–95.
22. Anthony Bourdain, *Kitchen Confidential: Adventures in the Culinary Underbelly* (New York: Harper Collins, 2000), 81.
23. Pinkard, *A Revolution in Taste*, 120.
24. Peterson, *Acquired Taste*, 193–194.
25. François Massialot, *Le Cuisinier Roïal et bourgeois* (Paris: Charles de Sercy, 1698), 284–285.

26. Horace Walpole, *The Letters of Horace Walpole to Sir Horace Mann*, Vol. 2, trans. Lord Dover (New York: George Dearborn, 1833), 91.
27. Peterson, *Acquired Taste*, 195–196.
28. Louis Saulnier and Théodore Gringoire, *Le Répetoire de la cuisine* (Paris: Flammarion, 1914).
29. Pinkard, *A Revolution in Taste*, 155–180.
30. Ibid., 173.
31. Ferguson, *Accounting for Taste*, 68–69.
32. Ian Kelly, *Cooking for Kings: The Life of Antonin Carême, the First Celebrity Chef* (New York: Walker, 2003), 201; Amy Trubek, *Haute Cuisine: How the French Invented the Culinary Profession* (Philadelphia: University of Pennsylvania Press, 2000), 18–20.
33. Ferguson, *Accounting for Taste*, 72–74.
34. Alain Drouard, "Chefs, Gourmets and Gourmands: French Cuisine in the 19th and 20th Centuries," in *Food: The History of Taste*, ed. Paul Freedman (London: Thames & Hudson, 2007), 274.
35. Timothy Shaw, *The World of Escoffier* (New York: Vendome Press, 1993); Kenneth James, *Escoffier: The King of Chefs* (Hambledon and London: Bloomsbury, 2012).
36. Tebben, *Sauces*, 59–60.
37. Michael Steinberger, *Au Revoir to All That: Food, Wine, and the End of France* (New York: Bloomsbury, 2011), 31–34; Pitte and Gladding, *French Gastronomy: The History and Geography of a Passion*, 147.
38. Tebben, *Sauces*, 63.
39. Pitte and Gladding, *French Gastronomy*, 149.
40. Patrick Rambourg, *Histoire de la cuisine et la gastronomie française* (Paris: Éditions Perrin, 2010), 283–299.

Selected Bibliography

Adamson, Melitta Weiss, ed. *Regional Cuisines of Medieval Europe: A Book of Essays.* New York and London: Routledge, 2002.

Drouard, Alain. "Chefs, Gourmets and Gourmands: French Cuisine in the 19th and 20th Centuries." In *Food: The History of Taste*, edited by P. Freedman, 263–300. London: Thames & Hudson, 2007.

Ferguson, Priscilla Parkhurst. *Accounting for Taste: The Triumph of French Cuisine.* Chicago and London: University of Chicago Press, 2004.

Montanari, Massmio. *Medieval Tastes: Food, Cooking, and the Table.* Translated by B. M. Archer. New York: Columbia University Press, 2012.

Peterson, T. Sarah. *Acquired Taste: The French Origins of Modern Cooking.* Ithaca, NY, and London: Cornell University Press, 1994.

Pinkard, Susan. *A Revolution in Taste: The Rise of French Cuisine.* Cambridge: Cambridge University Press, 2008.

Pitte, Jean-Robert. *French Gastronomy: The History and Geography of a Passion*. Translated by J. Gladding. New York: Columbia University Press, 2002.

Rambourg, Patrick. *Histoire de la cuisine et la gastronomie française*. Paris: Éditions Perrin, 2010.

Scully, Terrance. *The Art of Cookery in the Middle Ages*. Woodbridge and Suffolk: Boydell Press, 1995.

Tebben, Maryann. *Sauces: A Global History*. London: Reaktion Books, 2014.

Paul Freedman, *Sauces: The Basis for Classic French Cuisine* In: *From Garum to Mole: Sauces and Identity in the Western World*. Edited by: Andrew Donnelly, Beth M. Forrest, and Deirdre Murphy, Oxford University Press.
 DOI: 10.1093/9780190622138.003.0002

PART TWO

Sauces and the Self

3

What's Roman About Fish Sauce?

GARUM AND GARUM CONTAINERS IN EARLY ROMAN PORTUGAL

Joey Williams

GARUM, THE GENERIC modern name for a variety of ancient sauces, pastes, and condiments produced from fermented and salted fish entrails, was among the Romans' favorite foods. Garum found its way onto the plates of many Romans, either alone or mixed with other ingredients.[1] It was enjoyed by both the wealthy and the poor and was consumed by the Romans wherever they could produce or import it.[2] Archaeological evidence suggests that facilities for the production of fish sauce were concentrated along the Atlantic and Mediterranean coasts of Portugal, Spain, and France, although garum was also produced in the eastern Mediterranean, along the Black Sea, and in small batches wherever local regulations did not prohibit this on account of its stench.[3] Even Pompeii appears to have had a garum shop, and residents of that city also imported the sauce, in addition to consuming locally made versions. The Iberian Peninsula in particular appears to have dominated garum production in the Western Roman Empire. In many parts of Iberia, such as the region around Lisbon, garum production began almost as soon as the Romans arrived.[4]

The sauce also found its way into the pages of a host of ancient texts, thus testifying to its ubiquity in the Roman world.[5] From Pliny the Elder's *Natural History* (ca. 77 CE) and the poet Martial (latter half of the first century CE) to the philosophical epistles of Seneca (ca. 65 CE) and even an astrological treatise by Manilius (ca. 10–20 CE), Roman authors variously praise different grades of the sauce, complain of its smell, and bemoan its effects on diners' health. Martial sarcastically commends a rival for pursuing a woman who has eaten several helpings of an especially smelly garum.[6] Seneca warns of the dangerous effects that the salty, fermented sauce has on the stomach.[7]

Pliny, however, praises garum for its ability to season otherwise bland foods,[8] and Martial, in another poem, extols the sophisticates who enjoy garum produced in particular ports.[9] The fish sauce was variously reviled as putrid, unwholesome, and malodorous, but also a valuable, tasty, and nearly essential part of a Roman's meal.

Manilius's *Astronomica*,[10] Pliny's encyclopedic *Natural History*, and a tenth-century agricultural manual titled the *Geoponica*[11] give the most complete descriptions of garum's production. Fish, on account of their rapid decomposition, were often preserved by drying or salting in the Mediterranean region. The blood and entrails were similarly processed in brine, left in the sun for some months, and the liquid left at the top was strained. This liquid, garum, was fermented thanks to the natural enzymes left in the fish viscera. Fermentation in this way was an important method of preservation, especially with a food that was so prone to spoilage. While many varieties, grades, and recipes of fish sauce were used by the Romans, this appears to have been the standard method for its large-scale production. The garum could be mixed with herbs, spices, and wine, used as a base for sauces, or applied directly to a meal.

At times of great demand, some producers diluted their garum, while others, like Umbricius Scaurus of Pompeii, proclaimed that theirs was sauce of the highest quality *liquamen optimum ex officina Scauri*, the "the best liquamen from the workshop of Scaurus," according to the several surviving advertisements from this ancient entrepreneur.[12] Another advertisement, from a shipping container found in London, advertises liquamen, a form of garum, as *Liquamen Antipolitanum Excellens Luci Tetti Africani*, or Lucius Tettius Africanus's Excellent Liquamen from Antipolis.[13] That a container for garum produced in a city along the French Riviera would find its way to Britain is in itself an indication of the voracity with which garum was consumed and the esteem in which it was held. Further testifying to the popularity of Tettius's sauce is a container with an identical label found in Ostia, the port of Rome.[14] Tettius's garum was clearly a successful international product.

Consumed from Pompeii to London, garum was a quintessential Roman food, imbued with symbolic weight as both a product of Rome and a food consumed by Romans. Like many products of the Roman Empire, it was likewise a symbol of that empire and its people. Its production in and transport to the far-flung reaches of the Roman Empire were surely not lost on its consumers. Without Rome's empire, garum would not have reached Britain, would not have been produced in Portugal, and would not have fostered the international trade of Lucius Tettius Africanus. The possession of high-quality garum suggested sophisticated, wealthy tastes. The popularity of fish sauce even in the most remote regions of the empire suggests that many, including the colonized, wished to have a taste of what garum, and Rome, had to offer.

The Distribution and Consumption of Garum

Given garum's popularity, it is no surprise that the Romans produced it on an industrial scale. One of the largest fish-salting and garum-making sites lay on the Atlantic coast of Portugal at Troía. This site, located on a tidal estuary linking the Sado River with the Atlantic Ocean, contained dozens of deep and shallow salting vats, large ramps used to bring ships ashore for loading and unloading, and even a bath complex for the workers. All stone used in building Troía, not to mention the brick and concrete, had to be imported to the island from across the estuary. The fish sauce manufactory was perhaps kept at a distance from the community on the mainland because of the foul-smelling nature of its product.

While garum was also produced at numerous other sites in Iberia, North Africa, and elsewhere, Troía was especially important because the growth of the garum industry there coincided with the production of a distinct type of the Mediterranean's common shipping container, the amphora.[15] Current surveys of the area suggest that more than eighteen different sites along the Sado River produced the amphoras needed to transport Troía's garum.[16] These amphoras, known to archaeologists as Lusitanian amphoras, and their identification, typology, and distribution are used to analyze Roman economy and signal the consumption of, desire for, and social significance attached to garum.

Lusitanian amphoras, like all Roman amphoras, likely held multiple different products during their use-lives and may have been utilized for secondary purposes even after they were damaged or discarded. Thus, an amphora found on an archaeological site may have been originally intended to transport garum but may also have been used to transport other staples of the Roman diet, wine and olive oil. Yet their primary and original contents were invariably fish sauce. The association of this container with numerous Roman goods perhaps added to natives' conception of garum as an especially Roman product and made the amphora an emblem of one's access to these valuable foods and the social esteem they commanded.

Lusitanian ceramics, and thus Lusitanian garum, have been identified dating from the mid-first century CE through the third century CE both in Iberia and around the Mediterranean.[17] The Portuguese archaeologist Carlos Fabião has argued that Lusitanian amphoras were also transported into northern Europe, even as far as Britain, although clay from Lusitania is rarely recognized there.[18] Given the popularity of fish sauce among the Romans, it should come as no surprise that a great many Lusitanian amphoras have been recovered from Rome's port at Ostia.[19] Other examples have been identified in shipwrecks along the southern coast of France, off the Balearic Islands, and in the Strait of Bonifacio between Corsica and Sardinia.[20]

While rare, an increasing number of securely excavated sites puts the date of the first Roman-style amphoras produced on the western coast of Iberia between roughly 60 BCE and 25 CE, roughly concurrent with the Roman consolidation of their colonial possessions in Western Iberia.[21] These amphoras represent the earliest categorically Roman container shape made in Lusitania, and thus also represent an emerging market, both locally and regionally, for Roman foods produced along the Atlantic coast of Iberia. Like their successors, these early amphoras were likely intended to carry garum since they were produced near garum factories on the coast, although they were also reused to ship other products until other amphora production sites (and their concomitant industries) were established elsewhere in the peninsula. The presence of Lusitanian amphoras within the interior of Portugal and Spain is thus a good indicator of a growing desire for Roman food generally, and garum in particular, by the new colonists and native population.

Amphora Production and the Roman Colonization of "Farther Spain"

The first century BCE saw the culmination of decades of warfare, territorial negotiation, and growing cultural entanglements between Romans and natives in western Iberia. Between 80 and 72 BCE, a renegade Roman statesman named Quintus Sertorius occupied much of the Iberian Peninsula and waged a civil war against the Roman Senate. Following his failed rebellion, Rome appears to have taken a greater interest in the western half of the peninsula, then called *Hispania Ulterior*, or "Farther Spain," and the formerly gradual nature of Rome's appropriation of territory soon took up a quicker pace. The rich potential of the territory was noted, small settlements established, and new agricultural and extractive industries took hold. The reshaping of Farther Spain into the imperial province of Lusitania resulted from the culmination of many decades of cultural contact, colonial entanglement, and material exchange between Romans and natives.

Julius Caesar and his entourage began some of the most radical changes to the Roman administration of the coastal urban settlements, as well as the foundation of new inland colonial centers and the reorganization of the rural landscape. Caesar served as governor of Farther Spain in 61–60 BCE, and many changes in the peninsula originated around this date. The Sertorian War had resulted in much disruption in the western half of the Iberian Peninsula, and the survey and pacification of the countryside, which had long harbored resistance to Roman rule, began in earnest. Rome needed to reassert its authority, particularly in the most remote areas, and thus it is no surprise that the remains of numerous Roman military sites date to this period. These include the network of small forts and watchtowers that surveilled the roads and resources of the Alentejo, as well as the more substantial fortifications at sites like Castelo da Lousa and Monte da Nora.[22]

The period of Caesar's governorship also coincides with the beginnings of garum production on the western littoral. The industry's growth was likely facilitated by one Lucius Cornelius Balbus, Caesar's lieutenant during the years of his governorship.[23] Balbus was a member of the local ruling class and surely knowledgeable about the region. It was through Balbus that the Romans began to identify natural resources for exploitation, pacify and settle even the most remote areas, and intensify both agricultural production and the manufacture of fish sauce.

Among the first Roman-style material culture produced during Caesar's governorship were the Lusitanian amphoras used to transport garum. The first productions of these amphoras along the western coast appear to coincide with the year 61–60 BCE. The earliest containers bear some similarities with those produced by Roman workshops in southern Iberia.[24] This suggests that the first workshops of the western Iberian coast likely employed at least a few potters familiar with amphora production from elsewhere in the peninsula. Nevertheless, the wide variety of forms, shapes, and production techniques indicates that the very earliest Lusitanian ovoid amphoras were something of an experiment. Soon after the middle of the first century BCE, as the new administration and economy became entrenched, the Lusitanian potters established large production sites for amphoras. The fish sauce from western Iberia was, it appears, an increasingly hot commodity among those who wished to enjoy and be perceived enjoying Roman products in this new far western colony.

Lusitanian Amphoras in Colonial Alentejan Contexts

In addition to its reach into the western Mediterranean and northern Europe, garum from Lusitania was destined for more local markets. Riverine and overland trade brought the Lusitanian amphoras deep into the interior of Iberia, and examples are found at especially isolated inland sites from even the earliest moments of production. The remote Alto Alentejo region of Portugal is one such case study in the most rural, remote areas of the peninsula to be colonized by the Romans in this period. Examples of these amphoras have been recovered from both indigenous sites and among early Roman settlements. Following the governorship of Caesar and the investment of the local ruling class, including Balbus but extending to many others, demand for Roman-style products within the new Roman administration appears to have flourished both in urban areas and in the countryside.

These sites lie within a region that remains isolated and rural even today. By the end of the first century BCE, the area was reorganized into the Roman model recognized throughout the Mediterranean and Europe. It was transformed by an economic system based around large Roman villas and cash crops such as wine and oil. From the period immediately prior to this, however, archaeologists have uncovered numerous small and large Roman fortifications, watchtowers, and indigenous settlements, in all of which were found Lusitanian amphoras. Amid colonization of the territory and conflict over resources, the inhabitants of the region desired fish sauce from the coast. The consumption of Lusitanian garum represents the acceptance, perhaps unconscious, of the new colonial reality, the Roman administration, and the wider Mediterranean economy that was swiftly finding a new market in the peninsula's interior. What's more, these shipping containers were conspicuous examples of a household's attachment to the Roman diet, signaling their interest in new foods and perhaps the new colonial order. Eating fish sauce did not transform anyone into a Roman, but its presence indicates the growing taste for Roman products and the connections provided by their empire.

Early Roman sites along the Guadiana River and further inland commonly possess examples of Lusitanian amphoras. These include the fortification of Castelo da Lousa and the many different small forts and watchtowers like Caladinho, Castelo dos Mouros, Mariano, Monte do Almo, Outeiro da Mina, Santa Justa, and Soeiros. An especially large collection of Lusitanian amphoras (and local imitations) were found during the excavation of the Castelo da Lousa, a site likely established in the middle of the first century BCE in response to the need for an increased Roman administrative and military presence in the area. The large site, which dominated the heights and slope of a hill adjacent to the Guadiana River, was fortified with a central classically Roman-style atrium house built of un-mortared local stone. Its inhabitants, likely either a detachment of active soldiers or settled veterans, consumed Roman products transported up the Guadiana River in amphoras.

Given its proximity to garum production facilities on the western coast of the peninsula, it is likely that these amphoras were primarily carrying fish sauce. It is no surprise that those in the employ of the Roman army desired garum. Indeed, the fish sauce production facilities along the western coast of Iberia were probably originally intended to serve the expanding Roman population in the peninsula (and elsewhere in the Mediterranean). The presence in western Iberia of recent Roman immigrants, as well as the larger Mediterranean market, was likely a catalyst for its flourishing production.

Several indigenous sites provide good evidence for the importation of amphoras and thus the potential consumption of Roman garum during this colonial period. These include both large settlements such as Castelo Velho de Veiros, small farmhouses like Vidigueira, and indigenous shrines such as the one dedicated to the pre-Roman god Endovelicus at São Miguel da Mota.[25] The presence of the containers of Roman food products at indigenous sites suggests that at least some of the locals' tastes had begun to align with what Rome had on offer.

Purchasing and importing garum from the new factories along the western littoral of the Iberian Peninsula fostered both economic and social connections in this changing colonial environment. The introduction of Lusitanian amphoras indicates a growing taste for garum in the most isolated parts of the Iberian Peninsula during the first century BCE, just as the interior regions like Alto Alentejo were being colonized, reorganized, and reimagined by the Romans. Whether this new pattern of consumption was the result of a new taste for fish sauce among the locals, a desire for familiar foods among Roman settlers, or a combination of factors is best explored through the presence of amphoras from rural Alentejan sites from the early Roman colonial period.

Sites of Roman Identity, Amphoras, and Their Imitations

Two neighboring sites in Alto Alentejo provide a window into the consumption of Roman garum and other food products during the earliest decades of Roman colonization. The first is an indigenous site called Rocha da Mina, and the second is a Roman watchtower known as Caladinho. These two sites were under two miles apart, although rough terrain would have made traveling between them difficult. Of the two, Rocha da Mina appears to have been occupied first, but both sites were inhabited for a relatively brief period. Neither site survived long into the first century CE, when the territory was reorganized to accommodate a Roman model of agricultural production with large estates, slaves, and cash crops like wine and oil. These two sites provide a microcosm for the consumption of Roman foods like garum immediately prior to the Romanization of this region. Like Castelo da Lousa, they possess examples of local imitations of amphoras.

The settlement at Rocha da Mina is situated in a valley and surrounded by a stream and rolling hills near the town of Alandroal in Alto Alentejo. Rocha da Mina is a relatively small site made up of five rooms constructed of the local rock and implanted around a massive stone outcrop. This location makes it difficult to see the site from the surrounding area, and the addition of a fortification wall provides a degree of additional safety. This site was likely occupied by indigenous people who sought to avoid the insecurity that plagued the region in the first century BCE. Nevertheless, the assemblage contains a number of artifacts that suggest some contact with the Roman administration and the wider Mediterranean economy. These include both imported olive oil amphoras from the Guadalquivir River Valley as well as the earliest Lusitanian amphoras.[26]

In addition to the early Lusitanian amphoras, Rocha da Mina's collection of artifacts also includes a fragment from a locally made amphora that resembles the form of those produced on the Lusitanian coast. This piece is produced from the brown, rough, granitic clay commonly found in the area just to the west of Rocha da Mina. This clay was commonly used in indigenous storage jars from this region, but its use in an amphora is unusual. Amphoras were made to be hauled long distances in a ship's hold rather than overland, and were designed for the sea-going, far-trading cultures of the Mediterranean Sea, and their shape reflects that. Yet despite the ubiquity of amphoras around the Mediterranean, there are no suitably navigable bodies of water in the entire Alentejo that would have demanded an amphora—in fact, it is among the driest regions in Europe. Even the Guadiana River was so shallow that it better served pedestrian traffic rather than river boats. Like in the rest of inland Europe, it was no doubt much easier to transport products to the Alentejo in barrels, bags, and skins rather than heavy ceramic amphoras. While amphoras were imported to the Alentejo, the form is rather ill-matched to the region's transport and shipping needs. Sending them overland would have been difficult, expensive, and risked breakage in a cart traveling over rough roads. But some Alentejan potters produced local imitation amphoras for reasons that defy utility, and even the indigenous inhabitants of Rocha da Mina apparently preferred fish sauce when it was provided in containers of this shape. The production of these imitation amphoras indicates consumers' conscious desire for their Roman fish sauce to be noticed. The sauce may have been incorporated into indigenous cuisine, but the amphoras advertised the Roman nature of its contents.

The watchtower called Caladinho is positioned atop a hill and abutting a large outcrop in order to surveil the surrounding countryside, particularly the road that connected the Roman cities of Évora and Merída. Caladinho, like Rocha da Mina, was inhabited only for a short time, from the middle of the first century BCE into the first decades of the first century CE.[27] Caladinho represents part of the Roman response, likely made under Caesar and Balbus, to the aftermath of the Sertorian revolt and the instability, banditry, and apparent guerrilla warfare that gripped western Iberia during the first century BCE.[28] This watchtower and others like it provided security for the region and allowed for the reorganization of the territory according to a Roman colonial model.

The inhabitants of the tower, likely first-generation settlers, allied locals, or even a military detachment, desired Roman imports perhaps to an even greater degree than their neighbors at Rocha da Mina. Thirty-four fragments of early Lusitanian amphoras and a few rare examples of locally produced amphora imitation were recovered from Caladinho, alongside seventy-one examples of olive oil amphoras from southern Spain. Like the amphoras from Rocha da Mina and the other sites in Alto Alentejo, these would have had to have traveled either overland from garum manufactories in the west or up the Guadiana River from the ports to the south with the olive oil amphoras. In either case, the Lusitanian amphoras likely held garum from the western coast intended for the people at Caladinho, whether they were Romans or Roman allies. In this otherwise isolated colonial landscape, the residents sought the foods that would demonstrate their connection to the wider empire. And where they couldn't find the real fish sauce containers on offer, they found local potters who could make some rough approximations of the familiar shapes. Their consumption of fish sauce was all the more conspicuous in these amphora imitations.

Fish sauce was evidently so desired and prized at Rocha da Mina and Caladinho that inhabitants would go to the effort of importing it despite the distance, expense, and terrain-inappropriate containers involved. Perhaps garum, as a new product of a burgeoning empire, and its containers represented a way that even those in isolated, rural places like Alto Alentejo might connect with that nascent power. Fish sauce represents one entanglement between their own identities and Rome's military might as well as the urbane, cosmopolitan nature of its products. To consume garum was to remember its origin as a pan-Mediterranean food, and to acknowledge one's place in Rome's nascent pan-Mediterranean empire. It also came with the cachet of Roman sophistication, so much so that Alentejan consumers were willing to imitate both the sophisticated tastes of Rome and even the pots that contained it.

These amphoras, and their fish sauce contents, served the culinary desires of the new Roman colonists, the allied indigenous aristocracy, and the changing tastes of indigenous Alentejans now more firmly linked to the wider Mediterranean world. As an integral element of a Roman meal, fish sauce held a cultural significance for its consumers. For some it was a taste of home, and for others it was a new, foreign, and desirable flavor.

Eating fish sauce did not make one a Roman. But fish sauce was a product made possible by the Romans, enjoyed by the Romans, and freshly available to even the most isolated settlements in this new colonial territory. Garum was a particularly Roman food, one that carried with it an air of culinary sophistication, pan-Mediterranean internationalism, and complicity in Rome's growing empire in the first century BCE. For many in Alentejo, a Roman identity might grow from the increasing consumption of Roman products and ideas, but for others, such as the inhabitants of Rocha da Mina, a taste of the Empire's fish sauce was perhaps enough.

Garum Recipe

Adapted from the *Geoponica*

Mix the blood and entrails of fatty fish, such as mackerel, sardines, or anchovies, with salt, at a ratio of 1 part salt for every 8 parts fish. Add dried herbs to taste. Leave the mixture in a covered clay vessel for two months, preferably in the sun. Stir the mixture frequently during this time. Strain the mixture into a storage jar once evaporation has reduced it into a thicker liquid. Your garum is now ready to serve!

Notes

1. See Adamson, Chapter 1 in this volume.
2. See Robert I. Curtis, *Garum and Salsamenta: Production and Commerce in Materia Medica* (Leiden: Brill, 1991), 6–8.
3. Robert I. Curtis, "Spanish Trade in Salted Fish Products in the 1st and 2nd Centuries A.D.," *International Journal of Nautical Archaeology and Underwater Exploration* 17 (1988): 205.
4. Rui Mataloto, Joey Williams, and Conceição Roque, "Amphorae at the Origins of Lusitania: Transport Pottery from Western Hispania Ulterior in Alto Altentejo," in *Lusitanian Amphorae: Production and Distribution*, ed. Inês Vaz Pinto, Rui Roberto de Almeida, and Archer Martin (Oxford: Archaepress, 2016), 139–152; Victor Filipe, "Importação e exportação de produtos alimentares em Olisipo: As ânforas romanas da Rua dos Bacalhoeiros." *Revista Portuguesa de Arqueologia* 11 (2008): 318.

5. See Curtis, *Garum and Salsamenta*, 6–15, for a thorough accounting of the literary evidence for ancient fish sauce production in the Mediterranean.
6. Martial, *Epigrams*, 11.27.
7. Seneca, *Epistles*, 45.25.
8. Pliny, *Natural History*, 31.88–93.
9. Martial, *On the Spectacles*, 33.102–103.
10. Manilius, *Astronomica*, 5.667–81.
11. *Geoponica*, 20.46.
12. *L'Année Épigraphique 1998* (2001), no. 1998.352.
13. *L'Année Épigraphique 1984* (1987), no. 1984.618.
14. Fanette Laubenheimer, "The Contents of Amphorae Produced in Gaul in the Imperial Period," in *Roman Amphora Contents: Reflecting on the Maritime Trade of Foodstuffs in Antiquity*, ed. Darío Bernal-Casasola, Michel Bonifay, Alessandra Pecci, and Victoria Leitch (Oxford: Archaeopress, 2021), 252.
15. Tomasso Bertoldi, *Guida alle anfore romane di età imperiale: Forme, impasti e distribuzione* (Roma: Espera, 2012), 63; Françoise Mayet and Carlos Taveres da Silva, *L'atelier d'amphores d'Abul (Portugal)* (Paris: Diffusion E. de Boccard, 2002); Françoise Mayet, Anne Schmitt, and Carlos Tavares da Silva, *Les amphores du Sado (Portugal): Prospection des fours et analyse du matériel* (Paris: Diffusion E. de Boccard, 1996).
16. Sónia Bombico, "Salted-Fish Industry in Roman Lusitania: Trade Memories Between Oceanus and Mare Nostrum," in *Heritage and Memories of the Sea*, ed. Filipe Themudo Barata and João Magalhães Rocha (Évora: University of Évora, 2015), 21.
17. See Vaz Pinto et al., eds, *Lusitanian Amphorae*, for a recent discussion.
18. Carlos Fabião, "Cetárias, ânforas e sal: A exploração de recursos marinhos na Lusitania," *Estudos Arqueológicos de Oeiras* 17 (2009): 564–565.
19. Clementina Panella, "Appunti su un gruppo di anfore della prima, media e tarda età Imperiale," in *Ostia III: Le terme del Nuotatore: Scavo dell'ambiente V et di un saggio dell'area. Studi miscellenei*, ed. Andrea Carandini and Clementina Panella (Rome: De Luca, 1973), 460–633.
20. Robert Étienne and Françoise Mayet, *Salaisons et sauces de poisson hispaniques* (Paris: E. de Boccard, 2002), 189–192; A. J. Parker, *Ancient Shipwrecks of the Mediterranean and the Roman Provinces* (Oxford: Tempus Reparatum, 1992).
21. Filipe, "Importação e exportação de produtos alimentares em Olisipo," 318; Rui Morais and Carlos Fabião, "Novas produções de fabrico lusitano: Problemáticas e importância económica," in *Cretariae 2005. Salsas y Salazones de Pescado en Occidente durante la Antigüedad*, ed. Lázaro Lagóstena, Darío Bernal-Casasola, and Alicia Arévalo (Oxford: Archaeopress, 2007), 127–133.
22. Joey Williams, *The Archaeology of Roman Surveillance in the Central Alentejo, Portugal* (Berkeley: California Classical Studies, 2017).
23. César Carreras Monfort, "The Gaditan Elites and the Figure of L. Cornelius Balbus," in *The Western Roman Atlantic Façade: A Study of the Economy and Trade*

in the Mar Exterior from the Republic to the Principate, ed. César Carreras Monfort and Rui Morais (Oxford: British Archaeological Reports, 2010), 249.

24. João Pimenta et al., "Cerâmicas romanas do lado ocidental do castelo de Alcácer do Sal, 4: Ânforas de importação e de produção lusitana," *Revista Portuguesa de Arqueologia* 9 (2006): 304. These early Lusitanian amphoras, called "Ovoid Lusitan" by scholars, possess some features resembling both the Haltern 70 and Dressel 7 forms produced in the south of the peninsula. By the middle of the first century CE, this early form appears to have been superseded by the Dressel 14 form.
25. Rui Mataloto and Conceição Roque, "Um regresso, de passagem, ao Castelo Velho de Veiros," in *Actas do V Encontro de Arqueologia do Sudoeste Peninsular*, ed. Manuela de Deus (Almodôvar: Município de Almodôvar, 2012), 676.
26. Mataloto et al., "Amphorae at the Origins of Lusitania," 140–142.
27. Williams, *The Archaeology of Roman Surveillance in the Central Alentejo*, 85–88; Rui Mataloto and Joey Williams, "*Terra Sigillata Italica* from Caladinho (Redondo, Portugal)," in *Contextos Estratigráficos na Lusitania (do Alto Império à Antiguidade Tardia)*, ed. José Carlos Quaresma (Lisboa: Associação dos Arqueólogos Portugueses, 2015), 13–24.
28. Williams, *The Archaeology of Roman Surveillance in the Central Alentejo*, 101–107.

Selected Bibliography

Curtis, Robert I. *Garum and Salsamenta: Production and Commerce in Materia Medica*. Leiden: Brill, 1991.

Étienne, Robert, and Françoise Mayet. *Salaisons et sauces de poisson hispaniques*. Paris: E. de Boccard, 2002.

Mayet, Françoise, and C. Taveres da Silva. *L'atelier d'amphores d'Abul (Portugal)*. Paris: Diffusion E. de Boccard, 2002.

Vaz Pinto, Inês, Rui de Almeida, and Archer Martin, eds. *Lusitanian Amphorae: Production and Distribution*. Oxford: Archaeopress, 2016.

Williams, Joey. *The Archaeology of Roman Surveillance in the Central Alentejo, Portugal*. Berkeley: California Classical Studies, 2017.

Joey Williams, *What's Roman About Fish Sauce?: Garum and Garum Containers in Early Roman Portugal* In: *From Garum to Mole: Sauces and Identity in the Western World*. Edited by: Andrew Donnelly, Beth M. Forrest, and Deirdre Murphy, Oxford University Press. © Oxford University Press 2026.
DOI: 10.1093/9780190622138.003.0003

4

Sauces in Late Antiquity and the Ascetic Redefinition of the Discourse on Food, Health, and Pleasure

Emmanuelle Raga

"The world's a bleak place when there's no room for pleasure."
—MALCOLM GLADWELL, *Revisionist History*[1]

TOGETHER WITH A change in dress, a new diet became a standard element of the Christian conversion narrative.[2] Change in diet was marked by a search for greater austerity, plainness, and scarcity.[3] However, these specific dietetic choices depended on a variety of cultural factors. In fact, many Christian communities, ranging from ascetic monks to high clergy to pious nobility, had different normative needs, which has led to a profusion of discourse about food and diet in the late antique written sources.[4] The result is a wide and varied compilation of Christian norms regarding nutrition and its relationship with pleasure, health, sin, sociability, and contemplation. These norms evolved during the transition from a late Roman world to the new political, cultural, and religious configurations of the Early Middle Ages. Sauces, as one of the basic elements of the ancient diet and ancient cooking, were part of this conversation.

The growing predominance of Christian asceticism following the religious identity crisis of the fourth century meant that an ascetic understanding of Christianity was increasingly promoted as the most perfect form of life. Consequently, asceticism had a significant impact on the discourse regarding the legitimacy of the search for pleasure in food. As sauces were understood as something liquid added to a dish to make it more agreeable to the taste—and so to provide pleasure—they were one of the elements stigmatized by ascetic

Christian authors when providing new dietetic instructions. Not only did this restrict the space given to sauces in the diet of the faithful, but the new ascetic discourse on food also impacted the very definition of what was understood as a sauce.

Sauces in Classical Literature: Cooks and Physicians

In ancient Roman society, sauces were indispensable to the *cena*, or central course of the banquet, which consisted mainly of dishes of meat and fish served in elaborate sauces.[5] Sauces were the central element of recipe collections and a fundamental component of banquets, where food had to be delicious and luxurious. The most famous recipe collection of its day, the *De re coquinaria (On the art of cooking)*, was associated with the ancient culinary author Apicius (see Adamson, Chapter 1 of this volume). It was mainly a list of sauces.[6] In particular, Apicius's books on diverse types of meat (e.g., poultry, quadrupeds, shellfish, and fish) consist almost exclusively of lists of sauces to accompany all of the different types of animal flesh. In other words, for the author of the *De re coquinaria*, a recipe in general often meant a *sauce* recipe. The art of cooking was first of all the art of making sauces.

But sauces were also a usual part of the everyday diet in the ancient world. When Ausonius, the fourth-century poet and teacher from Bordeaux, wrote a poem on the "daily round," he included the following description of a sauce in this passage on his midday meals:

> *The Time for Directing the Cook*. Sosias, I must have lunch (*prandium*). The warm sun is already passed well on into his fourth hour, and on the dial the shadow is moving on towards the fifth stroke. Taste and make sure—for they often play you false—that the seasoned dishes are well soused and taste appetisingly. Turn you bubbling pots in your hands and shake them up: quick, dip you fingers in the hot sauce (*iure calente*) and let your moist tongue lick them as it darts in and out.[7]

This observation that sauces could be part of the everyday solitary meal is important. Food had two different purposes in the ancient world and was part of two specific sets of norms. On the one hand, food restored and nourished; on the other, food was shared and promoted social cohesion. The most expensive and sophisticated dishes were exclusively consumed in the context of the banquet, or meal where food and drink were shared in order to create, maintain, and strengthen social ties and networks. Banquets required the presence of at least one guest, meaning at least one individual external to the household. On the other hand, nutrition—the consumption of food destined to restore the body—happened outside the banquet and could take place whenever and wherever it was necessary. A very eloquent example of this dual approach to food is the following passage found in the life of the emperor Severus Alexander in the *Historia Augusta,* the collection of imperial lives likely written by a fourth-century anonymous author pretending to be different authors from the third century. On the daily schedule of the emperor, he says at one point:

> On coming out of the bath he would take a quantity of milk and bread, some eggs, and then a drink of mead. Thus refreshed, he would sometimes proceed to luncheon (*prandium*), sometimes put off eating until the evening meal, but more frequently he took luncheon.[8]

In the morning, the emperor would first get something simple to eat that refreshed and restored him, and then he would either attend or not attend a proper lunch, demonstrating that these forms of consumption served different purposes and were not mutually exclusive. Severus Alexander was one of the favorite emperors of the author of the *Historia Augusta* and is presented as the perfect sovereign in every aspect. This organization of daily food consumption is thus considered ideal.

These two uses of food were associated with two different professions, the cook and the physician. Making food taste good was the task of the cook, while making food healthy was the task of the physician. Physicians, however, did take the question of pleasure into relative consideration, and cooks often mentioned the dietetic advantages of certain foods or recipes in their work. Food for nutrition was chosen according to the guidelines of physicians and had to respond to physiological needs, while food for sharing was to be delicious, sophisticated, and flavorful in order to represent the status of the host and guests. In addition, food for nutrition did not have to be agreeable to the taste, to the point that a diet for the sick was often associated with a bad taste. As the first-century Greek biographer and philosopher Plutarch put it when quoting a fellow physician:

> The second, I think, concerned the food which you people serve to the sick. For he urged that we should partake of it and taste it from time to time, and get ourselves used to it in time of health, and not abhor and detest such a regimen, like little children, but gradually make it familiar

> and congenial to our appetites, so that in sickness we may not be disaffected over our fare as if it were so much medicine, and may not show impatience at receiving something simple, unappetizing, and savorless.[9]

Though the physician quoted here did not agree with this approach to diet, the passage attests to the fact that the diet of the sick was considered as generally "simple, unappetizing and savorless." Furthermore, the dichotomy between the social, pleasurable, and lavish consumption at the banquet and the solitary, pragmatic, and healthy consumption at any other time was associated with an alternation between excessive banqueting developing into sickness and solitary dieting leading to the restoration of health.

However, food for the sick did not have to be unappetizing. Some physicians argued that the taste of food was related to the health of a patient. In fact, according to the prominent second-century CE physician Galen, the tastier the preparation, the healthier:

> For we physicians aim at benefits from foods, not at pleasure. But since the unpleasantness of some foods contributes largely to poor concoction [meaning digestion], in this regard it is better that they are moderately tasty.[10]
>
> People who practise the culinary arts (of which activity I expect the physician not to be completely ignorant) prepare olives in a variety of ways. For among things that are equally healthy, the more pleasant is better for concoction.[11]

Galen also suggested that a patient eat soft fish with what he calls a white sauce:

> But, while the preparations from cooking pans are for the most part causes of a lack of concoction, that with white sauce is best for it. This dish is produced when, after ample water has been added, one pours on a sufficient quantity of olive oil and a small amount of dill and leek, and then partly boils it and adds just so much salt that the whole sauce does not appear salty. This is the recipe that is useful for convalescent, but the fried fish is also useful for people in perfect health, and next to this is that cooked on a brazier.[12]

Apicius also includes dietetic considerations and advice. For example, in the chapter on seafood, Apicius recommends a series of sauces, including the following: "Take as much cumin as your five fingers will hold; crush half of that quantity of pepper and one piece of peeled garlic, pour on liquamen and dribble on a little oil. This will correct and benefit a sour stomach and promote digestion."[13]

Some centuries later, in an important source for the study of food in late antiquity, Anthimus's *De observatione ciborum* (*On the Observation of Food*), the role of the cook and of the physician are even more intertwined. Anthimus was likely a sixth-century doctor, and author of a compilation of dietetic recipes written for the Merovingian king Theuderic, the eldest son of Clovis (see Adamson, Chapter 1 in this volume).[14] His work completely blends the dietetic and the gastronomic. It consists of a list of ingredients (vegetables, fruits, eggs, dairy products, poultry, fish, and meat) and informs the reader of how healthy they are to consume and whether they are advisable for weak, sick, and healthy people. Along the way, however, he includes cooking suggestions for many items, and occasionally a sophisticated recipe like this one appears:

> What is called in Greek *afrutum* and in Latin *spumeum* is made from chicken and egg white. Lots of egg white must be used so the *afrutum* becomes foamy. It should be arranged in a mound on a shallow casserole with a previously prepared gravy and diluted fish sauce underneath. Then the casserole is set over the charcoal and the *afrutum* cooked in the steam of the sauce. The casserole is then placed in the middle of a serving dish, and a little wine and honey poured over it. It is eaten with a spoon or a small ladle. I often add to this recipe some good fish or even some sea-scallops, because they are extremely tasty and are particularly plentiful around where I live. From clean scallops are made "snow balls."[15]

The presence of this seemingly pleasurable meal in Apicius suggests that sauces, even though destined to provide pleasure, were not excluded from dietetic recommendations in the ancient mentality. This is particularly important in late antiquity, when the morality and legitimacy of searching for a greater pleasure would be challenged.

Sauces in the Ascetic Age

Asceticism was not new to late antiquity, but the aggressive way in which it was promoted—as the way of life each person should aspire to as part of the widespread conversion to Christianity—was. The competitiveness of asceticism generated a race toward its most intense possible form. The renunciation of foods and pleasure was an important part of this competition.

The overrepresentation of asceticism in written sources gives us the impression that asceticism overcame all aspects of life in the Early Middle Ages. We must be aware that this vision is a distorted perception. Not everyone became an ascetic. Communities continued to use the sharing of delicious and abundant food as a tool for maintaining social networks and cohesion. But the pressure of asceticism was real. It is particularly visible in the work of Sidonius Apollinaris, one of the rare authors of the period who was not tempted by asceticism. Quite the contrary, it appears, as he repeats in various letters, that the best way to deal with Christian conversion as an aristocrat was to continue to honor the social responsibilities inherited with the family name. By this he meant to continue to form and maintain aristocratic social connections and friendships, or *amicitia*, which can only be kept alive by attending the banquets and parties of one's friends.[16] The fact that Sidonius repeatedly felt it necessary to praise the aristocrats who maintained their full participation in the aristocratic circles despite having become priests or bishops suggests that the disruptive pressure of asceticism on the old way of life was apparent.

This pressure can be seen as early as the second century, when early Christian authors such as Clement of Alexandria (c. 150–215 CE) and Tertullian (c. 155–240 CE) provided their readers with a series of guidelines surrounding food consumption. For both authors, the approach to food had more to do with the traditional Roman discourses on the "good life" than with the Christian religion, and for both, the important issue was that food should be simple and only sufficient enough to meet physiological needs while providing as little pleasure as possible.[17]

The change in diet reflects a more general change in the perception of the relationship between body and soul. The classical relationship between the soul and the body can be seen as that of a benevolent master and its disciple. The Christian ascetic narrative promoted a much more antagonistic and violent relationship between the two. The soul was in constant danger of succumbing to the temptations brought by the desires of the inferior body, and thus had to force it into submission with all necessary strength and violence.[18] Depriving the body of all sensual pleasure, even the relatively more acceptable pleasure drawn from eating food, was considered indispensable for achieving a true ascetic and contemplative way of life. As the monk John Cassian notes: "For not only is drunkenness with wine wont to intoxicate the mind, but excess of all kinds of food makes it weak and uncertain, and robs it of all its power of pure and clear contemplation. The cause of the overthrow and wantonness of Sodom was not drunkenness through wine, but fullness of bread."[19]

The innocent pleasure taken when replenishing the body with food, even with quite simple and unappetizing food, was considered the fuel of debauchery and the open door to every other sin. The point was not only to avoid all pleasurable foods but also to never feel replenished and always stay hungry. Consequently, the body that was never permitted to relax could be maintained and controlled only by the vigilant soul.

In general, the ascetic change in diet consisted of two things: adopting regular fasting, which at that time meant not eating anything until the end of the day, when one simple meal would be consumed, and excluding all foods that provided pleasure and were considered unnecessary for survival and detrimental to a life of contemplation. Consequently, the first foods to be excluded were the ones most associated with pleasure: meat, wine, and sauces. Meat was the first and most important food of the banquet. It was the quintessential food to be shared, and it was a food consumed almost exclusively for the pleasure it brought since it was not, except for the very special case of professional athletes, an aspect of a healthy diet.[20]

Wine had a more complex semiology. It was a vehicle for debauchery at banquets and always very perilous for morality when consumed in excess. It was also an indispensable element of the Eucharist. Because of the former and despite the latter, wine was a beverage that ascetics sometimes rejected. For example, the fourth-century Saint Martin of Tours completely stopped consuming wine when he adopted his ascetic and reclusive way of life.

Finally, as something added specifically to make a dish more pleasurable, sauces and seasoning were naturally part of what had to be removed from an ascetic diet. In fact, the notion of adding something to make food more agreeable was so frowned upon that the very definition of sauce appears to have been extended to any liquid added to help with swallowing, as is suggested by the following passage from the *Sayings of the Desert Fathers* (or *Apophthegmata*), a compilation of conversations with Christian desert ascetics from the fourth century:

> Abba Achilles came one day to Abba Isaiah's cell at Scetis, and found him in the act of eating something. He had mixed it with salt and water on a plate. The old man, seeing that he was hiding it behind some plaited reeds, said to him, "Tell me, what are you eating?" He replied, "Forgive me, Father, I was cutting palm-leaves and I went out in the

> heat; and I put a morsel into my mouth, with some salt, but the heat burnt my throat and the mouthful did not go down. So I was obliged to add a little water to the salt, in order to swallow it. Forgive me, Father." The old man said, "Come, all of you, and see Isaiah eating sauce (*juscellum*) in Scetis. If you want to eat sauce (*jus*), go to Egypt."[21]

A sauce (*jus* or *juscellum*), as it is understood here by Abbas Achilles, can consist of nothing more than saltwater added to a dish in order to make it easier to swallow. This action is strongly condemned by the desert father of Scetis, who proudly represented one of the more radical versions of Christian asceticism in late antiquity. If a monk in Scetis wished to eat with sauce, even this thin water, he should move out of the monastery to Egypt; in other words, to a place removed from Scetis's extreme and elitist asceticism.[22] It appears that this extreme asceticism led to a contextual transformation of the very definition of what constituted a sauce in this period. In the ascetic logic of extreme refusal and defiance toward any form of sensual pleasure, the notion of what constituted a sauce could be extended to any form of liquid added to facilitate swallowing. The same simple addition of salty water to a mash would hardly be considered a sauce by non-ascetic contemporary consumers, as we saw with Ausonius. Ausonius used *jus* to refer to a hot, bubbling, delicious sauce that took time and the work of a skilled private cook, not just the adding of plain water.

Sauces were also closely associated with the pleasure that banquets were intended to provide. The early Christian moralists confirm this association. Clement of Alexandria, the second-century theologian, for example, taught his disciples to despise the behavior of banqueters and criticized the thrusting of hands into the sauces.[23]

In addition, Apicius was perceived as decadent in late antiquity, and his sauces remained the symbol of the sophisticated aristocratic banqueting. When Sidonius Apollinaris laughed with a friend at the fact that a very simple man was going to be invited to his companion's table, he used Apicius as the symbol of the absolute in culinary sophistication:

> I can see it all as if I were there; the novelty of everything to one whose wits are not of the sharpest; his confusion as a stranger invited to make himself at home, or as a nervous guest drawn into conversation, or as a countrified fellow called on to take his part in polite gaiety, or as a poor man set down at a sumptuous board. It will be strange indeed to a man from these parts, where ill-cooked viands and too much onion (*crudos*

> *caeparumque crapulis esculento*) afford the only fare, to find himself as nobly regaled as if he had eaten his fill all his days at Apician banquets.[24]

To early moralizing Christian authors, the sauces of the banquet were a source of immoral pleasure and a tool of expression of social distinction and class contempt, both of which were to be condemned. However, sauces were not excluded entirely by all. Certain late antique ascetics found ways to incorporate the consumption of sauces into their religious identity. This was true even in a monastic setting, and even for the most ascetic monks of the desert. A passage written by John Cassian suggests that the more abundant use of oil and table salt, as well as adding something to nibble, like olives, figs, and prunes, transforms the austere ascetic daily meal into a celebration:

> When we had finished the duties of the day, and the congregation had been dismissed from Church we returned to the old man's cell, and enjoyed a most sumptuous repast. For instead of the sauce which with a few drops of oil spread over it was usually set on the table for his daily meal, he mixed a little decoction and poured over it a somewhat more liberal allowance of oil than usual; [. . .] Then he set before us table salt, and three olives each: after which he produced a basket containing parched vetches which they call *trogalia*, from which we each took five grains, two prunes and a fig apiece. For it is considered wrong for anyone to exceed that amount in that desert.[25]

In this context, Cassian also mentioned a peculiar tradition relative to the everyday lonely meal of the ascetics which is of interest to us here. He suggested that these ascetics had the habit of laying one single drop of oil in an otherwise flavorless broth, not to enhance the taste, but to deprive the ascetic of the satisfaction of having eaten a completely ascetic meal, thus avoiding being overwhelmed by a guilty pride:

> For each of them when he is going to partake of his daily repast, pours those drops of oil on, not that he may receive any enjoyment from the taste of it (for so limited is the supply that it is hardly enough I will not say to line the passage of his throat and jaws, but even to pass down it) but that using it, he may keep down the pride of his heart (which is certain to creep in stealthily and surely if his abstinence is any stricter) and the incitements to vainglory, for as his abstinence is practised with

> the greater secrecy, and is carried on without anyone to see it, so much the more subtly does it never cease to tempt the man who conceals it.[26]

This last passage aptly illustrates that the issue was not what was consumed, but whether pleasure was derived from consuming. The ascetics were not avoiding sauces and oil because they were inherently "impure," but rather, because they provided pleasure. If, however, they were added in such a small amount as to not enhance pleasure, they were most welcome, as they helped to avoid the sin of feeling pride.

Concluding Remarks

A sauce in late antiquity was something liquid added to a dish to make it more pleasurable. Pleasure was mandatory in order to properly receive guests at the table. A shared meal was a happy occasion that defined authority and status but was also meant to provide joy. However, the point at which food was made pleasurable enough to be called a sauce varied according to the level of tolerance to, precisely, pleasure. And since pleasure was the central obsessive issue in this age of strict asceticism, sauces are a useful tool for shedding light on the tensions and stakes of this period.

As it was with many other aspects of everyday life, sauces were inserted into the process of redefining the perceived relationship between pleasure and nutrition that was, in part, associated with the ascetic movement. While pleasure remained indispensable to the sociability of festive occasions, it also transformed into the main focus of the ascetic fight for redemption. Similarly, sauces were, as we have seen, both fundamental yet superficial for the same reason: they provided pleasure. Sauces thus were simultaneously rejected and coveted as indispensable because they provided pleasure. The newly dominant ascetic discourse challenged the legitimacy of sauces in healthy diets, even as it altered the definition of what could be called a sauce at all.

Sauce for an Ascetic

Inspired by the writings of John Cassian, a fifth-century monk

Ingredients:

A few drops of olive oil

Method:

Add a few drops of olive oil to your daily meal.
Mix and eat, but do not enjoy too much.

Notes

1. Malcolm Gladwell, "McDonald's Broke My Heart," *Revisionist History Podcast* S2E9, August 10, 2017. https://www.pushkin.fm/podcasts/revisionist-history/mcdonalds-broke-my-heart.
2. Robert Markus, *The End of Ancient Christianity* (Cambridge: Cambridge University Press, 1990).
3. See Veronika Grimm, *From Feasting to Fasting, the Evolution of a Sin: Attitudes to Food in Late Antiquity* (New York: Routledge, 1996); Teresa Shaw, *The Burden of the Flesh: Fasting and Sexuality in Early Christianity* (Minneapolis: Fortress Press 1998); Andrew McGowan, *Ascetic Eucharist: Food and Drink in Early Christian Ritual Meals* (Oxford: Clarendon Press, 1999); Bonnie Effros, *Creating Community with Food and Drink in Merovingian Gaul* (New York, Palgrave, 2002).
4. Susannah Elm, *Virgins of God: The Making of Asceticism in Late Antiquity* (Oxford: Oxford University Press, 1994); Richard Finn, *Asceticism in the Graeco-Roman World: Key Themes in Ancient History* (Cambridge: Cambridge University Press, 2009).
5. Florence Dupont, "Grammaire de l'alimentation et des repas romains," in *Histoire de l'alimentation*, ed. Jean-Louis Flandrin and Massimo Montanari (Paris: Fayard, 1996), 210.
6. The *De re coquinaria*, the collection though which Apicius's work was transmitted, was a combination of elements from two books written by Apicius and a Greek dietetic treaty (Jacques André, *L'Alimentation et la cuisine a Rome* [Paris: Klincksieck, 1961], 217). It was originally composed in the first century but circulated in the fourth in a modified version.
7. Translation from Joseph Pucci, "Ausonius' Ephemeris and the Hermeneumata Tradition," *Classical Philology* 104 (2009): 62.
8. Translation from David Magie, trans., *Historia Augusta, Volume I* (Cambridge: Loeb Classical Library, 1932), 239.
9. Translation from Frank Cole Babbit, *Plutarch: Moralia, II* (Cambridge: Loeb Classical Library, 1928), 221.
10. Translation from Owen Powell, trans., *Galen on the Properties of Foodstuffs = De alimentorum facultatibus* (Cambridge: Cambridge University Press, 2003), 105.
11. Ibid., 92.
12. Ibid., 142.
13. Translation from Joseph Dommers Vehling, trans. *Apicius: Cookery and Dining in Imperial Rome* (Chicago: Walter M. Hill, 1936), 217.
14. For Anthimus's identification, see Yitzhak Hen, "Food and Drink in Merovingian Gaul," in *Tätigkeitsfelder und Erfahrungshorizonte des Ländlichen Menschen in der Frühmittelalterlichen Grundherrschaft (bis Ca. 1000): Festschrift für Dieter Hägermann zum 65. Geburtstag*, ed. Brigitte Kasten (Wiesbaden: Franz Steiner Verlag, 2006) 99–110.

15. Translation from Mark Grant, *Anthimus: On the Observance of Foods* (Devon: Prospect Books, 1996), 63.
16. See Emmanuelle Raga, "Bon mangeur, mauvais mangeur. Pratiques alimentaires et critique sociale dans l'œuvre de Sidoine Apollinaire et de ses contemporains," *Revue Belge de Philologie et d'Histoire* 87 (2009): 165–196; Emmanuelle Raga, "The Impact of Christianity on Diet, Health and Nutrition in Late Antiquity," in *The Routledge Handbook of Diet and Nutrition in the Roman World*, ed. Paul Erdkamp and Claire Holleran (New York: Routledge, 2018), 229–242.
17. Blake Leyerle, "Clement of Alexandria on the Importance of Table Etiquette," *Journal of Early Christian Studies* 3 (1995): 123–141.
18. Jérôme Baschet, "Âme et corps dans l'occident médiéval: Une dualité dynamique, entre pluralité et dualisme," *Archives de Sciences sociales des Religions* 112 (2000): 5–30; Peter Brown, *The Body and Society: Men, Women and Sexual Renunciation in Early Christianity* (New York: Columbia Classics, 1988).
19. Edgar C. S. Gibson, trans., *A Select Library of Nicene and Post-Nicene Fathers of the Christian Church* (New York: Christian Literature Company), 235.
20. For more on meat, see Emmanuelle Raga, "Interdire la viande à la table monastique entre Antiquité tardive et haut Moyen âge en Occident: Un bricolage normatif autour de la problématique du plaisir," in *Religions et interdits alimentaires. Archéozoologie et sources littéraires*, ed. Béatrice Caseau and Hervé Monchot (Paris: PUPS, 2016), 1–11.
21. Translation from Benedicta Ward, *The Sayings of the Desert Fathers: The Alphabetical Collection* (Kalamazoo: Cistercian, 1984), 29.
22. The desert of Scetis is situated in today's Egypt but is understood as a specific and unique environment in the history of early asceticism and monasticism (see Helen Waddell, *The Desert Fathers* [Ann Arbor: University of Michigan Press, 1978]). Thanks to Jim Keenan of Loyola University Chicago's Department of Classical Studies for his advice on Scetis and the nature of Achilles's comment.
23. Leyerle, "Clement of Alexandria on the Importance of Table Etiquette," 126, 137.
24. Translation from O. M. Dalton, *The Letters of Sidonius* (Oxford: Clarendon Press, 1915), 114–115. Eating loads of onions (and loads of garlic) was in the ancient world a sign of rusticity, representative of the plain existence of the simple men (see André, *L'Alimentation et la cuisine a Rome*, 20) and was apparently the perfect opposite of the highly sophisticated mythical table of Apicius.
25. Translation from Gibson, *A Select Library*, 375.
26. Ibid.

Selected Bibliography

Anthimus. *De observatione ciborum, On the Observation of Food*. Translated by Mark Grant. Devon: Prospect Books, 2006.

Brown, Peter. *The Body and Society: Men, Women and Sexual Renunciation in Early Christianity*. New York: Columbia Classics, 1988.

Effros, Bonnie. *Creating Community with Food and Drink in Merovingian Gaul.* New York: Palgrave, 2002.

Grimm, Veronika. *From Feasting to Fasting, the Evolution of a Sin: Attitudes to Food in Late Antiquity*. New York: Routledge, 1996.

McGowan, Andrew. *Ascetic Eucharist: Food and Drink in Early Christian Ritual Meals.* Oxford: Clarendon Press, 1999.

Markus, Robert. *The End of Ancient Christianity*. Cambridge: Cambridge University Press, 1990.

Raga, Emmanuelle. "The Impact of Christianity on Diet, Health and Nutrition in Late Antiquity." In *The Routledge Handbook of Diet and Nutrition in the Roman World*, edited by Paul Erdkamp and Claire Holleran, 229–242. New York: Routledge, 2018.

The Sayings of the Desert Fathers. The Alphabetical Collection. Translated by Benedicta Ward. Kalamazoo: Cistercian Publications, 1984.

Emmanuelle Raga, *Sauces in Late Antiquity and the Ascetic Redefinition of the Discourse on Food, Health, and Pleasure* In: *From Garum to Mole: Sauces and Identity in the Western World*. Edited by: Andrew Donnelly, Beth M. Forrest, and Deirdre Murphy, Oxford University Press. © Oxford University Press 2026.
DOI: 10.1093/9780190622138.003.0004

5

Salsa, Sugo, e Intingolo

COOKING ITALIAN IDENTITY IN ARTUSI'S *LA SCIENZA IN CUCINA*

Fabio Parasecoli

"The best sauce you can offer your guests is a smile and warm hospitality."
—PELLEGRINO ARTUSI, The Art of Eating Well[1]

FEW BOOKS ENJOY the same renown in the recent history of food in Italy as Pellegrino Artusi's *La Scienza in cucina e l'arte di mangiare bene* (The Science in the Kitchen and the Art of Eating Well), first published in 1891. Although no publisher initially wanted to risk any capital on the project and the author had to pay for the first printing himself, the volume rapidly became a major success.[2] Through the fifteen editions Artusi revised himself before his death in 1911, the number of entries increased from 475 to 790, thanks to readers who constantly sent him letters, offering their own recipes, from throughout Italy. Artusi's work grew organically over two decades.[3] While maintaining its core inspiration and approach, the book evolved from the work of an individual (and a male who was not a professional cook or caterer) who was responding to the historical changes around him to a collective reflection of the transformations Italy was undergoing as a new country, at least from the material culture point of view. Although the royal government had not identified food and cooking as tools to influence citizens' lives (unlike the Fascist authorities a few decades later), Artusi's expanding book strongly suggests the relevance of culinary culture for nation-building at a time when Italy was still an abstract concept for many of those who found themselves within its borders. The growing collection of recipes from all over the country made it more tangible and part of everyday activities, at least for the middle class and mostly female audience he was writing for. Through food, Italy was not just a distant political structure but could be experienced and ingested in manageable and understandable dishes.

The country had officially become a unified kingdom in 1861, but the process of expansion continued with the 1870 conquest of Rome, previously belonging to the pope, and the World War I annexation of Trentino, Alto Adige, and Venezia Giulia in the northeast. Political integration under the Savoy king and a national government did not immediately usher in any sort of cultural or social unification, as Italy had been fragmented among numerous local dynasties and foreign occupants for centuries. It is against this background that, at the age of seventy-one, Artusi started working on *La Scienza in cucina*. Although the author makes no direct mention of politics, the desire to create a repository of dishes, practices, and culinary language that would make sense to all the newly minted Italian citizens is revealed by Artusi's frequent digressions and introductions to the recipes.

This chapter will examine how Artusi's attempt at creating a shared Italian cuisine as a reflection of the new unified country and its diversity was in tension with the influence of French culinary traditions, which were simultaneously respected as prestigious and rejected as foreign. To assess these dynamics, it focuses on how the author embraces sauces—including tomato sauce, the use of which was at the time still heavily identified as a southern custom—by defining them as Italian in relation to and at times in opposition to the French category of *sauce*, which Escoffier was systematizing in France in the same period.[4] Artusi's apparent lack of clarity resulting from the fragmentation of the category of sauce into *salsa*, *sugo*, and *intingolo* actually expands the semantic field to reflect the different traditions of Italy. By so doing, the author implicitly frames the creation of a shared canon of recipes—adapted and tamed as they may be in order to accommodate bourgeois culinary tastes—as an act of faith in the existence of Italy as a nation and as a cultural entity. The statement "We have made Italy, now we must make Italians," famously attributed to statesman and artist Massimo D'Azeglio, seems particularly resonant here.[5] The majority of the population of the newly unified country, especially the working classes, had little sense of what being "Italians" might mean. The king and the national authorities were often perceived as foreign and remote from local realities and everyday experiences. Thus it is not surprising that Artusi turned to food as a way to locate a shared material culture that could testify to Italy's very existence.

This chapter begins by outlining the history of *salsa*, *sugo*, and *intingolo* in the culinary literature of Italy, focusing especially on late eighteenth- and early nineteenth-century recipe collections. Such cookbooks provide the background for Artusi's reaction to the French influence and his attempt to give respectability and value to Italian cuisine. It then closely analyzes of Artusi's recipes for *salsa*, *sugo*, and *intingolo*, looking in particular at the emergence of tomato-based sauces, as these would acquire particular significance in the creation of an Italian national culinary identity.

Creating a National Culinary Language

At the end of the general introduction to his book, right before the recipes, Artusi included "an explanation of terms which, being Tuscan dialect, not everybody would understand."[6] He uses this section not only for that purpose but also to clarify words of French origin that he seemed to believe should belong to the Italian culinary language. Examples include *cotoletta* (*côtelette*), *mazzetto guarnito* (literal translation of *bouquet garni*, for which the common expression *odori* or "scents" is often used), and *sauté*, used not for the technique but the sauté pan. The presence of these terms points to the relevance of French culinary culture among the Italian upper and middle classes after the unification as the result of two centuries of a slow but steady penetration through a great number of cookbooks and the widespread presence of French chefs among the elites.

Artusi implicitly embraced the French cultural approach to food known as *gastronomie*, the critical and expert analysis and evaluation of food and cooking developed in France from the early nineteenth century as an expression of the bourgeoisie's search for its own sense of taste and cultural identity.[7] Demonstrating Artusi's familiarity with the French culinary arts, Brillat-Savarin's name appears three times in his book: the first time as author of the aphorism "To invite a guest is to assume responsibility for his happiness for the duration of his stay under your roof";[8] the second time to introduce a recipe for cheese fondue (*cacimperio*); and the third time in an explanation of the name of the Savarin dessert.

Some of Artusi's recipes, such as *zucca di zuppa gialla* (yellow squash soup), start with an *intriso*, which is manifestly a roux.[9] However, he is deeply ambivalent about French culinary hegemony, thus embodying the spirit of *Risorgimento*, the cultural and political movement that provided the ideological support to the process of national unification between 1848 and 1870. For instance, he gives the name of *zuppa sul sugo di carne* (soup with meat sauce) to the French *soupe mitonnée*, specifying that:

> some cooks, to give themselves airs, leaf through the phrase books of our unfriendly western neighbors for high-sounding names that mean

> absolutely nothing. According to them, I should have called this soupe *mitonnée*. Had I done so to please the multitudes who kowtow to foreign influences, filling my book with odd and exotic sounds, it would certainly have been much better received! For our own dignity, I have instead done my utmost to use our elegant, musical tongue and have called this soup by its name.[10]

In this paragraph, he connects the troubles he encountered while trying to publish his book and his attempt to use the Italian national language to create a shared culinary vocabulary with what he considers a widespread admiration and subservience to French cuisine. Using "elegant, musical" Italian is a matter of dignity and national pride, not only of expediency and cultural interest. In his choice of language and in his reflections about his choices, Artusi embraces what social scientist Michael Billig defines as "banal nationalism": everyday representations and embodied experiences of nationality, often connected with popular culture, from sports to anthems, flags, and, of course food.[11] Such nation-building techniques are crucial in the formation and effectiveness of "imagined communities" such as the nation-state, which otherwise would be emotionally and existentially removed from citizens' daily lives.[12]

At the same time, Artusi, well aware of the modernity of his culinary approach to his recipes, was eager to differentiate his work from previous writers. Discussing *L'arte di ben cucinare* (The Art of Cooking Well), written in the mid-1600s by Bartolomeo Stefani, a cook from Bologna working in the court of the Duke of Mantua, he describes that epoch as a time when "all manner of spices and herbs were widely used and abused, and sugar and cinnamon found their way into broth, boiled meat and roasts." He continued by musing, "should my Bolognese forerunner criticize me in the afterlife, I shall defend myself by telling him that things have changed for the better."[13] Nevertheless, at the opposite extreme, Artusi criticizes people for "beginning to omit herbs and spices even where they are necessary."[14] By doing so, he implicitly reclaims the culinary past of Italy as an important influence in the development of a national cuisine.

Artusi's book reflected not only the cultural and social values of the expanding middle classes of the new Italian state, but also their spending power and access to food. The author adopted an educational approach, mixing home economics tips and hygienic counsel with medical advice aiming at sobriety, temperance, and good management of the domestic finances. His tone was light and entertaining, offering side notes that allowed later readers to get a better sense of the material culture of the time. Artusi's text reveals how, in the last decades of the nineteenth century, bourgeois families had embraced the custom of the shared family meal that was slowly acquiring a structure based on the sequence of *antipasto* (appetizers), *primo* (usually a soup, or a pasta dish, less often rice), *secondo* (meat or fish) with *contorni* (side dishes, often vegetables), and dessert at the end.

Artusi wrote at a time when perspectives on food in Italy were changing, both culinarily and linguistically. Most rural dwellers, as well as large parts of the urban population, were illiterate, unable to speak standard Italian, and fiercely attached to their local vernaculars (which had been demoted by the new cultural authorities to the lower status of dialects, but were, nonetheless, often true languages). Italian, deriving from the work of Dante, Petrarch, and Boccaccio in the thirteenth century, was mostly used as a written language, and frequently was limited to the educated.[15] Linguistic gaps were only one aspect of Italy's fragmentation, which was also visible in dietary patterns. While the relatively small upper and middle classes had regular access to food, most Italians were undernourished. Around 80 percent of the working-class household budget was spent on food, with most concentrated on basic staples.[16] The diet of rural workers, which still constituted a large percentage of the population, was limited, both in terms of variety and calories. As wheat, fruit, and olive oil production was mostly directed to middle-class urban consumers, rural workers had access to corn (mostly in the form of *polenta*), barley, millet, buckwheat, beans, lentils, and fava beans. Chestnuts and chickpeas were frequently ground into flours to make porridges, dumplings, breads, and focaccias.

The end of the nineteenth century saw the ascent of food manufacturing companies catering to the new urban consumers. With the unification, internal borders and custom fees had been removed, easing the movement of goods, and pushing landowners to specialize their crops and sell them on a national market. However, most agricultural production was consumed locally. The first large, refrigerated warehouse was not inaugurated in Milan until 1897, pointing to the lack of efficient nationwide infrastructures for food distribution. Various companies under the nominal coordination of the central government managed the relatively small railway lines until 1905, when the system was unified under a single public organization. Reflecting these conditions, and despite the government's efforts toward nation-building in terms of infrastructure and production, food customs remained deeply local, especially for the lower classes, both urban and rural.

As a side effect of the mandatory military service that forced young men from all over the country to leave home for a few years to be stationed in unfamiliar destinations, the central government unintentionally contributed to the unification of food habits.[17] Italian military leaders clearly understood the importance of living conditions—and, in particular, food—for troop morale.[18] The issue of finding a diet that would satisfy soldiers from different geographical origins and social backgrounds led the military authorities to look for a safe middle ground. These tended to reflect rural foodways; for instance, breakfast included dried figs, nuts, cheese, olives, sardines, and fresh apples. For the first time, many recruits had access to three meals a day and victuals like pasta (with tomato sauce), closely connected with the burgeoning food industry, which became everyday items for recruits, identifying them with their direct experience of the Italian nation. From 1916, soldiers also gained access to coffee, which would turn into a mainstay of Italian food customs.[19] While the main goal of the Italian army was to reinforce the newly unified country from a military point of view, it had the unintended consequence of contributing to nation-building through the experiences—including eating—its male citizens shared as soldiers.

The Long History of Sugo *and* Salsa

It is against this background that Artusi wrote his cookbook, unintentionally reflecting the cultural and social debates that underlined the development of Italy as a newly unified country and the government's effort to strengthen the nation. To better understand the author's attitude and the way he positioned himself in the history and tradition of the cuisines of Italy, sauces offer a particularly interesting case, as these preparations were deeply rooted in local foodways and reflect Italy's culinary fragmentation. At the same time, thanks to the industrialization of the food system, they were becoming better known and used in their regional variations among the middle classes. Furthermore, sauces presented similarities and differences with French cuisine, against which Artusi was trying to define an Italian national culinary canon. He struggled to find a language that could be easily accessible in every corner of Italy, and sauces constituted both a cultural and a linguistic conundrum. What is the historical background for Artusi's use of the words *sugo* and *salsa*, both of which have been present in the Italian culinary vocabulary since its inception? How did the local traditions interact with foreign influences in the centuries preceding the publication of *La scienza in cucina*?

In the *Liber de coquina*, one of the first cookbooks written in Latin on the Italian peninsula at the end of the thirteenth century, probably at the French-influenced Anjou court of Naples, the word *salsa* is used in the contemporary sense of a condiment. For instance, in *de salsis pro auibus* (recipe 32, sauces for birds), *de salsa pro pullis assatis* (recipe 33, sauce for roasted poultry), and *de salsa pro columbis* (recipe 34, sauce for squab). However, *salsus* and *salsatus* are also still used to mean "salted," reflecting the original sense of the expression in Latin. The word *succus* (from which *sugo* derives) is also found in the sense of juice, in relation to fruits. The word *sapor* (flavor, from the verb *sapio*, to have taste of) is used as well to indicate preparations that today we would consider as sauces, such as the *sapor pullorum qui dicitur mustarda* (recipe 38, chicken sauce that is called mustard).

The Latin *salsa*, *succus*, and *sapor* were respectively translated into Italian as *salsa*, *succo/succhio*, and *sapore* when recipes from the *Liber de coquina* were redacted in vulgar Italian and included in the collections known as *Libro della cocina*, one compiled in Tuscany between the late fourteenth and the early fifteenth centuries, and one in the south in the early fifteenth century. The same vocabulary appears in the mid-fifteenth century in Maestro Martino's recipe collection and, a century later, in Bartolomeo Scappi's 1570 *Opera*. There, in book six, chapters twenty-eight and twenty-nine, the word *sugo* also indicates the juice dripping from meat, as the broth of castrated ram, or even the water in which vegetables have cooked.[20] Later in book six, chapter 156 refers to "a glass of *sugo* made of chards and spinach" added to a frittata.[21] *Salza* (spelled with a *z*) refers instead to recipes that required reducing by simmering liquids (including fruit juices, vinegar, and wine) until they reach a thicker consistency. The sauce of quince juice in book two, chapter 268, falls under this category.[22] In book two, chapter 272, however, Scappi also uses the word *salsa* for *salsa verde*, a mixture of finely minced parsley, spinach, mint, arugula, and other herbs crushed in the mortar with bread and vinegar.[23] The process is similar to the preparations that Scappi calls *sapore*, which still reflect the medieval use of thick sauces made with bread, acidic juices, great quantities of spices, and little fat.

Supported by lords and kings who displayed wealth and power by competing as patrons of refinement, arts, and literature, the Italian Renaissance originated a culinary world of unprecedented brilliance and originality. The new merchant and banking elites expressed their social aspirations through conspicuous consumption in the forms of fashion, architecture, objects, and food. However, Italy's fragmentation, as well as underlying economic and social tensions, eventually allowed European powers to take direct control of vast areas of the peninsula and to indirectly influence local politics. In the seventeenth century, Spain extended its direct control over Lombardy and Milan, Sicily, Sardinia, and the area of southern Italy comprising today's Abruzzo, Molise, part of Latium, Campania, Apulia, Basilicata, and Calabria. At the same time, the

Catholic Church, striving to stop the expansion of Protestantism, generated a religious and cultural atmosphere that contributed to snuffing out the creative spirit of the Renaissance. These developments were accompanied by a long-lasting economic stagnation, while wars, famines, and epidemics decimated the population. These events caused a reduction of commerce, which in turn slowed down banking and finance, two of the major sources of wealth in Italy. In the eighteenth century, Tuscany was bestowed on the dukes of Lorraine, relatives of the Hapsburg family. Meanwhile, Spain transferred Lombardy to Austria, and the Savoy dynasty of Piedmont took control of Sardinia. Finally, the kingdom of Naples passed to a member of the Spanish royal family, Charles of Bourbon, who established a local dynasty, independent but influenced by Madrid, that would rule over southern Italy and Sicily until 1861.

The Foreign Influences on the Food of Italy

Inevitably, foreign occupants profoundly affected local foodways, with the consequence that the cuisines of Italy lost their role as the European epicenter of culinary novelty and sophistication. As Italy's courts lost their position as *arbiter elegantiarum* in all things food, France emerged as the new engine of innovation. François Pierre de La Varenne's 1651 *Le cuisinier françois* reflected, and to some extent sanctioned, the transition from the Italian-influenced Renaissance cuisine to a new style that constitutes the basis for French culinary hegemony. While medieval-style sauces continued to appear in his work, La Varenne also introduced a different kind of preparation, based on the meat-cooking juices or broth with the addition of herbs, flour (or more rarely, fine breadcrumbs or *chevelure*), and at times egg yolks or fats for emulsification. With few exceptions, such as *sauce verte*, *sauce poivrade*, and *sauce Robert*, these new preparations are neither called *sauce*, nor do they appear in a separate section, but rather are placed within the recipes of which they are an important component as *liaison* (thickener and connector), such as in *ragoût* and *fricassée*. They reflected a preference for smooth textures, which was made possible also by the spread of the *potager*, a raised stove that allowed for better control over temperature than fireplaces.[24] As sociologist Jean-Pierre Poulain and food historian Edmond Neirinck observe, La Verenne's sauces ushered in the introduction of two important techniques: the fat-based roux and the reduction, both of which would be further developed in the following years, as the mysterious L. S. R's 1674 *L'art de bien traiter* and François Massialot's 1691 *Le cuisinier roïal et bourgeois* indicate. These foundational texts also included *jus*, which are simple *déglaçages* of meat cooking juices, and *coulis*, resulting from the straining (*couler*) of the jus through a sieve, after the addition of herbs and other ingredients such as mushrooms and almonds.[25] Over time, these techniques for *jus* and *coulis* would turn into building blocks of the nineteenth-century master sauces, as systematized by Carême.[26]

The foundational books of the second half of the seventeenth century, as sociologist Priscilla Parkhurst Ferguson points out, "exhibit a marked ambition to dictate practices."[27] They mark the beginning of the systematization of techniques and, later, of labor organization that was one of the reasons for the success of French cuisine in the following centuries, as well as its influence on culinary professions around the world.[28] Food historian Patrick Rambourg also argues that:

> with a greater ease of use and a better layout of the recipes, the evolution of cookbooks corresponds to the ordering of culinary activities. The professional organization that structures it and the growing will to rationalize the work of the cook will play a big role in the quality of French cuisine and its long-term duration. The culinary system created by practitioners allows them to prepare a great variety of dishes while keeping a certain freedom of creation.[29]

Sauces assume a more important role and greater visibility in the eighteenth century. For example, François Marin offers about fifty recipes in his 1739 *Dons de comus ou les délices de la table.*[30]

In Italy, in the meantime, several cookbooks reveal an enduring connection with local traditions. Among the best-known examples are Francesco Vaselli's *L'Apicio ovvero il maestro de' conviti* (Apicius, or the Master of Banquets, 1647), *La lucerna de corteggiani* (The Oil Lamp of Courtiers, 1634) by Giovan Battista Crisci, and *Lo scalco alla moderna* (Modern Kitchen Steward, 1692) by Antonio Latini, who worked for the Spanish viceroy of Naples and paid particular attention to the products of the southern peninsula. His book is the first to include recipes for tomatoes; they are all called *alla spagnuola* (in the Spanish style), suggesting that their culinary use had been introduced from Spain, where it was more or less established. Out of three, only one is a sauce; the other two are a casserole with veal, pigeon, and stuffed chicken necks, and a vegetable stew close to the modern Neapolitan *cianfotta* (not unlike a southern French ratatouille). A recipe similar to the latter would later appear in Francesco Gaudentio's 1705 *Il Panunto Toscano, ovvero la teologia gaudentina.*[31]

Latini's recipe for tomato sauce reads:

> Take half a dozen ripe tomatoes; place them on embers to roast, and when they are charred peel them carefully and mince them with a knife. You will add finely minced onions, as much as you like; chili peppers, also finely minced, *piperna* (wild thyme) in small quantity. Mixing everything together, season with a little salt, oil, and vinegar, which will make a very tasty sauce, for boiled meats or other dishes.[32]

This is very different from the tomato *sugo* or *salsa* found two centuries later in Artusi, as it resembles a Mexican-style *salsa*. The tomatoes are roasted, rather than cooked with the other ingredients, which are added later; furthermore, they are not strained.

Sauces presented under the name of *salsa* appear in chapter fourteen, entitled "Di salsa e sapori di diversi modi" ("Of Sauces and Sapori of Different Kinds") of Latini's *Lo scalco alla moderna.*[33] The title of the section suggests a distinction between the two terms, but the first recipe, *sapore o salsa di presciutto di porco* (pork ham sauce), seems to conflate them. In other cases, the word *sapore* appears to refer to preparations in which a main ingredient (mostly fruit, but also anchovies) is cooked with a liquid and other spices to obtain a fluid, smooth consistency, often strained through a sieve, that can be stored and served cold; *salsa* indicates instead a rougher texture with ingredients in small pieces, to be served warm or cold depending on the recipe. The sauce techniques that were being developed in France during the same period do not appear yet.

Despite the persistence of local tradition, from the late seventeenth century, the influence of French cuisine on Italian cookbooks developed in three directions: recipes and techniques, consolidation of taste, and a concern for appropriateness (heavily determined by considerations of education, class, wealth, and language). The beginning of this preponderance is marked by the publication in 1682 of *Il cuoco francese ove è insegnata la maniera di condire ogni sorta di vivande* (The French Cook, Where the Way to Season All Kinds of Foods Is Taught), which presented itself as the translation of La Varenne's major text but was, in reality, the adaptation of minor works of his. This kind of distortion was not a rare phenomenon, as *Il cuoco reale e cittadino*, also published in 1724, was supposed to be a translation of Massialot's volume, though it was far from faithful to the original.

The new trends in French cuisine were slowly embraced in Italy, at least among the elites who had seen their political autonomy and relevance wane in the face of increasingly stronger foreign presence. France was considered a central point of reference not only for the cooks of the upper classes, but also for those bourgeois intellectuals who wanted to embrace more modern and progressive models of consumption. As food and its consumption became expressions of cultural identity, the bourgeoisie tried to develop its own distinctive culinary taste. It expressed dislike for the intricate dishes of the old nobility and a growing appreciation for popular traditions, which were inevitably reinterpreted and filtered to meet their new standards of refinement. These new preferences partly echoed the French culinary fashion, which highlighted clear and distinct flavors, the separation of sweet and savory courses, fresh ingredients, and a much-reduced use of spice. In fact, well-to-do families often hired French chefs, considered more prestigious than the local professionals and obviously more familiar with the new French cuisine. Aristocratic families in Naples and Palermo called these chefs *monzù*, a local adaptation of the French word *monsieur*. These chefs became the interpreters of French food for the Italian elites and played a crucial role in the introduction of the so-called French-style service, with a first course of appetizers and soups, followed by a second course of several dishes all served at the same time, and then ending with desserts.

The Tension Between Cosmopolitanism and Localism

The influence of France became visible in new cookbooks that tried to adapt the French model to local recipes and ingredients. *Il Cuoco Piemontese perfezionato a Parigi* (The Piedmontese Cook Perfected in Paris, 1766), basically a translation of Menon's *La Cuisinière bourgeoise*, and *La cuciniera Piemontese* (Piedmontese Cooking Woman, 1771) indicated the role of the region of Piedmont as an important link between Italian and French culinary customs. Vincenzo Corrado, at the court of Naples, applied French techniques to southern ingredients in *Il credenziere di buon gusto* (The Tasteful Credenza Manager, 1778) and, above all, in his masterpiece *Il cuoco galante* (The Gallant Cook, 1773). While the book includes Neapolitan specialties like rice *sartù* (a meat-filled, dome-shaped rice dish), it has categories derived from French cuisine, such as *potaggi* (an Italian adaptation of the French word *potage*), *colì* (*coulis*), *puré* (purée), *ragú* (*ragoût*), and *budin*. A whole chapter is focused on *salse, sapori, marmellate, e geli* (sauces, jams, and jellies). Corrado explains: "*Salse* and *sapori* described in this treatise are not dishes but rather condiments, which were invented and served on the table with the goal of providing greater seasoning for a dish, or to give strength to tired stomachs, or to titillate the palate that wants to eat with more flavor, or more than necessary, or even without hunger."[34] *Salsa* differs from *sapore* because the former is served warm, and the latter cold.[35] As a consequence, most *sapori* are fruit-based, with the exception of one made with anchovies.

Corrado's inclusion of several tomato recipes in a short section dedicated to the vegetable in *Il cuoco galante* suggests that tomatoes had achieved wider acceptance by the second half of the eighteenth century.[36] What he called *salsa di pomodoro* required cooking peeled and chopped tomatoes with garlic, basil, and chilies, straining the mixture, adding olive oil and spices, and boiling it with vinegar and meat cooking liquid, as it was to be served with meat.[37] If the recipe is closer to contemporary tomato sauces in terms of technique, the presence of vinegar and meat juice makes it quite distinct. Corrado also provides the recipe for a *colì di pomodoro*, a condensed tomato sauce enriched with ham fat, broth, and toasted bread crumbs, strained through a sieve.[38]

In the decades preceding unification, cookbooks tended to reflect local practices and ingredients, like *Il cuoco senza pretese* (The Cook Without Pretensions, 1834), which was heavily influenced by Lombardy, and Ippolito Cavalcanti's *Cucina teorico-pratica* (Theoretical and Practical Cuisine, 1837), which in its second edition includes an appendix in Neapolitan dialect on the popular cuisine of Naples. The latter also contains one of the first references to a tomato sauce used as a condiment for pasta.[39] Other cookbooks, like *Il nuovo economico cuoco Piemontese e credenziere Napoletano* (The New Economical Piedmontese Cook and the Neapolitan Butler, 1822) and *Il cuoco milanese e la cuciniera Piemontese* (The Milanese Chef and the Piedmont's Female Cook, 1859), attempted to connect different regional traditions. However, French influences are evident across the board. *Il cuoco milanese e la cuciniera piemontese*, for instance, includes several recipes for purées. The book offers a whole section about *sughi spremuti* ("squeezed" sauces, that is to say, passed through a sieve); besides the ones of beef and veal (similar to those later found in Artusi), the author includes interesting recipes for *sugo* of *giambone* (using a derivation of the French word *jambon* instead of the Italian prosciutto), duck, and shrimp, as well as the recipe for a *sugo economico domestico* (a cheap *sugo* for the home), to which cured pork and chicken offal can be added. The section about sauces includes many classic French recipes, from *velouté* to *béchamel* (presented with the French name), to a *salsa di tomates* (again, the French word is used instead of the Italian *pomodoro*). The last is a purée of tomatoes cooked in broth with the addition of *sugo*, some flour, and butter, which is clearly more similar to Escoffier's sauces than to Artusi's.[40] The collection has only one other self-standing recipe for tomatoes, filled with bread and herbs and covered in a sort of egg fricassee.[41] The author asserts that tomatoes are a little fruit that comes from America, is also called *pomo d'amore* (love apple), and is used in *ragò* (from the French *ragoût*) *e salse*, as for instance in the *ragò alla finanziera*, an accompaniment based on mushrooms and truffles.[42] The author's lack of familiarity with tomatoes suggests that as late as 1859 the vegetable is still vaguely exotic in northern Italy.

The influence of French cuisine on the volumes intended for wider and less refined audiences seems less pronounced, although it is quite detectable in the north of the country, as it is in, for instance, the anonymously written *Il cuoco Piemontese ridotto all'ultimo gusto* (The Cook from Piedmont Adapted to the Most Recent Fashion), published in Milan in 1825. The French roux becomes *rosso*, as in *petto di vitello in rosso* (veal breast in roux).[43] The sauce section includes many French recipes, others without any indicated origin, one presented as "Italian," and one as "English." The author often refers to "the texture of the sauce," indicating that the readers are supposed to already know what it is like. The book also presents *sughi colati* (strained meat-based gravies, often with butter and flour, often used as ingredients in more complex preparations) and *intingoli*, which are quite similar to *sughi colati* but may also be vegetable- and seafood-based. However, the various categories of *sugo*, *intingolo*, and *salsa* are not clearly defined or differentiated, pointing to both the relevance of many local practices and the lack of systematization in the cuisines of Italy, which was one of the reasons why French culinary practices were considered more prestigious. Tomato is not listed in the chapter about vegetables, but it appears with the names of *tomate* and *pomo d'oro* in several recipes, such as a rice soup and a salted cod croquette dish, where a *salsa di pomodoro* is explicitly referred to, although no recipe for it is provided in book.[44]

Giovanni Brizzi's *La cuciniera moderna* (The Modern Female Cook), published in Siena in 1845, has a section for sauces where the ones in the French style are clearly marked as such, while the Italian character of the others is assumed.[45] The *sugo* and *colì* fall under the same category of what is used "to season foods," which also includes béchamel sauce (*bisciamella*) and a couple of *lesioni* (from the French *liaison*). Southern customs still appear relatively unfamiliar.[46] The word *maccheroni* is used both for pasta and for a sort of flour gnocchi with eggs and orange zest.[47] The collection includes two recipes for a tomato sauce that can last for a long time. One is concentrated tomato juice that can be kept covered in oil in a jar, and the other is tomato juice boiled in sealed bottles, which reveals the wide utilization of the appertization processes (that is, the destruction of microorganisms in food through exposure to very high temperatures in airtight containers) in domestic settings.[48] Tomato sauce appears as an ingredient, for instance in a *fagioli in umido* ("beans stewed in a tomato sauce"),[49] the *maccheroni alla napoletana con calamari* ("Neapolitan-style macaroni with squid"),[50] and the *zuppa di magro con sugo di pesce* ("meatless soup with fish sauce").[51]

Il re dei cuochi: trattato di gastronomia universale (The King of Cooks: A Treatise of Universal Gastronomy), written in 1868 by Giovanni Nelli (who actually wanted to remain anonymous), presents a very systematic—and very French—approach to cuisine, despite a declaration in the preface that the book is meant for "gastronomes, chefs, and female cooks," and that "the recipe collection is so abundant that it allows to adapt the expenses for the table to all conditions, from the most modest fortune to those have been kissed by luck." The volume is marketed as "indispensable for professionals but recommended also for housewives," who could use it to improve their skills and thus grow in reputation even if "the majority of instructions belong to the kitchens of the grand houses."[52] The names of many recipes are given in French together with Italian translations, and "sometimes using expressions from dialects."[53] Although the preface describes the book's language as "easy," a small glossary is provided for the more technical terminology, including terms for objects, ingredients, and techniques. In many ways, the author's decision to explain culinary vocabulary reflects the same necessities that led Artusi to include a glossary in his own book. However, the desire to establish a unified language, relatively free of foreign influences, is absent in Nelli, who was rather inspired by the practical goal of making his recipes understood by all sorts of readers. In fact, French terms such as *glaçe*, *quenelles*, *hors d'oeuvre* (instead of *antipasto*, used by Artusi), and *entrée* or *entremets* are included in the glossary, as they are widely used throughout the book.

In the historical digression that follows the book's preface, Nelli shows a certain patriotic pride, declaring that "no country is more blessed with the gifts of nature" than Italy, and that "we" are rich in great products, to the point that "our cheeses and *panettone* travel to the inhospitable steppes of Russia and to the faraway America." However, he is also convinced that "within a few years, the numerous and always growing relations that exists among European nations will make differences in cuisine disappear and there won't be but one way of cooking, as it happened for clothes."[54] Nelli appears much more cosmopolitan than Artusi. Many recipes also carry French and English names, while exotic ingredients such as tapioca, arrowroot, and curry are featured.[55]

Although Nelli does not explicitly state it, evidently he believes that this imminent culinary cosmopolitanism would be dominated by the French cuisine that also influenced the professional outlook of his own book. This is particularly evident in the sauce section. "In grand kitchens, sauces are prepared under the name of *grandi salse* (grand sauces) or *salse madri* (mother sauces), *sugo* or *coulis*, which are kept and added when needed to the other sauces in order to improve them or enhance them," he explains. "Sauces, which by nature are the accompaniment of entrees, have always been considered as the essential basis for good cooking," he summarizes, before then elaborating further on their categories: "the main ones are known under the name of *spagnola* (espagnole), *vellutata* (velouté), *besciamella* (béchamel) and *alemanna* (allemande)."[56] The debt to French culinary practices as Escoffier was organizing them in that same period is evident: many sauces start with a *rosso* (a roux), and *essenze* are distinguished from the *sughi* obtained by deglazing meat, as the former "need to be tastier, clear, and liquid."[57] Sauces are divided into *grandi salse* (grand sauces, the main classic French sauces) and *piccole salse* (everything else, including sauces from Italy, France, England, Germany, and even Russia).

Tomatoes are described as "refreshing and acidulous" and as enjoying "a special reputation, in particular because of the very tasty sauce that everybody uses."[58] These are two tomato sauces (*salsa*), one with vinegar and one without, and both ask for sauces such as *velouté* and *espagnole* as ingredients, thus reflecting the French influence.[59] Even the basic *purée di pomidoro*, the most similar to Artusi's *salsa di pomodoro*, calls for *velouté* or white sauce.[60] Tomatoes, *purée di pomidoro*, and *salsa di pomidoro* all appear as ingredients in many dishes, especially soups and pasta, suggesting that by the second half of the nineteenth century, before Artusi wrote his book, tomatoes were at least relatively common in kitchens all over Italy, both in their fresh and—increasingly—canned versions.

Artusi's Sauces

Artusi's categories reflect Italy's own culinary peculiarities and its cultural fragmentation, as is apparent in the small section on *Brodi, gelatina, e sughi* (Broths, Gelatin, and *Sughi*). His recipe for *sugo di carne* is similar to what Escoffier called *jus*, that is, juice.[61] Or, as it is named in Italian recipe collections from the same period, *consumato o consumé*, from the French word *consommé*, which names a reduced beef stock that is used as the basis for sauces, with the difference that Artusi includes thinly sliced cured pork belly in the recipe.[62] The French influence is evident also in the *sugo di carne che i Francesi chamano salsa spagnola* (the meat *sugo* that the French call Spanish), an interpretation of a classic *sauce espagnole* without tomato. Immediately after these French-inflected sauces, Artusi introduces the *sugo di pomodoro* (tomato sugo), for which he doesn't provide an actual recipe or indicate any specific uses, suggesting that readers were presumably familiar with it. Here is what Artusi says: "I will speak anon about tomato *salsa*, which must be distinguished from tomato *sugo*, as the latter is simple, i.e. made from tomatoes that are simply cooked and run through a food mill. At the most, you may add a small rib of celery and a few leaves of parsley and basil to tomato *sugo*, if you feel you must."[63]

The use of the word *sugo* for this preparation points to a different categorization of what the French would have called *jus*, *fonds*, and *sauces*. Artusi seems to employ the expression in its original meaning of *succo*, which refers to the juice that is extracted from something. The word is mostly used to indicate fruit juice in contemporary Italian. The etymologic dictionary by Pianigiani, published in 1907 and thus contemporary to Artusi's work, presents *sugo*, *succo*, and *suco* (which still exists in some Italian dialects) as synonyms, all derived from the Latin word *succus* (juice, sap, liquor), which in turns comes from the Indo-European root *sug-/suk-*, "to flow." They all refer to "the humor of plants, and what one gets by squeezing herbs, fruits, meat, and other things; metonymical: the flavor of something; metaphorical: the substance, the strength of something." Pianigiani instead explains *salsa* (deriving from the Latin *salsus*, salted) as "a semi-liquid condiment to pour on cooked foods, to improve or change their flavor."[64]

From this point of view, it makes total sense to use the same word *sugo* for both a meat *jus* and a simple tomato sauce, as they express the quintessential substance of the ingredients from which they derive. This approach points to Artusi's attempt at creating a repository of Italian recipes clearly distinguished from both the French-influenced Italian cookbooks from previous decades, and from the canonical French culinary repertory, where tomato sauce is a relatively late addition. In fact, it is absent in Carême's category of the *grandes sauces* (which were *espagnole*, *velouté*, *allemande*, and *béchamel*) and then added by August Escoffier as *sauce tomate*, which included a roux of flour, butter, and blanched pork belly, as well as a *fond blanc*.[65]

For Artusi, tomato-based sauces seem still connected to pasta in Southern dishes, such as the two recipes for *maccheroni alla napoletana* (Neapolitan-style macaroni). The first one is very rich, with ingredients such as raisins and pine nuts that harken back to previous epochs when savory and sweet were not so neatly separated in the cuisines of Italy. The meat, cooked in the tomato sauce to impart its flavor to it, is then eaten as a second course, pointing to the fact that at the time meat was a relative luxury for many families, including the bourgeois ones that are the main audience for Artusi's work. In describing the preparation, the author expresses his doubts about what he perceives as a *guazzabuglio di condimenti* (a messy mixture of condiments), while also guaranteeing its authenticity, revealing that he had learned the recipe from a family in Santa Maria Capua Vetere, near Caserta.[66] Overall, the author admits this macaroni recipe is not bad and "those who aren't devotees of simple foods may like them."[67] A second, simpler, meatless version of the recipe is also proposed to be used with *maccheroni lunghi* (long macaroni, possibly a sort of long *rigatoni*) or *penne.*[68] The desire to include recipes that fall outside Artusi's familiar culinary world, which for him were the traditions from Romagna and Tuscany, is a testament to his project of contributing to nation-building by providing his readers with a repository meant to reflect the whole of Italy (even though some locations, such as Sardinia, were left out). At the time, the connection between tomato-based sauces and pasta was far from established, and it was likely perceived as southern. Other pasta recipes, such as the *maccheroni alla Bolognese* (Bologna-style macaroni), call for a meat sauce without tomatoes.[69] It is worth noting that Artusi recommends to "boil the macaroni in a large pot, with much water, avoiding to overcook," later asserting that pasta is better and easier to digest if eaten *durettina*, that is "slightly hard."[70] In other words, pasta needs to be eaten *al dente*.

Curiously, the word *salsa* does not appear to refer to the tomato-based sauces in any of these recipes, and *sugo* is preferred. Why are these sauces for pasta not considered as *salsa*? Instead, the recipe for *maccheroni con le sarde alla siciliana* (Sicilian-style macaroni with sardines) describes the fish-based sauce as *salsa*. The vocabulary is further complicated by the word *intingolo*, which is literally a dipping sauce, and appears in the above-mentioned recipe for Bologna-style macaroni. The word *intinto*, a variation of *intingolo*, describes the condiment for the *pappardelle col sugo di coniglio* (pappardelle pasta with rabbit sauce) in the body of the recipe, while the word *sugo* is used in the title. The recipe actually includes tomato *sugo*, so it would seem it would fall under the category of *salsa*, at least in Artusi's prevalent use of the word. The word *sugo* is also used for the condiment of the *pappardelle colla lepre* (pappardelle pasta with hare), which calls for a *sugo di carne*, the meat sauce or *jus* we previously discussed. As a matter of fact, the preparation is also called an *intingolo*, despite its complexity and the presence of components that are recipes in themselves and need be prepared in advance. The word *sugo* appears again in the *spaghetti col sugo di seppie* (spaghetti with cuttlefish sauce) and in the *spaghetti coi naselli* (spaghetti with hakes). In the latter, the words *sugo* and *intingolo* once again seem to be used as synonyms.[71]

So, what is a *salsa*? How does it relate to its French counterparts, whose influence Artusi declares he wants to counter, and to other sauce-like preparations, such as *sugo* and *intingolo*? Unfortunately, even in the section that the author formally devotes to sauces (*salse*), there is no clear answer. Artusi lists a few classic French sauces, which he suggests were used in Italian domestic settings, among them the *revigote* (which he presents as a version of a *salsa verde* or green sauce), the mayonnaise (with an Italianized spelling, *maionese*), the hollandaise (*salsa olandese*), and the béchamel, for which he offers a simplified version under the name of *balsamella*. Overall, even when a sauce recipe reflects French culinary traditions and techniques, Artusi tries to make them more user-friendly, both in name and instructions. The author expresses particular annoyance at the grandeur of name of the *salsa alla maître d'hotel*, which he nevertheless does not Italianize, maybe to have the opportunity to gripe about it: "Such a pompous name for a little nothing (*una briccica da nulla*)! Yet the French claimed the right in this and other matters to impose the law; the habit became common, and it is now necessary accept it."[72] However, in his preface to the thirty-fifth printing of the collection, he grudgingly admits that French cookbooks are "less worse" than the Italian ones, which he describes as "fallacious or incomprehensible."[73] Artusi's patriotic sensibilities are conflated with his desire to present accessible and easy recipes, humbly introducing himself as a "simple dilettante" whose instructions can always be improved, as "practice is the best teacher," as long as one sticks to the best ingredients.[74]

The majority of the preparations in the sauce section of the book are to be used to accompany different kinds of meats, fish, eggs, and vegetables.[75] Only two are explicitly meant to season pasta: *salsa di magro per paste asciutte* (meatless sauce for pasta) and *salsa di pomodoro* (tomato sauce), the former containing *sugo di pomodoro* with additions of mushrooms, pine nuts, and salted anchovies. So, the word *sugo* is used to indicate a basic preparation that expresses the essential flavor of an ingredient. When the preparation gets even slightly more complicated, Artusi seems to prefer the word *salsa*, regardless of the national origin of the recipe, its ingredients, or its techniques. And in the case of the *salsa di pomodoro*, the main difference with *sugo di pomodoro* is the presence of minced onion, garlic, and olive oil, as the celery, parsley, and basil are the same as in the recipe of the *sugo* and the preparation for both requires cooking and passing the tomatoes through a food mill. The onion, garlic, and celery are prepared as a *battuto*, meaning that they need to be mixed with all the ingredients before cooking, rather than as a *soffritto*, in which case they would be browned in olive oil before adding the other ingredients.

While *sugo* ends up being a mere ingredient for other recipes, *salsa* is described as a more self-standing preparation, which "is good with boiled meat, is excellent, combined with sweet butter and grated cheese, on pasta, and for making risotto."[76] Although the difference would appear to be minimal, Artusi feels the need to differentiate between the two. It is unclear if he does so to reflect some culinary category that he took to be widely established, or to give a more systematic approach to his volume from a technical point of view, despite his stated goal to keep it simple. As *sugo* appears as an ingredient in various recipes, from *salse* to *umidi* or stews, it is presented as a building block of Italian cuisine, the way stocks and *fonds* are fundamental in French cuisine.[77]

In his section on *conserve* (preserves), Artusi also provides two recipes for tomato juice preserves, the first one *senza sale* (without salt) and the second one with sugar, basically a jam. In the recipe for the first one, the author states that tomato's juice "pairs well with so many dishes and it is such a good accompaniment to them that it is worth to make some efforts to obtain a good *conserva.*"[78] The recipe "without salt" is in fact quite laborious: it requires cooking *and* straining tomatoes, cooking the juice again to make it thicker ("until you pour a drop on a dish and it does not roll away"), pouring it into bottles that are to be sealed with corks and tied with twine, then finally boiling the bottles in large pots and waiting to remove them until the water in which they have been boiled is completely cold.[79] In this section, Artusi on the one hand indicates how the tomato has already become important in Italian culinary practices, while on the other hand he engages with the technological innovations of his time, pointing out that salicylic acid, of which he is quite suspicious, may be added to obtain a more liquid *conserva*, and that a budding industry of canned tomatoes already exists. By discussing tomatoes in all their forms—fresh, conserved at home, and canned in factories—Artusi implicitly expresses his desire to take into consideration products, customs, and recipes that until recently had been profoundly local. With this and similar gestures, the author manifests his interest in creating a new, shared culinary language and repertoire that could unify Italians' everyday experiences through taste and conviviality. By doing so, Artusi offers a modest but effective tool for nation-building, which would acquire greater relevance and visibility during the Fascist years.

Artusi constructs his more Italian, if not outright patriotic, approach within the context of culinary cosmopolitanism that transpires in nineteenth-century Italian cookbooks, regardless of their intended audience (professional or domestic) or their indebtedness to local cuisines. His frequent reflections point to both the desire to present recipes that are truly from Italy, freed from French influence, and the aspiration to give Italian cuisine the same respectability and technical systematization found in the French culinary canon, which is thus indirectly—and contradictorily—acknowledged as worthy of emulation. Artusi's aspiration to impart a greater scientific and logical organization to Italian cuisine is evident in the very title of his work and in frequent observations throughout the book. At the same time, the author strives to give a quintessentially Italian character to all the recipes, pointing to their regional origin as an expression of the culinary wealth of the new country. Moreover, as Alberto Capatti observes in his magnificently annotated edition, Artusi meant to organize the recipes in chapters, but he did not share the "rigid, progressive, and sectorial professional pedagogy" that dominated in other recipe collections from the same period and in which, for example, a greater number of sauces could be included in a separate chapter rather than provided, as Artusi does, within recipes that require them.[80]

Against this background, sauces are particularly interesting for assessing Artusi's debt to and desire for independence from French cuisine. The long history of mutual influence between Italian and French cuisines transpires in the very development of sauces as a culinary category, first under the late Middle Ages and Renaissance preeminence of Italy, and later with the French supremacy that started with the publication of La Varenne's book. As the seventeenth and eighteenth centuries saw a growing foreign presence in Italy, both the vocabulary and the practices around sauces expressed local, French, and Spanish elements, the latter expressed in particular with the use of tomatoes. This multiplicity of contributions generated both a great variety of recipes and visible confusion in terms of definitions and uses. Above all, it would appear that cookbook authors before Artusi were not really interested in clarifying such complexities, but rather were keen to offer a large variety of recipes. Italy as an administrative reality and as an ideological referent was absent from the lived experience of chefs and culinary professionals, who often operated for regional courts and took the political fragmentation of Italy for granted. During and immediately after the unification process, the culinary world appeared unresponsive to the political changes, looking at foreign influences as signs of desirable cosmopolitanism. Artusi's book marks a clear break with the past and the beginning of a new appreciation for food as an expression of Italian culture. Such an approach would become prevalent in the 1920s with the rise of Fascist nationalism and would reappear in books such Ada Boni's *Il Talismano della felicità*, first published in 1928. It is also partially thanks to Artusi's work that today we speak of "Italian cuisine" as opposed to "the cuisines of Italy," which is arguably a more accurate description.

***Salsa di pomodoro*, Recipe 125**

P. Artusi, *La scienza in cucina e l'arte di mangiar bene*

Translated by F. Parasecoli

There was a priest in a town in Romagna who meddled in everything and, insinuating himself into families, wanted to intervene in every domestic business. He was, on the other hand, an honest man, and because more good than bad came from his zeal, they let him do it. However, the witty populace had nicknamed him Don Pomodoro, suggesting that, as tomatoes show up in everything, so a good sauce made from this fruit would be a valuable help in the kitchen. Finely chop a quarter of an onion, a clove of garlic, a piece of celery as long as a finger, a few basil leaves, and enough parsley. Season it with a little oil, salt, and pepper; chop seven or eight tomatoes, and mix everything together on the flame. Stir from time to time and when you see that the sauce has condensed into a liquid cream, strain it with the sieve and use it. This sauce lends itself to very many uses. It is good with boiled meat, it is excellent for enriching pasta seasoned with cheese and butter, and it works well for risotto.

Notes

1. Pellegrino Artusi, *The Art of Eating Well*, trans. Kyle Phillips III (New York: Random House, 1996), 97.
2. Artusi reveals the fact of self-publishing in the introduction to the sixth edition in 1902.
3. I will be referring to three versions of the book. When quoting recipes verbatim, I will use the 1996 translation into English by Kyle M. Phillips III. However, as this is not a complete translation, I will use a 2017 Italian edition to access the missing portions, while providing my own translation. I will also reference a 2010 Italian edition to examine and quote the critical notes by the famed food historian Alberto Capatti.
4. See Freedman, Chapter 2, and Deutsch, Chapter 15, in this volume.
5. Charles L. Killinger, *The History of Italy* (Westport, CT: Greenwood Press, 2002), 1.
6. Pellegrino Artusi, *La Scienza in cucina e l'arte di mangiar bene* (Middletown, DE: Malaeska, 2017), 13.
7. Priscilla Parkhurst Ferguson, *Accounting for Taste: The Triumph of French Cuisine* (Chicago: University, 2004); Amy Trubek, *Haute Cuisine: How the French Invented the Culinary Profession* (Philadelphia: University of Pennsylvania Press, 2000).
8. Artusi, *The Art of Eating Well*, 97.
9. Artusi, *La Scienza in cucina*, 37.

10. Artusi, *The Art of Eating Well*, 46.
11. Michael Billig, *Banal Nationalism* (London: Sage Publications, 1995).
12. Benedict Anderson, *Imagined Communities: Reflections on the Origin and Spread of Nationalism* (London: Verso, 1991).
13. Artusi, *The Art of Eating Well*, 56.
14. Ibid., 55–56.
15. Martin Maiden, *A Linguistic History of Italian* (New York: Routledge, 1995).
16. Maria Luisa Betri, "L'alimentazione Popolare nell'Italia dell'Ottocento," in *Storia d'Italia, Annali 13: L'alimentazione*, ed. Alberto Capatti, Alberto De Bernardi, and Angelo Varni (Turin: UTET, 1998), 7.
17. Felice Baroffio and Alessandro Quagliotti, *L'alimentazione del soldato* (Torino: Tipografia Subalpina, 1960).
18. Assunta Trova, "L'approvvigionamento alimentare dell'esercito Italiano," in *Storia d'Italia, Annali 13*, 495–530.
19. Alberto Capatti and Massimo Montanari, *Italian Cuisine: A Cultural History* (New York: Columbia University Press, 2003), 118.
20. Bartolomeo Scappi, *Opera* (Venice: Appresso, Michele Tramezzino, 1570), 397.
21. Ibid., 412.
22. Ibid., 92.
23. Ibid., 94.
24. Susan Pinkard, *A Revolution in Taste: The Rise of French Cuisine* (Cambridge: Cambridge University Press, 2009), 108–110.
25. Jean-Pierre Poulain and Edmond Neirinck, *Histoire de la cuisine et des cuisiniers* (Paris: Delagrave, 2004), 35–38.
26. Maryann Tebben, *Sauces: A Global History* (London: Reaktion Books, 2014), 52–58.
27. Ferguson, *Accounting for Taste*, 37.
28. Trubek, *Haute Cuisine: How the French Invented the Culinary Profession.*
29. Patrick Rambourg, *De la cuisine à la gastronomie: Histoire de la table française* (Paris: Louis Audibert, 2005), 96.
30. Ibid., 102.
31. David Gentilcore, *Pomodoro! A History of the Tomato in Italy* (New York: Columbia University Press, 2010), 54.
32. Antonio Latini, *Lo scalco alla moderna* (Napoli: N.p., 1694), 444.
33. Ibid., 437–450.
34. Vicenzo Corraado, *Il cuoco galante* (Napoli: Russo, 1793), 141.
35. Ibid., 147.
36. Ibid., 164–165.
37. Ibid., 144.
38. Ibid., 16.
39. Massimo Montanari, *Il Mito delle origini: Breve storia degli spaghetti al pomodoro* (Bari: Laterza, 2019), 68.

40. Anonymous, *Il cuoco milanese e la cuciniera Piemontese* (Milano: Pagnoni, 1859), 52.
41. Ibid., 255.
42. Ibid., 77.
43. Anonymous, *Il cuoco Piedmontese ridotto all'ultimo gusto* (Milano: Silvestri, 1825), 79.
44. Ibid., 42, 221.
45. Giovanni Brizzi, *La cuciniera moderna: Opera gastronomica* (Siena: Mucci, 1845), 155–159.
46. Ibid., 30–35.
47. Ibid., 45, 59.
48. Ibid., 170.
49. Ibid., 69.
50. Ibid., 102.
51. Ibid., 103.
52. Anonymous, *Il redei cuochi: Trattato di gastronomia universale* (Milano: Logros, 1880), 12.
53. Ibid., 12.
54. Ibid., 23.
55. Ibid., 125, 140.
56. Ibid., 123.
57. Ibid., 129.
58. Ibid., 729.
59. Ibid., 148.
60. Ibid., 162.
61. Auguste Escoffier, *Le Guide culinaire: Aide-memoire de cuisine pratique*, 2nd ed. (Lagny: Eile Colin, 1907), 8.
62. Artusi, *La Scienza in cucina e l'arte di mangier bene*, 19.
63. Artusi, *The Art of Eating Well*, 24.
64. Ottorino Pianigiani, *Vocabolario etimologico della linguaa Italiana* (Roma-Milano: Albrighi, Segati & C., 1907).
65. Antonin Carême, *L'art de la cuisine française au dix-neuvième siècle*, vol. 3 (Paris: Paul Renuard, 1864), 1; Escoffier, *Le Guide culinaire*, 20.
66. Artusi, *La Scienza in cucina e l'arte di mangier bene*, 66.
67. Artusi, *The Art of Eating Well*, 77.
68. Artusi, *La Scienza in cucina e l'arte di mangier bene*, 66.
69. Ibid., 66.
70. Ibid.
71. Ibid., 76.
72. Ibid., 86.
73. Ibid., 3.
74. Ibid.
75. Ibid., 84–92.
76. Artusi, *The Art of Eating Well*, 99.

77. Artusi, *La Scienza in cucina e l'arte di mangier bene*, 46.
78. Ibid., 401.
79. Ibid.
80. Ibid., 287.

Selected Bibliography

Anderson, Benedict. *Imagined Communities: Reflections on the Origin and Spread of Nationalism*, rev. ed. London: Verso, 1991.

Artusi, Pellegrino. *The Art of Eating Well*. Translated by K. Phillips III. New York: Random House, 1996.

Artusi, Pellegrino. *La Scienza in cucina e l'arte di mangiar bene*. Edited by A. Capatti. Milano: RCS Libri, 2010.

Artusi, Pellegrino. *La Scienza in cucina e l'arte di mangiar bene*. Middletown, DE: Malaeska, 2017.

Billig, Michael. *Banal Nationalism*. London: Sage Publications, 1995.

Capatti, Alberto, and Massimo Montanari. *Italian Cuisine: A Cultural History*. New York: Columbia University Press, 2003.

Ferguson, Priscilla Parkhurst. *Accounting for Taste: The Triumph of French Cuisine*. Chicago: University of Chicago Press, 2004.

Gentilcore, David. *Pomodoro! A History of the Tomato in Italy*. New York: Columbia University Press, 2010.

Killinger, Charles. *The History of Italy*. Westport, CT: Greenwood Press, 2002.

Tebben, Maryann. *Sauces: A Global History*. London: Reaktion Books, 2014.

Trubek, Amy. *Haute Cuisine: How the French Invented the Culinary Profession*. Philadelphia: University of Pennsylvania Press, 2000.

Fabio Parasecoli, Salsa, Sugo, e Intingolo: *Cooking Italian Identity in Artusi's* La Scienza in Cucina In: *From Garum to Mole: Sauces and Identity in the Western World*. Edited by: Andrew Donnelly, Beth M. Forrest, and Deirdre Murphy, Oxford University Press. DOI: 10.1093/9780190622138.003.0005

6

"It's Maple Syrup Time!"

THE HARD WORK AND PURE PLEASURE OF REAL MAPLE SYRUP IN THE BACK-TO-THE-LAND MOVEMENT

Deirdre Murphy

IN THE WINTER of 1975, Bruce N. Coulter wrote an article for *The Mother Earth News* entitled "Sugaring: Amateur Style."[1] In it, he broke down carefully the tasks of syrup-making, starting with a description of the beginning of the maple tapping season. "How do you know for sure when the maple sap is ready to gather?" he asked. "Let's say that—some night in late February or early March—the temperature is below freezing as you go to bed. Then," he mused, "during the night, the wind changes and you find the mercury climbing, the snow melting and the sun coming up in a clear sky." This could only mean, as he revealed to his readers, that "[t]he 'run' has begun and you must be up and doing." Coulter went on to explain everything that had to happen next, from the initial step of tapping trees for sap to finally bottling the syrup. He didn't stint on the details of the work process. "To tap a maple tree you need a brace and a 7/16-inch bit, with which you bore a hole into the tree about breast high and two to three inches deep," he explained.[2] "The evaporating process is the heart and soul of the sugaring operation and your close attention must be devoted to maintaining a strong, steady fire," he cautioned and, "Now a word about vigilance," he warned, "Watch the evaporator like a hawk!" There was a lot to do here, he impressed upon his audience. Yet, at the conclusion of his how-to piece, he paused to affirm the process and celebrate its product: "Somehow, even if rain, snow, ashes and soot fall into the bubbling batch and soot gets in your eyes...somehow the syrup still tastes good...because it's a harvest you've reaped yourself from the bounty of Mother Earth."[3]

Presented in this way, the process of making maple syrup emerges as—all at once and together—an act of physical labor, an experience of gustatory pleasure, and an occasion of reverence for "Mother Earth." This multi-sided perspective is worth noting because it likely appealed to Coulter's intended audience as an ideal image of a pure experience, as marked by independent labor, a connection to nature, and a delicious final product. There is nothing extraneous here, no manager to heed, no factory to enter, no capitalist exploitation, no land degradation, no chemically processed foodstuff of unknown origin to wonder about.

For those most inclined to have been reading Coulter's article, a celebration of maple syrup was emblematic of a broader pursuit of purity—in living, in working, and in eating. *The Mother Earth News*, which published his piece, has been described as the "journal of record" for the back-to-the-land movement of the 1970s—that segment of the counterculture that had recently chosen to abandon the cities and suburbs in order to strike out on their own to set up farms in rural settings.[4] Back-to-the-landers lamented the industrial age into which they had been born as a defiled, polluted society. They dreamed of escaping it for something better, and they were drawn to writings such as Coulter's that were designed to help them figure out how to do the things they needed to do in order to survive and, hopefully, prosper. Such descriptions of *real* maple syrup—for Coulter's was far from unique—offered back-to-the-landers a distilled vision of a pre-industrial, arboreal version of a Garden of Eden in which the redemptive power of work could manifest and merge with their own newer understanding of humanity as deserving of those pleasures that were earned.

Maple syrup was a culmination of all that they had imagined clean living, hard work, and sweet rewards out in the country could be, and as such it is a sauce that defines their experience. Still, making maple syrup has never been easy. To understand the basic process is to be aware that it has always been dependent upon the convergence of unlike elements. There is climatic convergence: syrup-making begins as late winter just barely tilts into spring. This is the only time of the year, just a few short weeks, that trees can be tapped. As long as nighttime temperatures fall below freezing, and daytime temperatures rise above it, the sap will flow. But if either of those should change, the sap will either not rise in the tree (when it's below freezing both day and night), or it will become "buddy" and marked with off flavors (if daytime and nighttime temperatures both rise above freezing). There is also geographic convergence: syrup-making requires moving between civilization and wilderness, and throughout its long history, tappers have had to leave their camps, villages, or towns and head out into the woods to find a likely stand of maples. As slow-growing hardwoods, maples are not mature enough to be tapped until they are at least thirty years old. Consequently, they don't lend themselves to tight plantings of orderly rows in cleared fields that are the standards of mainstream agriculture. Finally, again, there is the convergence of human physical sensations: the laborious, mostly cold, often wet, and frequently solitary work of collecting sap, as well as the hours of standing over steaming vats as the sap evaporates down, all of which precedes the decadent pleasure of consuming the syrup amidst the warm comforts of the breakfast table.

These conditions and processes of syrup-making have not changed very much over the centuries, which is partly what drew back-to-the-landers to syrup-making.[5] There is only one way in which maple syrup is not a convergence, or a melding of distinct elements: its composition. *Real* maple syrup does not contain multiple ingredients. It is made largely by removing that which is unnecessary and retaining that which is essential. The entire point of evaporating maple sap, which is typically around 97 percent water and 3 percent sugars and traces of other organic matter, is straightforward: to produce a syrup that is 66 percent sugar.

By some accounts, this might disqualify maple syrup as a sauce. Here, there is no admixture of multiple ingredients, just the intense manipulation of one: maple sap. In popular discussions of sauces from the time period, the process of merging several ingredients is offered as one of the defining characteristics of sauce. In the introduction to its section on sauces, the 1975 edition of Irma Rombauer's *Joy of Cooking* tells readers just this. "All sauces, of whatever character... should be so skillfully blended that, like successful soups, they can be eaten all by themselves."[6] More recently, food studies scholar Maryann Tebben has argued in *Sauces: A Global History* that sauces have "certain core attributes," one of which is that they are "refined preparations (as distinct from raw materials)." Furthermore, they are not "ingredients but occupy a complementary role." Because of this, she finds, "Syrups, spice pastes, oils, vinegar and even salt... do not fit the definition of sauces because they are elemental ingredients."[7]

Such categorization is problematic. Maple syrup was the furthest thing from a "raw material," nor was it an "ingredient" (though it could be used as such). It was a sauce for back-to-the-landers, because they used it as such. When they described pouring the amber liquid over pancakes, waffles, French toast, *crêpes*, johnnycakes, oatmeal, or yogurt, they were using it as a sauce that added liquid and flavor to their enjoyment of those foods. "No one has really appreciated maple syrup," declared James Churchill, a contributor to *The Mother Earth News* in 1972, "until they've poured it... over wild rice on a cold winter morning with the snow piled deep around the cabin and the woodstove radiating a gentle heat."[8]

Such usage conforms to definitions offered in Tebben's and Rombauer's work, both of which classify sauce as distinct from the food it accompanies. While Rombauer's modern classic of American cookery actually does include "syrups" in its section on "sweet sauces," it also points out that sauces, whether savory or sweet, "compliment" food when they "enhance or heighten its intrinsic flavour," and "complement" it when they provide a desired contrast to its dominant flavor profile.[9] Similarly, Tebben understands sauces as "accompaniments, usually in smooth liquid form, that are applied to a dish in order to enhance its flavour."[10] Whether Churchill thought of his maple syrup as a "complement" or a "compliment" to his rice is unclear, but that he believed it added something vital, even transforming the dish into a transcendent experience, is not.

Ultimately, it is only the singularity of its composition over the inclusion of multiple ingredients that might give pause in considering maple syrup as a sauce. Yet it is precisely this characteristic that caused it to be revered by back-to-the-landers, and the paradox is one that I suspect would amuse them. If sauce is required to include multiple ingredients in order to be designated as such, then "pure" or "real" maple syrup that people worked so hard to concoct would not qualify, while adulterated or entirely fake syrup, which they derided repeatedly, would. Back-to-the-landers rejected so many of the norms of the twentieth century. Amidst a consumer culture that encouraged people to want more, they desired less, craved what was essential or "simple," and admitted to coveting nothing more than they could produce with their own labor. Maple syrup reflected this outlook and represented their aspirations. While Tebben has admitted that "there are some grey areas" when it comes to figuring out what counts as a sauce, with new ones being invented and long-standing ones evolving, their creation over time is "informed by cultural forces" such that, for example, "vegetarianism in Japan displaced fish sauce for soy sauce," and "rapid industrial growth in the U.S. encouraged ready-made, shelf-stable condiment sauces."[11] Labored over and savored by those who made it, the purity of a single ingredient is an intrinsic part of what made *real* maple syrup a really pleasurable sauce. Because of this, and perhaps retaining something of its revolutionary context from the back-to-the-land movement, it also stretches our understanding of what counts as sauce.

The Sources and Their Users

In 1950, homesteaders Helen and Scott Nearing published the first edition of *The Maple Sugar Book: Being a Plain and Practical Account of the Art of Sugaring Designed to Promote an Acquaintance with the Ancient as well as the*

Modern Practice, Together with Remarks on Pioneering as a Way of Living in the Twentieth Century. Running to nearly 300 pages of maple-centric advice, history, lore, and social commentary, it remains among the most comprehensive treatises on maple syrup ever written. *The Maple Sugar Book* quickly became an influential standard for back-to-the-land syrup-makers.[12] In addition to teaching the process of making maple syrup and the history of maple, the Nearings noted that their goal in writing the book "was to relate our experiment in homesteading and making a living from maple to the larger problem faced by so many people nowadays: how should one live?"[13]

The people who thought that maple syrup could be a good answer to that existential question were encouraged to approach the process with optimism, maintain a strong work ethic, and take pleasure in the natural world. In the Nearings' book, as well as another manual of small-scale independent maple syrup production, Noel Perrin's 1972 *Amateur Sugar Maker*, syrup-makers emerged as just these sorts of energetic figures. The type showed up in other places, too, such as when the subject of maple syrup was taken up with seasonal regularity in the pages of the iconic *The Mother Earth News*, which initially went to press in 1970 and has been in print in various iterations ever since. In these manuals and journal articles, physically demanding experiences seem to have given the syrup-makers a deep appreciation for the sauce. Migrating from winter to spring, from maple stand to plowed field, from boiling sap to freezing outdoor temperatures could test one's reserves of gruff stoicism and hippie gregariousness. When the Nearings asked, "how should one live?" they were far from the only ones to do so. This was such a common query that it became a catalyst for a new genre of literature: the counterculture DIY narrative. Throughout the 1960s and 1970s, the counterculture was awash in publications promoting visions of a society recreated to be more just, joyful, and cooperative.[14]

Among the counterculture generation, back-to-the-landers saw themselves as nurturers, energized by a spirit of discovery and driven to build new worlds. As members of communes or as individual families, they valued self-sufficiency when they set up homesteads. They enriched soil, spread compost, revered the food they grew, and were proud of the physical labor it took to get it.[15] They hoped they were doing everything right in building these new lives; often they weren't so sure.

In large part, their uncertainty was due to their timing as well as their upbringing. The back-to-the-land movement got its start at the tumultuous end of the 1960s and went on to flourish in the 1970s. Although its adherents rejected an urban industrial reality they defined as grinding and, at base, ill-considered, they did not necessarily see themselves as revolutionaries. They did not court public attention, and the explosive public conflicts that marked the era were not the sort of experiences in which they were likely to participate. The majority of them, it seems likely, came from the suburbs and cities, were white, and were college educated.[16] What they wanted most was to get out of the cities and to sustain themselves independently.

In this way, these back-to-the-landers were not unique. There have been several such movements throughout the history of the industrialized world.[17] In the United States, whether their participants referred to themselves as "new pioneers," or citizens of a "Green Earth," or adherents to "the simple life"—as they have done at various times and in various places—such "off the grid" movements have historically followed periods of economic downturn. Given this, those who have gone back to the land are more clearly understood as a recurring minority in the population who, when faced with economic calamities, heed the impulse to flee and take their chances striking out on their own.[18]

By the 1970s, in the midst of "Watergate, war in Vietnam, an oil embargo in 1973," expansion of the global population, and a host of environmental disasters, "back-to-the-landers added," as historian Dona Brown has summarized, "entirely new concerns to the old list: Pollution. Scarcity. An overcrowded planet."[19] In response, many scholars have estimated that over one million individuals in the United States formed a loose exodus to the countryside.[20] Once there, they self-identified as lovers of nature reaching back to connect with the pioneering spirit of their ancestors—minus the racism and colonialism, and with the addition of ecological sensitivity, they hoped. The problem was that they needed their efforts to produce their own food to succeed so that they could feed themselves, and they didn't always know what they were doing.

Fortunately, there were those who had expertise and wanted to share it with the newcomers. From their far-flung farms in rural America, more experienced individuals published "how-to" manuals and journal articles that gave advice on the intricacies of rural life. Not infrequently, they massaged it all with a folksy, romantic optimism designed to inspire ignorant others who followed their lead.

"The Warmth and Security That Self-Sufficiency Can Give You"

In 1975, *Mother Earth News* published another installment of a recurring column, "The Plowboy Interview." This one featured its founder, John Shuttleworth, as he explained some of the reasons why he and his wife, Jean, had started the publication. His central theme was self-reliance. To his readers, Shuttleworth touted "the warmth and security that self-sufficiency can give you when a seemingly endless stream of other people do not know how to raise or preserve the food they need or repair the equipment they have." As he continued, self-sufficiency was a thing to be pursued, and it was also part of a larger dynamic: "I was taught by example at the earliest possible age that it is good to share your surplus and your knowledge with those who need it."[21] Further, he saw self-sufficiency as part of an even larger framework. Those who were self-sufficient should take as their responsibility "the perpetuation of the planet and its fragile ecosystem," and accept as their "basic philosophy… that what's best for Earth and the preservation of its delicately interwoven web of life is, by definition, what's best for humankind. We *are* part of that web," Shuttleworth concluded, "no matter how grandly our species generally tries to ignore the fact."[22]

To summarize, Shuttleworth's expressed vision was far-reaching to the point that it correlated the self-sufficiency of the individual with planetary health. His ideas were also among the most prominent of the back-to-the-landers. They inspired and shaped their collective efforts. Here, those sentiments ring "grandly" with ambition for the movement.

The first essential step, though, was that people had to be able to take care of themselves. In their study of maple syrup, the Nearings had already made this declaration and testified that they found syrup-making to be particularly worthwhile because it provided a living and a "thorough-going education." As they declared, "We have earned from maple and… [w]e have also learned from maple." According to them, the endeavor molded a "complete" syrup-maker who "comprises in himself a woodcutter, a forester, a botanist, an ecologist, a meteorologist, an agronomist, a chemist, a cook, an economist, and a merchant. Sugaring is an art, an education, and a maintenance."[23]

When Noel Perrin published the *Amateur Sugar Maker* as a young homesteader in Vermont roughly two decades later, he appeared within its pages as the manifestation of Shuttleworth's hopes and the Nearings' beliefs. Perrin didn't say that making maple syrup was part of a greater scheme to save the planet, but he was measured in his efforts and in control of his learning process. It's easy to imagine that his evident fortitude and careful thought were exactly what Shuttleworth had in mind for the new pioneers of the day. At the start of his manual, Perrin explained that he wrote "in conscious admiration of Henry David Thoreau" (not surprising, since Thoreau was also very popular with the back-to-the-land set) because "he liked to see how much of a project one man can do alone, with just his hands and a few tools."[24] Perrin had that same curiosity, and it motivated him "to try my hand at sugaring." This was meant to be a serious experiment and besides, he confessed, "I like an edge of hard labor to my life."[25]

Taken together, these commentaries comprise a stalwart exhibition of back-to-the-land maple-supported self-sufficiency. The narratives they present are so encouraging and all goes so smoothly, perhaps excessively so. This is why Bruce Taub's memory is a sobering reminder of the steep learning curve that many back-to-the-landers encountered, with maple sugaring specifically and in their new environments more broadly. Taub was a member of the Earthworks commune in Franklin, Vermont, in the 1970s and, as he remembers, tapping projects were not always carried out fluidly:

> We were gathering heavily flowing maple sap on a glorious sunny day, temperatures in the high forties, using a three hundred gallon tank being drawn by our team of horses on a dray through the snow. Dozens of people were tromping through the woods pouring sap from the tap buckets into gathering buckets and unloading those buckets joyfully and speedily into the horse drawn tank. As we drove the first fully loaded tank back toward the sugar house the dray hit a hidden rock and tipped over pitching the gathering tank off the dray and onto its side. Though we only lost about twenty or thirty gallons of sap, the tank was far too heavy for us to right and reset on the dray, even with all the people power we had. So we set about unloading the sap we had gathered in the tank back into the gathering pails and then retraced our steps through the snow to the trees we had just harvested where we poured the sap back into the very buckets we had just unloaded. It was as if someone had taken a movie of our operation and was now playing the reel in reverse.[26]

Manuals and articles gave a lot of step-by-step advice on every aspect of sugaring because they had to; they were writing for people like Taub and his friends. As this memory underscores, though, all too often and very unfortunately, self-sufficiency was both an aspiration that back-to-the-landers worked toward and an immediate necessity. A partial list of chapters from the Nearings' *The Maple Sugar Book* indicates just how all-encompassing their advice could be: "Sugar from Trees," "Indians, the First Maple-Sugar Makers," "The Sugar Bush," "Sugar Tools and Equipment," "Maple Sap and Sap Weather," "Making Maple Syrup," "Marketing Maple Products," "The Money in Maple."[27] Such precision also characterized Perrin's manual and *The Mother*

Earth News articles as well. In her 1972 article, "Make and Market Maple Syrup: On Your Own Homestead," Sarah Funk provided very simple information: "warm days and cold nights will start the sap on its journey up the tree trunks. If there's a maple tree near your house, make an experimental taphole," she advised, "and watch until you see liquid oozing. That's your signal to get busy tapping."[28] At the same time, the article is painstakingly divided into topics that explained "Basic Equipment," "The Brace and Bit," "Spouts (Spiles) and Hooks," "Collecting Buckets and Covers," "The Holding Tank," "The Sugarhouse," "The Arch," "Tree Tapping," "Cooking Sap," "Finishing Syrup," and "Bottling Your Syrup," to name far fewer than half of her twenty-six subsections.[29]

As befits any tremendous undertaking for which one is not entirely prepared, back-to-the-landers maintained a sturdy optimism as they learned (or, at least they did when they wrote about it). They cheered each other on constantly. "Don't let the fainthearts discourage you with their warnings about back breaking labor and long, tedious cooking," Funk counseled. "Of course there's some work involved and patience required," she admitted, "but we've found that good things are worth waiting for... and sometimes it's the work which makes things even better!"[30]

Repeatedly, maple syrup enthusiasts assured one another that the process was "fun!" In a 1979 *The Mother Earth News* article entitled "We Make Tree Syrup in the Ozarks Too!," contributor Tom Hodges remarked, "When the season is over, of course, is when the real fun begins," because that's "when my wife and I strain our collected nectar." Overall, Hodges concluded, "we feel well paid for the pleasant time we spend in the woods."[31] Syrup-making remained fun even when, as writer Bruce Coulter recalled in his "Sugaring: Amateur Style," it wasn't the sort of fun that others could relate to: "One winter I was splitting logs in the backyard when a man drove up to make a delivery. He looked at the not inconsiderable pile of fuel and said, 'What's all this wood for?' " Coulter explained that in "a couple weeks I'll be using it to make maple syrup," and then recalled that his "visitor thought for a moment and then asked, 'What do you want to go to all the trouble for? You can get syrup in the stores.' " When Coulter responded that "I just do it for fun," the conversation was over: "the delivery man shook his head and climbed into his truck."[32]

What back-to-the-land syrup-makers found so compelling about the sauce was that it offered, as they described it, a potently seductive blend of realism and hedonism. One had to learn new skills and put them into practice working on the land, but there was also rich sweetness when it was done, not to mention the "fun" to be had along the way. More soberly, the Nearings cautioned that no one should get "the impression that sugar making is easy, or that the syrup pours from the tree full flavored and full bodied. . . . It involves arduous hard work, as anyone who has tried it will have found out."[33] Even so, they also acknowledged that it was "certainly sweet employment."[34]

Their reasons for describing it as such point to another way in which syrup-making could promote self-sufficiency: selling it. For many, marketability was part of the allure of syrup. The Nearings devoted two chapters to maple syrup as a source of income, while *The Mother Earth News* writers Susan Funk and Bruce Coulter also discussed selling as an option. Funk vouched to her readers that "[y]our syrup will probably sell itself if you let the word get around that it's available."[35] Noel Perrin, too, noted at the beginning of his manual that it was his intention "to earn a small part of my living by making syrup," and at the end he confirmed that he had been successful: "Most of the syrup we sold in New York City," and because "prices were high" that year, he had "made a decent sum of money."[36]

While none of the syrup-makers encouraged their readers to think of sugaring as a highly profitable scheme, they all touted it as a reasonably profitable means of extending one's income. According to the Nearings, sugaring was viable for new homesteaders because "the maple industry has always been carried on in houschold units. With minor exceptions," they asserted, "it can not be conducted as a large scale industry," for the obvious reason that the crop existed in disparate stands of maple trees in the forest.[37] For small homesteaders, this was an advantage because sugaring made use of land "ill suited to ordinary crop production."[38] Furthermore, they noted that sugaring made good use of the "energy of family and horses," who were "otherwise more or less idle at this time of year."[39] In other words, syrup-making could augment income during the period of the seasonal year when planting, tending, or harvesting crops was impossible. Whether this was "fun" or gave "a joyous sense of accomplishment," as Funk advocated that it could, it probably made life easier for those living at a remove from the established economic system.

Maple Syrup as Social Critique

The manufacture of maple syrup gained a heightened appeal for back-to-the-landers who saw the process as innately critical of the consumerism and industrial labor they wished to escape, and from the highly processed syrup that was either a blend of maple syrup and other sweeteners, or made only with imitation maple flavoring that had been created in a corporate-owned laboratory.[40] Admittedly, as a general rule, maple syrup does not conjure up images of fiery revolution. More likely, it brings forth visions of long weekend mornings, pillowy pancakes drenched in complex flavors of intense sweetness that linger only slightly viscously (the real stuff) or sticky plastic bottles stamped with pictures of log cabins nestled off in some imagined sylvan idyll (the fake stuff). For many, maple syrup is *the* flavor of cozy, pajama-clad homeliness, the quintessential sauce of the wholesome American breakfast table.

But there is another side to the story of maple syrup at mid-century, one in which its vaunted purity demonstrates the values of a movement that rejected the acquisitiveness and consumerism of the time period. This crystallizes early on with the Nearings and their *Maple Sugar Book*. Helen and Scott Nearing were defiant political radicals from an earlier and less forgiving time. She had been a classical musician, while he was a former economics professor, fired for his radical political leanings. When they abandoned the trappings of mainstream life and took up homesteading, first in Vermont and then in Maine starting in the 1930s, they supported themselves by farming and also by publishing books that explained how to take up homesteading, and why they thought people should. Their own rationale for doing so was informed by their distrust of capitalism and disgust with industrialization.

In *The Maple Sugar Book*, the Nearings lay bare the treacherous tendencies throughout the history of the American nation to devalue both humans and nature. They recount the processes by which "New lands in the Americas" had been "opened by railroads and hard roads and farmed by machinery" to the extent that "the United States is a country occupied by a few dirty, noisy cities... most free land is gone."[41] The resulting urbanized society was "artificial from top to bottom, imposing upon its victims a life pattern based on superficialities and upon an endless grind of routine that had as its chief purpose the fleecing of the poor and the weak for the profit of the rich and the powerful. Furthermore," their indictment continued, this society was "in general squalid and corrupt; ruthless" and composed of "policemanized concentration camps in which men and women were persuaded or compelled to live their lives."[42] The result of this society of "acquisition," as they termed it, was nearly incalculable loss:

> Once the commodity market is set up, it is the business of advertisers and salesmen to make the gadgets attractive. Buyers, to satisfy their acquisitive urge, need only one thing: money.... The would-be buyer

> takes a job, rents an apartment or room, dons the badge of serfdom—the business suit—and enters the city treadmill. He has exchanged his contacts with Mother Earth, with sunshine, starlight, cloud-decked sky, wind, driving mist and pelting storm, the light-drenched days and the gorgeous, silent, limitless nights for the floors, ceilings, walls, elevators, subways, one-way streets, teeming intersections, and traffic lights of man-made metropoli.[43]

Remember, the context for these criticisms was a manual on maple syrup. The Nearings' repudiation of mainstream culture here is strikingly, even poetically rendered. It was not, however, unique.

With more restraint, Perrin echoed some of these sentiments in his *Amateur Sugar Maker*. He, too, noticed that "[m]en are still trying to solve the problem of a livelihood by formulas more complicated than the problem itself."[44] For him, maple syrup was not a complication, but a treasured part of his seasonal year. His sense that tapping trees and boiling sap into syrup was "an annual rite, even an act of love" was linked to his perplexed and critical assessment of consumer culture.[45] Perrin admitted that there was always "the question of what I would be doing if I weren't sugaring." For himself, he didn't have a ready answer. For others, he found that it didn't look good: "I observe that my fellow teachers put in *their* spare time in March getting in a little late skiing, going to the movies, and watching hockey on television."[46] The result, as he saw it, was that they made no money and spent too much of what they did have: "what with their lift tickets and Head skis... their expenses often exceed mine." Finding this situation unacceptable, Perrin extended his scoff: "Nor do they wind up with a year's supply of syrup. On the contrary, most of them feel they can't afford decent syrup for their own pancakes.... The ones who mostly watch movies don't even dare eat pancakes, because they are afraid of getting fat. Whereas if they were... hanging out a few buckets they could eat what they pleased."[47]

For both Perrin and the Nearings, a society in which human experience was defined by the need to work in order to purchase things that may or may not be good for us, and that we may or may not even want, was deserving of pity or scorn. Maple syrup–making was their livelihood (at least in part), and so it makes a certain amount of sense that it would also become their platform for voicing social criticism. This was a more popular perspective than might be expected, as not one but two songs from the time period also correlate maple syrup with social discontent, hope for a more just society, and a profound connection to nature.

In 1971 Gordon Lightfoot released "Love and Maple Syrup," as part of his *Summer Side of Life* album, while in 1979 Pete Seeger came out with "Maple Syrup Time" on *Seasons and Circles*. Of the two, Seeger's is more emphatic in sounding a call for a revolutionary break from mainstream culture. He starts out cheerfully enough, though, and his first two stanzas offer instructions on the tapping and boiling processes:

First you get the buckets ready, clean the pans and gather firewood,
Late in the winter, it's maple syrup time.
You need warm and sunny days but still a cold and freezing nighttime
For just a few weeks, maple syrup time.
We boil and boil and boil and boil it all day long,
Till ninety seven percent of water evaporates just like this song
And when what is left is syrupy don't leave it too long
Watch out for burning! Maple syrup time.[48]

As the song winds on, the refrain "We boil and boil and boil and boil it all day long," is constant, and it is punctuated by the assurance that "Making it is half the fun," and there will be "satisfaction when it's done." By the conclusion, though, it's obvious that the directions given at the beginning have been part of a larger lesson:

I'll send this song around the world with love to every boy and girl,
Hoping they don't mind a little advice in rhyme.
As in life or revolution, rarely is there a quick solution,
Anything worthwhile takes a little time.
We boil and boil and boil and boil it all day long.
When what is left is syrupy, don't leave it on the flame too long.
But seize the minute, build a new world, sing an old song.
Keep up the fire! Maple syrup time.[49]

While Lightfoot was similarly inspired by maple syrup, his opening lines strike a romantic tone with their affirmation that "Love and maple syrup goes together/Like the sticky winds of winter/When they meet." From there, he too sketches an image of general discontent for, in this scenario, "lonely lovers" who are:

Looking for the world to be
Anything but what they see

Longing to be understood
By the heart that shapes the wood.[50]

While such imagery inflects the term "sappy" with new meaning, Lightfoot nonetheless draws upon themes similar to those taken up by the Nearings, Perrin, and Seeger. These "lovers" are defined by their dissatisfaction with the world as they experience it. By the end of the song they have retreated, and "go into the forest" where they gather "beneath the trees." In the last stanza they are even joined by many others:

In the north when winter's claw
Relaxes now to keep the law
Of nature in control
People come and stand in line
To rob the forest of her wine
But they don't feel the cold.[51]

Yet again, maple syrup (rendered here as the "wine" of "the forest") saves the day for those who want something more or better out of life. In all of these representations, social criticism slides from romantic despair to revolution, but it remains consistent. Overall, the expressions of discontent are so prevalent as to force the question: What was it about maple syrup that stirred such thoughts for those who retreated from the cities and suburbs in this era?

One answer has to be that the process of making maple syrup necessitates a direct reckoning with the social and industrial correlation of time and labor. Tapping and sugaring thwart established standards of industrial time for the obvious reason that this is not labor for which one could clock in or fill out a time sheet. Instead of set hours, there is the variable end of winter. Instead of recorded minutes, seasonal change is the governing standard for this sort of work. It is both inexorable (winter always ends and spring always arrives) and unpredictable (no one is ever sure how long the change from one to the other will take, what the weather will be like, or even precisely when it will happen).

As James E. Churchill described in his article, "Food Without Farming," from *The Mother Earth News* in 1972, "March is the time for sap to run in the maple trees," but "March in Wisconsin can be a beauty or a beast." If anything was certain in this season of indecision, it was that people could just as easily find themselves "picking tender greens from the sunny side of field knolls" as they might "spending the best part of the day shoveling through deep snow."[52]

A few years later, the editors of *The Mother Earth News* echoed Churchill's assessment. As they warned in an article entitled "Maple Syrup Recipe," from March 1978, although late in the "afternoon is the best time to collect the day's flow" of maple sap, no one should expect it "to run on a regular schedule. Some days you'll be lucky to find the bottoms of your buckets wet," while "on others, the pails will be running over before you get to them." In the end, they simply shrugged: "That's the way Mother Nature works."[53]

As all the articles and manuals referenced made clear, maple trees can be tapped only for short periods of the year—a few weeks, or even days, depending on conditions. Consequently, not even a calendar is of much use in determining when the seasonal work would start—only experience and awareness of weather and climate. As Bruce Coulter explained, "It isn't the demands of a sweet tooth or a desire to make money that motivates me to tap maple trees when spring arrives." Instead, he described a deeply romantic impulse: "like the one that prompts the Canada goose to lift from the waters of the Mississippi Delta country and wing his way to the breeding grounds around Hudson Bay. Perhaps," he concluded, "what drives me is an elemental instinct to produce with my own labor something from the riches of the good earth."[54]

Overall, producing syrup was marked for these commentators by an intimate awareness of natural rhythms. While this fostered a sensitivity to seasonal change, it also stood in direct contrast to the temporal and spatial dictates of industrial labor. In describing the beginning of the tapping season, for instance, Perrin's consciousness is consumed with the outdoors. He takes the measure of his world in a manner that is both expansive and immediate. "Fields won't be starting to green up until mid-April," and "[l]ilacs and apple-blossoms won't be out until mid-May," he considers. This is the context for understanding that he brings to the tapping season on one particularly clear "blue and gold day."[55] So too is his assessment that, "when you get home from town meeting at two or three in the afternoon, the temperature is up to sixty. Snow water is dripping from all the eaves, and you can almost hear the maples pumping sap. It is irresistible to hang a few buckets."[56] As Perrin saw the season, it was one of wonder: "a big maple with three or four buckets strung round it has a kind of flag-and-bunting festival look."[57]

This sense of connectedness could extend even further. As Perrin also found, boiling the sap in his sugar house for the long hours the process required turned out to be a community event. "Steam had been rolling out for about fifteen minutes... people in the village had had time to see it," he assessed. "I don't say they came pouring out of their houses and down to visit, but one or two at a time, a remarkable number did appear."[58] For the Nearings, too, the string of connections was obvious, and it began with their understanding that "what we have been developing is a source of livelihood from the earth—from maple as it happens." From this experience they found that it was "hardly possible to overemphasize the importance of this relationship with the earth, its rhythms, seasons, and cycles." From there, they too found that the process was "social because we have the time and means to share our livelihood and our lives.... Thus we play our part in setting up a good town, state, nation, world."[59]

Maple syrup–making appears to have functioned as a sturdy method of rejecting the demands and protocols of mainstream society because it conjured a far more powerful and appealing link: between conformity to the seasonal rhythms of the natural world, on the one hand, and a lived sense of community, on the other. In the end, maple syrup becomes a demonstration of the pleasure to be had in walking out of corrupt cities and back into nature, without wholly abandoning a sense of community. In this way, its production reveals maple syrup as an object worthy of reverence because it is transformative. It demonstrates the ability to pull the valued pieces of a human life into tight orbit with one another, and then to situate humanity within the larger scheme of the natural, not human-built, world.

Sweet Rewards

The culmination of everything, though, was the syrup itself. "It's almost superfluous to tell anyone how to use maple syrup," Sarah Funk remarked at the conclusion of her *Mother Earth News* article, but if anyone needed a hint, she offered that it was best "poured over pancakes, cornbread, yogurt, or a dish of fruit."[60] Nothing complicated, then, just a simple pour to transform a dish, mostly likely at the breakfast table. Contributor James Churchill similarly praised it as a worthy sauce. "I use maple syrup to cover wheat cakes in the morning, put it on my wholewheat bread," he recounted, and affirmed that it was "good eatin' anytime."[61]

It is evident that there were so many ways for this simple sauce to bring a rare pleasure. For instance, when Tom Hodges recounted the details of his sugaring season in *The Mother Earth News*, he described sitting down to a meal with maple syrup as the defining moment of the whole project. It was evidence of a job well and completely done: "Our 'sugaring season'... is officially closed," he declared, "when we remove all of the jugs, spigots, and nails from our trees, wash the equipment in preparation for next year's harvest, and treat ourselves to some homemade breakfast ambrosia."[62]

Beyond, or after, the physical challenges, then, maple syrup gained a strong and desirable aftertaste of rarity and purity. As Coulter described it, after all, maple syrup was pristine—a "bounty of Mother Earth," that he kept "for my own use or to give to friends." And as he whispered parenthetically, "(I get a smug feeling when they say, 'Oh, this is a lot better than the stuff you get in the stores')."[63] In fact, for George Lightsey, writing in *The Mother Earth News* in the winter of 1974 with his article, "Maple Syrup: The Cool Way," the only path to enjoying "real" and "pure" syrup was through his own efforts: "I've always thought of thick, golden pure maple syrup as one of the truly natural foods, even though I never tasted the real thing until I tried my hand at syrup production in the spring of 1971."[64]

Finally, when the Nearings reported that "[i]n the course of our journeyings . . . we meet many people who say, 'When can I get a taste of real maple syrup?,'" the issue, as they saw it, was one of purity.[65] And for most people, purity was rare: "The blended syrups and the chemical flavorings with which chain stores have been supplying them do not meet the demands of those who have once enjoyed the true maple flavor."[66] For many commentators, syrup gotten "in the stores" and not from their own efforts was, if not quite a thing of horror, not far from it either. Noel Perrin regretted that anyone would entertain "getting supermarket stuff which is 6 percent maple or 5½ percent maple or—this is superstition not flavor—2 percent maple."[67]

In 1973, though—a year after Perrin published his manual—the *National Maple Syrup Digest*, the official publication of the North American Maple Syrup Council, ran an article on consumers' reactions to table syrups. According to "Maple Syrup & the Blends," the situation was even more lamentable than Perrin or others surmised. First, the article's writer, David R. Marvin, recounted that blended syrups (in which maple was mixed with less expensive sweeteners, like cane sugar syrup) had been widely marketed in the United States since the end of the nineteenth century. Next, it reported on survey results that found consumers preferred "the taste of syrups made solely with artificial maple flavors!"[68] Finally, it reported that, overall, blended "maple-flavored" syrups were experiencing a drop-off in popularity: "sales are not growing as rapidly as population is, which reflects a change in consumer habits."[69] In summary, then, many consumers by the 1970s had never even tasted pure maple syrup, and to the extent that they liked maple syrup at all (based on their experiences with blends), they were accustomed to fake flavors—but not enough to keep buying as much syrup as they had in the past.

In the end, the "realness" or "purity" that back-to-the-land syrup-makers valued encompassed not the only the syrup that they poured, but also their own counterculture lifestyle choices. Purity in maple syrup was an obvious result of the "real" presence of actual maple trees in nature, but it was also a thing of intentionality: those who went back to the land had to seek it out and create it for themselves. Their ability to taste and find pleasure in the sauce they made marked out their own evolution beyond the reach of a corrupting mainstream consumer culture that had long ago abandoned the "purity" of natural environments. While the tastes of mainstream consumers altered to the point that they found greater pleasure in that which was artificial than that which was pure, back-to-the-landers had avoided this trap. Their enjoyment of the pure maple syrup they made was an assertion of their escape, one that they defined as a rare and hard-earned success.

DIY Maple Syrup from Sap

This recipe has been adapted from the websites *The Art of Doing Stuff* (https://www.theartofdoingstuff.com/how-to-make-maple-syrup/) and *Tap My Trees* (https://tapmytrees.com/collect-sap-make-syrup/).

You can collect sap from any variety of maple tree, although sugar maples are the most common (because their sap has the highest sugar content). This recipe is adapted for making syrup at home and after you have collected sap. Remember that the ratio of sap to finished syrup is approximately 40:1, so expect to enjoy a small quantity.

Equipment:

Food-safe storage containers for sap
Shallow pan with broad surface area to use for evaporation
A small amount of butter or vegetable oil
Ladle
Smaller stockpot or saucepan
Candy thermometer
Refractometer (optional)
Paper filters (available where syrup-making supplies are sold)
Glass jars or bottles
An outdoor heat source, such as a burner attached to a propane tank in your yard

Method:

1. Set up your outdoor heat source. Whether you use a burner and propane tank or choose another method, you need to generate a lot of sustained, concentrated heat. While you can make syrup on the stovetop in your kitchen, this is generally not advisable since the process of evaporation takes several hours and produces a huge amount of steam. Be warned: stories of steamed-off wallpaper abound in the annals of home syrup-making literature. Work on your stovetop only at the end of the process when you are finishing the syrup.
2. Place the shallow pan over your heat source and fill it not more than three-quarters full with sap.
3. As the sap boils, keep adding more sap from your storage container(s). Do this slowly, and try not to "break" the boil. Aim to keep your evaporation pan about one-quarter to half full at all time, and at a boil.
4. When the boil is going, it can be vigorous. If it rises quickly and is in danger of boiling over the sides of your pot, add a *small* drop of vegetable oil or a small bit of butter. The fat will calm the boil.
5. Once you have added all of the sap to your evaporation pan, continue to boil until an inserted candy thermometer reads approximately 213°F. By now there will be a lot less sap in the pan, and what remains will begin to take on a darker color.
6. At this point, the sap can be transferred to a small pot and brought inside to the stovetop in order to finish the boil.
7. Keep boiling until the sap reaches 7.1°F *above* the boiling point for water. Once this happens, you have made syrup. (Note that the standard temperature at which water boils is considered to be 212°F. However, this depends on the altitude of your location. If in doubt, boil some water, check the temperature, and be sure that your sap boils to 7.1°F over whatever that is.)
8. Maple syrup is considered to be syrup when it is no less than 66 percent sugar. If it is lower than this, it can spoil. If its sugar content is 67.5 percent or higher, the syrup can crystallize. If you wish to be precise, a refractometer will measure the brix (sugar content) of your syrup.
9. Pour your finished syrup through paper filters in order to remove sugar sand (solids produced during the evaporation process).
10. I find it easiest to store this small amount of syrup in the refrigerator, but if you want to bottle it, reheat syrup to between 179° and 190°F before pouring into sterilized bottles.

Notes

1. "Sugaring" and "Sugaring off" are colloquial terms for evaporating sap. Historically, they have been applied to both maple syrup- and maple sugar-making.
2. Bruce N. Coulter, "Sugaring: Amateur Style," *Mother Earth News* 31 (1975): 66.
3. Ibid., 68.
4. Donna Brown, *Back to the Land: The Enduring Dream of Self-Sufficiency in Modern America* (Madison: University of Wisconsin Press, 2011), 205; Jeffrey Jacob, *New Pioneers: The Back-to-the-Land Movement and the Search for a Sustainable Future* (University Park: Penn State University Press, 1997), 5. For more on the influence of *The Mother Earth News* on the back-to-the-land movement, see Jonathan Kauffman, *Hippie Food: How Back-to-the-Landers, Longhairs, and Revolutionaries Changed the Way We Eat* (New York: William Morrow, 2018); Kate Daloz, *We Are as Gods: Back to the Land in the 1970s on the Quest for a New America* (New York: PublicAffairs, 2016).
5. Until recently, anyway. For a disapproving account of the more recent innovation of reverse osmosis, see Noel Perrin, *Amateur Sugar Maker, 20th Anniversary Edition* (Hanover: University Press of New England, 1992), 104–105.
6. Irma Rombauer and Marion Rombauer Becker, *Joy of Cooking*, 6th ed. (New York: Scribner, 1975), 330.
7. Maryann Tebben, *Sauce: A Global History* (London: Reaktion Books, 2014), 13.
8. James Churchill, "Food Without Farming," *The Mother Earth News* 13 (1972): 74.
9. Rombauer, *Joy of Cooking*, 330.
10. Tebben, *Sauce: A Global History*, 13.
11. Ibid., 13, 14.
12. Kauffman, *Hippie Food*, 182–183.
13. Helen Nearing and Scott Nearing, *The Maple Sugar Book: Being a Plain and Practical Account of the Art of Sugaring Designed to Promote an Acquaintance with the Ancient as Well as the Modern Practice, Together with Remarks on Pioneering as a Way of Living in the Twentieth Century* (New York: John Day, 1950), xi.
14. Stewart Brand's *Whole Earth Catalog* fostered and celebrated counterculture experimentation. Even so, it was, as its title defined it, a catalog. Its driving purpose was to provide its readers with, as its slogan declared, "Access to Tools." Because it focused on materials more than practices, *The Whole Earth Catalog* is not a part of this study.
15. See Warren Belasco's discussion of food as an "edible dynamic." Belasco has used the term to locate the preparation and consumption of food as a site at which the "visceral, lived daily link between the personal and the political" became manifest for the counterculture as it experienced and created social change. Warren Belasco. *Appetite for Change: How the Counterculture Took on the Food Industry* (Ithaca: Cornell University Press, 1989), 317.
16. Brown, *Back to the Land*, 209.

17. While there have been several other back-to-the-land movements, this study is purposely limited. For a more comprehensive discussion of such movements, see Brown, *Back to the Land*.
18. Ibid., 209.
19. Ibid., 8.
20. Jacob, *New Pioneers*, 3. As Brown points out, though, we would do well to be skeptical of this number: "tracing that number back through the footnotes brings one to a single estimate extrapolated from the study of a small area in British Columbia in 1979." *Back to the Land*, 206.
21. John Shuttleworth, "The Ploughboy Interview," *Mother Earth News* 31 (1975): 7.
22. Ibid., 8.
23. Nearing and Nearing, *The Maple Sugar Book*, 246.
24. Perrin, *Amateur Sugar Maker*, 7.
25. Ibid., 8.
26. Quoted in Timothy Miller, *The Sixties Communes: Hippies and Beyond* (Syracuse, NY: Syracuse University Press, 2015), 209.
27. A "sugar bush" is the term for a stand of maple trees.
28. Sarah Funk, "Make and Market Maple Syrup: On Your Own Homestead," *Mother Earth News* 14 (1972): 34.
29. Ibid., 34–41.
30. Ibid., 42.
31. Tom Hodges, "We Make Tree Syrup in the Ozarks Too!: Another Approach," *The Mother Earth News* 55 (1979): 65.
32. Coulter, "Sugaring: Amateur Style," 67.
33. Nearing and Nearing, *The Maple Sugar Book*, 67.
34. Ibid., 234.
35. Coulter, "Sugaring: Amateur Style," 68; Funk, "Make and Market Maple Syrup," 42.
36. Perrin, *Amateur Sugar Maker*, 8, 102.
37. Nearing and Nearing, *The Maple Sugar Book*, 223.
38. Ibid., 220.
39. Ibid., 224.
40. R. E. Kremers, "Imitation Maple Flavor." United States Patent 2,446,478, filed October 6, 1944; issued August 3, 1948.
41. Nearing and Nearing, *The Maple Sugar Book*, 213–214, 216.
42. Ibid., 150, 237.
43. Ibid., 150, 214.
44. Perrin, *Amateur Sugar Maker*, 30.
45. Ibid., 94.
46. Ibid., 93.
47. Ibid., 93–94.
48. Pete Seeger, "Maple Syrup Time," Track 7 on *Circles and Seasons*, Rhino Entertainment, vinyl record, 1979.

49. Ibid.
50. Gordon Lightfoot, "Love and Maple Syrup," Track 10 on *Summer Side of Life*, Reprise Records, vinyl record, 1971.
51. Ibid.
52. James Churchill, "Food Without Farming," *The Mother Earth News* 13 (1972); 75.
53. "Maple Syrup Recipe," *The Mother Earth News* 50 (1978); 12.
54. Coulter, "Sugaring: Amateur Style," 69.
55. Perrin, *Amateur Sugar Maker*, 75.
56. Ibid., 71–72.
57. Ibid., 59.
58. Ibid., 81.
59. Nearing and Nearing, *The Maple Sugar Book*, 245.
60. Funk, "Make and Market Maple Syrup," 42.
61. Churchill, "Food Without Farming," 77.
62. Hodges, "We Make Tree Syrup in the Ozarks Too!," 65.
63. Coulter, "Sugaring: Amateur Style," 66.
64. George R. Lightsey, "Maple Syrup: The Cool Way," *Mother Earth News* 25 (1974): 42.
65. Nearing and Nearing, *The Maple Sugar Book*, 232.
66. Ibid., 232.
67. Perrin, *Amateur Sugar Maker*, 95.
68. D. R. Marvin, "Maple Syrup and the Blends," *National Maple Syrup Digest* 12, no. 3 (1973): 13.
69. Ibid., 12.

Selected Bibliography

Brown, Donna. *Back to the Land: The Enduring Dream of Self-Sufficiency in Modern America*. Madison: University of Wisconsin Press, 2011.

Coulter, Bruce N. "Sugaring: Amateur Style." *Mother Earth News* 31 (1975): 66–69.

Houriet, Robert. *Getting Back Together*. New York: Coward, McCann, and Geoghegan, 1971.

Jacob, Jeffrey. *New Pioneers: The Back-To-The-Land Movement and the Search for a Sustainable Future*. University Park: Penn State University Press, 1997.

Kauffman, Jonathan. *Hippie Food: How Back-to-the-Landers, Longhairs, and Revolutionaries Changed the Way We Eat*. New York: William Morrow, 2018.

Miller, Timothy. *The Sixties Communes: Hippies and Beyond*. Syracuse, NY: Syracuse University Press, 2015.

Nearing, Helen, and Scott Nearing. *The Maple Sugar Book: Being a Plain and Practical Account of the Art of Sugaring Designed to Promote an Acquaintance with the Ancient as Well as the Modern Practice, Together with Remarks on Pioneering as a Way of Living in the Twentieth Century*. New York: John Day, 1950.

Perrin, Noel. *Amateur Sugar Maker, 20th Anniversary Edition*. Hanover, NH: University Press of New England, 1992.

Shuttleworth, John. "The Ploughboy Interview." *Mother Earth News* 31 (1975): 6–9.

Tebben, Maryann. *Sauce: A Global History*. London: Reaktion Books, 2014.

Deirdre Murphy, *"It's Maple Syrup Time!": The Hard Work and Pure Pleasure of Real Maple Syrup in the Back-to-the-Land Movement* In: *From Garum to Mole: Sauces and Identity in the Western World*. Edited by: Andrew Donnelly, Beth M. Forrest, and Deirdre Murphy, Oxford University Press. © Oxford University Press 2026.
DOI: 10.1093/9780190622138.003.0006

7

Bixa orellana in Belize

FLAVORING POSTCOLONIAL CUISINE

Lyra Spang

BELIZE, ONCE A British colony devoted to timber extraction, is a small, culturally diverse nation bordered by Guatemala to the south and west, Mexico to the north, and the Caribbean Sea to the east. The only English-speaking nation on the Yucatán Peninsula, Belize brings together the cultures and qualities of the Caribbean and Central America in one country. The descendants of the ancient Maya live here, alongside more recent arrivals: mestizo blends of Maya and Spanish conquerors; the Kriol,[1] a product of the British colonial enterprise, who claim a mix of European and African ancestries; the Garifuna, descended from West African and Carib people, who are the original settlers of the Caribbean; Mennonites; and descendants of East Indian, Chinese, and North American immigrants.

Because of this diversity, to understand Belizean food, one must investigate how national identity is formed and represented in this Central American society. Thanks to colonial favoritism and the pervasive influence of what is called hegemonic nationalism, Kriol home cooking (epitomized by dishes such as rice and beans with stew chicken, potato salad, and fried plantain) plays a gatekeeping role in legitimizing ingredients and dishes as being Belizean. Most Belizeans consider an ingredient to be truly Belizean only if it has undergone a "kriolization" process, typically through use in a Kriol home kitchen and incorporation into Kriol recipes. Colonial history and cultural politics are essential to discussing sauces in Belize, for the making of a nation has much to do with the making of a sauce.

Despite the colonial hangover caused by the British divide-and-conquer approach to cultural diversity, in modern Belize the seed of one plant unites diverse groups. That plant is the shrub *Bixa orellana*, native to Central America and prized not just in Belize but in Guatemala, Honduras, and southern Mexico (Yucatán and Quintana Roo states). Once associated with the Maya peoples of Belize, and used by their ancestors long before European arrival, the seeds of this shrub flavor the most ubiquitous Belizean dishes. *Bixa orellana*, commonly called annatto or achiote, flowers once a year. When pollinated, these flowers turn into little pods about two inches long that are covered with soft spikes and filled with small seeds attached to a papery internal membrane. The seeds are covered with a bright orange paste full of the carotenoid bixin that intensely colors everything it touches. Removed from the seeds, the paste is used to flavor and color foods and cosmetics around the world.

Annatto paste and seeds have a distinctive earthy aroma and flavor that is hard to compare to other spices. In industrial food processing, pure annatto paste is most commonly used as a natural coloring agent in margarine and certain cheeses. Ubiquitous in Belize, *recado* seasoning is an annatto-based spice blend. The whole paste-covered seed is removed from the pod and dried, then ground with black pepper, allspice or clove, onion, garlic, oregano, cumin, salt, and sour orange or vinegar to form a thick paste called *recado rojo*. Another version, *recado negro,* incorporates carbonized ground corn tortillas to color the paste pitch black. Both types of *recado* are formed into blocks or balls and

FIGURE 7.1 A blend of dried annatto seeds, allspice seeds, cloves, dried oregano, onion, garlic, and vinegar waits to be ground into red *recado* paste.

Credit: Lyra Spang.

stored to be used as needed to flavor meats, soups, and other dishes. *Recado*-based gravies flavor many of Belize's most common and popular dishes.

These sauces are the focus of this chapter. Since independence in 1981 and the evolution of national and cultural identity in the 1990s, *recado*-based gravies have been legitimatized through Kriol home cooking as a uniting sauce and flavor found (often daily and at least occasionally) on all tables, in all districts, and across all cultures in Belize. This is a prime example of how an ingredient associated with a marginalized group (the Maya peoples) became nationalized through a creolization process. Before delving deeper into this tale of cultures, cuisines, sauces, and nationalism, let's take a brief look at the history behind modern Belizean foodways.

History

The indigenous Maya of Belize had complex regional cuisines before the Spanish conquest, but the little we know about them is derived from a few surviving artistic depictions, chemical traces left on ancient pots, and the home cooking of modern Maya descendants. After the arrival of the Spanish, their conquest of the Maya city-states, and systematic destruction of the written record, no ancient Maya cookbooks have survived, if they ever existed, although illustrations of chocolate-making and food preparation and names have been found in the Madrid Codex and the Calakmul murals.[2] Between disease, conquest, and the forced removal of Maya peoples from the region, the Maya population in Belize was reduced from millions to perhaps as few as 10,000 people. The survivors farmed far away from the British logging camps near Belize Town. The initial settlers of post-conquest Belize were a mixed bag of Europeans and African slaves who were more intent on culling the forest for valuable timber than in settling down and creating a local cuisine. Logging agreements between the British and Spanish (who controlled the region until 1851) restricted agriculture in the British settlement. As a result, Belizean cuisine was built in colonial times with less of the indigenous influence that is so important in adjacent Mexico and Guatemala. But *Bixa orellana* was one plant whose presence never disappeared from Maya yards, even as the Maya civilization toppled and Maya peoples were marginalized within the new colonial order.

Belize (originally called Honduras Bay, the Bay, and later British Honduras) was a rough frontier where imported barrels of flour and salted meat fueled the labor of immigrants and slaves.[3] Simple camp cooking included the staple called "pork and doughboy," made by boiling the salted meat with dumplings made from lard and flour.[4] The Baymen, as these loggers were called, and their slaves hunted, fished, and gathered wild food from the rain forest. Over time they added to their diets by planting gardens around the more permanent logging camps, but imported flour and salted meat remained the everyday food ingredients of timber extraction in Belize. The closest that camp cooks got to a sauce was the liquid left over in the pot after food was boiled, which was shared out equally to the diners.[5] Despite the salty flavor, this imported dish was considered "proper food" as compared to (fresher) local ingredients.[6] One-pot cooking in large iron pots made other kinds of dishes and sauces a rarity, though empty kerosene tins were often adapted to bake simple breads.

In Belize Town, the colonial center, this frontier food was supplemented in poorer homes by gardening and markets provisioned by hunters, fishers, and small-scale farmers in surrounding communities. Wealthier people, mostly European immigrants and the descendants of early settlers, clung to British and European continental food to demonstrate their class status and loyalty to the British crown. Imported sauces, such as Worcestershire, played an important role in creating a European diet from local ingredients. Bottles of prepared sauce from England and the United States started to appear in the eighteenth century, and imported ingredients like olives, anchovies, wine, and olive oil were used to make sauces following European recipes. These sauces apparently had the power to turn local fish, meat, and vegetables into acceptable simulations of European food.

Most of this elite class employed cooks, either slaves or their descendants, who were carefully taught to maintain European tables. Elaborate table settings and a series of courses eaten with proper decorum were probably more important than the actual ingredients of the food. From a few early newspaper accounts, it seems that employers and chefs often quarreled, particularly when chefs tried to introduce familiar foods from local markets.[7] Later, in the late nineteenth century, important meals for special occasions or with guests often entailed eating imported canned food, as well as choice local fish or fowl, covered with imported sauces like mushroom ketchup. This preference for European foods, no matter how expensive or badly preserved, persisted well into the late twentieth century, when it was finally challenged by Belizean nationalists.[8] Even today, imported salad cream is a key component in the dressing for potato salad, a popular Belizean Kriol side dish, and many Belizean cooks still use imported Worcestershire sauce in the pan gravies for stewed chicken and other meats.

Throughout the colonial era, there was an unrecorded alternative food system among the few Maya who had survived the wars and disease, and their descendants who returned from Mexico and Guatemala to form rural communities in the north and south of the colony. During Mexico's caste war in the 1850s, Yucatec Maya and mestizo refugees moved into Belize from southern Mexico and formed self-sufficient communities across the northern part of the colony. Mopan and Kekchi Maya communities dotted the inland south. They continued to grow indigenous staple crops of corn, beans, chili peppers, pumpkin, cassava, cacao, and herbs and spices, including *Bixa orellana*. Trading did occur between these communities and the colonists, but most of the food eaten in Maya rural households in the colonial days was produced within their farming communities. In the early nineteenth century, Garifuna exiles from the island of St. Vincent began to settle villages along the coast, bringing with them a subsistence system based on plantains and root vegetables like cassava and sweet potato and supplemented with local seafood and bush meat. By the end of the century, the countryside was dotted with self-sufficient Maya, Garifuna, mestizo, and Kriol communities. In these cash-poor villages, eating an imported diet was not an option; eating what one grew was a necessity and a sign of poverty.

In the early 1960s, Belize's "father of the nation," the Honorable George Price, who in 1964 was elected as premier for the home governance of the colony of British Honduras, urged Belizeans to reject imported British food and instead eat local fish and root crops as a way of demonstrating independence from British control. Price believed that eating locally sourced food was key to severing dependence on Britain, specifically on British colonial-era food systems. Developing Belizean food systems and local food security as a nation in the making would pave the way for independence from Britain. By then, however, local food had become strongly linked with poverty, and Price's message received a hostile reception. The anti-colonial movement promised a prosperity in which every Belizean would be able to afford an imported diet.[9] Even Belize's independence from England in 1981 did little to weaken the dominance of European cuisine, which was only challenged in the early 1990s with the growth and public emergence of self-described cultural and national identities. At this point, local flavors and spices, including *recado*, which were associated with poor rural farming communities, began to gain traction in middle-class Kriol kitchens. These postcolonial transformations have flavored and shaped the nature of sauces in Belize today.

Models of Nationalism

What do models of nationalism have to do with sauces? Ongoing tensions around cultural and national identity in Belize are expressed in many arenas, and food is a particularly tangible daily reminder of the cultural politics of this young nation. In a scant forty-four years since independence, the country has had to decide what it wants to be. It is an unusual place, once a little chunk of England surrounded by former Spanish territory, a land of diverse peoples who played both cricket and football (soccer), listened to reggae while lounging on the top of a Maya pyramid, ate tortillas made from hand-farmed corn as well as fluffy white Creole coconut bread made with imported wheat. Since independence, Belize, once administered by the British through the colony of Jamaica, has continued its historic Caribbean orientation through membership in the Caribbean Community and Common Market (CARICOM), but it is also an active member of the Central American Integration System (CAIS). Belize acts as a gateway between these two regions, straddling the line between Anglophone Caribbean and Spanish-speaking Central American identities and embracing both within its borders. The complexity inherent in this position affects many aspects of Belizean life, including cuisine.

As a young, diverse nation, one of the first questions facing the new country was how to integrate cultural and national identity. Anthropologist Laurie Kroshus Medina identifies three models of nationalism in her seminal work on Belizean national identity.[10] "Synthetic nationalism" was one of the first models to be employed by the Belizean government during the seven years of home rule leading up to full independence and immediately thereafter. This model attempts to create an overarching "national" Belizean culture that is different from and more powerful than each cultural group's identity and that blends traits of different cultural groups. This national "Belizean" identity aimed to supersede individual ethnic identities and soften cultural difference. This model was not successful, however, as many feared that the Kriol politicians who were promoting it would use it to discourage cultural expression of minority groups while promoting a national identity that overrepresented the dominant Kriol culture. By the mid-1980s, another approach had become standard in Belizean government, which remains the official model of Belizean nationalism to this day. Called "pluralistic nationalism," this model defines Belize and Belizeans as a harmoniously diverse and multicultural society, with each culture group possessing its own attractive cluster of traits—language, food, music, and "traditions"—in the context of an overarching national identity, what Richard Wilk calls "domesticated" or "safe" nationalism.[11] Well-groomed and socially acceptable diversity is an asset. This version of nationalism is what is taught in public schools across Belize and is used by the Belize Tourism Board in its publications and international advertising, urging visitors to experience "the many cultures of Belize." However, lurking below the surface, another model persists. Medina calls it "hegemonic nationalism" and labels it an "unofficial" model, which she claims has been embraced particularly by Kriol and Garifuna Belizeans in the face of large-scale "Spanish" (mestizo) immigration from surrounding countries such as Guatemala and Honduras.[12] Since 1981, over 35,000 Guatemalans, Hondurans, and Salvadorans have immigrated to Belize, swelling the numbers of Maya and mestizo-identified people in the country and causing the Kriol population to become a numeric minority by 1990. This discourse racializes Belizean identity, claiming that "Spanish" Belizeans (and often by extension Maya groups as well) are not real Belizeans and that only those with some degree of African heritage truly represent the nation.

Many Belizeans publicly endorse the pluralistic model. Support seems strongest among younger Belizeans, regardless of cultural background, who were born or grew up in an independent Belize. More and more Belizeans have parents from different cultural groups, and in the national census the number of individuals claiming multiple cultural affiliations is increasing.[13] Despite this, when put to the test, most Belizeans reveal some degree of hegemonic bias in their thinking. As part of thirteen months of field research on the cultural politics of food and nationalism conducted by the author in 2012–2013, fifty Belizean participants of different cultural backgrounds were asked to sort ninety photo cards showing images of different dishes found within Belize today, according to their level of perceived "Belizean-ness." Research participants consistently scored Kriol dishes and some Garifuna dishes as being "most Belizean," while many mestizo and Maya dishes were categorized as being "in between Belizean" or even "not Belizean."[14]

As demonstrated by this exercise, the most powerful cultural group in Belize continues to be the Kriol, the most socioeconomically and politically dominant group under the British colonial regime. For most of the history of the colony they comprised the largest population, and prior to and after independence in 1981 were associated strongly with the nation and Belizean identity.[15] Problematically but commonly described as a mixture of African and European immigrants, and thus a product of colonialism, they have long been associated with the birth of the nation from a British colony in the heart of Spanish territory.[16] This cultural and political dominance continues, even though, according to the 2010 census, Kriol people make up only 29 percent of Belize's population and the catch-all "mestizo" group accounts for 52 percent. Because of this dominance through hegemonic nationalism, Kriol home cooking plays a fundamental role in defining Belizean cuisine. In order for a flavor or sauce to be considered Belizean, it must be found in Kriol kitchens.

Cross-Cultural Saucier

In present-day Belize, the two most important sauces across the country are pan gravies flavored with the paste of the *Bixa orellana* seed and habanero-based hot sauces. Habanero hot sauces, both commercial and homemade, are found in most Belizean kitchens, where diners add them to taste to their own plate of food. Hot sauces contribute spiciness and acidity that balances the richness of the *recado*-based gravies that are the flavor base of all Belizean stewed meat dishes. *Recado*-based gravies, in turn, complement the core of the meal, the staple dish of rice and beans.

While today in Belize red *recado* can be found in almost every household regardless of ethnicity, this was not always the case. Only since independence has *recado* seasoning seeped into Kriol, and thus national, consciousness.

FIGURE 7.2 *Recado* balls.
Credit: Lyra Spang.

How did *recado* made from the seeds of *Bixa orellana* come to be Belizean instead of remaining a "cultural" seasoning employed only by Mestizo and Maya groups? An examination of the evolution of Belize's iconic national dish—rice and beans with stew chicken, fried plantain, and potato salad—serves as an example of how *recado* came to be kriolized, and thus nationalized, through its incorporation into stewed meat gravies. Throughout Belize today it is difficult to find a plate of stewed chicken with no *recado* in the pan gravy. When a visitor sits down to eat rice and beans and stewed chicken, the gravy, dipped right from the stew pot and ladled over a generous mound of rice and beans, has a particular taste. This flavor only exists thanks to Kriol home cooks' adoption of *recado* seasoning and is a clear demonstration of the enduring power of hegemonic nationalism.

Chalkboard menus across Belize resonate with lists of "stew chicken, pork, beef," "stew fish," and if you are lucky, "stew lobster" (sometimes described as "lobster creole" to sound fancier in more touristy areas). Stew beans, like their meaty counterparts, swim in a gravy that is well seasoned with herbs and spices and often contains a few choice pigtails for added porky oomph. Long-simmered dishes of stew chicken, beef, pork, pigtail, or even lobster and conch are almost always served as accompaniments to rice and beans.

Across Belize, much meat and seafood are treated the same way. First it is washed in lime juice or vinegar mixed with water to properly clean it and to ensure that the protein won't taste "renk" (rank). Animal flesh is not considered really clean until this is done. This practice originates in times before electricity and refrigeration were widespread as a way to disinfect meat or seafood that may have come in contact with flies and pathogens. It is then rubbed with a marinade mixture of lime juice or vinegar and red *recado*, sometimes supplemented with Season-All or salt and black pepper. This red *recado* and vinegar marinade is so popular that the internationally known hot sauce company Marie Sharp's bottles and sells it as "Belizean seasoning." To make the pan gravy typical of stewed meats, the meat is browned in fat (ideally coconut oil for proper Belizean Kriol flavor), the remaining marinade, onion, garlic, perhaps sweet pepper, and other seasonings are added along with water, and everything is cooked slowly until the meat is tender and the gravy is flavorful and slightly thickened. Stewed chicken in particular is historically associated with the Kriol people of Belize, but everyone, regardless of cultural group, now makes and eats stewed meats with a *recado*-spiced pan gravy. One can find these dishes in almost every Belizean owned restaurant in the country and abroad.

This original Belizean Kriol Sunday meal evolved in the days when fresh chicken dinner meant killing and a plucking a bird from one's own yard. The

FIGURE 7.3 Belize stewed chicken dish.
Credit: Lyra Spang.

tougher meat of these free-range birds was softened through the long stewing process, which also broke down cartilage and fat to create the flavorful pan gravy served with the dish. This sauce, a byproduct of the meat stewing process, moistens the relatively dry rice and beans or plain rice on the plate and is usually spooned right on top. Some sit-down restaurants put the gravy in its own little bowl for customers to pour over the plate of food as desired. If stewed beans are made instead of rice and beans, the beans and their gravy are also spooned over the rice to moisten it. Hot pepper sauce is then added to suit the diner's taste. Together with a side of potato salad (or coleslaw) and some fried ripe plantain, this dish forms what famed food anthropologist Sidney Mintz called a "signature" or "significant" food.[17] This is the one meal that most visitors are aware of through pre-travel research, as it is mentioned in all guidebooks and most websites about Belize.

As part of field research on food and nationalism in Belize, the author conducted food history interviews with over fifty Belizeans of different cultural backgrounds. This excerpt from an interview with a Kriol woman in her sixties is revealing of how older generations of Kriol Belizeans view the use of *recado* as a seasoning in making stewed meats. She is from the fishing-turned-tourism village of Placencia, located on a sandy peninsula far from the Maya communities inland.

INTERVIEWEE: . . . *recado* neva fi wi. Cuminos . . . inland mostly yu find cuminos and ting. Fresh thyme. We just start to get dem ting da sea front.
RESEARCHER: (when you say *recado* neva fi wi, who dah wi?)
INTERVIEWEE: Kriol. *Recado* fi Indian and Spanish, neva fi we.
RESEARCHER: (What did you used to season with?)
INTERVIEWEE: Salt and black peppa family. Dah sea da still usually salt and black peppa.

English translation:
INTERVIEWEE: . . . *recado* was never ours. Cumin . . . inland mostly you find cumin and things. Fresh thyme. We just started now to get these things on the seashore.
RESEARCHER: When you say *recado* was never ours, who are you referring to?
INTERVIEWEE: Kriol. *Recado* is for Indians (Maya) and Spanish (mestizo), not for us.
RESEARCHER: What did you used to season with?
INTERVIEWEE: Salt and black pepper family. By the sea it's still usually salt and black pepper.

Another Kriol interviewee from Belize City who is in her mid-thirties noted that her mother never used *recado* in making her stew chicken when she was growing up. Her mother considered *recado* to be a shortcut ingredient that "Spanish" (mestizo) people used just to add color to the dish, when the same color and better flavor would be achieved through properly browning the chicken. Some Kriol cooks from this older generation still refuse to use *recado* in stewing meats at home, but they are an exception. The addition to the iconic Kriol Sunday dinner of originally non-Kriol ingredients like red *recado* demonstrates how creolization has become equivalent to nationalization in Belize. But how exactly did this process take place?

Participants in the survey employed a number of criteria when determining how to categorize a particular food. Many subscribe at least partially to a hegemonic model of nationalism that predicated Kriol (and sometimes, to a lesser degree, Garifuna) culture and food as being more Belizean than that of other cultural groups. The presence of a food item in Kriol (and sometimes Garifuna) homes underlies many of the criteria used to determine the Belizean identity of a food. If participants looking at a picture of a dish or ingredient do not make an immediate association with a cultural group, they will evaluate its Belizean-ness based on other criteria: (1) Was the dish cooked by Kriol or (to a lesser degree) Garifuna people in their homes? (2) Is the dish made from ingredients that are produced in Belize? (3) Does the dish/food item exist elsewhere (as far as the participant is aware), or is it only found in Belize? (4) Is the food a staple—that is, does the participant believe that it is found in most homes and eaten almost every day by most people in the country, including Kriol people? (5) Is it found consistently on the menus of Belizean restaurants? (6) Is the food believed by the participant to have been made or invented by ancestors, living or dead, who are considered Belizean? (7) Did the research participant grow up eating the food at home?

These criteria are used to decide how Belizean a particular food item is. Some criteria carry more weight than others. In order for a food to be placed in the "most Belizean" category, most research participants felt it must be at least occasionally prepared (and thus transformed, legitimized, and nationalized) by Kriol people at home. If the food is not strongly associated with Kriol (or to a lesser degree Garifuna) cultural groups, the more of the other criteria it fulfills, the more likely that it will still be placed in the most Belizean category. In this way, Kriol home cooking acts as the legitimizer of Belizean identity, nationalizing dishes, ingredients, and seasonings.

Given the dominant role of Kriol home cooking, it is not surprising that the Kriol Sunday dinner was transformed into a national dish. Originally this meal was a special treat, particularly for cash-poor families. In an era of no refrigeration, it was an indulgence to have store-bought rice and beans and fresh meat, a refreshing change from home-grown cassava and other root vegetables, seafood, or imported salted meats common in the colonial era. But when the first self-identified Belizean Kriol restaurants opened to serve homesick Belizeans in Los Angeles and New York City in the early 1970s, this dish was suddenly available every day of the week to someone with a little money to spend.[18] By the end of the 1980s, stew chicken could also be bought during the week at Kriol-owned venues in Belize. New culinary entrepreneurs copied the successful menus of these first restaurateurs, and stew chicken became one of the most common plates to be sold at restaurants and trendy establishments across the newly independent country.

This exposed Belizeans from all cultural groups to the Kriol Sunday dinner, which was nationalized through its success as a restaurant meal. People from other cultural groups who did not typically eat rice and beans or stew chicken before learned to make these dishes (some while working as employees in Kriol-run restaurants), and some began making them at home. As a result, today in Belizean Maya homes located far from the historical centers of Kriol culture, a birthday or other celebration might be a reason to spend the money to buy some rice and make this iconic meal as a special occasion dish.[19]

This rapid nationalization of the dish in the last forty years has not gone unnoticed. As one research participant in her mid-thirties noted:

> Honestly Lyra I di eat stew chicken from when I small, from when I could eat I di eat stew chicken. I know dat when I da little girl stew chicken da one of di foods that everywhere serve inna every community inna every culture even the Indians have their version of stew chicken, I think it's across the board in Belize, across the cultural board.
>
> English translation:
> Honestly Lyra I have been eating stew chicken since I was small, from the moment I could first eat I was eating stew chicken. I know that from when I was a little girl (in the 1980s) stew chicken was one of the foods that is served in every community, in every culture even the Indians (Maya) have their version of stew chicken, I think it's across the board in Belize, across the cultural board.

We don't know whether it was Maya, mestizo, or Kriol cooks who first experimented with putting *recado* in their stew chicken. Whoever did it first, its use by Kriol home cooks since Belize's independence has legitimized it as a typical ingredient in the pan gravy that accompanies this signature dish. Kriol cooks have long experimented with and incorporated ingredients, seasonings, and even entire dishes from other cultures into their home meals, and many are proud of their ability to do so with finesse. This kriolization process transforms the ingredient by making it part of Belizean Kriol culinary tradition. Thus, *recado* became part of a dish that was then nationalized through Kriol-owned restaurants. One research participant explained it to me this way:

> We have one heavy, heavy, heavy Spanish influence inna Belize we inna Central America how could that not be part of our, become part of our culture and being, apart from the Kriol we have the Garifuna and the Spanish we adopt di meal and mek it our own, dey cook dey rice and stew beans just like we.
>
> English translation:
> We have a strong Spanish influence in Belize, we are in Central America, how could that not be part of our, become part of our culture and being. Apart from the Kriol we have the Garifuna and the Spanish, we adopt the meal and make it our own (and) they cook their rice and stew beans just like us.

She went on to say, "Again, you cannot be living in Belize which is in Central America and not have these foods pile over into your culture and adopt it and make it your own. I mean by origin it may not be most Belizean but it became most Belizean."

Recado has become Belizean through its incorporation by Kriol cooks into their recipes for stew chicken and other stewed dishes. By becoming part of the very sauce that flavors and moistens that Kriol Sunday dinner turned national dish, *recado* has gained its full citizenship and become a real Belizean at last. This nationalization process has been so successful that, to some, the use of *recado* in stew chicken is one of the things that *makes* it Belizean. A research participant in her late fifties said it best:

> Rice and beans with stew chicken is Belizean, I believe anytime you say stew chicken you di talk about Belize, other people mek chicken stew but not with di *recado* and other thing the way we mek it da Belize.
>
> English translation:
> Rice and beans with stew chicken is Belizean, I believe anytime you say stew chicken you are talking about Belize, other people make stew chicken but not with the *recado* and other things the way we make it in Belize.

A young research participant in her late twenties echoed this sentiment when discussing rice and stew beans with stew chicken:

> Uh yeah, I'm gonna go with Belizean on that one. One thing for me that makes things uniquely Belizean is the *recado* seasoning. I know it's called annatto but I don't think it's used the way we use it like in the stew chicken. Because of the *recado*, because of the stew beans the way the stew beans is [*sic*] prepared I think it's different.... I've had like Cuban black beans that might be a little similar, I've had rice and peas from Jamaica, I just, I don't know, I have a suspicion again that stew beans might be different here, the beans that we choose to stew, the red beans, and then you are combining it with the coconut rice and the stew chicken, so then you have Creole again combining with rain forest spice, I think representative of our geographic position, Creole and the rainforest... the whole Creole Latin American thing.

Conclusion

As the participant observed, Kriol stewed chicken flavored with "Latin" seasonings like *recado* reflect the unique position of Belize as a country that brings together both Central American (Maya and mestizo) and Caribbean (Kriol and Garifuna) cultures under one government. One could argue that today's recipe for stew chicken is an example of synthetic nationalism, where the dish represents different cultures successfully fused together into one national meal. However, the fears of the original opponents of synthetic nationalism can still be justified. It was Kriol dishes (rice and beans, stewed chicken), not Maya or mestizo ones, that ended up as the national meal, and it was Kriol incorporation of *recado* into Kriol home cooking that elevated it from a seasoning used by marginalized "Indians" and "Spanish" to being representative of the nation of Belize. As the Kriol research participant stated, Kriol cooks take non-Kriol ingredients or dishes and "adopt it and make it your own. I mean by origin it may not be most Belizean but it became most Belizean." Regardless of their cultural background, for most Belizeans, Kriol home cooking is still required to legitimize an ingredient as 100 percent Belizean. If Maya and mestizo people used *recado* in their stew chicken but no Kriol cooks did, it would not be considered a "Belizean" innovation, but rather a Maya or "Spanish" one. Hegemonic nationalism has not been defeated quite yet, but the incorporation of non-Kriol flavors into Kriol home cooking and their subsequent nationalization is at least some acknowledgment that Belize is and always will be a multicultural nation, spanning the regional division between the Caribbean and Central America. The ingredients in these gravies reflect that diversity and bring together in one sauce the flavors of the Caribbean and Central America. It is that *recado*-flavored sauce that wets coconut-milk-saturated rice and beans and makes them not Kriol, not mestizo or Maya, not Caribbean or Central American, but uniquely Belizean.

Stew Chicken

Recorded by Lyra Spang

Over twenty years ago a lady in Cayo District, Belize, wrote down this recipe for me when I told her she made some of the best stew chicken I had ever had. Since then, I have found out in talking to others that most people prepare their stew chicken with similar ingredients. This is something almost everyone, particularly in Belizean Kriol culture, knows how to make at home.

Ingredients:

The meat:

A whole chicken, cut into pieces, or conversely 4–5 chicken legs and thighs or breasts with rib meat, skin on. (Do not under any circumstances try to make this with boneless skinless chicken breast. In fact, I strongly recommend using either a combination of white and dark meat, or dark meat alone, for the best flavor.)

The vegetables:

Onion
Sweet pepper (green)

The seasonings:

Red *recado*
Garlic
Soy sauce
Worcestershire sauce
Ground cumin
Thyme
Oregano
Salt
Fresh ground black pepper
Bay leaf or allspice leaf (optional)
White vinegar (2 tablespoons)
Coconut oil (1–2 tablespoons)
Sugar (1 teaspoon)

Method:

1. Take the cut-up chicken, place in a bowl, and rub thoroughly with a mixture of about 2 tablespoons of vinegar and a piece of *recado* about the size of half an egg.
2. Add several tablespoons each of soy sauce and Worcestershire sauce and cumin, and dried thyme, oregano, and black pepper. Don't add salt yet.
3. Chop an onion or two and one large or two medium sweet peppers and chop up 3–5 cloves of garlic.
4. Heat the coconut oil in a large saucepan to medium high heat. Toss in the sugar. Add the chicken, skin side down, and brown, then turn and brown on the other side. Reserve the marinade from the chicken.
5. Add the onion, garlic, and sweet peppers, turn heat down and sauté until onion is transparent, then add the liquid from the chicken bowl, along with a glass or two of water, enough to almost cover the chicken.

6. Let simmer for 40 minutes to an hour, taste for flavor, and adjust seasonings as needed. You may need to add more soy sauce, Worcestershire sauce, or herbs to your taste. Add salt if needed.
7. Serve with rice and beans or stew beans and rice, fried plantains, and a little side salad (potato salad or coleslaw is classic) for a taste of one of Belize's most popular lunches.

Notes

1. I use the Kriol orthography recommended by the Belizean Kriol Language Project when referring to either the Belizean Kriol language or Belizean Kriol people. I use the word "kriolization" to refer to the generic "creolization" process in the specific context of Belize and to distinguish it from the generic terms "creole" and "creolization." In examples not specific to Belize I continue to use the generic terms.
2. Ramon Carrasco Vargas, Veronica A. Vazquez Lopez, and Simon Martin, "Daily Life of the Ancient Maya Recorded on Murals at Calakmul, Mexico," *National Academy of Sciences* 10, no. 46 (2009): 19246–19247.
3. Richard Wilk, " 'Real Belizean Food': Building Local Identity in the Transnational Caribbean Food," *American Anthropologist* 101, no. 2 (1999): 252.
4. William Dampier, *Dampier's Voyages* (London: E. Grant Richards), 1906, as quoted in Richard Wilk, *Home Cooking in the Global Village: Caribbean Food from Buccaneers to Ecotourists* (New York: Berg, 2006), 252.
5. Wilk, *Home Cooking in the Global Village*, 62.
6. Ibid., 61.
7. Ibid., 109–111.
8. Richard Wilk, "A Taste of Home: The Cultural and Economic Significance of European Food Exports to the Colonies," *Food and Globalization: Consumption, Markets and Politics in the Modern World*, ed. Alexander Nützenadel and Frank Trentmann (Oxford: Berg, 2008); Wilk, *Home Cooking in the Global Village*, 151–153.
9. *The Belize Billboard*, 1964. Cited in Wilk, " 'Real Belizean Food,' " 9.
10. Laurie Kroshus Medina, "Defining Difference, Foraging Unity: The Co-construction of Race, Ethnicity and Nation in Belize," *Ethnic and Racial Studies* 20, no. 4 (1997): 757–780.
11. Richard Wilk, "The Local and the Global in the Political Economy of Beauty," *Review of International Political Economy* 2, no. 1 (1995): 120, 128.
12. See Medina, "Defining Difference, Foraging Unity," 757–780.
13. Statistical Institute of Belize 2000, *Census Report*; Statistical Institute of Belize *Census of Belize, 2010*.
14. Lyra Spang, "A Real Belizean: Food, Identity and Tourism in Belize," PhD diss., University of Indiana, 2014.

15. At one point immediately after the Mexican caste war in the 1850s, a large influx of Mexican refugees into the northern half of the country tipped the balance in favor of the "Hispanic" or "Spanish" population, but in the later years of the nineteenth century the Kriol regained numerical dominance. See also Karen Judd, "Cultural Synthesis or Ethnic Struggle? Creolization in Belize," *Cimarron* 2 (1989): 103–105.
16. Ibid.; Assad Shoman, "Reflections on Ethnicity and Nation in Belize," *Proyeteco AFRODESC/EURESCL: Document de Travail* no. 9 (2010): 8.
17. Sidney Mintz, *Tasting Food, Tasting Freedom: Excursions into Eating, Culture, and the Past* (Boston: Beacon Press, 1996).
18. Wilk, " 'Real Belizean Food,' " 246.
19. Spang, "A Real Belizean."

Selected Bibliography

Carrasco Vargas, Ramon, Verónica A. Vázquez López, and Simon Martin. "Daily Life of the Ancient Maya Recorded on Murals at Calakmul, Mexico." *National Academy of Sciences* 106, no. 46 (2009): 19245–19249.

Judd, Karen. "Cultural Synthesis or Ethnic Struggle? Creolization in Belize." *Cimarron* 2 (1989): 103–118.

Medina, Laurie Kroshus. "Defining Difference, Foraging Unity: The Co-construction of Race, Ethnicity and Nation in Belize." *Ethnic and Racial Studies* 20, no. 4 (1997): 757–780.

Mintz, Sidney W. *Tasting Food, Tasting Freedom: Excursions into Eating, Culture, and the Past*. Boston: Beacon Press, 1996.

Shoman, Assad. "Reflections on Ethnicity and Nation in Belize." *Proyecto AFRODESC/ EURESCL: Mexico. Document de Travail* 9 (2010): 4–61.

Wilk, Richard. "The Local and the Global in the Political Economy of Beauty: From Miss Belize to Miss World." *Review of International Political Economy* 2, no. 1 (1995): 117–134.

Wilk, Richard. " 'Real Belizean Food': Building Local Identity in the Transnational Caribbean Food." *American Anthropologist* 101, no. 2 (1999): 244–255.

Wilk, Richard. *Home Cooking in the Global Village: Caribbean Food from Buccaneers to Ecotourists*. New York: Berg, 2006.

Wilk, Richard. "A Taste of Home: The Cultural and Economic Significance of European Food Exports to the Colonies." In *Food and Globalization: Consumption, Markets and Politics in the Modern World*, edited by Alexander Nützenadel and Frank Trentmann, 151–153. Oxford: Berg, 2008.

Lyra Spang, Bixa orellana *in Belize: Flavoring Postcolonial Cuisine* In: *From Garum to Mole: Sauces and Identity in the Western World.* Edited by: Andrew Donnelly, Beth M. Forrest, and Deirdre Murphy, Oxford University Press.
 DOI: 10.1093/9780190622138.003.0007

8

Sriracha and the Performance of Identity

Joshua Abrams

IN 2012, TWO years after having been named by *Bon Appétit* magazine as their 2010 "Ingredient of the Year," Huy Fong's Sriracha (Rooster) sauce sold 20 million bottles, putting it just outside the country's top ten best-selling condiments, and its sales have continued to climb from there.[1] Yet, unlike Hellmann's Mayonnaise, Frito Lay's "Tostito" Salsa, or Heinz Ketchup (the top three), Huy Fong is a family-owned business that to date has never advertised. Since then, its sales have continued to expand globally, in essence single-handedly creating and building a now highly competitive "Sriracha market" into which other manufacturers have attempted to enter. Indeed, although there are sriracha sauces that long predate Huy Fong's, the impact of this branded version has been so great that it has become a generic name for an Asian-inspired hot sauce of chili, garlic, vinegar, sugar, and salt. Versions are widely produced and stocked across the world, including by subsidiaries of the companies that produce the top three condiments (Unilever, PepsiCo, and Kraft Heinz, respectively). In late 2014, *Food and Wine* noted the incredible prevalence of Sriracha-based products introduced that year, including chips, popcorn, pizza, lollipops, beer, vodka, and even candy canes. Moving away from consumable products, Sriracha's iconic green-capped bottle, Rooster logo, and the company's resistance to marketing have left a space for the development of a culture of fandom. Although this fan culture is perhaps unusual in relation to food products, it has engendered at least two hardcopy fan-produced cookbooks and aficionado-made paraphernalia, including shirts, infant onesies, mobile phone cases, Halloween costumes, and—in one of the most unusual commercial partnerships—a 2016 Lexus Sriracha IS.[2] Among its admirers, Sriracha counts a global panoply of celebrity chefs, including David Chang, Daniel Patterson, and Jean-Georges Vongerichten, as well as celebrity trendsetters, such as it-girl Kylie Jenner, who tweeted an image of herself in a green wig and red sweater on December 1, 2015, with the comment, "Don't you just love Sriracha?"

How did what is, in essence, a branded product from a small manufacturer founded in 1980 in Southern California by a recent immigrant become so ubiquitous that its name has come to serve as a generic term across the board? This chapter argues that Sriracha has staked a claim not merely to its own "legitimacy," but as a foundational building block of performances of contemporary identity within a U.S.-dominated Western culture. By examining the history of its founding and early development, its adoption by the "foodie" community, and more recent local backlash against the company, Sriracha can be used to frame key transitional developments in negotiations of American identity over the past thirty-five years.

Diasporic Identity, Pan-Asian Immigration, and Asian Americanness

While U.S.-based consumer surveys indicate a general belief that this hot sauce is a traditional Asian condiment, people typically also have difficulty identifying its history. The name would imply Thai origins; Si Racha is a town located south of Bangkok on the eastern shore of the Gulf of Thailand, which produces a variety of hot sauce similar to, but distinct—sweeter and thinner—from the U.S.-produced sauce. There it is served primarily as a dip for local seafood. An interview in *Bon Appétit* magazine in 2013 asserts that an "original" sauce (Sriraja Panich) was developed in Thailand by Ms. Thannom Chakkapak in the early part of the twentieth century, although there is limited evidence of such claims. Various alternate explanations exist for the origin of that region's sauces, including its creation by migrant laborers from Myanmar, as well as possible domestic "homestyle" inventions. Yet the American-made product offers an equally oblique and mysterious history, which is surprising for something of such recent provenance and likely the result of active choices made by the company's founder, David Tran, in his development and production of the sauce.

Tran, who is ethnically Chinese, had been an officer in the South Vietnamese army throughout the 1970s. While he had experimented with producing and selling his own hot sauces locally, this was a small part of his life until the political change in Vietnam forced his evacuation. Tran sought passage for himself and his family aboard the Huey Fong, a Panamanian cargo ship, amidst what later turned out to be particularly scandalous circumstances within diasporic refugee politics, including a cache of smuggled gold worth almost $800,000.[3] The global press coverage and scrutiny around this crisis likely influenced Tran's determination to succeed on his own terms when he left Hong Kong shortly thereafter for the United States.

Settling in Los Angeles (after a brief stay in Boston, where he had attempted but failed to manufacture hot sauce), Tran found himself in the destabilized position of refugee/migrant, who not only needed to find a means to support himself, but also possessed a particularly complex political identity. Both his personal history and his itinerary likely meant that he understood himself as already possessing a hybrid Asian identity—bringing together his Chinese heritage (his family still spoke Cantonese), his Vietnamese life, and his troubled stopover in Hong Kong, then still a British Crown Colony. This blending of a specific Vietnamese identity into a more diffuse Asian-Americanness minimizes cultural difference to promote possibilities of assimilation, a position with which Tran may have found a natural, if likely subconscious, alignment on his arrival in Los Angeles.[4] This city, one of the key sites in defining a new notion of what it meant to be Asian-American and a cityscape in rapid development, was arguably the perfect city for him. Los Angeles in the 1970s, with its twin pillars of Hollywood and car culture, had long served as a city of the imagination, and was in the process of becoming the postmodern site par excellence. Alongside the growth of late capitalism, the greater Los Angeles area was experiencing a vast demographic change through a combination of pan-Pacific and Latin American migrations. Between 1970 and 1990, L.A. County's population shifted from 70 percent Anglo to 60 percent non-Anglo, making it a majority-minority area.[5] Paradigmatically "American," Los Angeles became ground zero for redefinitions of this identity at the end of the twentieth century. Tran's arrival coincided with this crucial moment of change and development.

Tran has never publicly discussed the design of the bottle explicitly, but it reflects not only his own hybrid identity, but the growing Asian-American hyphenate, serving to further distance the condiment from any notion of an "authentic" Asian original product. On the plastic squeeze bottle, Tran chose to list ingredients and suggest uses in a combination of six languages. Chinese, Vietnamese, French, and English traced his own hybrid biography and travels, while Spanish brought it firmly into its Southern Californian context. The sixth language is Thai, whose presence necessarily, but somewhat obliquely, referenced the chili sauces of coastal Thailand from which he drew some inspiration. The bottle itself is already Asian American, while helping consumers define this mode of identification.

The Sriracha bottle engages the diner actively in the production of taste. As with other condiments, it brings the act of saucing out of the kitchen and to the table. In so doing, the diner helps to define and refine a notion of Asian American identity, as one that draws from Asian identities, American identities, and their complex interweaving through histories of immigration and assimilation. The multilingual bottle's refuses one single, stable identity. Writing in 2013 in *Los Angeles Magazine*, David Chute perhaps overly venerates the bottle, although his claims might be seen to suggest that the bottle allows the diner to simultaneously inscribe the food and notions of personal identity:

> More than a mere utilitarian container, the bottle is a hot-sauce delivery system, and there's a tactile charge to squirting the contents onto your food, an action much more gratifying than the blup-blup-blup of throttling a glass bottle and forcing it to disgorge. Huy Fong has to be squeezed out because it's too thick and silky and stubbornly cohesive to pour easily; it has a slight gelatinous clinginess that ketchup lacks. You can decorate a serving of noodles as if you were frosting a cake, and the sauce won't separate and leak to the bottom of the bowl.[6]

While Tran had attempted several other products (the first was a sate sauce), and Huy Fong still manufactures several other condiments, including *sambal oelek* and chile garlic paste, it was this squeezable bottle that, along with its contents, may be seen as paradigmatic.

Huy Fong's Sriracha complicates the binary of an Asian-American product indigenous to the United States but distinct from white culture. Its ingredients are local to California, such as jalapeños and garlic, and include an American-style pre-processed garlic powder. Although the process of making it draws from Asian origins, it is malleable in its usage, staking a claim to distinct Americanness that arises out of the country's multiethnic fusion.

In seeking to find an opportunity to claim his "American Dream," Tran joined a long line of refugees and migrants who made names for themselves in culinary development. Having sampled the locally available hot sauces, Tran saw an opportunity to produce his own, launching Huy Fong in 1983. He took the name of the ship on which he had fled Vietnam and chose the rooster logo from his zodiac sign. Tran almost entirely self-funded the company after being rejected by more traditional funding sources. Yet he found himself in the midst of an explosive growth of Asian-owned businesses in Los Angeles, made possible through a variety of sources of capital such as the *tong tine*, an "informal lending club that allows immigrants to pool their money."[7] The existence of such alternative funding methods and the concomitant development of an Asian-American business community meant that Huy Fong was able to take advantage, both formally and informally, of such developments.

Tran initially sold this hot sauce door to door, primarily to Vietnamese restaurants, personally carrying buckets of samples to prospective clients. With this inexpensive and simple product, he was easily able to take a major role in the local market, replacing both non-Asian-style and imported Asian sauces. In the United States, hot sauces were widely available, but not prevalent, and dominated by two "Western" styles—Mexican and Louisiana/Cajun. While such broad categories necessarily oversimplify, the former (such brands as La Victoria and Pace) typically included dried or smoked chilis as well as spices such as cumin for a heavier flavor profile, and the latter (such as Tabasco and Crystal) generally included fermented peppers, vinegar, and salt, in a thick blend.[8] Sriracha is distinct, both in its consistency and in its taste. The addition of sugar has likely helped contribute to its uptake. As a more clearly Asian-based, but locally available condiment, it rapidly found a clear market niche, becoming ubiquitous across a variety of Asian-American restaurants, first within Los Angeles and then increasing beyond. Such developments were fundamentally connected to the growing Asian-American population across the nation, and the role of Los Angeles within the cultural imaginary.

As Los Angeles remained one of the primary points of entry for Vietnamese, and other Asian, immigrants—with Southern California's Camp Pendleton serving as a processing station—products produced in the city often became readily familiar to recent arrivals, many of whom would then leave for other communities, particularly Houston, New Orleans, Chicago, and Minneapolis. Once Huy Fong was able to establish a toehold in the Los Angeles market, its domestic spread through growing pan-Asian food markets was explosive, facilitated by built-in social networks of diasporic migrants through the country. Large Vietnamese communities were present in both Southern California and the Gulf states, both areas with strong historical connections to hot sauces.[9] Thus, mainstream diners in both areas, outside of the immediate target population, might have been more predisposed to spicy food than elsewhere in the country.[10] In these locations, Sriracha's Asian identity seems well positioned to have played off the two other regional hot sauces in the market. The marking of this as distinctly Asian American would not only have played into notions of taste and recognition, but also functioned as a way of marking identity within and around Asian-American communities.

As such, Sriracha could serve as a distillation of Asian-American identity, from the pasts of many diverse Asian cultures, in the same way Heinz Ketchup's 57 varieties is commonly used to refer to those with a mixture of backgrounds.[11] Huy Fong's Sriracha offers an Asian-American rejoinder to this, a claiming of Americanness that is also fundamentally Asian.

Growth and Foodie Culture

From the mid-1980s to the present, Huy Fong's sales skyrocketed, requiring progressively larger factory spaces to meet the growing demands for Sriracha. The company first expanded in its location in the Rosemead neighborhood of Los Angeles. Then it took over the former Wham-O toy factory (maker of the hula hoop and frisbee, among other iconic American products), before moving into its current home in nearby Irwindale. Why has the sauce experienced such explosive growth? What has made it so captivating, aside from a relatively opaque notion of "deliciousness" and the added presence of sugar that made it perhaps more consumer friendly than other capsaicin-based condiments? The answer lies in the development and articulation of a notion of "foodie identity," which sociologists Josée Johnston and Shyon Baumann frame as a complex interweaving of two stories. "The first narrative depicts good food as democratic.... The second story describes how food operates as a source of status and distinction for privileged eaters," which they suggest must be considered to be simultaneously "operat[ing] in tension."[12] Sriracha offers perhaps the perfect convergence of these ideas. Its growth models the rise of a more democratic relationship to food, notions of an identity defined through the performance of omnivorous eating habits, cultural capital, and questions around sustainability and industrial production. Those who identify as foodies have the privilege of social mobility and exercise commercial choice amidst conflicted notions of American identity and "ethnic authenticity."

In 1986, writer Jonathan Gold first launched his column of restaurant criticism, "Counter Intelligence," for the *LA Weekly*, a free alternative newspaper that had been around for less than a decade. Gold's tenure there (and at the *Los Angeles Times*, where he moved in 1990) was marked by a notable change in the very nature of food criticism, one that, like Meiling Cheng's reading of Los Angeles, drew upon the city as multicentric and polarized: "a Los Angeles owned by the current hegemony—whatever its constitution is—and surrounding it, edging from the margins, are *other Los Angeleses*."[13] Gold's criticism contributed to the move away from a narrative of a few dominant French or French-style restaurants and a *haute cuisine*–dominated understanding of value. The same early 1980s moment was also the peak of the rise of "California cuisine," symbolized in Southern California by Wolfgang Puck's Spago, which quickly became "the place to see and be seen" for Hollywood and wealthy elite. Simultaneously, the growth of Asian and Asian-American populations in the valleys offered an enormous and rapidly expanding range of culinary possibilities. Gold's reviews over the past thirty-plus years focused primarily not on restaurants for those with economic capital (Spago, for instance), but on places where diners obtain cultural capital by identifying out of the way "holes in the wall," where they could find more "authentic" expressions of cuisine from the patchwork ethnic map of Los Angeles. The map of the city that these reviews began to sketch was one in which cultural prestige began to be highlighted as accessible for both early adopters and those who found comfort outside of a limited "American" palate.

Through Gold and those who democratized food criticism in his wake, in particular through the rise of social media, a "class" of foodie based on notions of culinary distinction rather than explicit class background served to highlight new food trends and practices. The internet made possible sites like Chowhound and eGullet, which facilitated sharing of "discoveries" and the popularization of a broader array of restaurants than could be covered—even by Gold—from the late 1990s, as well as serving to make portable finds such as Sriracha more ubiquitously recognized and desired.

Sriracha lucked into, as well as helped to produce, a moment when an omnivorous food identity was rising. The markers of authenticity toward which Huy Fong's products gestured, such as its availability at small ethnic restaurants and grocers, played into this, leading to a snowballing expansion and near-ubiquitous recognition. It offered a rejoinder to more traditional condiments, making it the perfect entrée to "social mobility." Indeed, its taste played into this as well. Garlic, which much earlier had been critiqued as anti-American/immigrant, was by this point firmly ensconced as normal; the relatively mild chiles and the sweetness of sugar meant that it was immediately recognizable; but it was also clearly distinct and accessible, echoing mass market ketchup but with tomato replaced by chili.[14]

Yet, for all its positioning as authentic, Sriracha's positioning as American was utterly crucial to its success in becoming a marker of identity. Huy Fong invented a history of imagined authenticity but did so in a way that was not Asian, but rather Asian-American. Doing this allowed for the diner or chef to reimagine its use. The success of Sriracha and its rapid expansion beyond the Asian food market was based in large part on its versatility across cuisines. Throughout the newspaper and magazine discussion of it, the overriding idea is its varied utility, with it being used with everything from deviled eggs, Cuban sandwiches, and Bloody Mary cocktails to shrimp, roast squash, and garlic bread.[15] This openness allowed it to take hold of the cultural imaginary, allowing the chef or diner to blend the sauce's claim to adventure with a recognizably "domestic" dish. Throughout the company's history, this blend has remained crucial to the claiming of a so-called foodie identity, which, through the rise of social media and food television, has become simultaneously more central to the cultural zeitgeist.

In the post–Vietnam War moment of distrust of the "military-industrial complex," Huy Fong's anti-establishment positioning and the company's relative opacity allow the diner to, either explicitly or implicitly, claim a form of independence and heterodoxy. The lack of public information about the company, which is small and does not advertise, positions it as seemingly antithetical to the corporate practices of major companies such as Heinz; using Huy Fong's Sriracha then purports to potentially serve as a semi-hidden form of anti-capitalist protest, a performance that aligns with the stereotypical foodie demographic, legible to an "in-group," but culturally vague. Furthering this seemingly natural connection, as well, are the company's ties to local farms that provide the jalapeños, giving it a distinctively Californian farm-to-table identity associated with locavorism and anti-capital protest. Indeed, the basis of countercultural movements in the U.S. response to the Vietnam War suggests a form of reparation implicitly performed through using a sauce with a historical connection to this conflicted moment.[16] Sriracha both enabled and fostered the development of a "foodie" identity in the United States central to the turn of the twenty-first century.

Backlash and Re-Marking of "Americanness"

The end of the second decade of the twentieth century has seen a rise in nationalist populisms and a troubling hostility to immigrants across a number of major Western democracies. This racialized backlash was the context for a lawsuit against Huy Fong, which had been invited by the city of Irwindale in 2010 to move to a new $40 million dollar plant with favorable loan terms. Tran described the offer as "irresistible," despite the significant distance from their previous location and costs associated with moving.[17] The lawsuit served as a coded response to Sriracha, which clearly owed so much to the immigration histories of the second half of the twentieth century.

According to Ernesto Hernández-López in the *Seton Hall Law Review*, the development of a new factory for Huy Fong in Irwindale "was the largest commercial real estate project in Los Angeles in 2012... [and] noted for its green design elements."[18] Yet despite the significance of the invitation, public investment in it, and its recognition as the "Best Industrial Project" in Los Angeles from the *LA Business Journal*, the city of Irwindale sued Huy Fong shortly after they had moved in, claiming that the factory was "a public nuisance due to the emanation of odors and irritants from the Subject Property which are causing physical harm and discomfort for the people of the City of Irwindale."[19] This suit was eventually dropped after intense public pressure and a national media outcry; the dichotomy between the initial invitation and the legal challenge speaks clearly to rising prejudice, anti-immigrant backlash, and "nimbyism." As scholars Anita Mannur and Martin Manalansan articulate in a blog post from early 2014:

> As Martin Manalansan has written elsewhere, "smell in America... is a code for class, racial and ethnic differences." Yet cities are expected to function as odorless zones, both literally and psychically. Traces of immigrant excess must always be kept at bay and where food is concerned, difference must be managed to ensure that the kind of food one finds at the table is synchronous with the mandates of a multiculturalist ethos of eating. It must not appear "too foreign," "too different," "too oily" or too aberrant. In other words it must not be too offensive, lest it upset a carefully calibrated balance of acceptable multiculturalism.[20]

Sriracha's move and expansion threatened the racial and ethnic balance of this Los Angeles suburb. It is perhaps particularly worth noting that this is not simply a white/non-white binary, but traces a more complex story around Southern California's population and "acceptable multiculturalism." Irwindale's population is largely Latino, so this rejection might be seen to simultaneously produce nuanced narratives around both the decline of a "white majority" as well as the production of Asian Americans as a so-called "model minority," and the ways in which these have positioned Latino immigrants and communities within a context of mixed immigration. Returning once again to the historical presence of Mexican hot sauces in a U.S. context, the expansion of Huy Fong can not only be read as replacing Latino populations in such a historically racially inscribed area as Southern California, but also as a total inversion of historical race relations. It is through the complex political wrangling over something as seemingly simple as the production of Sriracha that "white Americans" could interpret changing racial politics as a loss rather than ongoing negotiations of identity. Beyoncé Knowles recalls the importance of spicy food in the ongoing discussion between languages of whiteness, privilege, and racial identity in her 2016 hit "Formation." She sings, "Earned all this money but they never take the country out me/I got a hot sauce in my bag, swag."[21] While she is perhaps speaking metaphorically, carrying and using Huy Fong's Sriracha has served as a key marker of identity over the past thirty-five years. Its portability—it is now even available in a keychain-sized bottle—and prevalence have served to move it from a growing Asian-American population to an omnivorous foodie population, creating an early twenty-first-century backlash that speaks disturbingly to race and perceptions of privilege.

Recipe for Homemade "Huy Fong"–Style *Tuong ot Sriracha*

Joshua Abrams, 2017

Ingredients:

1 pound mixed red and orange jalapeños
2 cloves garlic
1 tablespoon garlic powder
1 tablespoon palm sugar
2 teaspoons salt
1/3 cup rice vinegar

Method:

1. Stem jalapeños.
2. Place all ingredients except vinegar in food processor and blend until smooth.
3. Put purée in glass jar, cover with plastic wrap and allow to ferment (keep in a cool dark place for 4–5 days), stirring daily. Sauce will bubble as it ferments.
4. Mix with vinegar and blend again.
5. Bring to a boil and simmer, allowing sauce to thicken.
6. Strain and bottle.

Notes

1. Daniel Patterson, "Ingredient of the Year: Sriracha Hot Sauce," *Bon Appétit*, December 9, 2009.

2. Lexus, "Lexus Serves Up the Sriracha IS: Making a Hot Car Spicy," November 16, 2016, https://pressroom.lexus.com/lexus-is-sriracha-la-auto-show/.
3. Sophia Suk-mun Law, "Vietnamese Boat People in Hong Kong: Visual Images and Stories," in *The Chinese/Vietnamese Diaspora: Revisiting the Boat People*, ed. Yuk Wah Chan (London: Routledge, 2011), 118.
4. Jonathan X. H. Lee, *History of Asian Americans: Exploring Diverse Roots* (Santa Barbara, CA: Greenwood Press, 2015), 135–136.
5. Allen J. Scott and Edward J. Soja, eds., *The City: Los Angeles and Urban Theory at the End of the Twentieth Century* (Berkeley: University of California Press, 1996), 14.
6. David Chute, "Fire in the Bowl," *Los Angeles Magazine*, April 2001, 72.
7. Erin Curtis, "Cambodian Donut Shops and the Negotiation of Identity in Los Angeles," in *Eating Asian America: A Food Studies Reader*, ed. Robert Ji-Song Ku, Martin F. Manalansan, and Anita Mannur (New York: New York University Press, 2013), 17.
8. For a broader history and exploration of hot sauce styles and histories, see Dave DeWitt and Chuck Evans, *The Hot Sauce Bible* (Freedom, CA: Crossing Press, 1996); and Denver Nicks, *Hot Sauce Nation: America's Burning Obsession* (Chicago: Chicago Review Press, 2017).
9. For chili sauces and Saint Domingue—which directly impacted foodways in the Gulf—see Costura, Chapter 10 in this volume.
10. Nadia K. Byrnes and John E. Hayes, "Personality Factors Predict Spicy Food Liking and Intake," *Food Quality and Preference* 28 (2013): 213–221.
11. Frank H. Wu, *Yellow: Race in America Beyond Black and White* (New York: Basic Books, 2001), 263.
12. Josée Johnston and Shyon Baumann, *Foodies: Democracy and Distinction in the Gourmet Foodscape* (London: Routledge, 2010), 1–2.
13. Meiling Cheng, *In Other Los Angeleses: Multicentric Performance Art* (Berkeley: University of California Press, 2002), 16.
14. The broader hot sauce market has grown exponentially over this same time period, and while this fact is clearly linked to the rise of Sriracha, there are a number of factors suggesting an interwoven relationship rather than one solely of causality in either direction. (For the increase in sales of hot sauce from 2000 to 2014, see Roberto A. Ferdman and Ritchie King, "The American Hot Sauce Craze in one mouth-watering chart," last modified January 28, 2014, https://qz.com/171500/the-american-hot-sauce-craze-in-one-mouth-watering-chart/.)
15. See, for instance Ben Dewey, "The 31 Best Sriracha Recipes of All Time," *Bon Appetit*, last modified July 26, 2017, https://www.bonappetit.com/recipes/slideshow/best-sriracha-recipes-ever; Rebecca Nicholson, "I Ate Sriracha Hot Sauce on Everything for an Entire Day," *The Guardian*, last modified June 30, 2015, https://www.theguardian.com/lifeandstyle/wordofmouth/2015/jun/30/i-ate-sriracha-hot-sauce-on-everything-for-an-entire-day.
16. For a discussion of the linkage of countercultural ideas to this, see Johnston and Baumann, *Foodies*.

17. Joe Mathews, "What Makes Sriracha Stink? It's Not the Sauce. It's Cities Like Irwindale," Zocalo Public Square, last modified December 5, 2013, https://www.zocalopublicsquare.org/2013/12/05/what-makes-sriracha-stink/ideas/connecting-california/.
18. Ernesto Hernández-López, "Sriracha Shutdown: Hot Sauce Lessons on Local Privilege and Race," *Seton Hall Law Review* 46 (2015): 189–242.
19. *People ex rel. Irwindale v. Huy Fong Foods Inc.*, 2013. http://lawblog.justia.com/wp-content/uploads/2015/05/sriracha_complaint.pdf.
20. Anita Mannur and Martin Manalansan, "Dude, What's That Smell? The Sriracha Shutdown and Immigrant Excess," From the Square, last modified January 16, 2014. https://www.fromthesquare.org/dude-whats-that-smell-the-sriracha-shutdown-and-immigrant-excess/.
21. Beyoncé Knowles, "Formation," Track 1 on *Lemonade*, Columbia Records, 2016.

Selected Bibliography

Chan, Yuk Wah. *The Chinese/Vietnamese Diaspora: Revisiting the Boat People*. New York: Routledge, 2011.

Cheng, Meiling. *In Other Los Angeleses: Multicentric Performance Art*. Berkeley: University of California Press, 2002.

Hernández-López, Ernesto. "Sriracha Shutdown: Hot Sauce Lessons on Local Privilege and Race." *Seton Hall Law Review* 46 (2015): 189–242.

Law, Sophia Suk-mun. "Vietnamese Boat People in Hong Kong: Visual Images and Stories." In *The Chinese/Vietnamese Diaspora: Revisiting the Boat People*, edited by Yuk Wah Chan, 116–130. London: Routledge, 2011.

Nicks, Denver. *Hot Sauce Nation: America's Burning Obsession*. Chicago: Chicago Review Press, 2017.

Scott, Allen J., and Edward W. Soja. *The City: Los Angeles and Urban Theory at the End of the Twentieth Century*. Berkeley: University of California Press, 1996.

Joshua Abrams, *Sriracha and the Performance of Identity* In: *From Garum to Mole: Sauces and Identity in the Western World*. Edited by: Andrew Donnelly, Beth M. Forrest, and Deirdre Murphy, Oxford University Press.
 DOI: 10.1093/9780190622138.003.0008

PART THREE

Sauces and the Other

9

A Matter of Haut Gout

THE RAGOUT IN ENGLISH PRINT CULTURE

India Aurora Mandelkern

DERIVED FROM THE old French word *ragouster*—"to revive the taste"—the ragout entered the English lexicon during the mid-seventeenth century.[1] It came into being as an elastic food category rather than a specific recipe; according to the *Oxford English Dictionary* (OED), a ragout could be "a highly seasoned dish, usually consisting of meat cut into small pieces and stewed with vegetables." More simply, it defines a ragout as "a sauce or relish."[2] The *Petite Larousse Illustré* defines *ragoût* as "a dish of meat, vegetables, or fish, cut into pieces and cooked in a spicy sauce."[3] There was, of course, a whole class of dishes that intersected and overlapped with the ragout: *fricassees*, *olios*, and *terrines* of various kinds, but for many, the ragout was the catch-all, the universal archetype, the symbol of everything that French cuisine represented. In many ways, it was the Enlightenment's equivalent of chop suey in the twentieth-century United States: foreign, mysterious, resistant to classification.

Many cultures served dishes that could qualify as a ragout of some kind—writers occasionally referred to Persian or even Chinese dishes in this way—yet the ragout's pedigree was unmistakably Gallic. La Varenne, the grandfather of modern French cuisine, defined a ragout as "any sauce, or meat prepared with a haut goust [*sic*], or quick or sharp taste." His successor, François Massialot, called it a "high season'd dish, after the French way." Ragouts were the secret sauces of French cooking. They anointed *poupetons* (essentially a meat "cake" that was bound with egg, baked, and then reversed onto a serving dish) and accented *filets mignons*. They were poured over *brusoles* (seasoned veal steaks that were then baked) and drizzled over *farces* (an early modern form of stuffing).[4] They imbued French cooking with art and technique but remained morally and medically suspect. The 1702 English translation of

François Massialot's famous cookery tome, *The Court and Country Cook*, proclaimed on its cover to divulge the recipes for "the most exquisite a la mode ragoos," yet the ragout nevertheless had to be vindicated in the book's opening lines. Some attributed "the shortness of man's life . . . to his departure from the simple and frugal manner of living of our first parents, and to the vast quantities of exquisite ragoo's and sauces, that are continually coveted."[5] Fortunes had been lost, lives had been destroyed, and empires had fallen thanks to its rich and seductive flavors.

This ambivalence isn't all too surprising. French cookery in England was laden with political baggage.[6] Not only were the two countries at war intermittently throughout the eighteenth century, but French culture was also the center of domestic debates about the morality of consumption and whether it could be civilized. Of course, Britons also were introduced to many other new foods during the first half of the eighteenth century, about virtually all of which they had an opinion. Newspapers hailed the arrival of West Indian sea turtles and Oriental soy sauces on one page, while they lambasted the follies of foppish epicures on the next. Yet nothing stirred more heated alimentary debates than the "new" style of cookery brought across the Channel. Discussed and debated in poetry, plays, songs, and novels, French cookery celebrated man's ascendency over nature while exposing the depths of his depravity. Some saw it as a civic achievement, a demonstration of the reason and ingenuity that divine providence had bestowed upon men. Others linked it to the decadence and despotism of the absolutist court, threatening the virility of British bodies and minds.

This chapter examines the ragout's loaded status in eighteenth-century print culture. Drawing from cookbooks and travelogues, fiction and poetry, advertisements, and moral weeklies, the following pages examine how the rhetoric surrounding ragouts animated deep-seated questions about the civic identity, the human sense of taste, and its impact on the body and social relations. They focus less on the ragout's culinary evolution, which have been explored elsewhere, and more on what the ragout emblematized. Understood as a thick, rich, highly seasoned sauce with simmering meat, and imported from abroad, ragouts raised latent anxieties about appetite and desire. It was specifically ragout's sauce (as opposed to the meat) that not only affected one's ability to navigate a luxury-saturated world but also threatened to blur status distinctions in an increasingly complex society. By tricking the senses and seducing the imagination, the ragout-as-sauce illuminated the darkest corners of human nature.

When the first ragouts appeared in England, it was amidst a society colored by deeply held medical and moral beliefs that had shaped attitudes toward eating for centuries. Dieticians still quoted early Church fathers who had regarded the sense of taste as a symptom of humankind's inherently sinful nature. (Body and soul were essentially at war with one another, and human eating habits manifested this fallen state.) Religious leaders still invoked the enjoyment of food and drink as evidence of the materialism of epicurean thought. Epicurus's famous motto, spoken in the first book of Corinthians—"let us eate and drinke, for tomorrow we die"—was repeated in sermons, almanacs, and eventually newspapers as a way to underscore his libertinism, anti-authoritarianism, and renunciation of divine interference in the world. English advice literature correlated gentility with the ability to eat only when hunger compelled it, without capitulating to the pleasures of brutish animal sensations.[7]

The first ragouts arrived in a society conditioned to believe that too much alimentary variety was dangerous. Venetian nobleman Luigi Cornaro decried the addictive powers of opulent banquets in his influential dietary treatise, *La Vita sobria* (1558), which was cited frequently in English literature.[8] Only by abstaining from everything but bread, broth, and eggs (egg whites in particular were considered "insipid" and lacking in flavor) could the palate's discriminatory capabilities be restored. Temperance could even restore one's enjoyment of food to a prelapsarian level of sensitivity. Elizabethan physician Thomas Moffett concurred. Forty years of nothing but dry, white manna was undoubtedly beneficial for the Jews, although he was certain they complained terribly, he wrote in his influential and oft-cited dietetic manual *Health's Improvement*, which went through numerous editions.[9]

The God-given discriminatory powers of the tongue were critical to health, for the tongue evaluated what matched an individual's unique constitution before food was ingested. But the mind was easily corrupted. Of all the "false passions" to which man was susceptible, Cornaro argued that the pleasures of eating were the most dangerous and the least avoidable sins.[10] His English contemporary, physician William Bullein, claimed that a predilection for highly seasoned sauces underscored a man's inner depravity; God was known to curse the epicure with an insatiable love of these foods.[11] Even by the eighteenth century, nutritional choices continued to be rationalized using this language. Once "corrupted with our souls," Huguenot iatrochemist Daniel Duncan wrote, the mouth, being the "principal Gate by which our Friends and Enemies enter," lost the ability to separate the salubrious from the merely sensual.[12] We thus must not believe "that Partial Councellor Taste," Duncan cautioned, "which seeking nothing but Pleasure, never gives its Approbation to unpleasant Things, how useful soever they may be."[13]

By the dawn of the eighteenth century, many of these long-standing beliefs about food, flavor, and desire were redoubled as waves of foreign comestibles were brought to England from abroad.[14] The acculturation and consumption of new stimulants such as chocolate, coffee, and tea became institutionalized among elites in new types of public spaces. Foreign fruits and spices, once obscure curiosities cultivated in private physic gardens, became coveted edible luxuries displayed at fashionable tables. And modern systems of cooking, particularly from France, became mainstays of fashionable homes.

Until the Renaissance, differences in social strata exerted a greater impact on European culinary styles than did national differences. Dishes like the *blancmange* (a chicken, rice, sugar, and almond dish) or *pottage* (the boiled stews of cereals, vegetables, and meat) were equally known on both sides of the Channel.[15] Over the seventeenth century, however, national standards of identity begin to emerge. As early as 1615, John Murrell's *New Booke of Cookerie* suggests an English reliance on dried fruits and spices, while French recipes tended to embrace *verjuice* (sour juice of unripe grapes or crab apples) and herbs.[16] As Paul Freedman has pointed out Chapter 2 in this volume, the new style of French cookery pioneered by La Varenne and Nicholas de la Bonnefons during the 1650s and 1660s accelerated these nascent differences, increasingly calling upon sweet herbs, wine, garlic, cream, and butter, as opposed to the dried fruits and exotic spices that had been so prevalent in Renaissance cooking.[17]

Food textures also became smoother and silkier than the sauces of the Renaissance, thanks in part to the use of roux or beaten egg yolks as thickeners in lieu of simmered breadcrumbs. Raised stove *potagers*, or stewing stoves, had been present in English kitchens for over a century, but they became indispensable for maintaining the low to medium amounts of heat required for sauces to emulsify, a feat that was nearly impossible to accomplish in a traditional fireplace.[18] The presence of the *coulis* (or cullis), a strongly flavored reduction prepared from pounded and strained meat juices to which bouillon and wine were then added, contributed both texture and flavor, imbuing dishes with what was known as *haut gout*, a word that begins to appear in English texts during the mid-seventeenth century.[19] Defined in the OED as a "high or piquant flavor," *haut gout* wasn't a specific taste as much as an idea of rich, pungent, and highly seasoned properties that could not be put in words.[20] These properties were closely intertwined with the ragout; La Varenne had used the term to define it in the first place.

Indeed, the ragout was the touchstone of this new approach to cooking. Varenne's *Le Cuisinier francais*, translated into English in 1653, listed ninety-four ragouts in the table of contents. Massialot's *Court and Country Cook*, translated in 1702, included over one hundred. While not necessarily more time-intensive than English recipes—cullises took considerable time and effort to prepare but could be made ahead and stored for later use—ragouts presupposed a higher level of culinary sophistication, manifested in harder-to-obtain ingredients such as truffles and champagne, or multiple steps of blanching, frying, thickening, and straining.[21] Considerably more complex than the everyday gravy, ragouts called attention to a divergence in national culinary values. As British cookery became increasingly associated with a "plain and easy" amalgam of tradition and practicality (channeled in impressively large joints of meat, pies, puddings, and seasonal vegetables and fruits), French cookery came to be associated with a formal system of rules and processes for combining basic ingredients into cullises and sauces, the elementary building blocks from which a great many dishes could be prepared.[22]

Some Britons welcomed the rise of French cookery, regarding it as a technology for replicating polite society's desirable qualities: harmony, balance, emotional restraint. Others expressed reservations. Polite literature frequently depicted the French cook as a malevolent trickster who manipulated flavors with mysterious essences and quintessences, or strange techniques of straining and degreasing, imbuing the craft with an abstruse, alchemical identity.[23] It lambasted the French cook's penchant for making "kickshaws," an English bastardization of *quelque chose*—in other words, an embellished yet completely indecipherable "something." For culinary patriots, the new cuisine was synonymous with profligacy and waste. "Me can give you the Essence of five or six Ham, and de Juice of ten or twelve Stone of Beef," boasts a foolish French cook in a 1738 play, *Sir John Cockle at Court*, "all in de Sauce of one littel Dish."[24] Hannah Glasse famously devoted an entire chapter in her well-known *The Art of Cookery Made Plain and Easy* (1747) to the frivolity of French sauces. "This dish I do not recommend making," she commented under a recipe entitled "The French *Way of Dressing* Partridges," which required pounding twelve perfectly good partridges in a mortar and simmering them in champagne, "for I think it is a jumble of trash."[25] In all realms of print culture, the constant pounding, reducing, and straining of stately haunches of meat into delicate sauces and cullises became powerful criticisms of the French social body. By wasting vast quantities of food that easily could have fed entire parishes, French cookery eroded the systems of patronage and obligation that upheld social harmony.

The modern gentleman inhabited a society where cuisine had been severed from need and was engineered to please the passions. "Fami[shing] the belly to gratify the pallat," one writer recounted in *A Succinct Description of France*, 1700. "For Sauce rather than Diet," said another.[26] The vogue of French cookery, "and every other Country that has anything remarkably delicious, high, or savoury in Food," celebrated Scottish physician and dietary authority George Cheyne wrote, had subverted the "natural" medical function of cooking. "Made Dishes, rich Soop [*sic*], high Sauces, Baking, Smoaking [*sic*], Salting, and Pickling, are the Inventions of Luxury, to force an unnatural Appetite, and encrease [*sic*] the Load, which Nature, without Incentives from ill Habits, and a vicious Palate, will of itself make more than sufficient for Health and long Life."[27] Some medical writers believed that this new alimentary environment made diseases more deadly than they once had been, rendering traditional remedies less effective.[28]

It was a story that had been heard before. Many emphasized the parallels between the vogue for French cooking in England and the culinary decadence of imperial Rome, which peregrinated through literary culture as a cautionary tale.[29] Echoing the words of Seneca and Horace, both of whom had described longings for the simplicity of the Republican diet, English writers linked the adoption of foreign foods to the decline of civic virtue. In his popular poem *The Art of Cookery, in Imitation of Horace's Art of Poetry* (1709), William King, a High Church Tory satirist highly critical of the ascendant Whig order, conflated the growing scholarly interest in Roman foodways with the abandonment of the "natural" English diet of goats, cabbage, and simple puddings in favor of champagne, "stinking cheese," and "French Kick-shaws or Oglios brought from Spain."[30] For King, modern French cuisine was just the latest iteration of the twelve-hour banquets, the wine-fueled orgies, and the extravagant feasts of dormice and peacock brains that had heralded the demise of the imperial Roman civilization. "No sooner did the Romans come to feed on these made Dishes," the Oxford-trained physician William Wagstaffe wrote in 1719, "but their Courage and Resolution, and all the Virtues of the Intense Cato and their Daring Ancestors, began to melt and to dissolve, like Anchovies in a Sauce, and to dwindle till their whole Empire was devour'd at a Meal, by the Goths and Vandals."[31]

Not only did ragouts threaten the longevity of empires, but they also preyed upon individual bodies and minds. These concerns converged in public discussions of taste—understood in terms of the physical palate as well as the faculty of judgment—that animated efforts to organize and evaluate the increasingly complex eighteenth-century commercial landscape of new cultural activities and luxury goods.[32] In this environment, gustatory discernment became a powerful measurement of cultural refinement. Like a good eye for painting or sculpture, the palate represented subjective discriminative abilities that neither conformed to traditional benchmarks of education and status nor made themselves available for purchase. Not only was it a useful metaphor for aesthetic taste—Joseph Addison famously likened it to the ability to identify individual ingredients within a blend of tea, while David Hume compared it to a seemingly hereditary ability to detect traces of rust and leather within a barrel of wine—but the palate also demonstrated the embodied, physiological nature of refinement.[33] Little wonder that great wits, sensitive to art, music, literature, and conversation, also tended to be epicures. Physicians attributed this to their softer, springier, "less curiously modulated" nerves, which heightened the intensity of sensory experiences.[34] (A woman's nerves also were believed to be softer and more sensitive as to explain a more delicate and emotional nature.) Cookery writers also proclaimed a sensitive palate to be a mark of refinement. Massialot described the sense of taste as a "Ray of... Reason and Intellect." Without a discerning palate, one could neither manage the appetite nor appreciate the technical elegance of modern cuisine. Patrick Lamb, the official cook to Queen Anne and a contemporary of Massialot, concurred. A "vicious palate," he wrote in the preface to *Royal Cookery* (1710), cannot be a "proper judge of tastes."[35]

Still, if discerning the ragout's ingredients was an exercise in enlightened discrimination, Britons rarely had much success. This rich and extravagant "made dish" challenged English values of tradition and transparency, embodied in the near sacred status of the roast. Indeed, the haunch of roast beef was defined in opposition to the ragout, as seen in Henry Fielding's 1734 ballad, "The Roast Beef of Old England."[36] A large haunch of beef could be easily understood with the senses. Its size gestured to the fecundity of the English countryside and the technical ingenuity needed to produce it. Even antiquarian and naturalist Martin Lister, an outspoken advocate of French cuisine, acknowledged England's superior "management of meat."[37] Deconstructing the French ragout, however, was much harder to do. The mysterious techniques behind its preparation mirrored the dangerous qualities of modern French society: irrational, despotic, deceitful, grotesque. Others saw it as an edible vehicle for popish superstition: a jumble of strange and discordant ingredients that became even more muddled when mixed together.[38]

"TASTE is now the fashionable Word of the fashionable World," quipped the satirical newspaper *Common Sense* in 1738. "But where and what that Taste is, is not quite so certain." Indeed, the piece continued, the desire to exhibit refinement and style led men to abandon reason altogether: building houses that didn't shelter, listening to discordant music, "eat[ing] nothing they like, for the sake of eating in Taste."[39] This was a recurrent image in eighteenth-century satire: the new generation of eaters so addicted to the social prestige of French cookery that they proclaimed likings for foods that their palates would otherwise reject. The notion of *haut gout* was a case in point. It gestured to the artificial inscrutability of fashionable foods, their flavors rendered pleasant by custom alone. In the satirical play, the *Comical Don Quixote* (1702), the stench of garlic breath could deal a man a "double death," yet added a "curious hautgoust" to one's dinner.[40] Alexander Pope anthropomorphized gluttony as a woman in his 1735 "Epistle to a Lady" and made *haut gout* her nose. "If a lump of soot falls into the soup ... stir it well," Jonathan Swift sarcastically advised in his 1731 *Directions to Servants*, "and it will give the soup a *high French taste*."[41] *Haut gout* gnawed at vanity rather than hunger, exploiting the newfound fluidity of the English caste system. As taste sensations were so private—no one could truly know what one's companion experienced—the foppish parvenu would likely hide his grimace; that is, until custom transformed disgust into pleasure, and what once failed to qualify as food was reinvented as an acquired taste.

For medical writers, connoisseurship of ragouts was more serious still, poisoning the body as well as the mind. Cheyne attributed the "high" flavors of ragouts and continental made dishes (as well as coffee, tea, rich wines, and spirits) to their abundance of salts: the volatile, crystalline substances that made up all matter.[42] Salts were necessary for life—even water was composed of them. Yet the wrong salts clustered in the wrong quantities could coagulate and block the nervous channels, interfering with digestion and overstimulating the sexual appetite.[43]

Prolonged consumption of these harmful foods could also destroy the faculties of sensory discrimination altogether. Taste pathologies—loss of taste, heightened sensitivity, pica or "absurd tastes" for inedible substances such as chalk or dirt—were hardly new phenomena. For centuries they had indicated a spectrum of ailments ranging from divine possession to humoral imbalances to the improper production of saliva.[44] Taste phantoms and dramatic changes in chemosensory sensitivity also signaled a disordered mind. (Considered to be naturally more passionate, sensuous, and impressionable than men, women had historically been associated with abnormal gustatory predilections.)[45] In the eighteenth century, taste pathologies began to be elaborated with new anatomical realism. In 1706, Daniel Duncan, a Montpelier-trained physician, published a lengthy treatise contending that high concentrations of sulfurous salts found in coffee and tea burned off the tongue's nervous endings, just like a depilatory removed the skins from animals. The burns soon hardened into calluses, preventing the tongue from tasting and setting in motion a vicious cycle of habituation that operated by diminishing returns. "In eating [the victims] have not the lively and nice Taste that other People have," Duncan concluded. "Deficiency is common to them, and to all those who abuse Ragoo's, Confections, Wine, and other strong Liquors."[46]

Over the next two decades, the seat of taste pathologies migrated from the tongue to the nervous fibers that coursed throughout the body, which came to explain all kinds of sensations, feelings, and emotions. Springy and elastic nerves denoted a heightened responsiveness to sensory stimuli, a witty, curious, and more emotional demeanor, and generally higher intelligence. Yet a diet rich in highly seasoned foods weakened the nerves' natural elasticity, blunting flavor sensations. (In some cases, one physician posited, the same "vitious Diet" could also excessively *relax* the nerves, causing bland foods to taste like fire or pepper.)[47] Today physicians associate *ageusia*—loss of taste—with loss of the desire to eat, often leading to weight loss and depression.[48] Historically, however, it portended the opposite kind of behavior, exhorting eaters to chase the original high by consuming ever-greater varieties and quantities of pungent foods. Sensitive-nerved men of taste—elites most likely to be exposed to fashionable cuisine in the first place—were most at risk, as George Cheyne pointed out in the opening lines of *The English Malady* (1734). "Addresses of this kind are generally a sort of ragous and olios, compounded of ingredients as pernicious to the mind as such unnatural meats are to the body," he wrote in his dedication to his patron. "But I know that your lordship's taste is too delicate, and your Judgment too chaste to be able to bear such cookery."[49] Piqued by curiosity, reinforced by society, and habituated by custom, ragouts called attention to the enduring presence of animal appetites in the most refined and civilized of minds.

Given the ragout's ephemeral pleasures, pleasures intensified by their brevity, making rational nutritional decisions based on flavor became a forlorn hope. The best way to control the tendency to overindulge was to abandon the ragout and other "made dishes" in favor of bland, simple foods. "If we would enjoy a sound state of health, and preserve a vigorous old age," Nicholas Robinson warned, we should refrain from tasting such delicious morsels, "least their too frequent repetition impair the constitution."[50] Given the temptations posed by exotic and flavorful cuisine, it is little wonder that Cheyne counseled his patients "to eat and drink by our EYE," instead of their fallible palates, whether by measuring out separate portions, or by counting mouthfuls one by one.[51]

It isn't clear how seriously to take these satires. Vented to a rapidly growing reading public, these cheaply printed tirades were written primarily with polite entertainment in mind.[52] In fact, many eighteenth-century newspapers saw no conflict in advertising the same courtly cookbooks that they also condemned in the following pages. Still, it is worth asking why—among a wide spectrum of new ingredients, dishes, and food customs—the ragout became the proverbial symbol for everything that was decadent, foreign, and corrupting.

After all, English cookbooks featured plenty of native sauces and gravies. Yet the ingredients were fewer, the cooking times were shorter, and the recipes, on the whole, were less complex. Nor were English sauces ever as important as the meats that they were made to adorn. The French ragout, by contrast, was practically defined by the sauce, which itself was a powerful marker of cultural identity. After all, sauces are often where a cuisine's unique flavor principles reside, that is, the repetitive combinations of ingredients that demarcate one culture's cuisine from another.[53] Thick and viscous, lacking shape or form, sauces made foreign flavors familiar. This is underscored by the prolific body of advertisements for bottled sauces that ran during the eighteenth century. *Opsonium Regium*, or the "King of Relishes," sold in London during the 1720s at the astronomical price of three shillings per bottle, was advertised to "gentlemen that travel the Roads, where they seldom or never meet with any good Sauce."[54] Only so much as "[a] spoonful [of it] . . . put into any made Dish, as Ragouts, Fricassees," the ad claimed, "gives them such an agreeable Flavour and Taste as surpasses Imagination." By the century's end, London oilmen packed and sold dozens of exotic sauces at the shortest notice for colonists from India to Jamaica, allowing Britons to season the dangerous foods of foreign climates with the metropolitan taste of home.

An extended sojourn in England caused the ragout to acculturate as well. By the 1760s and the 1770s, the ragout recipes published in cookbooks appeared with fewer ingredients and pared-down instructions. The *coulis* lost ground to catchups and lemon pickles, which were cheaper and easier to prepare oneself.[55] The ragout evolved into a stew or hash that could be made quickly in large quantities.[56] Ragouts evolved on the other side of the Channel as well, as a smaller number of sauces or *fonds* began to replace the dozens of *coulis* that had been so central to eighteenth-century cooking. Marie-Antoine Carême, writing in the aftermath of the French Revolution, still included ragouts in his influential work on the new *haute cuisine*, but he regarded them primarily as ornaments for other dishes, with little detail or nuance. Alexis Soyer, the French celebrity chef who made his name working in England, treated them in much the same way in his *The Gastronomic Regenerator* (1846), lumping them into a broader category of sauces and garnitures designed to be poured over other dishes. Escoffier barely mentioned ragouts at all in *Le Guide culinaire* (1903); when the first English translation was published four years later, they had vanished altogether.

Ragouts no longer have the cultural cachet that they once had, but they still have a place in French cooking.[57] Prepared with anything from meat to fish to vegetables, poached in water, thickened with stock, or seasoned in a variety of ways, today's ragouts are versatile comfort foods, far cries from the daring feats of appetital engineering for which they were originally named. Indeed, it's easy to forget that ragouts helped create France's reputation as a paragon of high culture, which, for better or worse, has remained true to this day. Yet there are still similarities in spirit. Poured over starches, accenting meats, and sometimes eaten on their own, ragouts still lend flavor and a hint of surprise to whatever they adorn, seducing us to eat a little more than we should.

Ragout de Salpicon, or Forced-Meat Ragout

The Professed Cook: Or, the Modern Art of Cookery, Pastry, and Confectionary
B. Clermont, 1769

This is a Mixture of several sorts of Meat cut into dice, such as Sweet-breads, fat Livers, Ham, Truffles, Mushrooms, &c. which you put all together into a Stew-pan, with a good bit of Butter, a faggot of sweet Herbs, two Cloves, and two or three Shallots; soak them some time, then add Veal Cullis, Broth, Pepper and Salt; simmer it till the Meat is done, and the Sauce much reduced; skim it well. You may serve this by itself, or with any sorts of brazed Meat. — Many more things may be added to this Ragout, as Beef-palates, Artichoke-bottoms, Cocks-combs, Lambs-stones, small Eggs, &c. &c. taking care to boil the hardest sufficiently, before it is mixed with the rest; and that Breasts of roasted Poultry and Girkins chopped together, be in it only long enough to warm without boiling.[58]

Notes

1. Randall Cotgrave's *A Dictionarie of the French and English Tongues* (London: Adam Islip, 1611) mentioned the haricot "mutton sod with little turneps, some wine, and tosts [sic] of bread crumbled among," the fricassee "any meat fried in a panne," and fricandeaux "short, skinless, and daintie puddings or quelquechoses, made of good flesh and hearbes chopped together, then rolled up in to the forme of Liverings, and then boyled," but no ragouts (n.p.). Historians often regard the haricot, which derives from the old French hallicoter, or "to cut into tiny morsels," as the ancestor of the ragout.
2. James Murray, *The Oxford English Dictionary*, Vol. VIII (Oxford: Oxford University Press, 1933), 110.
3. Claude Augé, *Petit Larousse Illustré* (Paris: Librairie Larousse, 1906), 822.
4. See Massialot's glossary in *The Court and Country Cook* (London: W. Onley, 1702), 10–16.
5. Ibid., 20–22.
6. Nor were Britons unified in their opposition. French cookery was closely associated with the cosmopolitan, enterprising habits of the Whig Party, while traditional English roasts were associated with the Tories.
7. Steven Shapin, "How to Eat like a Gentleman: Dietetics and Ethics in Early Modern England," in *Right Living: An Anglo-American Tradition of Self-Help Medicine and Hygiene*, ed. Charles Rosenberg (Baltimore, MD: Johns Hopkins University Press, 2003), 21–58.
8. Cornaro's treatise, like its author, has had a long and remarkable life. Originally published in 1558 as *Trattato della vita sobria*, within several years of its publication, his writings had sparked fervid controversy throughout the Veneto but were endorsed by numerous physicians throughout the Continent. First published into English in 1633, his work has since become a fixture in the history of longevity science.
9. Thomas Moffett, *Health's Improvement* (London: T. Osborne), 363.
10. Luigi Cornaro, *Sure and Certain Methods of Attaining a Long and Healthful Life: With Means of Correcting a Bad Constitution etc.*, 3rd ed., trans. W. Jones (London: Richard Gunne, 1740), 30.
11. William Bullein, *A briefe and short discourse of the virtue and operation of balsame with an instructions for those that have had their health to preserve the same. Whereunto is added Doctor Bullins diet for health* (London: John Perin, 1585), 7.
12. Daniel Duncan, *Wholesome Advice against the Abuse of Hot Liquors* (London: n.p., 1706), 5. Iatrochemistry was a sixteenth- and seventeenth-century school of thought that employed chemistry to understand medicine and physiology.
13. Ibid. Duncan did not advocate complete abstention from these substances, yet believed the problem was that sufferers mistook them for medicines.
14. Neil McKendrick, John Brewer, and J. H. Plumb, *The Birth of a Consumer Society: The Commercialization of Eighteenth Century England* (Bloomington: Indiana

University Press, 1982); Maxime Berg, *Luxury and Pleasure in Eighteenth Century Britain* (Oxford: Oxford University Press, 2007).

15. Compare, for example, "To Force a Legge of Lambe, on the French fashion" with "A Fridaye's Pye." This is also further discussed in Terence Scully's *The Art of Cookery in the Middle Ages* (Woodbridge: Boydell Press, 1995), 196–235.
16. Courtly French and English cuisines were never identical, however; differences in respective spices and flavorings were evident as early as the fourteenth century. See Gilly Lehmann, *The British Housewife: Cookery Books, Cooking and Society in Eighteenth Century Britain* (Blackawton: Prospect Books, 2003), 36–37.
17. Susan Pinkard, *A Revolution in Taste: The Rise of French Cuisine 1650–1800* (Cambridge: Cambridge University Press, 2010); Jean-Louis Flandrin, *Arranging the Meal: A History of Table Service in France* (Berkeley: University of California Press, 2007); Barbara Wheaton, *Savoring the Past: The French Kitchen and Table from 1300–1789* (Philadelphia: University of Pennsylvania Press, 1983).
18. Pinkard, *A Revolution in Taste*, 108, 148. Pinkard has argued that the raised stove *potager* helped evenly distribute these precise levels of heat. However, the *potager* was introduced far before the ragout became a mainstay of cuisine, so it was unlikely to have caused this new style of cooking (Ivan Day [food historian] in conversation with the author, November 15, 2016).
19. Similar to the coulis was the essence, particularly essence of ham, which was made with ham and onions, thickened with roux, and strained through sieves.
20. English writers also associated *haut gout* with foods high in sulfuric compounds: garlic and onions, *asafoetida*, and spices known for their seductive, lingering odors. It was also used to describe a panoply of exotic flavors; in 1739, for example, the breakage of a bottle of soy sauce en route to the Custom House had elicited coverage in five different newspapers. Described to the public as "a rich Catchup," it was proclaimed to confer "the highest gust of any Sauce in the World."
21. Ivan Day, personal conversation, November 15, 2016.
22. Steven Mennell, taking a cue from Norbert Elias, has argued that these changes helped distinguish the elites from the lower classes that had recently gained access to plentiful amounts of meat and spices. Stephen Mennell, *All Manners of Food: Eating and Taste in England and France from the Middle Ages to the Present*, 2nd ed. (Urbana: University of Illinois Press, 1995).
23. For the relationship between eighteenth century *nouvelle cuisine* and chemical, see Sean Takats, *The Expert Cook in Enlightenment France* (Baltimore, MD: Johns Hopkins University Press, 2011) who traces the status of the cook from an imitator of elite dishes into a virtuoso/artist who employs his own mind, and E. C. Spary, *Eating the Enlightenment: Food and the Sciences in Paris* (Chicago: University of Chicago Press, 2012), 195–242.
24. Robert Dodsley, *Sir John Cockle at Court* (London, n.p., 1738), 7.
25. Hannah Glasse, *The Art of Cookery made Plain and Easy* (London: N.p., 1747), 53.
26. Robert May, *The Accomplisht Cook* (London: R. Wood, 1665).

27. George Cheyne, *An Essay on Health and Long Life* (London: George Strahan, 1724), 28–29.
28. Many early modern physicians also believed that the men and women of antiquity enjoyed longer life spans than they did. See Harcouet de Longeville. *Long Livers: A Curious history of such persons of both sexes who have liv'd several ages, and grown young again*, trans. R. Samber (London: J. Holland, 1722). For the sociological implications of these beliefs and their dietetic impact, see Steven Shapin, "Descartes the Doctor: Rationalism and Its Therapies," *The British Journal for the History of Science* 33, no 2 (2000): 131–154.
29. This was heightened in the early eighteenth century when Martin Lister, in 1705, released a new limited edition of *Apicii Coelii de Opsoniis et Condimentis,* popularly referred to as "On the Soups and Sauces of the Ancients."
30. Anita Guerrini has explored these dietary debates in "Health, National Character and the English Diet in 1700," *Studies in History and Philosophy of Biological and Biomedical Sciences* 43, no. 2 (2012): 349–356.
31. William Wagstaffe, *A Letter from the Facetious Dr. Andrew Tripe at Bath to his Loving Brother the Profound Greshamite* (London: J. Morphew, 1719), 29–30.
32. Scholars today believe that the concept of aesthetic taste originated sometime between the fifteenth and seventeenth centuries, somewhere between the court of Versailles and the Iberian Peninsula. Concretized among the *precieuses* of the seventeenth century French court, the concept of *le gout* eschewed pedantic academic learning in favor of ineffable forms of knowledge and rhetoric. In England, this concept evolved in the city as opposed to the court: in taverns and coffee-houses, assembly rooms and concert halls. In the absence of sumptuary laws, English canons of taste served to unofficially refine and regulate the unbridled consumption of luxury goods. see John Brewer, *The Pleasures of the Imagination: English Culture in the Eighteenth Century* (New York: Farrar Straus Giroux, 1997).
33. Joseph Addison, "Essay No. 409," *The Spectator* (London), June 19, 1712; David Hume, "On the Standard of Taste," in *Four Dissertations* (London: A. Miller, 1757).
34. Nicholas Robinson, *A System of Spleen and Vapours* (London: A. Bettesworth, W. Innays, and C. Rivington, 1729), 62–63; George S. Rousseau, "Nerves, Spirits, Fibers: Towards Defining the Origins of Sensibility," in *Studies in the Eighteenth Century III*, ed. Robert F. Brissenden and John C. Eade (Toronto: University of Toronto Press, 1973), 137–157; John Mullan, "Hypochondria and Hysteria: Sensibility and the Physicians," *The Eighteenth Century*, 25, no. 2 (1984): 141–174; Graham J. Barker-Benfield, *The Culture of Sensibility: Sex and Society in Eighteenth Century Britain* (Chicago: University of Chicago Press, 1992).
35. Patrick Lamb, *Royal Cookery, or, the Complete Court Cook* (London: Abel Roper, 1710), 2. This work drew on his service in the courts of Charles II, James II, and William III. The book was extremely popular, going into four editions.
36. The title was also the subtitle of a 1748 painting by William Hogarth.

37. Martin Lister, *A journey to Paris in the year 1698*, 3rd ed. (London: Jacob Tonson, 1699), 158. Lister believed that French meat, thanks to the drier air, was leaner than British meat, giving it a saltier taste more suited for stews and broths.
38. Thomas Gordon likened French cookery to "the Latin mass, and nobody knew what was in it: He therefore wish'd that Soups and Ragouts were out of Fashion, for that, in his opinion, they savour'd strangely of Popery and Wooden shoes." See *The humorist, being an essay on several subjects* (London: W. Boreham, 1720), 212–213.
39. Anonymous, "Taste," *Common Sense: Or, the Englishman's Journal*, Vol. II, 8–15 (London: J. Purser, 1738), 8.
40. Thomas D'Urfey, *The Comical History of Don Quixote* (London: J. Darby, 1729), 164. In *Acetaria: A Discourse of Sallets*, John Evelyn had referred to garlic and "other Hautgouts" as noxious substances, so repulsive that they had once been served to punish men for crimes (London: B. Tooke, 1699), 52.
41. Jonathan Swift, *Directions to Servants* (London: R. Dodsley, 1745), 41.
42. Spary, *Eating the Enlightenment*, has argued most forcefully for the classification of ragouts and other made dishes, coffee, and spirits in one category as "stimulants."
43. Young and tender plants, by contrast, had very few dangerous salts and thus were healthier (see Cheyne, *An Essay on Health and Long Life*; Guerrini, "Health, National Character and the English Diet in 1700").
44. Joan the Meatless, the subject of a fifteenth-century anti-Lollard treatise penned by Thomas Netter (d. 1430), supposedly did not eat for fifteen years other than at the Eucharist and could differentiate between one thousand consecrated and unconsecrated bread, which she did "not by divine inspiration but by a certain skill of her senses, since she had such a horror of all bodily food that she could not tolerate its taste or smell." See Caroline Walker Bynum, *Holy Feast and Holy Fast: The Religious Significance of Food to Medieval Women* (Berkeley: University of California Press, 1988), 35–37, 91–92. In the eighteenth century, disordered tastes also became powerful symptoms of the new nervous diseases such as hysteria and hypochondria, which were believed to disproportionately affect women. John Maubray, *The Female Physician, Containing all the Diseases incident to that Sex, in Virgins, Wives, and Widows; Together with Their Causes and Symptoms, Their Degrees of Danger, and Respective Methods of Prevention and Cure* (London: James Holland, 1724), 81–84.
45. Constance Classen, *The Color of Angels: Cosmology, Gender and the Aesthetic Imagination* (London: Routledge, 1998), 76–77.
46. Duncan, *Wholesome Advice against the Abuse of Hot Liquors*, 106.
47. Robinson, *A System of Spleen and Vapours*, 283.
48. Norman Mann, "Management of Taste and Smell Problems," *Cleveland Clinic Journal of Medicine* 69, no. 4 (2002): 329–336; Carl Philpott and Duncan Boak, "The Impact of Olfactory Disorders in the United Kingdom," *Chemical Senses* 39, no. 8 (2014): 711–718. There is no clear connection between loss of taste or smell

and weight loss; Barbara Stuckey, *Taste: Surprising Stories and Science About Why Food Tastes Good* (New York: Atria, 2012), 301–302.

49. Cheyne, *An Essay on Health and Long Life*, 163.
50. Robinson, *A System of Spleen and Vapours*, 150.
51. Cheyne, *An Essay on Health and Long Life*, 39–40, 226.
52. Nor were they necessarily surprising. As Jack Goody, in *Cooking, Cuisine and Class: A Study in Comparative Sociology* (Cambridge: Cambridge University Press, 1982), has argued, luxurious foods and "high" cuisines are virtually *defined* by the presence of some unceasing moral or political opposition to them.
53. Elizabeth Rozin, *The Flavor-Principle Cookbook* (New York: Hawthorn Books, 1973).
54. "Opsonium Regium" appears in several advertisements running in the *Daily Post* (London) in the winter and spring of 1731.
55. Catchups in the eighteenth century could be made from a variety of ingredients, unlike the modern tomato-based product. Such varieties included Seville oranges and walnut catchup, green walnut shell catchup, oyster catchup, and English catchup (vinegar, garlic, anchovies, and spices). See Charlotte Mason, *The Lady's Assistant for Regulating and Supplying her Table* (London: J. Walter. 1780), 298–299. *Catchup*, *catsup*, and *ketchup* all refer to a sweet-and-sour flavored condiment and entered the English language at the end of the seventeenth century, with *catchup* being the most common in the eighteenth century, *catsup* becoming the most common spelling in the nineteenth and first half of the twentieth century, and *ketchup* being the most common spelling since the mid-1970s. See Bentley, Chapter 12 in this volume.
56. In *Mrs. Beeton's Book of Household Management*, the ragout is defined as "a stew or hash."
57. The *Larousse Gastronomique*, originally published in 1938, defined ragouts as dishes "made from meat, fowl, or fish cut in pieces of regular shape and size, browned or cooked without coloring and with or without an accompaniment of vegetables." Today, the brown ragouts are prepared by frying meat lightly, sprinkling with flour and adding stock, meat juices, or water. Blanc ragouts, or *à l'anglaise*, have no thickening—basically poached.
58. Clermont, *The Professed Cook*, 305–306.

Selected Bibliography

Berg, Maxine. *Luxury and Pleasure in Eighteenth Century Britain*. Oxford: Oxford University Press, 2007.

Brewer, John. *The Pleasures of the Imagination: English Culture in the Eighteenth Century*. New York: Farrar Straus Giroux, 1997.

Cheyne, George. *The English Malady*, 3rd ed. London: G. Strahan, 1734.

Guerrini, Anita. "Health, National Character and the English Diet in 1700." *Studies in History and Philosophy of Biological and Biomedical Sciences* 43, no. 2 (2012): 349–356.

Lehmann, Gilly. *The British Housewife: Cookery Books, Cooking and Society in Eighteenth Century Britain*. Blackawton: Prospect Books, 2003.

Massialot, François. *The Court and Country Cook*. Translated by J. K. London: W. Onley, 1702.

May, Robert. *The Accomplisht Cook*. London, R. Wood, 1665.

McKendrick, Neil., John Brewer, and J. H. Plumb. *The Birth of a Consumer Society: The Commercialization of Eighteenth Century England*. Bloomington: Indiana University Press, 1982.

Pinkard, Susan. *A Revolution in Taste: The Rise of French Cuisine 1650–1800*. Cambridge: Cambridge University Press, 2010.

Shapin, Steven. "How to Eat like a Gentleman: Dietetics and Ethics in Early Modern England." In *Right Living: An Anglo-American Tradition of Self-Help Medicine and Hygiene*, ed. Charles Rosenberg, 21–58. Baltimore, MD: Johns Hopkins University Press, 2003.

India Aurora Mandelkern, *A Matter of* Haut Gout*: The Ragout in English Print Culture* In: *From Garum to Mole: Sauces and Identity in the Western World*. Edited by: Andrew Donnelly, Beth M. Forrest, and Deirdre Murphy, Oxford University Press. © Oxford University Press 2026. DOI: 10.1093/9780190622138.003.0009

10

Hot Sauce and Colonial Degeneracy

MAKING OF THE SELF IN THE EIGHTEENTH-CENTURY FRENCH CARIBBEAN

Maureen Costura

ACCORDING TO TRADITIONAL Haitian folklore, there were once two men named Ti-Malice and Bouki. In the many Haitian stories in which these two appear, Ti-Malice is the quintessential trickster, lazy and conniving, and regularly outsmarting himself as he seeks to take advantage of his slower, greedy friend Bouki. These two are often associated with animal characteristics, with Bouki being equated to the hyena in African folklore, while Ti-Malice takes on the role of the hare. In one story, Ti-Malice becomes tired of Bouki always showing up and demanding a share of the lunch he is about to eat. Ti-Malice decides to teach Bouki a lesson and prepares a sauce (or *sos*, in Haitian Creole) with a large amount of highly spicy chili peppers. When Bouki comes by looking for lunch, Ti-Malice serves him this sauce, thinking to drive his friend away for good. Unfortunately, Bouki loves the spicy sauce so much that he runs through the village telling everyone that they need to come to Ti-Malice's house to try his special, delicious new sauce.

Sauce (or Sos) Ti Malice ("Little malice" or "mischief" sauce) is a Haitian staple, found across the island in kitchens and restaurants, and it is often the subject of articles, cookbook recipes, and postings on immigrant websites.[1] It is a food that is quintessentially Haitian, signaling belonging and homecoming to many. However, Sauce Ti Malice is a product of a particular period of historical development and reflects the preoccupations of the population that created it. It also reflects an embodied tension specifically related to food: the anxiety over the prospect of becoming what you consume, of embodying the traits associated with particular foodways. Sauce Ti Malice and the sly folktale relating its origin story are a perfect vehicle for the discussion of preoccupation with the act of becoming a new person, belonging to a new place, that was widely written about by European colonists in colonial Haiti (then known as Saint Domingue) and was also acknowledged by both free people of color and the enslaved individuals of the island.[2]

In the mid- to late eighteenth century, just prior to the Haitian and French revolutions, the European scientific community was engaged in a debate over the origin of different human ethnic groups and races. The Comte de Buffon, a renowned naturalist and encyclopedist whose works influenced later scientists, including Lamarck, Cuvier, and to a limited extent Darwin, suggested quite seriously that the origin of these "races" was in their exposure to environmental differences, specifically those that came from the climate, soil, and food produced. Buffon's writing brought the whole idea of the colonial project as a civilizing influence into doubt, since according to his theory, any civilized individual subject to the environmental conditions of a new place would, over time, degenerate to more closely resemble the original inhabitants. This theory of colonial degeneracy was the backdrop against which climate was experienced and food was consumed or shunned, praised or ignored, throughout the French colonial world.[3]

Colonial Saint Domingue

In the late eighteenth century, the island of Saint Domingue was the driving force of French mercantile wealth and the crown jewel of the French colonial empire. Called "the Pearl of the Antilles," Saint Domingue was a literary, musical, artistic, and scientific powerhouse, all built on the labor of brutalized men, women, and children of African descent. That brutalization, and the need on the part of the elites to rationalize and excuse the treatment of these individuals, gave rise to a society full of contradictions and tensions. The tensions would come to a head with the outbreak in 1791 of the Haitian Revolution, which remains the only entirely successful slave revolt in the New World. However, in the years leading up to the Revolution, the attempt to reconcile the observable realities of life in such a quintessential slave society—the violence, quick and agonizing deaths, and the prevalence of epidemic disease and failure to thrive of a substantial portion of the population—preoccupied a good proportion of the French and Creole citizens of Saint Domingue. Failure to thrive was not solely ascribed to the diseases that were endemic to the island, although they were acknowledged as a major component. Instead, many explanations also focused on the unsuitability of the total environment—the climate, the soil, the food—for European bodies. According to Buffon's theory, which was widely accepted in French society, the Caribbean environment in which these individuals of European descent lived would have a subtle, intrinsic effect on their forms, skin colors, and characters. This effect included a change in their susceptibility to diseases. Until individuals adapted or degenerated to suit the environment of Saint Domingue, they needed to protect themselves. Those who were attempting not to degenerate, and who wished to remain wholly European, with all the privileges that implied, would never fully adapt and were considered far more at risk to the island's endemic diseases.

Newly arrived Europeans or those who became ill were advised to adapt their diets in order to mitigate the effects of the environment on their bodies. These dietary adaptations included shunning chili peppers, vinegar, warming spices, and alcohol. While behaviors or food choices could be blamed for disease, those who were so fortunate as to survive and acclimate to the island had further challenges. As these survivors became part of the fabric of society, the concern was that the society itself would depart from the European ideal and a new people, or race, would emerge. This new race became known as Creoles, with a further division between those known as European Creoles, born in the colonies of European descent, and African Creoles, those born in the colonies of African descent. If Europeans and Africans are imagined to be entirely different races, as Buffon and his contemporaries did, then the two forms of Creoles were a step closer together, and also a step closer to the indigenous people of the islands, who over time all the colonists would come to resemble.[4] This change, and the fear and attempts to avoid colonial degeneracy on the part of the French colonists and their descendants, can be illustrated through the vehicle of hot sauce, particularly Sauce Ti Malice and related vinegar-based hot sauces and recipes. These hot sauces serve as an integral part of numerous recipes both historically in Saint Domingue and in modern Haiti. Some of these recipes include *picklise* (a spicy pickle sauce), *griot* (pork seared and then braised in Sauce Ti Malice), and *tassot* (marinated beef served with Sauce Ti Malice, rice, and beans).

The negative influence of the climatic conditions of Saint Domingue did not end with the French occupation of the island. The characteristics attributed to individuals of Saint Domingan descent spread with the refugees of the Haitian Revolution to other areas of the French colonial Caribbean and into New Orleans. Following the outbreak of the Haitian Revolution, many Saint Domingan individuals made their way to the U.S. port city, which was similar enough in climate and culture to offer a welcoming environment to former Saint Domingans.[5] While political and cultural concerns in New Orleans are not identical to those of Saint Domingue, it still makes a reasonable and welcome proxy for discussions of life in Saint Domingue.

Nomenclature and the classification of individual status was a preoccupation during the eighteenth and early nineteenth centuries. Terms of identification were fluid, contested, and laden with political, economic, and social implications. In simplified terms, people of European descent who were born in Europe occupied one social rung, Creoles of European descent the next, followed by free people of color, often referred to as either *affranchis*, *sang-mêlé*, or *gens de couleur libres* (there is considerable overlap between this group and the African Creoles, people of African descent born in the New World, who were often but not inevitably enslaved), and finally the enslaved men and women brought directly from Africa. Individuals could also be assigned status based on an obsessively detailed examination of their racial makeup, as recounted in Moreau de Saint Méry's *Description topographique, physique, civile, politique et historique de la partie française de l'isle Saint Domingue* (1789), in which the lawyer and chronicler describes 128 different racial mixes for Europeans and Africans.

Aside from racial and national designation, there was also the consideration of economic status. According to François Wimpffen, an explorer and French Army captain who lived in Saint Domingue from 1788 to 1790, enslaved people called a European or European Creole with great wealth a *grand blanc*, while one without substantial holdings was a *petit blanc* or a *blanc noir*.[6] Europeans who became acclimated to Saint Domingue might lose sufficient status to be simply classed as Creoles, perceived as having less compelling ties to the metropole. The strength and demonstration of these ties was of great importance to those at the top of society, although by the outbreak of the Haitian Revolution these ties were beginning to chafe and perhaps loosen.

Ethnogenesis in Saint Domingue

The loosening of ties between the New World French-descended Creoles and their homeland can be termed *incipient* or *liminal ethnogenesis*, or the self-identification of a new social group with its own traits and characters. This has a long academic background, beginning in the nineteenth century as a "response to European ideologies of national and racial purity. Ethnogenesis theories proposed instead that all modern nations arose from ongoing cultural interactions and waves of migration, each new ethnic form emerging from multiple predecessors."[7]

In Saint Domingue and throughout the French colonial world, a new ethnic identity was emerging, that of the Creole. This person, born in the New World and subject to its influences, might or might not have been *sang-mêlé* (which usually referred to an individual of African and European parentage) or *métis* (which often referred to an individual of indigenous and European parentage), but according to Buffon's process of colonial degeneracy was inevitably becoming more similar to those of mixed descent than he or she was to their European forebears. According to Buffon, this in turn led to that individual being better suited to thrive in the climate and disease environment of the colonies. Colonial degeneracy could be resisted by avoiding as many of the influences of the new locale as possible, especially vinegar-based hot sauces like Sauce Ti Malice.

This incipient ethnogenesis through colonial degeneracy was interrupted by both the French and Haitian revolutions, and eventually the culture of the emergent ethnic group was largely incorporated into broader American culture by the arrival of large numbers of migrants from the United States following Napoleon Bonaparte's sale of the Louisiana territories. Perhaps aspects of the culture continued, but the emergent sense of Creole solidarity and their dominance of social, political, and economic life fractured under the different racial and cultural understandings of the Americans.

The traits ascribed to this emergent Creole ethnic group were remarkably uniform and have continued to form part of the mythology surrounding the most visible former French colonial territory in the United States, New Orleans. The majority of New Orleans's nineteenth-century reputation derived from the high numbers of Saint Domingan refugees who settled there between 1791 and 1809, when Cuba expelled the last of the Saint Domingans. The traits associated with them—hospitality, cheerfulness, lasciviousness, violence, and preoccupation with honor—were predominantly ascribed to the Creole population, which derived from exiled Saint Domingans. In Haiti itself, descriptions of character are largely overshadowed by narratives of warfare and violence during the Haitian Revolution.

Buffon's Theory

Buffon was a believer in monogenesis, the idea that all human beings descended from one origin. Like other European writers of the period, Buffon claimed that those original humans must have been Caucasian, with other, later groups of individuals degenerating from this natural state as a result of environmental influences and diet. Buffon claimed that life forms from one climatic zone often fail to thrive or have their natures altered by prolonged residence or growth in another area. In particular, he singled out the fate of European plants and animals in the New World. He claimed that in both the founding members of these species, and their descendants, the versions of them found in the New World are inevitably smaller, weaker, and less able to thrive than those same species in their "natural," European environment.

> American animals we shall perceive... not only the number of species is smaller, Animated nature, therefore, is in this portion of the globe less active, less varied, and even less vigorous; for by the enumeration but that in general they are inferior in size to those of the old continent; not one animal throughout America can be compared to the elephant, rhinoceros, hippopotamus, dromedary, buffalo, tiger, lion, &c.[8]

While a great deal of research has been done on colonial degeneracy and Buffon, even the best accounts leave out the role that food and the consumption of food played in exacerbating or speeding the changes that were called degenerate. Buffon blamed colonial degeneracy explicitly on the prolonged effects of climatic and dietary exposure to the New World environment itself. This exposure was made worse by the consumption of life forms that had acclimated to this environment, which is to say, plants and animals native to the New World. By consuming the native fruits of the non-European climate, Europeans became degenerate even more quickly than they otherwise would, based solely on exposure to the new climate.

> From every circumstance we may obtain a proof, that mankind are not composed of species essentially different from each other; that on the contrary, there was originally but one species, which, after being multiplied and diffused over the whole surface of the earth, underwent diverse changes from the influence of the climate, food, mode of living, epidemical distempers, and the intermixture of individuals more or less resembling each other; that at first these alterations were less conspicuous, and confined to individuals; that afterwards, from continued action; that these varieties have been perpetuated from generation to generation, in the same manner as deformities and diseases pass from parents to their children, and that in fine, as they were first produced by a concurrence of external and accidental causes, and have been confirmed and rendered permanent by time, and by the continued action

> of these causes, so it is highly probable that in time they would gradually disappear, or become different from what they at present are, if such causes were no longer to subsist, or if they were in any material point to vary.[9]

In this, Buffon is merging the modern European notion of *terroir*, which is defined as the combination of climate geology and human interaction with place in shaping foods, with medical understandings of the mid- to late eighteenth century. In Buffon's mind, the character and physical state of individual people—whether they were sick or well, moral or immoral, impulsive and passionate, or placid and mellow—was due to the ways in which outside influences, literally born of the soil, worked on innate predilections. This degeneracy impacted not just physical appearance and health, but behavior and character as well, in a reflection of the Galenic understanding of humors. Those subjected to the climatic heat and moisture of Saint Domingue would inevitably find their own qualities of heat and moisture exacerbated, impacting both their physical health, whether through humoral or miasmatic influences, and their mental qualities or characters. When they reinforced this with unwise consumption of foods from the island's tropical *terroir*, they found themselves more greatly and swiftly impacted.

Disease in Saint Domingue

The first impact of foreign and colonial *terroir* was on the health of a newly arrived individual. The question that preoccupied the French colonial establishment in the eighteenth century was whether or not people of European descent could thrive in Saint Domingue. While there was also concern for the financial expenditure on enslaved people who seldom lasted beyond three years, this was not a question of medical possibility but of disease and blame. Enslaved individuals were accused of innate laziness and failure to successfully adapt, and they were watched closely to make sure that they did not self-harm, either by action or inaction, during their acclimation to the physical and social climate of Saint Domingue. This became a matter of concern especially during the Seven Years' War, which cut off easy access to the slave ports of Africa and forced the slave owners of Saint Domingue to tend to, rather than replace, their enslaved workers.[10] While the death of enslaved people caused financial consternation, the failure of European individuals to thrive in Saint Domingue caused a far greater concern among the colonial elites.

Medical practice among the colonial elites was in a period of transition. Although formal medical practitioners had been disputing Galenic practices and understandings since the seventeenth century, the concept of "humours persisted de facto among practitioners."[11] Galenic medicine ascribed the occurrence of disease to imbalances of the humors, the outward expression of which were the fluids of blood, black bile, yellow bile, and phlegm. The humors in turn were influenced by a variety of factors, including the ambient temperature, the force of the sun's heat, and the foods consumed by the afflicted individual. Although unfashionable by the end of the eighteenth century, it is still easy to detect the influence of Galenic medicine in the fears and advice given to newly arrived and long-term residents of Saint Domingue. For instance, one humoral treatment common in Saint Domingue involved rubbing mercury on people being treated for yaws (a bacterial infection) to induce sweat, an excess of the melancholic humor believed to cause the disease.[12]

While Galenic practices were still the norm, Enlightenment understandings of medical practice were becoming fashionable among Saint Domingue's elite. As a result, the two systems of practice are often found mixed together in unexpected ways, depending on the age, economic status, and training of both "patient" and practitioner. These practices were influenced by a climatic or miasmatic system, which borrowed from Buffon's theory of colonial degeneracy and race formation. The colonial environment was rife with swamps, uncultivated wastelands, and rotting vegetation, all of which created miasmas that caused disease. A variety of antidotes to these miasmas were proposed, including the burning of gunpowder, a reliance on scented cloths, and smelling salts. To strengthen oneself against these miasmas, it was still considered important to support one's humors through proper diet and behavior.

According to medical doctors, philosophers, and scientists such as Buffon, Saint Domingue was a particularly difficult place to acclimate to due to its presence within the Torrid Zone. Located close to the Equator, this zone was home to the greatest concentration of miasmas possible, as the air was full of rotting vegetation, heat, too much moisture, and blazing sunlight. These were the same traits that allowed planters to grow sugar cane, the most profitable product of the island. While in Galenic terms sugar was a universally beneficial food, according to the miasmatic system, sugar and the cane vinegar and rum it produced were dangerous, especially when reinforced with dangerous chili peppers and other native foods. While medical professionals railed against the consumption of these foods, elites apparently found them irresistible, judging by the number of times the injunction to avoid them had to be repeated. This combination provoked the sanguine and choleric humors, while the diseases exuded by the landscape killed many. Moreau noted in his 1789 account of the island that "Saint Domingue is very murderous."[13] Fevers in particular were feared and often infected newly arrived Europeans. "In general, Europeans, upon their arrival, pay tribute to a malignant, but conditioning, fever. They can hope afterwards to enjoy good health, provided they do not give way to excesses, injurious everywhere, but fatal in the islands."[14] Fevers, which were believed to be caused by an excess of hot blood, were treated either by bloodletting or by simply bathing the head of the afflicted person with cool water and cooling herbs. Enslaved Africans were considered better suited to the island because they also came from the Torrid Zone, as is shown in the poetic memoir of the unidentified Creole of Saint Domingue, who wrote in defense of slavery: "Thanks to... the thickness and oiliness of skin, which Providence has wisely given these races of the Torrid Zone, they can prudently brave the climate which would in a short time kill the European."[15]

As a result of the high numbers of Europeans arriving in Saint Domingue who were afflicted by fevers, epidemic disease, and ultimately death, medical practitioners were repeatedly expected to weigh in on the proper treatment of new arrivals. The advice that they gave is reflective of the contemporary state of medical knowledge. New arrivals were to avoid too much physical activity, retreat to the mountains immediately, where the air was considered cleaner, and especially to avoid those foods and drinks that would exacerbate the negative ill effects of the climate. "If all new arrivals showed the precaution of remaining in the more elevated region a few months, they would avoid, no doubt, the necessary danger of becoming acclimated."[16] Any foods that were considered to have a heating effect on the blood were to be shunned. This included alcohol, meat, warming spices such as cinnamon and allspice, and any food that was native to the island, like tomatoes or cassava. The greatest condemnations, however, were reserved for those who consumed foods that were seasoned with spicy chilies or chili sauces like Sauce Ti Malice. This was at once a food native to the Torrid Zone and one that was considered to have an undeniably heating effect on the individual. In theory, this sauce could do a great deal of mischief to the system of the unacclimated European consumer, which might explain some of its evident popularity among enslaved Saint Domingans of African descent. Just as Ti Malice tried to make his food unpalatable for the lazy, thieving Bouki, perhaps enslaved Saint Domingans could render their food undesirable or unsafe for Europeans with the addition of spice.

Disease, Passions, and Chili Peppers

Europeans who were becoming degenerate, or acclimated to the colonial environment, were altering not just their physical natures but their emotional and mental natures. Foods that were enflaming to the body were also enlivening to the libido, prompting medical practitioners to entreat their patients to avoid sexual activity. According to historian Karol Weaver, doctors "therefore warned their patients to avoid dangerous foods—most especially spices and strong drink—and to restrain their passions."[17] A European who was fully acclimated to this landscape was often considered "very lazy, a little vain, prodigal, inconstant, and a libertine; but his faults are redeemed by important qualities which cause him to be loved and esteemed. He is a good friend, sincere, generous, and brave to temerity; he has a natural intelligence, taste for the arts, and his hospitality is praised by all who visit our isle."[18]

These characteristics were considered similar to those of the indigenous peoples who had also inhabited this zone, both in the New World and in Africa. A Captain Bossu, writing in 1790, states that the indigenous peoples of the New World "feed on lizards, serpents, crabs, turtles and fishes, which they season with pimento, and the flour of manioc. Lazy to an excess, and accustomed to the greatest independence, they detest slavery, and can never be rendered so useful as the Negroes. For the preservation of their liberty they make every exertion; and when they find it impossible, will rather die of hunger or despair than live and be obliged to work."[19] These same traits—lazy, independent, and defiant—were used by Moreau to describe Creoles born in the New World. "Used to having strong wills, they (Creoles) are angered by obstacles, and when the latter disappear, they are thoughtless once again."[20] In the humoral system, these traits belong to the sanguine or choleric humors, and were reinforced by both the climatic heat and the piquancy of the chili pepper commonly used in cooking in both indigenous and colonial New World society. Saint Domingan Creoles "reject the wholesome foods and prefer the salty things brought from Europe or the viands of the country, prepared in a novel way and known under even more novel names."[21] They are weak because they have "destroyed their stomachs" with indigenous foods.[22]

Chili peppers, or capsicums, are native to the New World, first domesticated in Mexico at least 6,000 years ago, although there are disputed sites that might push that date back further.[23] Archaeologists have identified four separate strains of chili peppers, implying four separate domestication events over a period of time. Of these four, modern diners are most familiar with the capsicum annum. Other strains include the yellow lantern chili, the tree chili, and the amarillo pepper used widely in modern Peruvian cuisine. Some scientists have argued that the piri-piri, or Tabasco chili, is a fifth domesticate, although this has yet to be widely accepted.[24]

What is well documented is that one variety of chili pepper was in widespread use on Saint Domingue throughout the colonial period. This chili pepper, known as the Haitian pepper or the Bonda Man Jacques, is a chinense or yellow lantern chili, closely related to the habanero. (Habanero simply means that the pepper was first identified in Havana, implying that this pepper may have had a widespread use in the Caribbean during both historic and possibly pre-Columbian times.) It is a fiercely spiced pepper measuring 200,000–300,000 on the Scoville scale, and it is widely used in stews and soups, particularly the Caribbean version of court bouillon. Modern Haiti preparations using this pepper include the relish *picklise*, where the chilies are soaked in vinegar with vegetables; *rougaille de tomates*, a salsa-like dish that uses chilies, onion, and ginger; and a stew called *blaff*, which involves garlic, lime juice, chilies, and allspice. All or most of these ingredients would have been considered "heating" foods according to the Galenic system, and few were of European origin, making them doubly suspect. Although there are few descriptions of lower-class or enslaved Saint Domingan cuisine at the time of the Haitian Revolution, most of these ingredients, including allspice, chilies, tomatoes, and ginger, were included in the list of foods that new arrivals should avoid.

Sugar and Cane Vinegar

The other food item often connected to Saint Domingue is sugar and its byproducts, including various forms of rum and cane vinegar. Sugar (at least in the form of alcohol), like chilies, is considered a hot food in Galenic medicine, though sugar promotes sanguine behavior such as hospitality and affability, while chilies provoke choleric anger.[25] Sugar was also strongly associated with Saint Domingue, as it was the major source of wealth on the island and the crop that made Saint Domingue the producer of one-eighth of the wealth of France. One distinguishing characteristic of life in Saint Domingue was the extent to which all inhabitants had access to and relied on sugar and its byproducts of rum, cane vinegar, and molasses.[26] This reliance on sugar and sweets marked out Creoles especially, while rum manufacture lagged on the island due to the protectionist policy of metropolitan France, which used legislation and taxation to protect its *eau-de-vie* producers. Without the outlet of legal rum production, excess or spoiled cane juice was often used for cane vinegar, which forms the liquid basis of *picklise* and Sauce Ti Malice. So, while sugar manufacture provided wealth and status to the elite, and enslaved people could be harshly punished for the theft of sugar, rum and cane vinegar were the undesirable failures or cast-offs of the sugar manufacturing process, a fitting matrix for colonially degenerate hot sauces.

Sugar was sanguine, while the damaging chilies, garlic, and mustard were seen as choleric. However, sugar in the refined form of alcohol was still heating to the blood. Hence, although sugar itself could be consumed without damage to the European characteristics of the individual, rum, its cheaper derivative *tafia*, and cane vinegar, which was basically unconcentrated rum, were considered dangerous to people acclimating to the heat and humidity of torrid Saint Domingue.

Cuisine in Saint Domingue

Due to the chaos and displacement of the Haitian Revolution, it is difficult to reconstruct when the different preparations entered the culinary lexicon of Saint Domingue. Those who wrote about the island were overwhelmingly white European or European Creole males, and the few dishes they recount almost always strongly emphasize European food preparations norms. The occasional mention of a food being "heavily seasoned" or "spiced with pepper" could imply the use of chili and vinegar sauce preparations like Sauce Ti Malice, but there is no way to prove that from the descriptions. Dishes that are described in detail in *My Odyssey*, the anonymous first-person account of the outbreak of the Haitian Revolution, are obviously partially European in origin, like the elaborate forerunner of *turducken*.[27] However, that elaborate dish of meats within meats was placed on a "highly seasoned salad" that could imply something like a *picklise*.

The *picklise* or the pairing of *grillade* with Sauce Ti Malice or other vinegar-chili pepper infusions can be assumed to derive from the culinary tradition of the enslaved rather than the slaveholders, and as such it is difficult to claim any great understanding of pre-Haitian Revolution foodways from such brief descriptions. However, Haitian folktales can give some insight into why and how these highly seasoned sauces were valued in Haitian (and likely Saint Domingan) culture. In addition to the popular story of Sauce Ti Malice, there is also the classic folktale of the "Whee-ai!" In it, Bouki encounters an old woman (or man) eating food by the side of the road. He asks her what she's having, distracting her and causing her to bite her tongue. She cries out "Whee-ai!" Bouki spends the rest of the day going around asking people what "Whee-ai" is, and where he can get some. Finally, Ti Malice gets so tired of Bouki asking that he cooks up a stew with a sauce made from whole chili peppers and gives it to Bouki. When Bouki bites into a pepper he starts to yell, and Ti Malice informs him, "There's your Whee-ai!"[28]

Bryan Wagner, in his recent book *The Tar Baby: A Global History*, examines a classic tale of the antebellum American South's versions of Bouki and Ti Malice, B'rer Fox and B'rer Rabbit.[29] He theorizes that these stories are primarily about understanding food and who controls access to food. The tales of Bouki, Malice, and the sauces are a sly way of describing the use of hot sauce to draw boundaries around those whom food belongs to. The chilies mark the food as belonging to New World Creoles—a disguised sort of ethnogenesis inherent in every burning bite.

While European colonists feared the humoral and degenerate influences of spicy foods, people of African descent embraced their use. In the story, Ti-Malice's attempt to keep his spicy food for himself backfires as Bouki and, through him, the rest of the community become acclimated to the spicy hot sauce. Today Sauce Ti Malice is seen as an essential part of Haitian cuisine, the necessary condiment.

Wet Nursing and Acquired Degeneracy

Despite their fear of colonial degeneracy, capsicum and its derivative sauces were not consumed only by people of African descent. The consumption of these sauces is hinted at by European Creoles as well, despite the dangers associated with consumption. Why would elite individuals consume, even clandestinely, foods associated with degeneracy? The fault was described as both the result of their climatically influenced degenerate natures and the failings of enslaved women. European Creole exposure to spice was blamed in large part on the diet and humoral tendencies of their wet nurses. Wet nursing was widespread in eighteenth-century France: "Of the 21,000 births registered in Paris in 1780, only 5 percent of them were nursed by their own mothers."[30] Many infants with elite parents were placed with rural tenants, dependents of their parents' estates. This translated easily into reliance on enslaved wet nurses among Europeans and Creoles in Saint Domingue.

Wet nursing was already a concept fraught with emotional complications, with reformers accusing those who used wet nurses of being murderously lacking in maternal instinct. How much more problematic, then, was the concept of the enslaved wet nurse, one who was already part of a class often accused of opportunistically killing their own infants so they could slake their sexual appetites? Even when the child thrived under such care, the damage to their humoral natures was assured. Enslaved wet nurses, according to Wimpffen, "seldom reached the period of weaning without communicating to the infant they nourish, the venom of corrupted milk, and the vices of the temperament to whose lascivious and fiery nature, forced continence has added fresh fuel."[31]

The Creole child, then, was as a result of their birth, milk, common food, and the climatic and miasmatic influences under which they were raised, disadvantaged over the European child raised in the more Temperate Zone of Europe. Male children were naturally more disadvantaged than females, since the woman's "hot blood" more readily acclimated to Saint Domingue, and they had the benefit of being able to lose menstrual blood to offset the excitation of the blood brought on by spicy food and hot weather. As the young Creole Gentleman of *My Odyssey* claims, "They possess our virtues and our vices with the modifications that belong to their sex."[32] Besides, girls and women were not supposed to be able to display the rationality and self-control of men. While the climate could cause European Creole women to lose their "freshness," while early marriage and sex, along with imprudent food choices, could sap them of vitality, Creole women were still seen as "delightful," if over-prone to torturing enslaved women.[33]

This ingrained distrust of the Creole is seen in many European colonial societies. The Creole was nourished by different food, their nature transmitted to them through the bodies of their wet nurses. They were people who were grown in a different soil with a different climatic influence and therefore were of a character that differed noticeably from the European "original." They were, simply put, colonially degenerate. The careful parent would seek to mitigate the influences of the *terroir* in which their child was conceived, often sending the mother back to France to give birth in the ancestral family lands, and procuring a wet nurse there. Others would keep their children with them until school age, then send them off to France for years or decades, to allow them to be seen as truly French, with roots that went deep into the soil of the mother country. However, according to Moreau, this seldom worked:

> Entrusted to France, to persons to whom they are strangers, or even to mercenary individuals who sell their profits at higher prices than they are worth, they (Creoles) haven't even a hope of profiting from the imperfect schooling which they get.... Bored, they count one by one

> the days passed in exile from their father's roof, and count impatiently those days that remain until the end of the term.[34]

Those Creoles who spent much of their lives in metropolitan France often took pains to establish that, even as they profited from their connection to Saint Domingue, they didn't really feel at home there. "I was astonished not to discover within me that sentiment of impatience which carries one's thoughts to the place of his birth," wrote one.[35] This determined cosmopolitanism may have served to reassure the friends of Creoles that this individual had not succumbed to degeneracy, that they were in fact still European and therefore trustworthy.

Conclusion

The repeated warnings against chili peppers and other spicy and heating foods are found throughout French colonial literature and represent more than a dietary choice. They are a clear reflection of the profound unease with the colonial project and its chances of success. The colonists, while they might become wealthy, powerful, and succeed in supplying the metropole with all of its desires, did so only by risking the very identities that allowed them to succeed. Their European natures, which eighteenth-century science claimed were the natural result of their environment, gave them an inborn right to conquer and rule, yet made them unsuited for the environments where these colonial projects were carried out.[36] However, in those places where Europeans became acclimated—whether through mixing of blood, imbibing of humors through breastmilk or food, or simply long exposure to the climate and soil of the new land—those European natures would subside. The colonial project would fail as a new people arose.

That this ethnogenesis was well underway in Saint Domingue is argued for by the recurring descriptions of European visitors, who characterize Creoles as sanguine, choleric, hot-tempered, honorable, and lascivious. It is shown by the later political acts of the European colonists, who, unable to believe that enslaved Africans could effectively organize and rise up against the colonial order, accused the *sang-mêlé* Creoles of masterminding the insurgency. The colonial European elite always believed the Creole to be essentially "other," as shown by the long retention of essentialized terms for describing Creoles after their flight from Saint Domingue to New Orleans.

The Creole consumption of spicy sauces, made with indigenous chili peppers and fermented or spoiled cane vinegar, and associated with African-derived folk heroes like Bouki and Ti Malice, was seen as accelerating the onset of colonial degeneracy and endangering the colonists' health. They were seen as a threat to the colonial system itself, since the changes in mood and character that they brought on would drive colonists further from their European roots and hasten the day when the colony could no longer be thought of as French at all.

Picklise

This is a fresh spicy pickle sauce still widely used in Haiti, found at food stalls, homes, and local restaurants. Adapted from Mona Menager, *Fine Haitian Cuisine.*

Ingredients:

4 cups of thinly shredded mirliton squash (use cabbage if mirliton is unavailable)
2 medium thinly sliced carrots (you can add any vegetable that pickles well, including bell peppers, radishes, or beets; I do not recommend tomatoes, because they change the consistency of the dish, but they are used widely in Haiti)
1 small onion or 4 shallots, thinly sliced
1–3 Bon Ma Jacques or Habanero peppers, thinly sliced or pounded to a paste
1/4 cup of Steen's Louisiana cane vinegar
1 teaspoon salt
1/8 teaspoon of ground black pepper

Method:

In a large non-reactive bowl, place mirliton squash, carrots, onions, and peppers. Toss together until well mixed.

Sprinkle cane vinegar, salt, and ground pepper over the vegetables. Mix thoroughly and set aside for one hour before serving.

Notes

1. Mirta Yurnet-Thomas, *A Taste of Haiti* (New York: Hippocrene Books. 2002), 47; Mona Cassion Menager, *Fine Haitian Cuisine* (Coconut Creek: Educa Vision, 2005).
2. While we have some evidence that enslaved individuals were discussing these issues, as is usually the case when discussing people laboring under the restrictions and deprivations of enslavement, most of the evidence of their engagement in this debate is filtered through the words and worldviews of the European colonists.
3. Georges Louis Leclerc, comte de Buffon, *Buffon's Natural history, containing a theory of the earth, a general history of man, of the brute creation, and of vegetables, minerals,*

&c. &c. From the French, with notes by the translator (London: H. D. Symonds, 1797–1807), 3:326; 4:348.

4. For an example of this thinking in Belize, see Spang, Chapter 7 in this volume.
5. Shannon Lee Dawdy, *Building the Devil's Empire: French Colonial New Orleans* (Chicago: University of Chicago Press, 2008); Nathalie Dessens, *From Saint Domingue to New Orleans: Migration and Influences* (Tallahassee: University Press of Florida, 2010).
6. François Alexandre Stanislaus Wimpffen, *A Voyage to Saint Domingo, in the Years 1788, 1789, and 1790*, trans. J. Wright (London: T. Cadell, Junior, and W. Davies, 1817), 108.
7. Barbara Voss, "What's New? Rethinking Ethnogenesis in the Archaeology of Colonialism," *American Antiquity* 80 (2015): 655.
8. Buffon, *Buffon's Natural history*, 4:350.
9. Ibid., 4:352.
10. Karol Kimberlee Weaver, *Medical Revolutionaries: The Enslaved Healers of Eighteenth-Century Saint Domingue* (Urbana: University of Illinois Press, 2006), 55.
11. Noga Arikha, *Passions and Tempers: A History of the Humours* (New York: Harper Collins, 2007), 232.
12. Weaver, *Medical Revolutionaries*, 50.
13. Ibid., 19.
14. Althea de Puech Parham, ed. and trans., *My Odyssey: Experiences of a Young Refugee from Two Revolutions by a Creole of Saint Domingue* (Baton Rouge: Louisiana State University Press 1959), 39.
15. Ibid., 24.
16. Ibid., 39.
17. Weaver, *Medical Revolutionaries*, 103.
18. Parham, *My Odyssey*, 35.
19. Buffon, *Buffon's Natural history*, 3:176.
20. Médéric Louis Élie Moreau de Saint-Méry, *A Civilization That Perished: The Last Years of White Colonial Rule in Haiti*, ed. and trans. I. D. Spencer (Lanham, MD: University Press of America, 1985), 32.
21. Ibid., 35.
22. Ibid.
23. See Charles R. Clement, William M. Denevan, Micheal J. Heckenberger, André Braga Junqueira, Eduardo G. Neves, Wenceslau G. Teixeira, and Willam I. Woods, "The Domestication of Amazonia Before European Conquest," *Proceedings of the Royal Society B: Biological Sciences* 282 (2015), 1–9; Kurt Michael Friese, Kraig Kraft, and Gary Paul Nabhan, *Chasing Chiles: Hot Spots Along the Pepper Trail* (White River Junction: Chelsea Green Publishing, 2011), 156; and Pilcher, Chapter 14 in this volume.

24. Friese, Kraft, and Nabhan, *Chasing Chiles*, 158.
25. Arikha, *Passions and Tempers*, 2007.
26. Moreau, *A Civilization That Perished*, 35; François Alexandre Stanislaus Wimpffen, *A Voyage to Saint Domingo, in the Years 1788, 1789, and 1790*, trans. J. Wright (London: T. Cadell, Junior, and W. Davies, 1817), 108.
27. "They carried a litter upon which was placed a trough, on which was a whole veal, well roasted, and gently settled on a highly seasoned salad. The aforesaid calf was split from head to tail, and this opening was elegantly tied with pink ribbons. The trough was placed before the carver of that day, who untied the ribbons. The veal was separated enough to let be seen in his flanks a sheep prepared in the same manner but tied with blue ribbons. In the mutton was an enormous turkey with green ribbons. In this turkey was a capon tied with yellow ribbons, and the capon contained as many ortolans as there were guests. Imagine our further admiration and enthusiasm when, upon opening the little birds, which were encircled with strips of bacon rind, we found favors of different colors, each containing a marinated oyster!" From Parham, *My Odyssey*, 56.
28. Alcée Fortier, *Louisiana Folktales: Lupin, Bouki, and Other Creole Stories in French Dialect and English Translation* (Lafayette: University of Louisiana at Lafayette Press, 2011). Other versions have Ti Malice fooling Bouki by placing cactus leaves into a bag and telling him the Whee-ai was inside.
29. Bryan Wagner, *The Tar Baby: A Global History* (Princeton, NJ: Princeton University Press: 2017).
30. Sarah Hrdy, *Mother Nature: A History of Mothers, Infants, and Natural Selection* (New York: Pantheon Books, 1999), 351.
31. Wimpffen, *A Voyage to Saint Domingo*, 102.
32. Parham, *My Odyssey*, 35.
33. Moreau, *A Civilization That Perished*, 31–34.
34. Ibid., 27–28.
35. Parham, *My Odyssey*, 9.
36. Rebecca Earle, *The Body of the Conquistador: Food, Race, and the Colonial Experience in Spanish America, 1492–1700* (Cambridge: Cambridge University Press, 2012).

Selected Bibliography

Buffon, Georges Louis Leclerc, comte de. *Buffon's Natural history, containing a theory of the earth, a general history of man, of the brute creation, and of vegetables, minerals, &c. &c. From the French, with notes by the translator*. London: H. D. Symonds, 1797–1807.

Earle, Rebecca. *The Body of the Conquistador: Food, Race, and the Colonial Experience in Spanish America, 1492–1700*. Cambridge: Cambridge University Press, 2012.

Menager, Mona Cassion. *Fine Haitian Cuisine*. Coconut Creek: Educa Vision, 2005.

Moreau de Saint-Méry, Médéric Louis Élie. *A Civilization That Perished: The Last Years of White Colonial Rule in Haiti*. Translated and edited by I. D. Spencer. Lanham, MD: University Press of America, 1985.

Parham, Althea de Puech, ed. and trans. *My Odyssey: Experiences of a Young Refugee from Two Revolutions by a Creole of Saint Domingue*. Baton Rouge: Louisiana State University Press, 1959.

Voss, Barbara. "What's New? Rethinking Ethnogenesis in the Archaeology of Colonialism." *American Antiquity* 80 (2015): 655–670.

Weaver, Karol Kimberlee. *Medical Revolutionaries: The Enslaved Healers of Eighteenth-Century Saint Domingue*. Urbana: University of Illinois Press, 2006.

Wimpffen, François Alexandre Stanislaus. *A Voyage to Saint Domingo, in the Years 1788, 1789, and 1790*. Translated by J. Wright. London: T. Cadell, Junior, and W. Davies, 1817.

Maureen Costura, *Hot Sauce and Colonial Degeneracy: Making of the Self in the Eighteenth-Century French Caribbean* In: *From Garum to Mole: Sauces and Identity in the Western World*. Edited by: Andrew Donnelly, Beth M. Forrest, and Deirdre Murphy, Oxford University Press.
DOI: 10.1093/9780190622138.003.0010

II

"To Change This Sauce Would Be Little Short of Heresy"

THE GEOPOLITICS OF "RANCID" OLIVE OIL IN NINETEENTH-CENTURY SPAIN

Beth M. Forrest

IN THE 1873 *Dictionary of Cuisine*, French writer Alexandre Dumas offered a menu comprising many sauce-laden dishes, including Lobster á l'Américaine, Plaice á la Sauce Normande, Mackerel Maître d'Hôtel, Sautéed Kidneys with Burgundy [sauce], Scrambled Eggs with Kidney Gravy, and Hearts of Lettuce á l'Espagnole (without oil or vinegar). Of the last he explains:

> This is a memento of Spain. There the vinegar has no bouquet, and in exchange *the oil has a rancid odour.* It is impossible, therefore, to eat salads, even when the heat and the dryness of the air give you a violent appetite for fresh, raw vegetables.
>
> Well, I took care of this by substituting yolks of eggs for the oil, and lemon juice for the vinegar. This mixture, suitably seasoned with salt and pepper, made an exquisite salad, which we finish preferring to our own French salads.[1]

Dumas's biting critique of a dressing that he flippantly names as Spanish, in which he supplants not just two ingredients of the sauce but rather the *core* two ingredients used—for reasons of bad taste—is not an isolated case of critical Iberian assessment in his book. Elsewhere, he notes that the wine in Spain is kept in goatskins "which give it an abominable flavour" and that he has traveled "much" in Spain, "where you eat badly."[2] The only acceptable sauce *á l'espagnole* then, according to this erudite observer, exists when the two ingredients in the recipe that are processed are replaced by ones that remain crude and unadulterated. In the case of a dressing for salad, vinegar and oil are exchanged with those in purely natural form, egg and lemon. Not only would these latter ingredients act as a safe substitute for the unctuousness and acidity in the sauce, but their very essence of remaining in an unrefined state emphasizes for the reader the idea that these are foodstuffs that even the Spanish cannot mismanage.

English travel writer Richard Ford, in his 1847 book, *The Spaniards and Their Country*, however, disagrees with Dumas's opinion on Spanish sauce for salad. He staunchly declares that using an egg in the dressing is simply heretical and instead instructs one to add four times the oil to a seasoned mixture of vinegar and water. Although he is in the minority, he confides that the result will be the one thing that is "truly delicious in Spain."[3] Moreover, Ford explicitly defines sauce as an embodiment of culture when he recalls a conversation he once had with a Spanish cook. "Let me smell and taste the salsa," he implored her, even as he described the sauce before her as one composed not only of "oil, wine, and nutritive juices," but also of her essence. For him, she "whose mind, body and spoon were absorbed in a single mess [meal]" was also part of the sauce.[4] To Ford, olive oil was as much as part of the sauce as the person who made it and, in this moment, oil-based sauce and its consumer enter into a cyclical relationship. This sauce becomes the expression of Spain, and those who eat it personify the sauce and the culture.

For many writers in the nineteenth century, food reflected national character and helped them to understand and explain the geopolitical situation of a nation. As these preceding characterizations reveal, though, in the case of Spain, this was particularly true with regard to sauce and, even more specifically, olive oil as the principal ingredient within sauces. To make matters more complicated, one frequent—almost rote—observation of writers in the nineteenth century was that, while olive oil was prevalent in Spain, it was also rancid. This rankness (of a natural ingredient, or what we may understand to be an economic resource against the backdrop of the Industrial Revolution) infused the food and assaulted the senses, they reported, while its very essence captured the inert character of Spain itself. The cause, it seemed, was rooted in both politics and religion. Historian Henry Charles Lea, in an 1898 *Atlantic Monthly* article, "The Decadence of Spain," argued that the downfall of the Spanish Empire, which began in the sixteenth century and culminated in the nineteenth century, was due to its "pride," "indolence," and, notably, "spirit of conservatism which rejected all innovation in a world of incessant change, a world which had been sent by the Reformation spinning on a new track, a world... in which modern industrialism was rapidly superseding the obsolescent militarism of Spain."[5] Indeed, writers buttressed these sentiments with similar cultural characterizations-cum-culinary portrayals.

Therefore, while Dumas's attitude can be understood as a continuation of French culinary exceptionalism, which had burgeoned by the early nineteenth century, his comments were emblematic of a much broader perspective. Likewise, Ford's romantic image of the rustic cook and a pre-industrial Spain was equally problematic in its construction of the intrinsic connection between culture and cuisine. As both cases suggest, olive oil in sauces became a symbol of Spanish culture and society in the nineteenth century, and the fact that it was often understood to be rancid highlighted the very essence of everything that was perceived to be wrong with Spain. Ford asserted these connections in another one of his books, the exceedingly popular 1846 *Gatherings from Spain*: "It has been said of our heretical countrymen that we have but one form of sauce—melted butter—and a hundred different forms of religion, whereas in orthodox Spain there is but one of each, and, as with religion, so to change this sauce would be little short of heresy."[6] The sauce to which Ford refers is a version of *sofrito*, which he explains consists of olive oil, garlic, red peppers, and saffron. The color of the sauce, according to Ford, is a "rich burnt umber," the same hue that he observed not only in Murillo's painting, but also Spanish clothes, Spanish houses, and Spanish wives. He continues, "This sauce has not only the same colour, but the same flavor everywhere; hence the difficulty of making out the material of which any dish is composed."[7] The sauce, the base of which is olive oil, permeates all of the food and all of the country. It is both an actual sauce and metaphorical idea of "saucing" the country.

Sauces in Spanish cuisine uniformly took olive oil as their base. So ubiquitous was olive oil as a foundation across culinary applications, and even used singularly as sauce, that at times it even became a stand-in representative for Spanish cuisine and culture. When writers foreign to Spain commented on olive oil–based sauces, or even olive oil as a sauce, they did so against the backdrop of an Industrial Revolution that was well developed in Western Europe but late in spreading to the nation. Their comments on the rancidity of the ever-present olive oil were a way of illustrating how Spanish politics and religion, perceived as decadent and rejecting progress, caused the once powerful empire to fall so swiftly and completely. This chapter aims to offer an overview of the role of olive oil as sauce by looking at traditional Spanish sauces and olive oil in historic recipes to show its ubiquity; to present how foreign writers have constructed a narrative around Spanish sauces and olive oil; and to consider the implications of this narrative against the backdrop of geopolitics in the late eighteenth and nineteenth centuries.

Olive Oil as Sauce

Sauces played a prominent role in Spanish cuisine, as the 1859 cookbook, *Tratado completo y práctico de confitería y pastelería* (The Complete and Practical Treatise of Confectionary and Pastry), published in Barcelona, notes:

> the preparation of dressings called sauces, etc.... is very useful in the kitchen sector, its preparation demands a lot of attention and in knowing how to use it with taste and opportunity, it has been the cause of what pastry chefs and cooks have enjoyed an almost immortal fame; so we gladly give principle to our culinary task, explaining the sauce.[8]

Furthermore, traveler and writer Richard Ford remarked that the cuisine of Spain was in particular need of sauce, asserting that:

> Wherever meats are bad and thin, the sauce is very important; it is based in Spain on oil, garlic, saffron, and red peppers. In hot countries, where beasts are lean, oil supplies the place of fat, as garlic does the want of flavor, while a stimulating condiment excites or curries up the coats of a languid stomach.[9]

In Ford's passage, the terms "sauce" and "condiment" are used interchangeably.[10]

In addition to olive oil being a sauce in its own right, olive oil was, and remains, the omnipresent ingredient in Spanish sauces. In the December 2015 issue of *Lucky Peach* magazine, food writer Marian Bull offers a list of regional and national Spanish sauces that serve as a loose equivalent to the more globally known French ones, promoted and codified by Carême and Escoffier, in the early nineteenth and twentieth centuries, respectively.[11] Many of these sauces appear in Spanish cookbooks in the nineteenth century, and all of them highlight the universality of olive oil, as every sauce listed includes it as an ingredient. In fact, olive oil is the only ingredient that appears in all of the sauces—eleven in total—that Bull includes. First, there are "The Building Blocks": *sofrito*, onions and tomatoes cooked in olive oil (the sauce that Ford mentions); and *picada*, a flexible combination of nuts, bread, and garlic, which are ground and fried in olive oil.

Next, she offers regional sauces of the Basque and Catalan regions: Basque sauces include *pil-pil*, made from olive oil, in which cod (typically salted) has been poached, leaving a gelatin, which is then emulsified into a sauce, while *salsa de tinta* is made by slowly poaching onion in olive oil, adding squid ink, and flavoring it with green pepper and/or tomato sauce. *Salsa verde* is another Basque sauce, in which garlic infuses olive oil, to which flour and parsley are added to make a roux, followed by fish stock (the 1850 cookbook *El Libro de cocina* includes a recipe for *salsa verde* that is a mixture of herbs with oil, vinegar, and mustard). *Salsa vizcaína* concludes the Basque sauces; it also begins with oil-poached onion, to which *choricero* (a sweet, red pepper) is added and pureed, again with green pepper and/or tomato sauce. Catalan sauces are the third category, which consists of *romesco*, a thick mixture of almonds, hazelnuts, *piquillo* peppers, olive oil, and vinegar; and *allioli*, a simpler version than the Italian one, composed of only oil, garlic, and salt.

Bull's final grouping of mother sauces are those universally found across Spain. The first, béchamel, uses butter and flour as a base in its French form. In Spain, however, the butter is commonly replaced with oil.[12] Furthermore, béchamel's most frequent use in the Spanish kitchen is when the sauce becomes the base for *croquetas*, which are then fried in oil.[13] For example, both *El Libro de cocina* (1850) and the Catalan *Tratado completo y práctico de confitería y pastelería* (1859) offer recipes for *croquetas*, the latter including *croquetas de crema*, *croquetas de sesos* (brains), and *croquetas de aves* (birds), all of which are to be fried "in very good oil, or lard."[14] The second universal sauce Bull names is *refrito de ajo*, made from frying garlic in oil and mixing the oil with vinegar (or another acid) to finish dishes. The final sauce listed is *salsa española*, a meat stock with pureed vegetables, which begins with vegetables fried in oil. *Salsa española* appears in many cookbooks of the nineteenth century, including *El Libro de las familias de cocino española, francesa y americana* (1871), although the 1854 cookbook *La Cocinera del campo y de la cuidad* calls for the use of butter and notes that this sauce is "for when you have to give a great meal," perhaps because parts of it were translated from a French edition or in an affirmation to the French culinary influence of the nineteenth century.[15]

These examples, of course, all abide by the traditional French understanding of a sauce, but if one considers the popular definition of a sauce, which is a liquid or semi-liquid substance served with food to give moisture and flavor, the possibilities are broadened. The same holds true if using the definition of the first edition of the *Oxford English Dictionary*. It defines sauce as: "Any preparation, usually liquid or soft, and often consisting of several ingredients, intended to be eaten as an appetizing accompaniment to some article of food

†Formerly occas. applied to a condiment of any kind."[16] This, then, challenges the epistemology of sauce in three areas: first, it rejects the notion that a single ingredient, albeit less common, cannot be a sauce; second, by stating that sauce is an accompaniment—meaning it is either supplementary or complements a food—does not preclude the possibility of food being served in a sauce; third, it documents that the categories of sauces and condiment historically have been used interchangeably. Therefore, the addition of olive oil to a dish can be understood in certain applications *as* a sauce, while foods served in olive oil can also be seen as being served *in* a sauce, and, when authors in the nineteenth century discuss condiments, they could very well mean sauce in our modern usage. As an article in the 1829 *The United Service Journal and Naval and Military Magazine* explains, in one Iberian recipe:

> *Take your tureen* and fill it with slices or crumbs of bread, pour over them a strong garlic soup as long as they will absorb it, and then... fill the tureen with oil! which must not be, if you wish to have a real Spanish dish, from Provence or Florence, but thick, unctuous, and rancid, and if possible, of a crimson tint, from the olives being over ripe when pressed; in default to this, to come nearer the true original relish, you may add a little of the best spermaceti from your hall lamp.[17]

The article also condemns the larger role of oil in Spanish cuisine:

> cookery may be at once condemned as *ultra-gros,* and oil and garlic must be considered in the ascendant in their culinary horoscopes: indeed these so completely overwhelm the taste of the meat, that it becomes only a vehicle for gorging these ingredients... they eat, and drink, and sleep, on *acéyte* and *ajo.*[18]

There is no question that olive oil is a sauce for the soup, providing additional moisture and an undeniable (even if questionable) flavor; it sauces the food.[19]

The 1854 *La Cocinera del campo y de la ciudad* includes the recipe "*Carne de vaca cocida, al aceite,*" which was served with "*una salsa hechas al aceite,*" or beef cooked in a sauce made with oil; "*Pernil asado,*" for which pork is marinated in salt, pepper, and olive oil with sage and good quality vine wine (from Malaga or Madeira) for two to three days; and an "Exquisite Salmorejo" that is finished with olive oil before serving.[20] The 1848 *Novisimo manual de cocinero* includes Cantabrian sardines that are preserved in oil (to be eaten they are put to the fire with crayfish). After plating, they are drizzled with fine oil and garnished with chopped pickles and capers.[21] "Cooked vegetable salad or Macedonian vegetables with oil" from the same cookbook illustrates the use of oil as a finishing sauce on vegetable salads, raw and cooked alike.[22] Fried artichokes use olive oil twice, as a cooking medium and as part of a sauce, according to a recipe in the 1854 *Novisimo diccionario-manual del arte de cocina*.[23] In all of these cases, olive oil is the emblematic sauce of Spanish cuisine. William Davidson, in his 1843 *A Treatise on Diet*, is unequivocal that olive oil was a sauce in and of itself. He explicitly states, "[olive] oil is chiefly employed as a sauce or condiment in dressing fish, salad, &c..." as well as being a substitute for butter.[24] Notice that he does not say that it is an ingredient *in* the sauce or condiment, but rather its role is *as* a sauce. Davidson's assertion that olive oil can be a stand-alone sauce also appears earlier, in Charles Gibbon's *A New Family Encylopædia* of 1831. These examples all support the historic understanding of sauce.

Olive-oil-as-sauce can go one step further in the context of nineteenth-century gastronomic writing. In contemporary observation of Spanish cuisine by non-Spaniards, writers consistently describe Spanish dishes as oleaginous and rancid; both, they argued, could be attributed to the pervasive presence of olive oil. If the culinary definition of sauce is to give moisture and flavor to a dish, then olive oil in nineteenth-century Spain can, indeed, be culturally understood as saucing the nation. Both moisture and flavor (meaning aroma or odor), after all, also occur outside of the mouth and eating and are present in the broader environment of a place and people.[25] It represents a cuisine and the individuals who chose to eat that food. On the frontispiece of *Novisimo diccionario-manual del arte de cocina*, the book is promoted as written by a "discipline of Brillat-Savarin," further suggesting that, indeed, the book is not only about recipes, but that the recipes communicate ideas about the people who eat the food. In the case of Spain, the narratives centered on olive oil are but one way "to consider the affective nature of 'Othering' through sensual descriptors of disgust, whether it be aroma or taste, for the senses are not apolitical."[26]

A Rank Country

The reason for olive oil's culinary omnipresence within sauces and as a sauce itself stems from the vast cultivation of olives in Spain. The 1851 Spanish text, *Instruccion para el pueblo: Cien tratado*, under the heading "Oleaginous Plants," states, "But in ours, where such an amount of olive trees exists and so much is the abundance of the fruit that they give, is the true oil, the olive oil, at such a comfortable price that hardly any other could hardly be sold."[27] By the mid-eighteenth century, small-scale peasant producers dominated olive production and, rather than planned orchards, the trees grew in scattered groves, as part of subsistence farming and living.[28]

This marked presence of olive oil in Spain did not go unnoticed by English and American travelers to Spain in the late eighteenth to mid-nineteenth centuries. William Jacob, merchant and parliamentarian, observed that even the wheat fields surrounding Seville were intermixed with olive trees.[29] One traveler writing in 1840 under the *nom de plume* XYZ, upon arriving in Andalucía noted that on "the richer and more fertile land" were "large olive plantations."[30] British travel writer G. A. Hoskins, in his *Spain, as it is* (1852), mentions passing olive farms on his way to Alcalá de Guadaira, observing olive groves around Valencia and Callbató and that the hills approaching Ronda were covered with olive trees.[31] Caroline Cushing, wife of the U.S. ambassador to Spain, reported that one of many olive groves in Bailén contained 60,000 trees.[32]

Travelers also noted the use of olive oil in Spanish cuisine. Jacob, in his letters documenting his travels through the south of Spain in 1809–1810, remarked that olive oil "answers the purpose of butter."[33] Cushing relates that while staying at an inn in Burgos, both meat and vegetable were fried in oil and kept in earthenware pots of oil. British writer George John Cayley, in his mid-nineteenth-century trip to Spain, was served eggs fried in oil and *migas* ("bread-crumbs steeped in water and sprinkled with salt, with hot oil poured over it in which a little bit of garlic has been boiled") for breakfast. He also had a much more tempered evaluation of it:

> The English have a strange unfounded prejudice against oil, and in favour of butter, which is as near as possible the same thing, only that oil is a clean, pure, vegetable fat, which keeps better, and is infinitely easier to have than good butter.... Butter is not good after three days' keeping; and accordingly is much oftener eaten bad than good. Nevertheless, good butter is a good thing; and we eat it, because we know it to be so.... But of oil, from unfamiliarity, we have an abhorrence.[34]

Travelogues published during this time commonly reveal the presence not just of olive oil but rancid oil.[35] For example, Robert Maccoun, in his article "Journeyings in Spain in 1852" printed in *The Knickerbocker*, remarked that:

> The Spanish *cuisine* is really execrable. Every article placed before you is stewed, and strongly impregnated with rancid oil, garlic, saffron, and red pepper; and the newly-arrived stranger, whose stomach is unaccustomed to such high-flavored condiments, is obliged to fall back upon boiled eggs, bread, and cheese.[36]

Cushing notes, "the oil is often extremely old and rancid. Indeed they [the Spanish] generally prefer the rancid oil to the sweet, as they say they are enabled to perceive the taste more sensibly."[37] T. Adolphus Trollope noted in an 1848 letter that, of the many tourists who travel to Bayonne, France, few will travel across the Pyrenees, due to their imagination of Spain as "a land exclusively peopled by sanguinary banditti, living wholly on rancid oil and garlic."[38] The influence of olive oil, however, went far beyond the table. XYZ suffered from the "noxious aromas that engulfed the entire Spanish capital city. According to our author's estimation, the air in Madrid was composed of the usual oxygen, hydrogen, and nitrogen but here there were also equal parts of rancid olive oil and garlic."[39] Rancid olive oil was not simply the aroma of Spanish sauces, or even Spanish cuisine more broadly. For our anonymous traveler, it was the aroma of Spain itself.

These comments were hardly limited to dilettante travelers. Well-regarded horticulturalist Arthur Young, in his 1802 *Gleanings from Books on Agriculture and Gardening*, differentiated olives not according to specific varieties but to place: Provence olives were the "best kind for pickling, and for making of oil," the Italian olive "produces, in warm seasons, some fruit in England," olives from the Cape of Good Hope were "a hardy sort," while the Spanish olive "makes rank flavored oil."[40] In the case of Spain, however, it is unclear whether the rankness stemmed from the olive or the oil-making process. A few years later, an English military surgeon in the Spanish service, Henry Milburne, writing about the British in Spain during the Napoleonic War, even felt the need to include commentary on the Spanish cuisine with a scathing critique saying, "As to their cookery, nothing can possibly be more disgusting to an English palate, most of their favourite dishes being seasoned with articles, amongst which, garlic and rancid oil generally compose."[41]

Oleaginous Spain

British government minister James Busby, better known for introducing the grape-vine to Australia, toured Spain and France in 1825. While on the continent, he remarked on the use of olive oil in the Mediterranean kitchen as a condiment. He also acutely perceived cultural attitudes toward the aesthetics of olive oil:

> Oil is the almost universal substitute for every purpose to which butter is applied with us, and milk is seldom or never used. There are, perhaps, few prejudices stronger than that of the English against the general use of oil, which they are accustomed to consider as a very gross kind of condiment; and perhaps there is no prejudice more unfounded. For surely the pure vegetable juice of the olive is far from being inferior, in delicacy, to butter, the animal fat of the cow; and there can be no doubt, that oil is also more wholesome and congenial to the human constitution, in a hot climate, than the latter. This district [Roussillion in South-east France] is not celebrated for the quality of its oil, but they do not, as in Spain, consider rancidity a merit.[42]

Busby's observations are particularly insightful due to his background in viniculture and viticulture. In his earlier book, *A Treatise on the Culture of the Vine, and the Art of Making Wine* (1825), he reveals himself to be a connoisseur who has an intimate understanding of the integral role of the senses in detecting slight differences, in particular regarding aroma. His interest in organoleptic qualities continues with an investigation of the environmental and cultural influences that impact such distinctions between foods and wines. While this may seem benign, it is not.

Goût de terroir or "Taste of Place," as Amy Trubek has argued, is the combination of three interlocking ideas surrounding the particular taste and flavor of certain food and drink as tied to a location: the influence of the physical environment, in this case, the soil and climate that allows olive trees to prosper in the Mediterranean; the cultural environment, or the role/impact that people have throughout the entire process of making a product; and the belief, that the end-product is unique and/or special from other similar foodstuffs.[43] Notably, the concept of *goût de terroir* surfaced during the same time period under discussion, in French author Le Grand d'Aussy's *Histoire de la vie privée des français* (1789) and reiterated by Brillat-Savarin in his *La physiologie du goût* (1826), among others. The writers both captured and shared the ephemerality of taste through their texts while promoting the connection of taste (biology) and "Taste" (aesthetics) with agricultural practices and place.[44] Typically, however, people understand *terroir* in relation to unique foodstuffs in rural France and are framed as positive attributes.

In the case of Spain and its nineteenth-century olive oil, conversely, *goût de terroir* offers a scathing commentary on poor farming, the bad taste of the culture in which is it produced, and the poor quality of the final product. For example, as the 1855 *Encyclopædia of Domestic Economy* (a guide to all topics tied to households) explains, it is the human element that most impacts the final product:

> Much depends, not only on the quality of the fruit, but also on its being exactly in the proper degree of maturity; if not sufficiently ripe, the oil has a bitterish taste; if too ripe, the oil is fatty. After the oil has been expressed, it is necessary that it be separated from the mucilaginous matter that accompanies it.... If it be immediately put carefully into clean glass flasks, and secured from the air, it undergoes no farther change. The common oil put into casks cannot be preserved above a year and a half or two years.... But a contamination of a pernicious kind by lead is said to occur from its having been kept in leaden cisterns, either in Spain, where this is practiced, or in this country [United States]. Good olive oil should be inodorous, insipid, soft, and agreeable in the mouth.[45]

English pharmacologist Jonathan Pereira notes that olive oil, or sweet oil, is "an unctuous fluid, of a pale yellow or greenish-yellow colour. When of good quality, it has scarcely any smell. Its taste is bland and mild." He also declares that of all the European olive oils, "Spanish oil is the worst."[46]

The 1851 *Official Illustrated Catalogue* of the World's Fair, held at London's Crystal Palace, documented the ten Spanish olive oils that were on display for the exhibition, and specifically explains that it is "almost a universal condiment with her people," except:

> the oils of Spain are more celebrated for their abundance than for their quality; but this circumstance is the result, exclusively, of the methods of their fabrication, which are kept up by the taste of the people—fond of mucilage—and by the dearness of all the means of land carriage.[47]

The entry continues with confidence, "[b]ut nothing would be more easy than for the Spanish oil producers to obtain good clarified oil, without any mucilaginous or empyreumatic [smoky/burnt] flavor."[48] British merchant William Jacob also commented that the delay between harvesting the olives and pressing them causes "great detriment" to the color of the oil.[49] While all of the organoleptic qualities are evaluated, the most prevalent commentary on Spanish olive oil focuses on taste, in particular its bitterness, and flavor (which is primarily from aroma), the latter of which would include rancidity.[50] Traditional positive attributes of olive oil, namely "fruitiness," derives from the natural state of the olive, the variety of drupe (stone fruit) grown, or the blending of different olive varietals. This was true in the nineteenth century, where several publications on exhibitions, including the 1851 World's Fair and the United States International Exhibition of 1876, offer commendations to olive oil producers (both Spanish entries as well as other nations) for their fruity flavor.[51]

The negative attributes, however, are most often linked to the processing of the olives into oil, both when they are processed and the processing method, as well as the storage of the olive oil after processing. In the nineteenth century, most writers did not malign the quality of the Spanish olive (with the notable exception of Arthur Young), which largely negates the possibility that environmental factors poorly impacted the quality of the final product. In fact, several writers praised Spanish olives, perhaps most notably in French politician and writer Alexandre Louis J. Laborde's text in *A View of Spain*, translated and published in 1809. He wrote:

> Spanish *olives* are generally excellent in their flavour; but there are gradations in this excellence. Those of Aragon are sweeter than those of Catalonia; and those of New Castile surpass both. The olives grown in the kingdom of Valencia are the most beautiful and large, and containing less oil are more agreeable to the palate. Those of Estepa, in the kingdom of Seville, are very small; but they afford a very fine and delicate oil: those again in the vicinity of Seville are as large as pigeon's eggs; but of very inferior quality to the preceding, and afford a smaller quantity of oil: yet they are preferable for eating after they have been well seasoned.... Those grown in the districts of Alcala and Guadayra, in the kingdom of Seville, are larger and finer than any in Europe, and the best adapted for pickling.[52]

Because olives begin to deteriorate as soon as they are harvested, immediate pressing reduces both oxidation (tied to rancidity) and fermentation or rotting, causing fustiness. Ideally, pressing will occur within 24 hours of harvesting olives, and not more than 36 hours. Correct storage of oil, away from sunlight, and relatively immediate consumption also limit oxidation. This oxidation either before pressing or after processing causes rancidity. In many cases, it appears that, in nineteenth-century Spanish olive oil production, the delay before pressing most severely impacted the oil's flavor. Busby reported that olives sat for a full fifteen days between harvesting and processing, which was nothing compared to a report in the 1913 issue of *American Medicine*:

> The olives of Spain are magnificent fruit, but the methods employed by the natives result in a coarsened, almost rancid product. The Spanish method is to pile the olives up and leave in a heap to decay for six months or more before pressed. This suits the National taste for strong, rancid oil.[53]

Looking at writings across the nineteenth century, then, it was most likely the oxidation caused by the delay in milling the olives that led to rancidity. William Jacob, writing a full century earlier, in 1809–1810, had also promoted this assessment, writing:

> The oil of Spain, however, is much less pure than that of France and Italy, though the fruit from which it is made, is greatly superior. This inferiority arises principally from the length of time the olives are kept, piled in heaps, before they are ground, whence, in this warm country, they ferment and become in some degree putrid.[54]

The same issue also appeared in British pharmacist and botanist Benjamin Maund's 1825 book, *The Botanic Garden*, and was oft-repeated: "Spanish olive oil, however, is inferior to other kinds, from the circumstance of the time which elapses between the gathering and the grinding of the olives."[55] According to Sir John Talbot Dillon, storage was also an issue, "from their little care in putting it into proper vessels, and carrying it about the country in skins, the oil in general is wretchedly bad" so much so that "such thin fermented matter hardly [is] deserving the name of oil."[56]

Collectively, then, the evaluation of Spanish olive oil and the reason for its perceived deficiencies illustrates an underlying narrative in which the natural bounty is good but man's labors negatively impact it. This understanding of the cultural influence on a foodstuff very much extends and complicates the second component of *terroir* by considering the adverse influence of human action (or in this case, inaction).

In *A Complete System of Modern Geography; or, the Natural and Political History of the Present State of the World* (1816), Irish-educated Francis Ennis surveys the universe, before considering continents and nations more specifically. While the emphasis is on the landscape of a nation, he—not surprisingly—considers the human interaction and activity within the nation. Here the intersection of environment, culture, and judgment can be seen. After speaking to the Spaniards' positive attributes, in which he suggested that they have a natural dignity and are full of rectitude, Ennis reported that they are:

> exceedingly slow—they lose the opportunity at hand by devoting to the deliberation the time which should be actively employed. Lazy—whole regions which might be productively cultivated are disregarded while thousands of able hands, like the animals for whom nature provides without toil, lie baking in the sun, and are called to work only by actually necessity. Bigoted and superstitious—the [*sic*] bear unchristian enmity to those who differ from them on the principles of religion.[57]

This moral construct of inertia and strict religious orthodoxy as tied to sensorial qualities of olive oil in Spain—especially rancidity in this case—happened at a crucial moment in history. First, beginning in the mid-eighteenth century and taking hold across the nineteenth, European and American upper- and middle-class culture shifted in its attitude toward the sense of smell. At its most benign, olfaction was simply " 'silenced' in modernity," but a more extreme view tied unpleasant odors to disease and sickness, which included "moral and mental degeneracy."[58] Since most contemporary writers discussed rancid olive oil in relation to the Spanish as one homogenous group, the commentary gains greater consequence, in that the rancidity of olive oil was understood as a larger cultural deficit. Returning to the unknown travel writer, XYZ, writing in 1840:

> On inquiring into the reason of the oil [in Spain] being so offensive, (for the olives are plenty in the warmer districts, and excellent in quality), we were told there were not presses enough in the country, and that heaps of olives lay therefore waiting their turn, till they become rancid. What a tale of inertness and apathy did this trifling explanation tell! At all events, the Spaniards now from long habit, like the article thus produced, and would not willingly, I believe, exchange it for better; and,—though I do not join in the sentiment of the propounder [*sic*] of the "*de gustibus nil disputandum*," being of opinion that tastes and dispositions *are* both disputable and important,—I would leave

> them their garlic and oil in peace, if I found food for eulogy in more important points.[59]

This attitude was not restricted to olive oil itself; rather, olive oil became a tangible example of Spanish inferiority. It is here that the association of rancid olive oil with Spain becomes most problematic: the sensorial offenses of rancidity intersect with a simultaneous development, the Industrial Revolution. Spain lagged behind both England and the United States in introducing efficient models of production. Jacob explains:

> The right of possessing an olive mill is a feudal privilege belonging to the lords of particular manors, and to such mills all the olives grown in the district, often a very extensive one, are obliged to be carried. Here they remain in heaps, waiting their turn to be ground, from October and November, when they are gathered, till the month of January, and sometimes February, and consequently become rancid, to the great detriment both of the colour and the flavour of the oil. The stones of the olive produce some oil, which is equally transparent with that of the pulp, but of a more acrid flavour; and as the farmers are anxious to produce as large a quantity as they can, the two kinds are mixed, by which means the whole becomes tainted.[60]

Indolent Oil

The senses, which included the biological sense of taste and the cultural attitudes toward "Taste" (as part of aesthetics), reflected individual attitudes toward food choice and collective sensibilities toward national cuisine. The field of gastronomy that blossomed in the early nineteenth century asserted that people are a reflection of the food that they eat. Since olive oil serves as a base for sauces and Spanish cuisine, it was representative of the Spanish people. If it was rancid, so too were the Spanish.

Taken altogether, however, published discussions of the rancid olive oil that was used as sauce or in sauces in early nineteenth-century Spain extend beyond gastronomic or even national sensibilities. Rather, they overlap with larger political discourses on political economy, industrialization, and nation-state-building. Spain, in the sixteenth century, had ruled over an empire with lands that extended to the Americas, East Indies, and the Spanish Netherlands, and included as well control over the Portuguese Empire from 1580 to 1640. Along with this vast amount of land and people, the influx of riches back to

Spain had been unprecedented. Yet, by 1808 Napoleon was ruling over Spain, and by 1825, most colonies in the Americas had gained their independence, including Mexico and Peru. The once affluent nation's economy sharply declined by the seventeenth century and lagged behind Western Europe well into the nineteenth century.

Late eighteenth- and nineteenth-century scholars tended to take two parallel approaches in explaining the economic and political decline of Spain. First, historians critiqued the nation as being apathetic toward both agriculture and commerce, often suggesting the role of Catholicism in creating such a position. For example, Scot William Robertson in his *History of America* argues that "the enormous and expensive fabric of their ecclesiastical establishment... greatly retarded progress of population and industry."[61] This attitude became a prevailing understanding of Spanish society in the United States, as well. The 1793 *American Universal Geography*, used in classrooms across the United States, wrote that "not only [were the Spanish] 'bigoted Catholics' subject to 'despotic monarchy' but lazy, indolent people prone to 'the practice of every vice.'"[62] William Prescott, one of the most illustrious American historians of the nineteenth century and a specialist in Spanish history, assigned particular blame to Philip II (r. 1556–1598), whose religious zealousness and political despotism obstructed Spain's advancement into the modern world. Prescott understood Philip's policies as hindering the "individual enterprise" that would cause a prosperous nation. Yet Philip's death did not usher in much change.[63] Indeed, the entry "Olive Oil" in the 1844 *Dictionary, Practical, Theoretical, and Historical, of Commerce and Commercial Navigation*, explains:

> The machinery employed in expressing the oil is of the rudest kind, and no doubt, numerous improvements might be introduced, not only into this branch, but into that of cultivating the olive tree. The peasantry, however, and... those who stand higher in the scale of fortune and rank, are too often but boors in intellect, are obstinate in their attachment to old practices.[64]

A second explanation given for the backwardness of Spanish economics and politics comes from romantic writers who appear more positively inclined toward the Spanish. They, conversely, praised its traditional and rural economy, picturesque landscape, and exotic people, but still retained a strong and negative assessment of its religious and political institutions. Richard Ford, writing about Spanish peasants milling grain for bread, suggests that an

English traveler may see the scene as poetic. But his Spanish companion, "bred and born under unshorn beams, is chilly as an icicle, indifferent as an Arab: he passes on the other side, not only not admiring, but positively ashamed; he only sees the barbarity, antiquity, and imperfect process; he is sighing for some patent machine made in Birmingham."[65] This "othering," a blend of orientalist and medievalist assumptions, promoted the idea that it was Spain's history—Arab, Muslim, absolute, Catholic; that is, *Spanish*—that had caused its present condition: old, stale, rancid. The very essence of both Spanish olive oil and national character were products of place and culture.

Geopolitical Sauce

By the late eighteenth century, the spirit of innovation had impacted olive oil producers in France, Italy, and Portugal with the replacement of beam presses with mechanical mills. This change sped the production and ended traditional practices of letting olives ferment between harvesting and milling. Older olives had been thought to produce more oil, as well as being easier to mill, but industry reformers sought to alter the mindset of farmers. They aimed to change the nature of the olive oil that was produced as well as the method, which, they argued, was actually less expensive, more efficient, and produced more oil.[66] In addition, this low acidity olive oil was clearer, sweeter, and easier to preserve. Coupled with the quick production after harvest, mechanically processed olives reduced the rancidity and made the olive oil more valuable in both industrial applications and on the dining table.

These changes were late in coming to Spain. The hydraulic olive oil press was not introduced there until 1833, with large-scale modernization not occurring until the late nineteenth century.[67] Even after the presses were introduced, Spain lacked the infrastructure to efficiently transport the heavy machinery to where it would be needed. Finally, James Busby, our previously mentioned British government minister and viticulturalist, noted that good olive oil could be made in Spain, but "[t]he fine oil produced by the Marquis [del Arco Hermoso, who had adopted the Florentine method of making oil] is not relished by his country men; they say it has no taste, and prefer the rancid oil which they have been accustomed to use."[68]

For American farmers and horticulturalists in the new republic of the United States, as well as for the English, the search for an oil (or fat) that was suitable for many industrial uses was of particular concern in the nineteenth century. Olive oil was increasingly seen as a commodity, and harnessing it could strengthen both personal wealth and the national economy.

Myriad authors wrote about this, including John Locke in his 1679 treatise *Observations upon the Growth and Culture of Vines and Olives; The Production of Silk; The Preservation of Fruits* (reprinted in 1766) and Peter Chazotte in his 1821 treatise *Facts and Observations on the Culture of Vines, Olives, Capers, Almonds, &c. in the Southern States.*[69] Thomas Jefferson also praised olive cultivation in a 1787 letter, noting that the price of olive oil "is equivalent to many pounds of flesh by the quantity of vegetables it will prepare and render fit and comfortable food." He continued, "Having been myself an eyewitness to the blessings which this tree sheds on the poor, I never had my wishes so kindled for the introduction of any article of new culture into our own country."[70] Jefferson's commentary was entirely about the olive oil production in France and Italy.

Therefore, it was both manufacturing as well as a culinary demand for quality olive oil that tied discussions of political economy to olive oil. In particular, British and Americans were in pursuit of an oil to replace melted lard for a gustatorial fashion of the time: fresh salad.[71] England had adopted fresh salads during the previous century, as noted by the publication of John Evelyn's 1699 *Acetaria: A Discourse of Sallets*, which was reprinted in 1825 in *The Miscellaneous Writings of John Evelyn.* In it, he writes that for the dressing one must have "the oyl, an Ingredient so indispensably and highly necessary... with an eye rather of a pallid olive green, without smell, or the lease touch of rancid, or indeed of any other sensible taste or scent at all."[72]

Indeed, in 1854 *The Favourite*, a collection of miscellaneous essays and short stories, also included recipes, among them Richard Ford's "Spanish Salad." The composition of the "sauce," as they called the dressing, metaphorically draws on a Spanish proverb. Four people were needed; a "spendthrift for oil," "a miser for vinegar," "a counsellor [*sic*; and sometimes written as statesman] for salt," and, to stir it up, a "madman."[73] It is perhaps no coincidence that the proverb includes references to economics, politics, and a madman, who in Voltaire's definition is one with a "malady which necessarily hinders a man from thinking and acting like other men."[74]

Spain, unlike the rest of Western Europe, was an empire fallen. Its decimated economy was understood to be the result of absolute rulers, a free-spending church, and lazy citizens, while other nations (in particular, the United States and England) saw themselves as prospering through industriousness and thrift. The very essence of rancid olive oil that appeared so prominently in Spanish sauces was understood to be a tangible manifestation of everything wrong with Spain in the nineteenth century. Rancid olive oil, the sauce of Spain, flavored cuisine, country, and people. Yet, if the contemporary historians and writers on Spanish cuisine were to comment as to why rancid oil remained commonplace, they may very well have argued that for the Spanish to change this sauce, it indeed would be—for the Spanish themselves—heresy.

Recipe for Spanish Salad

From Richard Ford's 1847 book *The Spaniards and Their Country*.[75]

Take lettuce, or whatever salad is to be got; do not cut it with a steel knife, which turns the edges of the wounds black, and communicates an evil flavor; let the leaf be torn from the stem, [and] throw [it] away as it is hard and bitter. [Wash and dry the lettuce.] Take a small bowl, put in equal quantities of vinegar and water, a teaspoonful of pepper and salt, and four times as much oil as vinegar and water, mix the same well together; prepare in a plate whatever fine herbs can be got, especially tarragon and chervil, which must be chopped small. Pour the sauce over the salad, powder it with these herbs, and lose no time in eating.

Notes

1. Alexandre Dumas, *Dictionary of Cuisine*, ed. Louis Colman (New York: Avon Books, 1958), 160. My italics.
2. Ibid., 17.
3. Richard Ford, *The Spaniards and Their Country* (New York: Wiley and Putnam, 1847), 134.
4. Ibid., 132.
5. Henry Charles Lea, "The Decadence of Spain," *Atlantic Monthly* (July 1898), 37.
6. Richard Ford, *Gatherings from Spain* (London: John Murray, 1846), 120.
7. Ibid., 120.
8. C. P. y A., *Tratadó completo y práctico de confiteria y pasteleria* (Barcelona: Imprenta y Libreria Politécnica de Tomás Gorchs, 1859), 318. "La confeccion de los aderezos llamados salsas, etc. es de mucha utilidad en el ramo de cocina, su preparacion exige mucha atencion y en el saberlos emplear con gusto y oportunidad, ha sido causa de qu cuchos pasteleros y cocineros hayan gozado una fama casi inmortal; así es que damos con gusto principio á nuesta tarea culinaria esplicando las salsa."
9. Ford, *Gatherings from Spain*, 120.
10. Indeed, many examples of using the terms "sauces" and "condiments" interchangeably, or sauce being understood to be a type of condiment, appear during this time period. In an ad for Lea and Perrins's sauce, the ad reads "Worcestershire sauce. This delicious condiment" (*The Medical Times and Gazette* 1866, 33).

11. Marian Bull, "The Mother Sauces of Spain." *Lucky Peach*. December 3, 2015. https://web.archive.org/web/20160306234000/http://luckypeach.com/the-mother-sauces-of-spain/.
12. Alicia Rios, "Olive Oil, Balsamic Medium," in *Oxford Symposium on Food & Cookery: The Cooking Medium*, ed. Tom Jaine (London: Prospect Books, 1986), 101–110.
13. Roden writes that croquettes made "with ham, chicken, salt cod, and seafood, or even cheese—are served in every tapas bar and restaurant." Her recipe calls for either sunflower or olive oil for deep-frying them. Claudia Roden, *The Food of Spain* (New York: Harper Collins, 2011), 166.
14. C.P. y A., *Tratado completo y práctico de confiteria y pasteleria*, 346–347.
15. Lara Anderson, *Cooking Up the Nation: Spanish Culinary Texts and Culinary Nationalization in the Late Nineteenth and Early Twentieth Century* (Suffolk, UK: Boydell & Brewer, 2013), 15–41.
16. Henry Bradley, *New English Dictionary*, Vol. 8 (Oxford: Oxford University Press, 1914), 182.
17. "A Hussar's Life on Service," *The United Service Journal and Naval and Military Magazine*, Vol. 1 (London: H. Colburn, 1829), 571.
18. Ibid., 571.
19. Food historian Alicia Ríos argues that olive oil is the "medium" of Spanish cuisine, meaning the substance through which sensory impressions are realized. It is used for basting, the pouring of a liquid/sauce over roasted dishes, and baked fish. Grilled meats are seared first in olive oil before grilling. Furthermore, olive oil is drizzled over gazpacho before serving and used to dress cold salads and warm vegetables. This was true in the nineteenth century as well. "Olive Oil, Balsamic Medium," 101–110.
20. *La Cocinera del campo y de la ciudad ó nueva cocinera económica* (Madrid: Don F. de P. Mellado, 1854), 40, 58–59.
21. Jacobo Berenguer de Mongat, *Novísimo Manual de Cocinero: Arte de La Nueva Cocina, Puesto al alcance de toda clase de personas* (parte segunda) (Barcelona: De la V. É H de Mayol, 1848), 110–111.
22. Ibid., 120–121. The roux-based sauces call for butter or grease, at a time when French food was seen as the gastronomic pinnacle of haute cuisine and on many of the suggested menus the authors suggest fresh butter on the table as well as the frequent call for olives. "Ensalada de legumbres cocidas ó macedonia de legumbres con aceite."
23. *Novisimo diccionario-manual del arte de cocina* (segunda edicion) (Barcelona: Libreria de Casimiro Miralles, 1854), 11–12. In a modern experiment for Serious Eats, a website that uses science to explain cooking, artichokes were fried in olive oil and the neutral canola oil. The tasters wholly agreed that the olive oil imparted a distinct flavor, although when pan-searing a meat with olive oil and serving with a sauce, the flavor was much less perceptible. https://www.seriouseats.com/2015/03/cooking-with-olive-oil-faq-safety-flavor.html/.
24. William Davidson, *A Treatise on Diet, Comprising the Natural History, Properties, Composition, Adulterations and Uses of the Vegetables, Animals, Fishes, &c. Used as Food* (London: John Churchill, 1843), 208.

25. Barbara Stuckey, in *Taste: Surprising Stories and Science About Why Food Tastes Good* (New York: Atria, 2012), argues that flavor is a combination of taste, aroma, and texture/mouthfeel, although more often flavor is seen as the equivalent to aroma. See Davide Panagia, *The Political Life of Sensation* (Durham, NC: Duke University Press, 2009).
26. Beth Forrest, "'A Tealess, Beerless, Beefless Land': Sensing and Tasting Spain in Late Eighteenth and Nineteenth-Century British Travelogues," in *Space, Taste and Affect: Atmospheres That Shape the Way We Eat,* ed. Emily Falconer (New York: Routledge, 2020), 95.
27. *Instruction para el pueblo: Cien tratado* (Madrid: Establecimiento Topografico de Mellado, 1851), 2389. "Mas en el nuestro, en donde tal cantidad de olivos existe y tanta es la abundancia del fruto que dan, se halla el verdadero aceite, el aceite de oliva, á un precio tan cómodo, que dificilmente podria venderse mas barato ninguno otro."
28. Juan Infante-Amate, "The Ecology and History of the Mediterranean Olive Grove: The Spanish Great Expansion, 1750–2000," *Rural History* 23 (2012): 161–184. Furthermore, olive oil for consumption was not the only product obtained by the olive tree, but rather it supplied a range of usable products, from light oil and pomace oil (which includes tiny fragments of pits, skin, and flesh) to firewood to olive leaves to be used as animal fodder. Busby reports that a decent yield from an olive tree is 3–4 *fanegas* (or Spanish bushel) each, an estimated 55.5 liters of olives, and, when pressed, produces 4.5 gallons of oil. James Busby, *Journal of a Recent Visit to the Principal Vineyards of Spain and France* (London: Smith, Elder and Cornhill, 1834), 30.
29. William Jacob, *Travels in the South of Spain: In Letters A.D. 1809 and 1810* (London: J. Johnson and Co., 1811), 125.
30. XYZ, *Spain, Tangier, etc. Visited in 1840 and 1841* (London: Samuel Clarke, 1845), 187.
31. George Alexander Hoskins, *Spain, as It Is*, Vol. 1 (Paris: A. and W. Galignani and Co., 1852), 113.
32. Caroline Cushing, *Letters, Descriptive of Monuments, Scenery, and Manners in France and Spain*, Vol. II (Newburyport: E. W. Allen & Co., 1832), 185.
33. Jacob, *Travels in the South of Spain*, 149.
34. George Cayley, *Las Alforjas* (London: Richard Bentley, 1853), 68–69.
35. Carrie Evangeline Farnham also notes the prevalence of this commentary, saying, "The rancid oil and garlic gave no little annoyance," *American Travellers in Spain: The Spanish Inns, 1776–1867* (New York: Columbia University Press, 1921), 34.
36. Robert Maccoun, "Journeyings in Spain in 1852," *The Knickerbocker*, February 1853, 98–99.
37. Cushing, *Letters, Descriptive of Monuments, Scenery, and Manners in France and Spain*, Vol. II, 37.
38. Adolphus Trollope, *Impressions of a Wanderer in Italy, Switzerland, France, and Spain* (London: Henry Colburn, 1850), 321.

39. XYZ, *Spain, Tangier, etc.*, 102.
40. Arthur Young, *Gleanings from Books on Agriculture and Gardening*, 2nd ed. (London: W. Smith, 1802), 272.
41. Henry Milburne, *A Narrative of Circumstances Attending the Retreat of the British Army Under the Command of the Late Lieut. Gen. Sir. John Moore* (London: T. Egerton, 1809), 100–101.
42. Busby, *Journal of a Recent Visit to the Principal Vineyards of Spain and France*, 72.
43. Amy Trubek, *The Taste of Place: A Cultural Journey into Terroir* (Berkeley: University of California Press, 2009).
44. Ibid., 21–22; Priscilla Parkhurst Ferguson, "A Cultural Field in the Making: Gastronomy in 19th Century France," *American Journal of Sociology* 104, no. 3 (1998): 597–641.
45. Thomas Webster and Mrs. William Parker, *An Encylopædia of Domestic Economy* (New York: Harper & Brothers, 1855), 468.
46. Jonathan Pereira, *The Elements of Materia Medica, or Pharmacology, and General Therapeutics*, Vol. IV, pt. 1 (London: Longman, Brown, Green, and Longmans, 1855), 667.
47. Robert Ellis, *Official Descriptive and Illustrated Catalogue of the Great Exhibition of the Works of Industry of All Nations*, 1851, Vol. III (London: W. Clowes and Sons, 1851), 1339.
48. Ibid.
49. Jacob, *Travels in the South of Spain*, 150.
50. Stuckey also describes the aroma of rancidity as akin to waxy crayons.
51. *International Exhibition, 1876 Reports and Rewards*, Vol. IV, ed. Francis Walker (Washington, DC: Government Printing Office, 1880), 262–276.
52. Alexandre Laborde, *A View of Spain*, Vol IV (London: Longman, Hurst, Rees, and Orme, 1809), 94.
53. "Olive Oil, the Oil of a Thousand Values," *American Medicine* 19 (1913): 454.
54. Jacob, *Travels in the South of Spain*, 150.
55. Jonathan Pereira, "Lectures on Materia Medica, or Pharmacology, and General Therapeutics," *London Medical Gazette* 20, no. 10 (1837): 376.
56. John Dillon, *Travels Through Spain* (London: R. Baldwin, 1782), 343.
57. Francis Ennis, *A Complete System of Modern Geography; or, the Natural and Political History of the Present State of the World* (Dublin: James Charles, 1816), 761.
58. Constance Classen, David Howes, and Anthony Synnott, *Aroma: The Cultural History of Smell* (New York: Routledge, 1994), 4; Alain Corbin, *The Fragrant and the Foul* (London: Pan Macmillan, 1994).
59. XYZ, *Spain, Tangier, etc.*, 33.
60. Jacob, *Travels in the South of Spain*, 150.
61. As quoted in Richard Kagan, "Prescott's Paradigm: American Historical Scholarship and the Decline of Spain," *The American Historical Review* 101 (1996): 426.

62. Ibid., 426.
63. Ibid., 429.
64. John McCulloch, *A Dictionary, Practical, Theoretical, and Historical, of Commerce and Commercial Navigation* (London: A. Spottiswoode, 1844), 902.
65. Ford, *Gatherings from Spain*, 116.
66. Massimo Mazzotti, "Enlightened Mills: Mechanizing Olive Oil Production in Mediterranean Europe," *Technology and Culture* 45, no. 2 (2004): 291.
67. Sheila Palomares Alarcón, "19th Century Industrial Architecture Related to the 'Olive Grove Revolution' in the Province of Jaén, Spain," in *Modernity, Frontiers and Revolutions*, ed. Maria do Rosário Monteiro, Mário Ming Kong, and Maria João Pereira Neto (Boca Raton, FL: CRC Press, 2018), 58.
68. Busby, *Journal of a Recent Visit to the Principal Vineyards of Spain and France*, 34. This raises an important question of whether Spanish olive oil was rancid or simply strongly flavored. I argue that, in the end, it did not matter as the narrative constructed by non-Spanish writers framed olive oil as rancid.
69. John Locke, *Observations upon the Growth and Culture of Vines and Olives: The Production of Silk: The Preservation of Fruits* (London: W. Sandby: 1766), 51; Peter Charzotte, *Facts and Observations on the Culture of Vines, Olives, Capers, Almonds, &c. in the Southern States* (Philadelphia: J. Maxwell, 1821), 18.
70. Thomas Jefferson, "From Thomas Jefferson to William Drayton," Library of Congress, 36, no. 6231 (1787).
71. The American public ultimately settled on cottonseed oil—Crisco—once the industry could figure out how to remove its odor (one of rancidity) as part of creating neutral aesthetics at a low cost. David Shields, "Prospecting for Oil," in *The Larder: Food Studies Methods from the American South*, ed. John T. Edge, Elizabeth Englehardt, and Ted Ownby (Athens: University of Georgia Press, 2013), 57.
72. John Evelyn, *The Miscellaneous Writings of John Evelyn, Esq.*, ed. William Upcott (London: Henry Colburn, 1825), 765.
73. "Rceipes" [*sic*], *The Favourite*, Vol. 1, no. 127 (London: Partridge, Oakey, and Co., 1854), 127.
74. Voltaire, *A Philosophical Dictionary*, Vol IV, 2nd ed. (London: John and Henry L. Hunt, 1824), 383.
75. Ford, *The Spaniards and Their Country*, 134.

Selected Bibliography

Busby, James. *Journal of a Recent Visit to the Principal Vineyards of Spain and France*. London: Smith, Elder and Cornhill, 1834.

Classen, Constance, David Howes, and Anthony Synnott. *Aroma: The Cultural History of Smell*. New York: Routledge, 1994.

Ferguson, Priscilla Parkhurst. "A Cultural Field in the Making: Gastronomy in 19th-Century France." *American Journal of Sociology* 104, no. 3 (1998): 597–641.

Ford, Richard. *Gatherings from Spain*. London: John Murray, 1846.

Forrest, Beth. "'A Tealess, Beerless, Beefless Land': Sensing and Tasting Spain in Late Eighteenth and Nineteenth-Century British Travelogues." In *Space, Taste and Affect: Atmospheres That Shape the Way We Eat*, edited by Emily Falconer, 85–98. New York: Routledge, 2020.

Infante-Amate, Juan. "The Ecology and History of the Mediterranean Olive Grove: The Spanish Great Expansion, 1750–2000." *Rural History* 23 (2012): 161–184.

Kagan, Richard. "Prescott's Paradigm: American Historical Scholarship and the Decline of Spain." *The American Historical Review* 101 (1996): 423–446.

Lea, Henry Charles. "The Decadence of Spain." *Atlantic Monthly* 82 (July 1898): 36–46.

Mazzotti, Massimo. "Enlightened Mills: Mechanizing Olive Oil Production in Mediterranean Europe." *Technology and Culture* 45, no. 2 (2004): 277–304.

Rios, Alicia. "Olive Oil, Balsamic Medium." In *Oxford Symposium on Food & Cookery: The Cooking Medium*, edited by Tom Jaine, 101–110. London: Prospect Books, 1986.

Shields, David. "Prospecting for Oil." In *The Larder: Food Studies Methods from the American South*, edited by John T. Edge, Elizabeth S. D. Engelhardt, and Ted Ownby, 57–75. Athens: University of Georgia Press, 2013.

Trubek, A. 2009. *The Taste of Place: A Cultural Journey into Terroir*. Berkeley: University of California Press.

Beth M. Forrest, *"To Change This Sauce Would Be Little Short of Heresy": The Geopolitics of "Rancid" Olive Oil in Nineteenth-Century Spain* In: *From Garum to Mole: Sauces and Identity in the Western World*.
Edited by: Andrew Donnelly, Beth M. Forrest, and Deirdre Murphy, Oxford University Press.
 DOI: 10.1093/9780190622138.003.0011

12

Ketchup as a Vegetable

CONDIMENTS, CULTURE, AND THE POLITICS OF SCHOOL LUNCH IN REAGAN'S AMERICA

Amy Bentley

KETCHUP IS ARGUABLY the United States' most ubiquitous condiment. Open any American's refrigerator and you're likely to see a ketchup bottle, or two, lurking in the inside door shelf or tucked away with the odd assortment of pickles, mayonnaise, and mustard. In fact, nearly everyone—97 percent—has a ketchup bottle in the fridge, most likely the Heinz brand.[1] Americans purportedly spend more money on salsa, but in terms of sheer volume, ketchup exceeds it, as we purchase some 10 billion ounces of ketchup annually—almost three bottles per person, per year.[2] Bright red in color, tangy, sweet, salty, and replete with a "meaty," tomatoey umami hit, ketchup provides color and flavoring accents, as well as aroma and texture cues that are familiar and comforting.

We slather ketchup on French fries, hamburgers, and hot dogs (though ketchup with the latter is, for many, anathema), but the uses go well beyond backyard cookout and sports arena fare. Ketchup also goes on eggs, mac and cheese, breaded and fried clam strips, and chicken fingers, and is frequently an ingredient in sauces and casseroles. Those who may not consider ketchup their go-to fast food condiment may opt for "fry sauce," a ketchup/mayo mixture with deep regional loyalty in the Mountain West.[3] In fact, ketchup's sweet overtone and bright color nicely complements and provides an accent for the American industrial diet, contrasting with its salty/fatty character and enhancing the already sweet flavor profile of much of our food.

While ketchup (some use the spelling "catsup") originally began as a fermented fish sauce in early China (without tomatoes), it traveled via the English navy around the world and found a home in the British motherland. British sailors bought the sauce, called *ke-tsiap* or *ke-tchup* by seventeenth-century Chinese and Indonesian traders, to provide relief for their dry and mundane hard tack and salt pork, and the condiment spread through the British Empire. Upon returning to England, sailors and others experimented to recreate the complex flavors of the sauce, substituting nuts, mushrooms, or shallots for the fish.[4] It was, and still is, a condiment meant to liven up standard, potentially stodgy meat and potato dishes.

There was no commercial tomato ketchup, however, until it landed in the United States. Ketchup became truly American once it was wed with the tomato and bottled industrially. An early ketchup recipe containing tomatoes appeared in Britain in 1817, which in addition to calling for "a gallon of fine, red, and full ripe tomatas [*sic*]," included anchovies, shallots, salt, and a variety of spices.[5] American tomato ketchup's original flavor profile was both less sweet and less sour that its later iterations. Because bottled ketchup easily became fermented and also spoiled relatively quickly, industrial producers found that adding extra vinegar helped preserve it. More sugar was added to balance the vinegar's sourness, and through the twentieth century ketchup gradually became sweeter in its flavor profile.[6]

By the early twentieth century, tomato ketchup had become "entrenched as the primary and most popular of condimental sauces, its appeal to Americans deep and widespread."[7] The "Esperanto of cuisine," as food historian Elizabeth Rozin describes it, given its ubiquitous presence, ketchup early on functioned as a great equalizer with its "special and unprecedented ability to provide something for everyone."[8] In our day, she notes, "it is accepted and enjoyed for its very 'Americanism,' [*sic*] its use largely constrained and limited by foods and products experienced and perceived as American in their preparation and presentation."[9] In short, ketchup marries perfectly with largely brown and beige, fat- and salt-forward American food: breaded and fried meats, salty potatoes.

In the 1870s, United States manufacturers began producing ketchup, and by the early 1900s, Heinz was the leading producer, selling 5 million bottles per year.[10] Today, Heinz reigns supreme, holding 60 percent of U.S. market share.[11] Heinz ketchup is in snack bars, chain restaurants, and down-home diners. Even some fancier restaurants plant bottles of it on each table because diners ask for it. Heinz, the platonic ideal of ketchup, according to Malcolm Gladwell, dominates because it is the perfect balance of sweet, salty, sour, and umami, a precisely calibrated product that is difficult to replicate.[12]

Not only do Americans recognize ketchup as the classic and iconic American condiment, so too does the rest of the world, which (for better or worse) regards it as emblematic of U.S. cuisine in general. Famed chef José

Andrés remarked that "everyone else in the world still thinks of American food as ketchup." Instead of being ashamed of it, Andrés noted, "It's time to embrace and celebrate ketchup."[13] Similarly, Elizabeth Rozin praised it as a "godsend" to American food: "a genuine American innovation, providing both visual and gustatory brightness and excitement, adding an aesthetic dimension to food that was little more than basic nourishment."[14] In good American fashion, the condiment has been exported abroad and made its way into numerous foreign cuisines in novel ways.

Recognizing ketchup's distinct, democratic, yet exalted place in the landscape of American food, then, is important to understanding the power of the 1981 "Ketchup as a Vegetable" debacle—how ketchup came to symbolize the malevolence of the economic policy of the Ronald Reagan presidency. This chapter illuminates this moment as it was framed through the media, then delves more deeply into the government's controversial recommendations regarding school lunch, and finally revisits the iconic power of ketchup unmoored from its American roots and extending across the globe.

Ketchup as a Vegetable: The Event and Its Aftermath

The event that became known as the "Ketchup as a Vegetable" incident was an attempted policy change gone awry, one part of the larger plan to dramatically alter the nature and process of government food assistance programs against the backdrop of overall budget restructuring of the era.[15] In 1981, the first year of President Ronald Reagan's administration, the government was deep in the throes of "Reaganomics," the economic policy focusing on overall reduction of government spending, taxes, and regulation. David Stockman, director of the Office of Management and Budget (OMB), orchestrated the plan to dramatically cut the federal budget, shrink government size, and slash taxes—especially for the wealthy. According to the prevailing economic theory known as supply-side or "trickle-down" economics, with their extra capital the wealthy would then invest in and create businesses that would boost the economy and employ and benefit the average citizen. That summer Congress passed and the president signed the budget, known as the Omnibus Budget Reconciliation Act of 1981. The budget sought to control spending in large part by consolidating most federal expenditures into block grants, which were transferred to the states for ultimate allocation. The Act also dramatically reduced budgets across the board, apart from the defense budget, which was significantly increased.

Apart from the Department of Defense, all federal agencies, including the United States Department of Agriculture (USDA), were each charged with cutting their budgets by several billion dollars.[16] Within the USDA, federal school lunch expenditures were to be chopped by one-third, from $4.5 billion to $3 billion. As Congress authorized the cuts, it also specified that the USDA should nonetheless maintain the current nutrition standards of the federal school lunch program. In the summer of 1981, a USDA Taskforce Group, overseen by Food and Nutrition Service (FNS) administrator (and Reagan appointee) William Hoagland, met to put together a set of proposals enabling the reduction in costs. Because the USDA was mandated to meet an October 1st deadline, the beginning of the new budget year, the Task Force had just twelve weeks to produce the school lunch reformulations with proposals that would maintain nutrition standards at two-thirds of the cost. Federal law requires that such legislative proposals be made public a month in advance to allow sufficient time for comment. To meet that deadline, the school lunch revisions, apparently with OMB approval, were published on September 4, 1981, on page 4452 of the Federal Register.[17]

The proposed recommendations sought to simplify local record keeping as a way to reduce costs, but they also included several changes that allowed for flexibility in what was to be served for the midday meal. Prior to this, federal guidelines mandated that school lunches had to contain a minimum of five items: one serving of bread, two of fruits and/or vegetables, one dairy serving, and one meat serving. USDA guidelines also determined adequate serving amounts and appropriate items. The combined items were to meet one-third of RDAs (Recommended Dietary Allowances), as determined by the USDA.

These school lunch requirements represented a conventional, mid-century definition of a meal. It consisted of what anthropologist Mary Douglas termed "A + 2b," "A" being the larger portion of protein (usually meat) and 2b being sides, usually a green vegetable and a starch of some sort, such as potatoes, corn, or rice.[18] A slice of bread was useful in sopping up gravy or juices, and milk was a common beverage, especially for children.

For its time, the new proposed guidelines recommended a somewhat startling list of ways to alter this conventional model. These included reducing meal sizes; offering certain substitutes for meat and vegetables; allowing changes in meal patterns; and reconciling differences between allowable breakfast items and lunch items. Specific changes included allowing tofu, cheese, and nuts to substitute for meat; allowing pretzels, donuts, pie, and other grain-based items as bread substitutes; reducing the requirement that school lunch meet one-third of the RDAs to one-fourth of daily needs; allowing such condiments as pickle relish to count as a vegetable; and allowing one tablespoon of tomato paste to count as an equivalent to one-fourth cup of tomato juice, considered a standard vegetable serving. Ketchup (or catsup) was not mentioned by name, though the regulations did state that "tomato concentrate" would qualify as a vegetable. It did not define the term further.

Thus, as part of the Reagan administration's attempt to slash $1.5 billion from children's nutrition funding, the recommendations were worded (whether deliberately or unintentionally) so as to conceivably allow for designating ketchup as a vegetable for its school lunch programs. If it was not deliberate, then naming pickle relish as a vegetable certainly opened the door to claiming "condiments" as a category to be the equivalent of vegetables. Though perhaps an absurd idea to most school lunch providers across the country, this change enabled the USDA to eliminate one of the two vegetables required to meet minimum food and nutrition standards, and thus shrink costs considerably. While the proposal included other changes that involved similarly dramatic category shifting, these received only minor attention compared to the idea of the salt- and sucrose-laden condiment ketchup as an equivalent to a bona fide vegetable.

After the recommendations were published in the Federal Register, a wave of publicity ensued, which began quietly but quickly reached an intense furor. The following day, September 5, two small items appeared in the *New York Times* mentioning the proposed school lunch changes, discussing them in terms of shrinking portions and lowering nutritional standards. "Smaller school lunches have been proposed by the Agriculture Department for the federally subsidized lunch program in schools throughout the country," matter-of-factly explained one story. "The proposal would abandon a goal set at the program's inception 35 years ago: to serve lunches that give children one-third of the recommended dietary allowances for a variety of nutrients," indicated the other.[19]

Five days after the recommendations were published in the Federal Register, the word "ketchup" first came into play. "When Is Ketchup a Vegetable? When Tofu Is Meat," ran the *Washington Post* headline on September 9. The first sentence framed the story: "The federal government, in major new changes for the nation's school-lunch program, wants to call ketchup and pickle relish vegetables, offer tofu as a substitute for meat and serve peanut butter or nuts as main dishes at noon."[20] Columnist Russell Baker quipped, "The authors of this plan are now debating whether school-lunch costs can be whittled further by counting ketchup on the French fries—

the number of French fries would also be reduced—as a second vegetable. That way you wouldn't have to squander money by supplying peas if the little chiselers insist on ketchup for their fries."[21]

Consumer advocacy groups went into high alert, as did Congress, which scheduled education subcommittee meetings to delve into the school lunch program revisions. The food industry watchdog group the Center for Science in the Public Interest (CSPI) issued its own press release September 11, the headline of which read, "USDA Undermines the Nutritional Integrity of School Meals." "The Department of Agriculture," the release began, "has proposed changes in the school lunch program that would diminish not only the quantity but the quality of foods served. The new regulations would allow schools to serve cakes, cookies, doughnuts, pies, corn chips, or pretzels in place of bread; and condiments such as pickle relish and tomato paste instead of a vegetable." Notably, the release did not use the word "ketchup"; rather, it focused on the changes to the bread requirement and another that eliminated the option of low-fat milk (only allowing whole milk was proffered as a cost-saving measure).[22]

Yet within two weeks the media focused squarely on the ketchup as a vegetable part of the proposal. Echoing a popular Burger King advertising slogan, "Hold the pickles, hold the relish, special orders don't upset us," the *Washington Post* ran an article with the headline, "U.S. Holds the Ketchup in School."[23] Pun-filled titles and phrases in newspaper stories multiplied: "Shrinking Lunch, With Relish," "The Emperor's New Condiments," and "Reagan's Nouvelle Cuisine for Kids."[24]

To highlight the seeming absurdity of these recommendations, several Democratic senators, including Patrick Leahy of Vermont, held a photo opportunity on September 24, just under three weeks after the proposal announcement (Figure 12.1). Invited reporters and photographers documented a row of senators consuming a lunch based on the new recommendations for kindergarteners: a tiny meat-and-soybean patty, a slice of bread, a few French fries, ketchup, and a partially filled glass of milk.[25]

Some GOP members of Congress were outraged as well, including Senator Henry J. Heinz, a Republican from Pennsylvania whose family-owned business, H. J. Heinz Company, manufactured the leading ketchup. On September 25, Heinz took to the Senate floor and called the whole proposal "ludicrous." "Ketchup is a condiment," he said. "This is one of the most ridiculous regulations I ever heard of, and I suppose I need not add that I do know something about ketchup and relish, or did at one time."[26]

FIGURE 12.1 Senate Democrats dine on school lunch. Jimmy Carter Presidential Library, Roddey Mims Collection, 1976–82, 9/24/81 (T-30630), NAID: 152023.

The same day as Heinz's condemnation on the Senate floor, the White House withdrew the proposal. Reagan, though never publicly addressing or defending the subject, detested the increasingly bad publicity and, as his administration realized it had lost the public relations battle, sought to change the subject. "Charging that the Agriculture Department 'not only has egg on its face, but ketchup, too,' the *Washington Post* reported, "Budget Director David A. Stockman . . . ordered the withdrawal of proposed federal rules that would have listed ketchup and pickle relish as vegetables in school lunches." The article continued, "[Stockman] said the controversial guidelines, which also would have allowed the substitution of soybean cakes for hamburger and doughnuts for bread, were the result of a 'bureaucratic goof.' "[27]

Stockman's attempt at damage control raised the ire of Secretary of Agriculture John Block, who immediately went to the White House to meet with the president, expressing his disapproval of the proposal's demise without his knowledge and consent. Angered by Stockman's dismissive remarks, Block in a public statement sought to at least defend his agency's original purpose and intentions. "The president and I both feel that the intent was sound and in step with the administration's goal to reduce regulation and return flexibility to the local units of government."[28]

In a subsequent press conference, an aide to Block awkwardly attempted to defend the recommendations. "There was a great misunderstanding in the land as to how these regulations are viewed," the aide reported. "I think it would be a mistake to say that ketchup per se was classified as a vegetable.... Ketchup in combination with other things was classified as a vegetable." When asked what those other things were, he replied, "French fries or hamburgers."[29]

By November, the administration had moved to adopt an "offer versus serve" model, one that had been in existence at the high school level, as a way to save money and reduce portion sizes and plate waste. Students would only have to take three out of five items available, a policy still in practice. "'Certainly we've taken care of the condiment issues,' [Food and Nutrition Service administrator] William Hoagland said, a reference to the earlier proposal for counting ketchup and relish as a vegetable."[30] The *New York Times* noted, "Initially White House officials maintained the proposals were being misunderstood and misrepresented, but eventually they decided to recommend their withdrawal."[31]

Throughout this three-and-a-half-week period, from the time the administration published its recommendations for altering school lunch to meet budget cuts to its withdrawal of those recommendations and shift to the "offer versus serve" option, nutrition "experts" and child advocacy groups voiced their vociferous criticism. "Ketchup as a Vegetable" became the shorthand for the entire set of proposed changes to school lunches. The head of the Field Fund, a leading liberal philanthropic organization, indicated that her strong motivation to fight Reagan administration recommendations "could be explained in one word—ketchup."[32]

The Food Research Action Center (FRAC), a nonprofit advocacy group based in Washington, D.C., was instrumental in defeating the school lunch cuts. FRAC employee Lynn Parker, who had participated in the USDA Task Force meetings that came up with the school lunch changes, publicly criticized them. Several years later, Parker described her experience: "I was thinking [of the recommendations in terms of] collective purchasing of food and similar things to reduce costs.... But it was clear from the first day that the USDA wanted us to cut the portion sizes in school lunch programs." She also noted, "They also wanted ketchup and other condiments to be counted as vegetables."[33] Parker had attempted to work "with members of the committee to make sure that the report stated that the recommendations were made only for economic reasons and that they didn't have a sound nutrition basis." When the recommendations resulted in reducing portion sizes of fruits, vegetables, and grains, Parker "led the FRAC campaign against the proposed regulations." According to her recollections, " 'Ketchup as a Vegetable' became the campaign line."[34]

Ultimately, USDA FNS executive Hoagland took the fall for "Ketchup as a Vegetable," as he was "lashed on Capitol Hill and skewered by the White House which removed him from his job two days before Thanksgiving," according to a *New York Times* story. Hoagland felt betrayed by those higher up who seemed to blame him and his committee for conceiving of the idea in the first place. Later confessing anger and depression over the incident, Hoagland defended his original recommendations on the grounds that they were misinterpreted: "It's an insult to me and to the school lunchroom officials to say that we would even consider forcing kids to eat ketchup as a vegetable." Seemingly unable to consider that the proposal might have been so poorly conceived and written as to allow for such a laughable substitution—even if that was not the committee's intention—Hoagland suspected that "Ketchup as a Vegetable" might have been "hatched in the imaginations of nutrition advocacy groups."[35]

So powerful was "Ketchup as a Vegetable" that debate and analysis of the incident continued throughout the Reagan years and beyond, taking on a life of its own. The Public Health Association, deriding the Reagan administration's effect on public health policy, argued that "if Congress had followed the Administration's proposals, [school lunch budgets] would have been down another third with school children eating ketchup and relish as vegetables. How can anyone believe that the Reagan Administration wishes to prevent disease or promote health or preserve public health in America?"[36]

Through the rest of the twentieth century and into the twenty-first, "Ketchup as a Vegetable" remained an easy symbol of a world of haves and have-nots. A 1986 *New York Times* letter to the editor commenting on the Hands Across America program (a feel-good event that raised money for charities by creating a giant human chain across the country) observed, "As President and Mrs. Reagan joined the human chain on the White House lawn, I couldn't help remembering the proposal of Mr. Reagan's Administration to make ketchup the equivalent of a vegetable in school lunch programs."[37] George Bush Sr.'s 1988 presidential campaign was dogged with references to "Ketchup as a Vegetable." The *Los Angeles Times* reported, "Referring to [Bush]'s statement last Friday that last month's rise in the unemployment rate was 'statistically almost irrelevant,' [Kitty Dukakis, wife of Democratic nominee Michael Dukakis] said it was 'not surprising, coming as it did from the standard-bearer of the party that thought ketchup was a vegetable.' "[38]

Humorist Calvin Trillin couldn't resist coupling former President Richard Nixon's well-known fondness for a lunch of ketchup over cottage cheese with "Ketchup as a Vegetable." "Only now does it become clear that the school lunch decision," ribbed Trillin, "then considered a public relations disaster, may have reflected some shrewd strategic planning: The Reagan Administration's policy on ketchup may have been the beginning of the [post-Watergate scandal] public rehabilitation of Richard Nixon."[39] In reporting on the 1999 discovery of the health benefits of lycopene, found in, among other things, ketchup, *Consumer Reports* mused, "In 1981, President Ronald Reagan was widely ridiculed for trying to pass off a popular condiment as a school-lunch vegetable. Now if the latest ad campaign [which highlighted lycopene] from condiment maker Heinz is right, ketchup fans may have the last laugh."[40]

Physical Properties, Cultural Meanings

The matter was seemingly over in a matter of weeks, yet the legacy of "Ketchup as a Vegetable" continued to live on. For Baby Boomers at least, it remains a part of the lexicon, emblematic of government ineptitude, and more specifically, an attempt to cheat the poor and children of basic nutritional needs for the benefit of the wealthy. For many it became a symbol of the "let them eat cake" attitude of the Reagan years, though for others it was representative of the partisan wrangling common in Washington politics. To better understand why ketchup emerged as a symbol of Reaganomics requires looking at the physical nature of ketchup, as well as its cultural meanings.

In the mid-twentieth century, Heinz ketchup ingredients listed on the label were as follows: "Made from fresh ripe tomatoes, spices, granulated cane sugar, bottled vinegar, onions, salt."[41] Before a 1990 labeling law was passed, food manufacturers only had to list the ingredients in order of volume, so it's impossible to tell the specific amount or proportion of sugar, for example, in each bottle, only that cane sugar was the third most prevalent ingredient after tomatoes and spices. Heinz, along with other ketchup makers, began substituting high fructose corn syrup for sugar in the 1980s.

In the 2010s, Heinz ketchup labels list ingredients as: "Tomato concentrate made from red ripe tomatoes, distilled vinegar, high fructose corn syrup (HFCS), corn syrup, salt, spice, onion powder, natural flavoring." Further, the label, as required by law, contextualizes the micro- and macronutrients in a serving of ketchup. According to the information, a one-tablespoon serving of ketchup contains twenty calories, zero grams of fat, 160 mg of sodium (a fairly hefty 7 percent of daily requirements), 4 grams of carbohydrate in the form of sugar (2 percent of daily requirements), and 2 percent of vitamins A and C for a day. Heinz contracts with farmers to grow the tomatoes, processes them into concentrate, and turns the concentrate into ketchup.[42] Since 2010, Heinz has also sold other ketchup products, including "Simply Heinz," containing no HFCS, an organic version, and a low-sugar variety, as well as a Sriracha-flavored ketchup.

A small irony of "Ketchup as a Vegetable" is that tomatoes are botanically categorized as a fruit, not a vegetable. Even so, an 1893 federal court ruling classified tomatoes as a vegetable "for commercial purposes," given that the "ordinary meaning" of vegetable was defined as a food "served at dinner in, with, or after the soup, fish, or meats which constitute the principal part of the repast, and not, like fruits generally, as dessert." This means that, legally, fruits that are commonly served as dinner items can be called vegetables, at least when it comes to trade and commerce. This is why tomatoes, cucumbers, squashes, and peppers are all sold as vegetables, even though according to their botanical properties they are fruit.[43]

"The whole idea is ludicrous," Senator Heinz had pronounced from the Senate Chamber, "ketchup is a condiment." Why is the thought of categorizing ketchup as a vegetable so ridiculous? Because of its texture and thickness? Because ketchup contains sugar and salt that compromise its nutritional value? Because it is commonly consumed as an accoutrement to food and not considered a food item itself?

Ketchup is indeed a condiment, thickly textured, with a concentrated flavor that functions as an accent to other foods. Elizabeth Rozin reminds us that "[k]etchup, along with its large and extended family of condiments, sauces, spices, and seasonings, has little to do with nourishment per se, but involves rather the pervasive practice of enhancing or altering or intensifying the flavor of food."[44] It would be difficult to consume ketchup alone in great amounts, say, an entire soup bowl of ketchup, because of its concentrated taste. As a condiment, it conflicts with our idea of what a vegetable as a component of a meal is supposed to be because of its texture, concentration of flavor, the manner in which a vegetable is consumed, the usual quantity consumed at one sitting, and the nutrition we expect from it.

In Douglas's "A + 2b" meal formula, a condiment functions as an accent to "A"; it is not meant to be consumed independently as a "2b," that is, a major component of a meal. Usually the condiment flavor is too concentrated to function as a side vegetable alone.[45] We are not comfortable with, for example, ordering a plate of just a condiment, say ketchup or mustard, at a restaurant—that would defy standard notions of a meal, as well as the understood function of a condiment. A condiment such as ketchup may contain similar ingredients and be close in texture to a pureed soup, which is of course perfectly acceptable to order alone, but "condiment," as we know, indicates a specific set of physical properties, uses, and psychological meanings.[46] This helps explain why the senators' press conference lunch—tiny little hamburgers with ketchup and French fries on the side, supposedly functioning as a vegetable, was such a symbolically powerful performance of the administration's proposed cuts to school lunch.

We're also not terribly comfortable admitting that French fries are one of the most commonly consumed "vegetables," especially by children, even infants as young as nine months old.[47] While potatoes are quite healthy, containing vitamins C and B-6, calcium, protein, and fiber, when processed into French fries or potato chips—which is how Americans consume 70 percent of their potatoes—the excess salt and fat diminish its overall nutritional profile. Tomatoes are also healthy, but similarly, 77 percent of the tomatoes Americans consume are processed into sauce or ketchup, both of which are most often prepared with added salt and sugar. USDA data indicates that 90 percent of Americans aren't consuming an adequate number of vegetables daily, and half of what vegetables they do consume are potatoes and tomatoes, mostly in the form of French fries, potato chips, and ketchup.[48] While Americans love their French fries and ketchup, few consider them "healthy vegetables," in the same category as, for example, green beans or squash. Thus, to consider fries and ketchup "the vegetables" in children's school lunches creates strong internal dissonance.

Further, ketchup has, for many, become a symbol particularly of children's food. Perfectly complementing the hamburgers and French fries in diners and fast-food joints, ketchup became firmly entrenched in the landscape of American fast food over the twentieth century. As ketchup's sweetness increased, it came to be a condiment particularly appealing to, and eventually marketed to, children. Restaurants and fast-food joints developed "kids' menus" replete with hamburgers, chicken nuggets, and French fries, all accompanied by ketchup.

While still undeniably "American," ketchup, like many American products, has made its way into other cultures and cuisines, and in so doing, its meanings and uses have changed. Outside the United States, ketchup has expanded from its status as mere condiment to a full-fledged sauce and even an ingredient for recipes. While North America dominates the global ketchup market, Europe is second, followed by Asia. Ketchup consumption is steadily increasing in developing countries, fueled by the international growth of fast-food chains and the popularity of Western-style diets in general.[49] Ketchup is a full-fledged element of the emerging Asian fusion cuisine known as *yōshoku*.[50] Known in Japan as "Western Food," yōshoku restaurants serve such hybrid, ketchup-centric dishes as *naporitan*, cooked spaghetti that is rinsed in cold water, then stir-fried with vegetables in ketchup, and *omurice*, an omelet lying over a mound of ketchup-flavored rice, and of course the *hambagu* (the Japanese version of a hamburger patty, usually served without a bun). Swedes pour ketchup as a sauce over pasta, a dish known as "Depression spaghetti" and consumed by some in the United States in the 1930s as well as today.[51] Given these expanding uses and meanings of ketchup, it's interesting to consider how Swedish and Japanese consumers categorize ketchup: As a condiment only? As a sauce? As a legitimate substitute for a vegetable?

Regardless of the global expansion of ketchup, in 1980s America ketchup was still predominantly identified as a ubiquitous and much-loved condiment, an accompaniment, but not a stand-alone food, to nationally recognized and familiar foods especially loved by children. The thought of feeding children, especially low-income children, ketchup as a vegetable, even if this was not the direct intention or outcome of the proposal, was weirdly Dickensian in its implications and thus damning to the Reagan administration. Other recommendations issued at the same time—cookies and pie for breakfast, replacing low-fat milk with whole milk just as childhood obesity levels were beginning to climb—in retrospect seem at least as bad if not worse than tomato paste counting as a vegetable. Yet at the time, for the media as well as for the general public, all else paled in comparison to the idea of serving ketchup as a vegetable for school lunch.

My close reading of the original recommendation persuades me that the intention was to count one tablespoon of "tomato paste," reconstituted in a dish such as pasta with tomato sauce, as a vegetable. This substitution may be logical and nutritionally sound. However, that change combined with the "condiments such as pickle relish as a vegetable" recommendation, allows for a plausible interpretation potentially applying to ketchup as well.

Perhaps the reason we remember "Ketchup as a Vegetable" has less to do with Reagan and his administration's intention, and more to do with its manifestation as a very powerful lodestone of criticism. The "tomato paste" recommendation was deliberately exaggerated, though not without some basis, because of a groundswell of dissatisfaction with so many other policies, including slashing domestic spending for social programs, as well as the general directive to change, and in doing so diminish, nutrition and food programs for many who needed it the most.

Looking back at the entire set of 1981 recommendations with over forty years of perspective, the meat substitutes, not yet mainstream and even somewhat controversial at the time, received minimal comment from nutrition and child advocacy groups or the popular press. Some letter writers to newspapers voiced their approval of plant-based or dairy substitutes for meat. "After reading of the Department of Agriculture's plan to change from meat to tofu and nuts as an 'austerity' move," wrote Chris and Joanne Lynt of Alexandria, Virginia, "Is it possible that [we] actually agree with something this administration is proposing? Our children would run a lower risk of heart disease and circulatory problems if this diet were implemented. But please don't let on that we radical-health-food-vegetarian-hippies agree with a Reagan policy. They might change their minds."

Today the meat substitutes outlined in the 1981 school lunch proposals make a great deal of sense and were in fact approved in the 1990s (nuts and nut butters in 1995, and tofu in 1998). Another of the proposals, counting protein sources from a variety of dishes instead of requiring that there be one larger serving of protein, also makes sense, in that it dramatically expands the notion of an "acceptable meal." So, for example, school cafeterias could serve a chicken barley soup with grains, vegetables, and a small portion of chicken, but milk or some cheese served separately could factor into the protein requirement. The proposal to count cookies and donuts as bread portions seems the most egregious recommendation, yet received minimal attention at the time. This is perhaps because in the early 1980s Americans had not yet experienced the sharp increases in sugar intake through growing soda consumption, or realized the accompanying obesity rates that would become apparent in the 2000s. Also, of course, the spotlight was squarely turned on "Ketchup as a Vegetable," with everything else in the background. Given ketchup's iconic nature, its firm tradition as a condiment accompanying American fast food, and its dearth of nutrients, "ketchup as a vegetable," a recommendation not even specifically cited, blocked out numerous recommendations—some progressive, some clearly regressive with regard to nutrition, others more neutral—and became the symbol of an administration gone wrong.

There are further interesting postscripts to this story. First, in 1998, seventeen years after the ketchup incident, salsa, by all accounts a more nutritious condiment but a condiment nevertheless, was approved as a vegetable for school lunch. Government officials, understandably nervous about the announcement, were defensive in their statements on the subject. "Ketchup is really mostly sugar and vinegar," said one Agriculture Department official, speaking on condition of anonymity. "This is not the same because... (salsa) is essentially a vegetable salad." Second, in 2011, "Ketchup as a Vegetable" returned to the media spotlight as Congress sought to block the Obama administration's attempt to increase the amount of tomato paste that could count as a "vegetable," from two tablespoons to a half a cup. Frozen pizza makers, who supply school districts with millions of pizzas per year, balked at the thought, since the increased amount would exclude their product from meeting the new nutrition standards. A "Pizza as a Vegetable" controversy ensued, and pizza lobbyists won.[52]

School lunch is still a fraught political and economic battleground for government, nutrition advocates, and food product manufacturers. Academics, the public health community, farm bill activists, and hunger and nutrition organizations have identified school lunch as an entity still in need of reform. Ketchup will remain part of school lunches, though whether as a condiment or something more remains to be seen. Meanwhile, Americans in general, as well as a growing portion of the global population, are still in love with ketchup.

How To Make Fry Sauce

Meagan Splawn, thekitchn.com, 2022
Makes about 2 1/2 cups

Ingredients:

2 cups mayonnaise
1/2 cup ketchup
1 tablespoon pickle brine, preferably from bread and butter pickles
1 teaspoon Worcestershire sauce
1/4 teaspoon kosher salt
1/4 teaspoon smoked paprika
Pinch cayenne pepper

Instructions:

1. Stir together the mayonnaise, ketchup, and seasonings. Place all the ingredients in a medium bowl and whisk to combine.
2. Refrigerate the sauce for at least 30 minutes. Cover the sauce and refrigerate at least 30 minutes but preferably 8 hours.
3. Serve with fries. Serve the sauce cold with hot fries for dipping.

Notes

1. Statista, "U.S. Population: Which Brands of Catsup/Ketchup Do You Use Most Often?," 2016, https://www.statista.com/statistics/278061/us-households-most-used-brands-of-catsup-ketchup/.
2. Carl Bialik, "Ketchup vs. Salsa: By the Numbers," *Wall Street Journal*, September 20, 2007, https://www.wsj.com/articles/BL-NB-191/.
3. Zee Krstic, "A Brief History of Fry Sauce, Utah's Favorite Condiment," *Eater.com*, 2018, https://www.eater.com/2016/8/6/12054512/fry-sauce-ketchup-mayo-utah-condiment/.
4. Dan Jurafsky, *The Language of Food: A Linguist Reads the Menu* (New York: W. W. Norton, 2014), 54.
5. Ibid., 60.
6. Elizabeth Rozin, *The Primal Cheeseburger: A Generous Helping of Food History Served Up on a Bun* (New York: Penguin, 1994); Rico Gagliano, "A Brief History of Ketchup," *The Dinner Party Download*, September 25, 2014, https://www.dinnerpartydownload.org/ketchup/.
7. Rozin, *The Primal Cheeseburger*, 108.
8. Ibid.
9. Ibid.
10. Andrew Smith, *Pure Ketchup: A History of America's National Condiment* (Columbia: University of South Carolina Press, 1996).
11. Statista, "U.S. Population: Which Brands of Catsup/Ketchup Do You Use Most Often?"; Javier E. David, "The Ketchup War That Never Was: Burger Giant's Link to Heinz," *CNBC.com*, 2013, https://www.cnbc.com/id/100464841/.
12. Malcolm Gladwell, "The Ketchup Conundrum: Taste Technologies," *The New Yorker*, September 6, 2004, https://www.newyorker.com/magazine/2004/09/06/the-ketchup-conundrum.
13. Julia Moskin, "'Pass the Ketchup' Could Bring Surprises," *New York Times*, August 9, 2011, https://www.nytimes.com/2011/08/10/dining/building-respect-for-ketchup.html.
14. Rozin, *The Primal Cheeseburger*, 107.
15. Susan Levine, *School Lunch Politics: The Surprising History of America's Favorite Welfare Program* (Princeton, NJ: Princeton University Press, 2008).
16. Ronald Reagan, "Address Before a Joint Session of the Congress on the Program for Economic Recovery," February 18, 1981, Online by Gerhard Peters and John T. Woolley, The American Presidency Project, https://www.presidency.ucsb.edu/node/246567. The Omnibus Reconciliation Act of 1980, signed by President Carter, also had provisions to reduce the amount of school lunch reimbursement by 2 cents per meal, but did not call for such steep budget cuts, nor did it reassign allocation as block grants.
17. Elaine S. Povich, "Budget Director Nominee Approved School Lunch Ketchup Plan," UPI Archives, September 22, 1085, https://www.upi.com/Archives/1985/09/22/

Budget-director-nominee-approved-school-lunch-ketchup-plan/8218496209600/; *Federal Register* 46, no. 172 (September 4, 1981): 44452–44457.

18. Mary Douglas, "Deciphering a Meal," *Daedalus* 101 (1972): 61–81.
19. "News Summary," *New York Times*, September 5, 1981, https://timesmachine.nytimes.com/timesmachine/1981/09/05/issue.html; Robert Pear, "US Acts to Shrink School Lunch Size in Economy Move," *New York Times*, September 5, 1981, https://www.nytimes.com/1981/09/05/us/us-acts-to-shrink-school-lunch-size-in-economy-move.html.
20. Ward Sinclair, "When Is Ketchup a Vegetable? When Tofu Is Meat," *Washington Post*, September 9, 1981, https://www.washingtonpost.com/archive/politics/1981/09/09/q-when-is-ketchup-a-vegetable-a-when-tofu-is-meat/7d305f0c-3cc9-480a-a119-e9307dd5ff91/.
21. Russell Baker, "The Gipper, Scrooge, and Santa," *New York Times*, September 12, 1981, https://www.nytimes.com/1981/09/12/opinion/observer-gipper-scrooge-and-santa.html.
22. CSPI News Release, "USDA Undermines the Nutritional Integrity of School Meals," *CSPI Archives*, September 11, 1981.
23. Mary Thornton and Martin Schram, "US Holds the Ketchup in Schools," *Washington Post*, September 26, 1981, https://www.washingtonpost.com/archive/politics/1981/09/26/us-holds-the-ketchup-in-schools/9ffd029a-17f5-4e8c-ab91-1348a44773ee/.
24. All of these occurred within the same year. "Shrinking Lunch, With Relish," *New York Times*, September 14, 1981, https://www.nytimes.com/1981/09/14/opinion/shrinking-lunch-with-relish.html; Francis X. Clines and Bernard Weinraub, "Briefing," *New York Times*, September 28, 1981, https://www.nytimes.com/1981/09/28/us/washington-talk-briefing-029632.html; Ellen Goodman, "Reagan's Nouvelle Cuisine for Kids," *Washington Post*, September 15, 1981, https://www.washingtonpost.com/archive/politics/1981/09/15/reagans-nouvelle-cuisine-for-kids/7a7139d4-4269-43e3-971f-8f7dfa7db5c2/.
25. "Senate Democrats Dine on School Lunch; 09/24/1981," *Roddey E. Mims Collection*, 1981, https://www.docsteach.org/documents/document/senate-democrats-dine-on-school-lunch.
26. Thornton and Schram, "US Holds the Ketchup in Schools."
27. Ibid.
28. Ibid.
29. Ibid.
30. "Reagan Gets New School-Lunch Plan," *Washington Post*, November 18, 1981, p. A17.
31. Steven R. Weisman, "Reagan Abandons Proposal to Pare School Nutrition," *New York Times*, September 26, 1981, https://www.nytimes.com/1981/09/26/politics/reagan-abandons-proposal-to-pare-school-nutrition.html.
32. Kathleen Teltsch, "Reagan Is Assailed by the Field Fund," *New York Times*, November 29, 1981, https://www.nytimes.com/1981/11/29/nyregion/reagan-is-assailed-by-the-field-fund.html.

33. "Alum Makes a Difference Inside the Beltway: Lynn Parker M.S. '75." *Cornell University Nutrition Program Alumni Newsletter*, n.d.
34. Ibid.
35. Francis X. Clines and Phil Gailey, "Briefing," *New York Times*, December 24, 1981, https://www.nytimes.com/1981/12/24/us/briefing-145112.html.
36. Anthony Robbins, "Can Reagan Be Indicted for Betraying Public Health?" *American Journal of Public Health* 73, no. 1 (1983): 12–13.
37. Paul Kellogg, "Feeding the Hungry Is a Federal-Sized Job," *New York Times*, June 3, 1986, https://www.nytimes.com/1986/06/03/opinion/l-feeding-the-hungry-is-a-federal-size-job-346786.html.
38. David Lauter, "Dukakis, Bush Kick Off Campaign's Final Drive Democrat Pledges to Return Prosperity to Middle America," *Los Angeles Times*, September 6, 1988, https://www.latimes.com › archives › la-xpm-1988-09-06-mn-1747-story.html
39. Calvin Trillin, "Uncivil Liberties," *The Nation* 250, no. 17 (April 30, 1990): 586.
40. "Does Ketchup Cut the Mustard?" *Consumer Reports on Health* (April 1999): 2.
41. "Heinz Ketchup: A Flavorful Message in a Glass Bottle," *State Museum of Pennsylvania*, 2015, https://web.archive.org/web/20150916090313/http://statemuseumpa.org/pennsylvania-icons-heinz-bottle/.
42. Julie Jargon, "Seeking Sweet Savings: As Ethanol Boosts Corn Price, Heinz Develops New Tomatoes To Reduce Syrup in Its Ketchup," *Wall Street Journal*, October 2, 2007, https://www.wsj.com/articles/SB119129220836546096.
43. *Nix v. Hedden*, U.S. Supreme Court, 1893. https://prezi.com/bs6gf3odrmit/copy-of-nix-v-hedden/?webgl=0.
44. Rozin, *The Primal Cheeseburger*, 86.
45. Douglas, "Deciphering a Meal"; Sidney Mintz and Daniela Schlettwein-Gsell, "Food Patterns in Agrarian Societies: The Core-Fringe-Legume Hypothesis," *Gastronomica* 1, no. 3 (2001): 40–52.
46. David Wayne Thomas, "Sauce, a la Carte," *Harper's Magazine* 36 (1996): 36.
47. See Amy Bentley, *Inventing Baby Food: Taste, Health, and the Industrialization of the American Diet* (Oakland: University of California Press, 2014), especially chapter five.
48. Roberto A. Ferdman, "How Much Do Americans Love French Fries and Ketchup? A Lot More Than You Think," *Washington Post*, September 21, 2015, https://www.washingtonpost.com/news/wonk/wp/2015/09/21/this-is-how-much-americans-love-french-fries-and-ketchup/.
49. "Ketchup Market—Growth, Trends and Forecasts, 2025–2030," *Mordor Intelligence*, 2025, https://www.mordorintelligence.com/industry-reports/ketchup-market.
50. Norimitsu Onishi, "Spaghetti Stir-Fry and Hambagoo: Japan Looks West," *New York Times*, March 26, 2008, https://www.nytimes.com/2008/03/26/dining/26japan.html.

51. "Spaghetti with Ketchup," Swede and Sour Kitchen, 2013, https://theswedeandsourkitchen.wordpress.com/2013/03/24/spaghetti-with-ketchup/; "Ketchup Spaghetti (AKA "Depression Spaghetti")," 2006, http://www.convergingcuisine.com/?p=28.
52. Marion Nestle, "Ketchup as a Vegetable? Think Again," *The Atlantic*, November16,2011.http://www.theatlantic.com/health/archive/2011/11/ketchup-is-a-vegetable-again/248538/.

Selected Bibliography

Bentley, Amy. *Inventing Baby Food: Taste, Health, and the Industrialization of the American Diet*. Oakland: University of California Press, 2014.

Douglas, Mary. "Deciphering a Meal." *Daedalus* 101 (1972): 61–81.

Jurafsky, Dan. *The Language of Food: A Linguist Reads the Menu*. New York: W. W. Norton, 2014.

Levine, Susan. *School Lunch Politics: The Surprising History of America's Favorite Welfare Program*. Princeton, NJ: Princeton University Press, 2008.

Nestle, Marion. "Ketchup as a Vegetable? Think Again." *The Atlantic*, November 16, 2011. http://www.theatlantic.com/health/archive/2011/11/ketchup-is-a-vegetable-again/248538/.

Rozin, Elisabeth. *The Primal Cheeseburger: A Generous Helping of Food History Served Up on a Bun*. New York: Penguin, 1994.

Smith, Andrew. *Pure Ketchup: A History of America's National Condiment*. Columbia: University of South Carolina Press, 1996.

Amy Bentley, *Ketchup as a Vegetable: Condiments, Culture, and the Politics of School Lunch in Reagan's America* In: *From Garum to Mole: Sauces and Identity in the Western World*. Edited by: Andrew Donnelly, Beth M. Forrest, and Deirdre Murphy, Oxford University Press.
DOI: 10.1093/9780190622138.003.0012

PART FOUR

New Directions

13

"Feeling-Up" the "Ingreasements" as Foundations of Sauces

THE CULINARY GENE IN AUSTIN CLARKE'S *PIG TAILS 'N' BREADFRUIT*

Meredith E. Abarca

THE REFERENCE TO the foundation, or fond, of a sauce is not intended to echo the eighteenth-century French gastronomical principle of using stocks for making an array of sauces. The fond I speak of is the ingredient that makes a sauce *worth its salt*, which happens to be salt. According to food historian Michael Symons, the "word 'sauce' originates in the Latin for 'salt.' "[1] Symons speculates that the very invention of sauces has occurred as a means by which to add salt in order to flavor and preserve desired food tastes. He further argues that a sauce is *worth its salt* when it functions as the "very glue of society" by balancing the "cultural-specific, repetitive [basic techniques and] flavor combinations" that mark the "distinctiveness of any [national or ethnic] cuisine."[2] As Symons describes it, then, salt is the catalyst that brings out the nuances of culturally identifiable flavors embedded within the ingredients of any given sauce. What Symons does not specify, however, is the kind of salt that holds the responsibility of balancing a sauce's flavors and, more elementally still, shapes the complex perception of flavor through taste buds by binding physiological responses to historical, cultural, and social relationships. Salt added in the processes of preparing and consuming food can originate in so many places. It can form in salt mines, be produced by salt waters, or can come from our bodies—hands, fingers, mouths.

Placing the body as the source of salt in a sauce enables reflection upon the idea of an inherited and culturally specific "culinary gene," a concept described by Austin Clarke in his memoir *Pig Tails 'n' Breadfruit*.[3] By *sauce*, I refer to the liquid that is created as a byproduct while something is being cooked, or the creation of a liquid substance to enhance the flavors of a dish. To such a sauce, the amount of bodily salt added for proper flavoring is measured through an embodied form of knowing. It is the addition of this salt that makes a sauce taste better. Simultaneously, it symbolically and materially links the historical, social, and cultural values of a people to the ingredients they use, their methods of cooking, and their reasons for preparing and sharing certain foods. All of these adhere to and are transmitted through the mineral content of this particular kind of salt.

The initial carrier of a culinary gene is the first "chef" to feed us, our biological mothers. This gene passes on an embodied knowing through a secretion process in which the salt within the food a mother eats transfers to the child she carries in her womb. Unlike other genes, a culinary gene continues to be passed on after birth, as mothers prepare food for their offspring, thus conditioning children's palates to like or dislike certain flavors. In this process, the secretion of salt from the cook's hands and fingers to the food she is making is absorbed by those who consume it. As this is happening, these eaters are also adding salt from their own bodies in the form of salivation.

Through the interconnected acts of cooking and eating, bodily forms of salting help convey a genealogy linking contemporary cooks with the original inventors of a given dish. Bodily salt plays a significant role in bridging cultural and historical lineage through both preparation and consumption. Austin Clarke's culinary memoir, *Pig Tails 'n' Breadfruit*, in which he presents the fond that flavors Barbadian food as a process of "feeling-up" the "ingreasements" (ingredients) offers an illustration of the transmission of bodily salt. For Clarke, it begins with the act of "feeling-up" food. In this action, the verb *to feel* carries three distinct meanings. First, it refers literally to feeling food through an array of sensations: textures, spiciness, sweetness, softness, sourness, tartness, bitterness, sharpness, and so on. The second refers to the emotions felt while cooking or eating, and from memories of previous experiences and the emotions that marked them: pleasure or anxiety, joy or sadness, excitement or disgust, curiosity or anxiety, nostalgia or reassurance. Third is feeling the rhythms that come with an array of culinary tasks: gathering ingredients, preparing foods, and daily rituals of consumption.

Clarke introduces the concept of "ingreasements" to suggest that what makes a recipe is not a list of ingredients, but the processes of gathering foodstuffs and flavoring, the end result of which is a prepared dish. In the second page of his memoir, he writes, "whatever it is we cook, we call it food, in the sense that any combination of any ingredients ('ingreasements'), of whatever quality, that we put into a pot and cook is food."[4] The interjection of the word "grease" underscores how the oils that release from meats, seeds, and plants are part of the seasoning and sauce produced in the process. Since the implements of measuring and mixing all the items added to a pot are the fingers and hands as food is being "felt-up," the secretion of bodily salt is also part of the flavoring of food.

An example of the seasoning created by the "grease" released from "ingreasements" is given in Clarke's description of the origin of "bu'n-bu'n" a term that comes from "burnt, without the letter 'r' and the letter 't' and used in all strata of Barbadian society." Clarke states:

> The bun-bun is the layer of food stuck to the bottom of the pot. It contains, in coagulated form, all the ingreasements that went into the "seas'ning" of the food: the oil, the pieces of meat that fell to the bottom, all the good things. And the present-day popularity of bun-bun suggests its culinary delectability, or sweetness.[5]

Sweetness, throughout Clarke's memoir, is not a reference to a sugary taste of food. It refers to Clarke's mnemonic sensory process that recalls the communal actions of gathering ingreasements according to seasons, social, and economic circumstances:

> The dynamics of social status and the strong effect it had on our lives, the communal nature of our villages, and the routine and schedule of harvesting the land and of the neighborhood butcher determined when ingreasements . . . were available to everyone, and therefore what you would eat on a given day of the week.[6]

Clarke introduces the term "ingreasements," therefore, to underscore that what defines Barbadian cooking is determined by the availability of foodstuffs. How these dishes develop a historical and cultural significance transmitted from one generation to the next is by seasoning "ingreasements" though the process of "feeling-up" the food that is being cooked. It is by "feeling-up" the "ingreasements" that a person's bodily salt flavors the sensations, emotions, and motions expressed while cooking and absorbed while eating.

"Feeling-Up" the "Ingreasements"

Austin Clarke (1934–2016), a writer, broadcaster, civil rights leader, literature professor, and diplomat, was born in Barbados and raised by a single mother.

A scholarship took him to Toronto, Canada, a place where he lived most of his life, with occasional absences to return to Barbados and to temporarily live in the United States and in Italy.[7] Despite having spent most of his adult life outside of Barbados, it's the food of his birthplace that left a lasting culinary effect on his life.

Clarke's opening line captures the totality that food plays in his sense of cultural self. "Food. Is a word that defines my life."[8] By placing a period between the word "food" and the verb "is," he makes two sentences: one capturing a complete thought in a single four-letter word; the other, by leaving the subject out, shows an ambiguous and complex process as to how and why food defines his life. As he reminisces and writes about the defining aspects food has for him, he shows how it connects him to the culture of Barbados, to the historical residue of colonization, and to the flow of global economies. Most significantly, Clarke shows the process of learning to embrace a heritage expressed through his mother's embodied culinary knowing. He elaborates the lessons conveyed about social relations and historical perceptions: how food—gathering it, cooking it, and consuming it—creates culture. His mother's cooking nourished his physical body, but it also shaped his character. As he recalls his childhood, he states, "[t]he food my mother cooked was never intended only 'to stop a hole' in my belly. More importantly, she had it in her mind that her food was to make me 'feel good,' make me grow into a strong young man and give me 'big, big brains.'"[9] Adulthood and geographical distance make it possible for Clarke to recognize how his mother's lessons influence his food memories, his culinary practices, and the stories he (re)creates to speak about how food defines his character.

Clarke's memoir conveys his esteem for the value of "feeling-up" food as a method of embodying and incorporating knowing, because he shows how people can become aware of history and culture as it is conveyed through such a form of knowing. Embodied or incorporated bodily knowing underscores a form of awareness that is understood by *feel*, often referred to as "intuition," or the "gut reaction." While intuitive knowing can be dismissed as subjective, capriciously individualistic, and therefore not of value to others beyond the person with a given intuition, judging food by the combining of available ingredients, both in the process of cooking and consuming it, by *feel*, as Clarke's memoir shows, challenges this philosophical dismissal. To know by *feel* reflects the affects (energies, emotions, judgments) that others before us have added in the form of their bodily salt to the sauces (food), and then transmitted to us through the flavors of the foods that we now prepare and consume. In the process of consumption, the saltiness of our saliva gland results in a seasoning process similar to that of "bun-bun" in that the flavor of the residue of all the ingreasements we consume is enhanced by our saliva. This then engages the mnemonic process in remembering the food we eat.

This *feel* of affect is exchanged through smell. Philosopher Teresa Brennan, in *The Transmission of Affect*, challenges what she calls the foundational fallacy of Western thought, the notion that as individuals we are intellectually and emotionally self-contained. She shows how the transmission of affect is a process by which "the emotions of affect of one person... and [the] energies these affects entail can enter into another" person.[10] Affect does not refer to the words used to articulate emotions such as satisfaction, love, hunger, or disgust. Affect deals with the force of energies an emotional state creates.[11] The sources of affective energies come from people's social milieu, but the effects of such energies are experienced biologically and physically. It is the field of neurology that explains how smell allows for a transmission whereby people become alike by alignment of nervous and hormonal systems through a process called chemical entrainment. This chemical exchange, which "works mainly by smell," is an unconscious olfaction that carries information and thus signals and produces reactions.[12] Clarke sums up the *feel* of affect when he recalls that women who "fed [him] from their pots" over the years transmitted so much more to him in this manner than food alone: "[I]n my heart, in my blood and in my mind, I carried all the conversations and all the eccentricities of my mother, my aunts, cousins, and grandmothers, these strong, beautiful, black, light-complexioned, and white women who nurtured me,... loved me and turned me into the man I am today."[13]

The mineral contents that produce the bodily salt that flavors the affects transmitted through "feeling-up" food are the socioeconomic and historical circumstances that led to the invention and techniques used in particular culinary practices. In his discussion of "Pepperpot," a one-pot dish whose name "conjur[es] up all kind o' herbs and spices and meats and voodoo and witchcraft and myths," Clarke provides the history of the signature "ingreasement" to make pepperpot, cassava, and how its use binds diverse culinary practices.[14] The Amerindians of Guyana taught the Black slaves taken from Barbados to Guyana to roam "the bush looking for diamonds and silver," to remove the toxicity of cassavas, and to use them as the "essential ingreasement in pepperpot, which keeps it lasting and lasting for days without going bad and gives pepperpot its dark colour and body."[15] After explaining the cultural, social, and economic shock experienced by both Amerindians and African slaves in Guyana, Clarke sums up what pepperpot has come to mean for both of these groups:

> So, when you talk 'bout pepperpot, a dish of great national-cultural significance, the only food that is really Guyanese, you talking about revolution. Communism, social and racial dislocation, political strife, and the Indians, Africans, and British that make up the Guyanese population. Only a nice plate o' Guyanese pepperpot can bring these... fractious fractions together, make them siddown at the same political table.[16]

But to *feel* the history of these "fractious factions," Clarke admits,

> you... have to ask God to help you find a woman willing and able to cook you the real McCoy in a Guyanese home. This meal will have, in its preparation and sweet seasoning, the sweat and perspiration of cultural truth and myth. You will get from her hand the true taste of the country.[17]

Aware that most of his readers are in North America, Clarke, after giving a recipe for making pepperpot, suggests an imagined process to feel at least part of the history embedded in the flavors of this dish:

> Whilst eating this pepperpot, pause in your delight. Close your two eyes for a moment, and into your mind will come the sparkling images o' silver and diamonds, frankincense and even myrrh and mirth, reflecting the roots of myths and culture in the [Guyana] bush.[18]

To know by *feel* and to transmit the feel of affect, therefore, is to link "the deeply personal with the social and to know that 'like the heart, [it] beats beyond our [cognitive] capacity to control it'; it is 'a lifeline between the past and the future.' "[19] The body carries a social totality archived on its "surface[,] its tissues," and its senses that is expressed and transmitted by the process of "feeling-up" the "ingreasements" of a dish that later are tasted in the very sauce created while such a dish is being cooked.[20]

As Clarke sets out to trace his culinary heritage, he shows how an incorporated knowing and an inscribed knowledge about history, culture, politics, and economics come together to develop his food consciousness that connects him to the culinary histories of Africans once enslaved in the West Indies. This kind of food consciousness links bodily knowing with cognitive awareness. It does not privilege one over the other, but shows how bodily knowing informs our thoughts and rationalizes our actions.[21] In his study about how societies remember, anthropologist Paul Connerton draws a distinction between incorporated knowing as practice and inscribed knowledge as information. He categorizes incorporated practices as those "conveyed and sustained by ritual and performances."[22] The performativity of incorporated knowing is linked to "habitus" of practices, feelings, values, and behaviors. Furthermore, transmission within incorporated knowing, whether this is intentional or not, takes place during the time a particular activity occurs—the moment of making a dish, the moment of sharing it, the moment of consuming it. All of these moments are flavored with bodily salt of those "feeling-up" the "ingreasements," as well as those eating the food.

A central difference between inscribed knowledge and incorporated bodily knowing, as Connerton presents it, is that inscribed knowledge is a cognitive process of understanding information. The sources of such knowledge come from the analysis of texts presented in the form of written documents, oral transmissions of information, and images. Often, the gathering of inscribed knowledge reflects a conscious effort to know. Clarke shows this form of acquired knowledge, for instance, when he speaks of the economic politics and migration routes involved in the Triangular Trade. He begins the chapter "Breadfruit Cou-Cou with Braising Beef" in this manner:

> Captain Bligh was one o' the people who sail from England to Africa, carrying nails and muskets and knives and silk top hats to trade with the Africans, for slaves. And he would take these slaves to the Wessindies, and exchange them for sugar and molasses and rum . . . and sail back to England with these riches, thereby completing the Triangular Trade.[23]

The gathering of inscribed knowledge here addresses a history of trade where Africans exchanged other Africans as a human commodity. Clarke traces how the logic of economic policies at the beginning of the West Indies' history is based on creating an equal exchange value among commodities that include muskets, knives, humans, sugar, molasses, and rum.

The transmission of a culinary historical and cultural awareness by which Clarke defines his life via food interlaces both inscribed knowledge and incorporated knowing. It is a food that "originated in the days of economizing and slavery—two powerful factors in any consideration of Barbados culture and folklore. Food rituals were based on the cultural intricacies of availability and foodstuffs."[24] Such rituals, necessary in producing food, are expressed in the performance of "feeling-up" the "ingreasements." The links that Clarke makes through the development of his food consciousness, therefore, show how incorporated knowing is affective, and how such affective energy influences the cognitive process by which inscribed knowledge is understood.

Clarke's theory of "feeling-up" and the development of his food consciousness show the degree to which it *is* the bodily salt added to food through the process of secretion and absorption that enhances a sauce flavored with historical and cultural significance for a given group of people. The coded information in a culinary gene helps recognize flavors that provide a bodily self-understanding of how "alimentary identities" are linked to histories and cultural practices that assist in defining a "sense of belonging to multiple, and sometimes overlapping, segments of society."[25] Clarke's memoir shows how a culinary gene maintains a feeling of heritage by which cultural traditions are continued and transformed. Most importantly, a culinary gene transmits a sensory way of knowing history and culture through food, where the initial lessons are passed from mother to child.

The saltiness of our own bodies can be thought of as an inherited culinary gene on two levels. Both of these observations expose the source that provides the deposits of salt that our bodies accumulate and then transfer to the foods we prepare and consume. The first is our predisposition to be receptive to certain flavors and textures that results from the frequency of their consumption; this predisposition is often based on a generational continuum. The method of seasoning our food often echoes our mothers' cooking; which is patterned after their mothers', and so on. Without specifically addressing the power a mother's cooking has in influencing the palate of a child, cookbook writer Elizabeth Rozin and psychologist Paul Rozin frame this predisposition as "culinary themes." For them, such themes define how most "of the world's people seem to belong to well-marked cuisine groups that create culinary products with distinctive and describable gustatory themes."[26] Clarke speaks of such themes—pig tails, meal-corn cou-cou, souse, pepperpot, pelau—but does not forget that it was women who "were always cooking [and] as these women cooked, they talked about the food they were cooking and whether they should try a different assortment of spices, a different combination of ingreasements." In this way, a person's cultural culinary themes are learned, expanded, and developed in the act of cooking and eating.

Not forgetting that women are responsible for establishing a group's gustatory themes leads to the second observation regarding the presence of a culinary gene. This refers to the mechanism by which the influence of a type of gene-like code is transmitted and recognized from one generation to the next: food's flavors. The first transmission takes place before birth. Studies have shown how a pregnant woman's food flavor preferences "are transmitted through the amniotic fluid in the womb to the fetus and . . . after birth this transmission can influence later flavor preferences" in all stages of life: infancy, childhood, adolescence, and adulthood.[27] It is also at the beginning stages of life when transmission of emotions connected to flavors takes place. A mother's body does not simply transmit the chemical components flavoring the food that she consumes while pregnant, but she also communicates the emotional significance she associates with those foods. "The learning of these preferences in *utero* and their emotional expressions are therefore incorporated into [the olfactory] hardwired system" of each individual.[28] The emotional sources embedded in food's flavors range from the familial to the cultural to the historical realm.

Memory and the olfactory "hardwired system" are integrally linked in the recognition of culturally and historically based culinary themes. Sociologist Cruz Miguel Ortíz Cuadra proposes the notion of the "palate memory," and chef and food historian Michael W. Twitty uses "blood memory" to explain two specific kinds of memory enabling such recognition. Ortíz Cuadra demonstrates, in *Eating Puerto Rico: A History of Food, Culture, and Identity*, how "palate memory" is linked to "a mother's cooking, [to] the frequent repeating of various diets and meals," which become the basis for a familial or cultural group's culinary themes.[29] All of these well-marked culinary themes, for him, are both stored and retrieved through our palates. In *The Cooking Gene*, Twitty sees "blood memory" as the substance of resurrection.[30] He writes:

> My entire cooking life has been about memory. It's my most indispensable ingredient, so wherever I find it, I hoard it. I tell stories about people using food, I swap memories with people and create out of that conversation mnemonic feasts with this fallible, subjective mental evidence. Sometimes they are people long gone, whose immortality is expressed in the pulp of trees also long gone and in our electronic ether. Other times they are people who converse with me as I cook as the enslaved once cooked, testifying to people and places that only come alive again when they are remembered. In memory there is resurrection, and thus the end goal of my cooking is just that—resurrection.[31]

For Clarke, these types of memories are activated by the process of "feeling-up" the "ingreasements."

While culinary themes gain their significance from the social milieu that brought them into existence and from the circumstances that allow them to be recreated or modified, it is a mnemonic process that recognizes and recreates such themes. Portraying as symbiotic this relationship between society and the body, Ortíz Cuadra in his book shows how and why palate memories evoke "fixation[s] on flavors and taste, and—at times—sensations of estrangement" by connecting "food and dishes with vital experiences and remembrance."[32] Similarly, for Twitty, blood memory represents a geneo-geography that allows him to trace and then connect to his culinary ancestry.

Going beyond reminiscing about his palate and blood memories, Clarke theorizes about food's significance in the history and culture of Barbados and the role his mother plays in the development of his food consciousness. The first recollection he shares with his readers about his mother's culinary teachings is the difference between *food* and *haute cuisine*, a distinction that underscores the value of cooking by *feel* and the process of transmitting such incorporated knowing to others. He recalls that the food defining his life is not " 'hot-cuisine,' as [his] mother called that kind of French sophistication with sauces and garlic.... 'What do the French-people know about cooking food?'... 'We talking about *food*, boy. Food!' "[33] It is not the mastery of elaborated technical skills that enhances the addition of garlic to a sauce that makes *food*. For his mother, it is the olfactory system that makes food. Clarke writes, "Taste and smell are important distinctions in my mother's definition of what food really is. Food to her, as to me, is something very special. Almost supernatural. Something that blends in with the culture of the place I was born."[34]

Making the olfactory system define what becomes food is significant in a number of ways. Taste and smell, known together as the gustatory system, are responsible for giving information to the brain about the chemical composition of the flavors of a given food through a process known as transduction. Because for Clarke's mother it is the "fingers and hands" that "are the implements for measurement," a person's bodily salt is part of the chemical composition flavoring the food being tasted and smelled.[35] Since the olfactory system is connected to the brain pathways that trigger emotions and memories, what gets flavored and deciphered through taste and smell is the *feel* by which something is prepared, cooked, remembered, and transmitted from one person to another.

The olfactory system, the hands, fingers, and palate (the producer of saliva), serve as the transmitter of the culinary gene. Clarke sums up the intersection of the olfactory system, emotions, and recollections as an incorporated bodily knowing expressed by "feeling-up" food:

> Taste is the thing. And touch. Tasting and touching. Feeling is stretched to include "feeling-up" the food: touching the fish; pulling

> out the entrails of a chicken with your fingers; peeling potatoes and slicing them with a knife while holding them in your hand—not using a gadget that ensures precision of cut and duplication of each slice.[36]

By feeling-up food and thus adding bodily salt, a culinary gene's DNA is passed on from one generation to the next. Its origin is embedded in the living history of concrete social realities. A culinary gene contains information of learned culinary skills, symbolic rituals practices of cultivating, gathering, preparing, and sharing food. It also contains the DNA that codes flavors and textures that become a foundation of knowledge archived in people's palate memories. This culinary gene transmitted by feeling-up food is what Clarke describes as a privilege he inherited from a diet of slaves who once lived in Barbados.

Privilege of Bodily Knowing

After describing the process for cooking pig tails and salted beef, served on rice cooked with fresh okra, Clarke writes:

> When you survey the contents of the pot, after you have taken off the lid and open-she up, such a waft of historical and cultural goodness going blow in your face! Such a strong reminder from the slave days, such a powerful smell of Barbadian hot-cuisine, is going to greet you that your mouth is bound to spring water and salivate, in a contemporaneous salvation of salivation.[37]

Here Clarke is adding another liquid substance that flavors the taste and texture of food, a bodily "ingreasement," if you will: anticipatory salivation. While this particular "ingreasement" is rather private and intimate, what allows the recognition of the flavors that provoke such salivation is not. Clarke describes this particular dish as "the backbone of existence for we [Barbados]. It was consumed regularly all over Barbados."[38] The aroma of "historical and cultural goodness" that provokes a "contemporaneous salvation of salivation," as an added final bodily "ingreasement," underscores a bodily transmission and recognition of cultural and historical context. The word "salvation" is key in this recognition. The salvation provoked by the aromas of pig tails, salted beef, and rice cooked with okra serves to transmit a culinary knowledge that carries a way of knowing beyond the limits of words.

The chapter that introduces this dish is titled "Privilege," and the opening lines draw attention, once more, to the difference between incorporated knowing and inscribed knowledge. Clarke begins the chapter by recalling a phone call he once received on a Friday night:

> "Mr. Clarke, do you know what 'privilege' is?" It was seven o'clock on a Friday evening, and the voice on the other end of the telephone was that of the prime minister of Barbados, the Right Honourable Errol Walton Barrow, PC. I was his adviser on internal political affairs. Whenever he addressed me as "Mr. Clarke" instead of "Austin" or "Tom," I knew immediately I was in serious political trouble.... "Privilege, sir," I began uncertainly, "is... ahm... a right, sir. Or an advantage. Privilege, Prime Minister, could be an immunity granted to a person, or to a group, or..." "Austin," his booming voice came through the telephone, but in a more jocular tone and with some amusement in it, "not *that* kind o' privilege! I mean *real* privilege." Real privilege?[39]

The *real* privilege that the prime minister was referring to is the dish of pig tails and salted beef. By defining privilege as a concept, Clarke's initial response speaks of an inscribed knowledge of such a term. But here, the prime minister speaks of a privilege understood through an incorporated knowing that takes place by making and eating "Privilege" in the form of a dish.

Once Clarke is presented with a plate of "Privilege," he describes how the liquid used to boil the okra is then used to cook the rice, after which it is mixed with the juices of the meat. The end result is that, when they are swallowed, the pieces of meat go "down smooth, smooth, smooth, slippery like raw oysters."[40] He translates the sensations and emotions embedded in the smoothness and slipperiness as an incorporated knowing that Barbardians are privileged to carry within their bodily salt. Clarke articulates the *feel* that eating "Privilege" evokes as an expression of historical, economic, and identity politics:

> Barbadians have always known that the food we eat is "slave food," based on leavings or left overs, the remnants of the better cuts of meat eaten by the Plantation owners. The Amurcans would call it soul food, but I would argue that we Wessindians, and Barbadians in particular, had come to soul food long before African Amurcans, African Canadians and Africadians.
>
> Slave food is an older concept of black aesthetics and black culture than is soul food. We was eating it before the 1960s, when Amurcans

> discovered that they was no longer 'coloured' or 'Negro,' but was black and beautiful and interested in African culture. We have known for a long time that we was beautiful, although we didn't know or care one damn that we was black.... Slave food doesn't have a damn thing to do with the soul or with 'black is beautiful.' It has *everything* to do with the belly.[41]

For Clarke, that which in the United States is known as "soul food" reflects an inscribed knowledge. Soul food for him is a concept, not the food itself. Soul food converts culinary practices borne out of specific histories and cultural context into an ideological discourse of identity politics. Clarke doesn't suggest that the concept of soul food is not useful within discourse on Africanized identity politics. After all, not only did he teach "African Amurcan Literature" at Yale, but he embraced "the black Amurcan and black Amurcan culture" to the point of "trying to speak like a black Amurcan" and considering himself "to be as much a Southerner as a Barbadian."[42] However, slave food, as he argues, represents an incorporated transmission of knowing that is experienced by its flavors, its texture, and its taste all *felt* in the belly.[43] Through this bodily knowing, "privilege," the dish, becomes the backbone of a people's cultural practices affirming their histories. He underscores how slave food is rooted in a bodily knowing by reaffirming:

> One thing about cooking that comes from slave days is that you have to feel-up everything.... You have to touch-up the food and love-up the food. Rub your two hands over the pig tails and the salt beef, together with the seasoning. If you do not touch-up and love-up the meats and the ingreasements, your food is not going respond and taste sweet when it done.[44]

By "feeling-up," adding the saltiness of the hands, and "loving-up," infusing food with sensations/emotions, a continuity with the past is maintained; it is the cook's palate memories that guide the flavoring of the food.

Clarke goes on to explain how the *feel* gained from eating "Privilege" transforms into inscribed knowledge, something he does throughout his memoir. By situating the origins of staple dishes as slave food, he helps his readers remember culinary processes linked to specific historical, cultural, and economic realities. For example, in describing the origins of how "Privilege" was first prepared, Clarke tells his readers:

> In colonial times, which followed the days of slavery, practically all the food we use to eat had to come from Away—from England, Canada, and Australia. Since colonized people were considered second-class to the people from Away, the food was also second-class, or of an inferior quality. Some of it, like the meat, had to be cured in brine. You would have to salt down your own pig tails and inferior cuts of beef in a barrel of brine, and leave them to settle and season for a few days before they turn into tasty meats that could be used for making Privilege.[45]

The contextual knowledge that Clarke describes here, long past colonial or slavery times, is also found in Kensington Market in Toronto or the Brooklyn Market in New York. In these markets of the Away places, where first-rate meats are found, it's possible to buy pig tails and salt beef "already season-up and soak-down in brine."[46] But in order to enhance the taste of pig tails and salt beef bought in the Away markets, and thus taste the flavoring of a culturally based culinary gene, Clarke states: if "you want a really nice piece o' pig tail or a sweet cut o' salt beef, you have to roll up your two shirtsleeves, up to your two elbows, take off your wristwatch and the sliver bracelets, and put your two hands down deep inside that brine-barrel."[47] This practice adds bodily salt not only to the brine-barrel, but most importantly to the pieces selected to make "Privilege" at home. Clarke is guided by his incorporated knowing and his inscribed knowledge to affirm his right to savor the present-day privilege of eating the food that once sustained slaves in Barbados.

Listening as Clarke Does

Clarke's last chapter, "Frozen in Time," speaks to the importance of remembering that our incorporated knowing is filled with cultural and historical information transmitted not by words but by *feel.* The last dish Clarke mentions in this chapter is "African Chicken," which one of his friends "christened" "Chicken Austintecious."[48] This particular recipe rekindled Clarke's desire to cook and eat chicken. What had turned off his appetite was "the enormous amount" of chicken he "used-to eat whilst growing up in Barbados."[49] While teaching at Yale University in 1968, he learned to make this recipe from a student, a "black-Amurcan (hyphenated in them days) who was re-discovering Africa, a political strategy to combat the degradation and segregation he and others was experiencing through the slow pace o' 'racial integration.'"[50]

"African Chicken" calls for "chicken parts: legs, the neck, the wings, the thighs, the back" and, once they are cleaned and dried, a little salt and lime juice are added to them. The sauce requires "an onion, green onions, fresh thyme, cloves o' garlic, fresh ginger, brown sugar, pepper, fresh red peppers, cream, mayonnaise and peanut butter." All of these "ingreasements" need to be "rub-in" on the chicken parts "using your ten fingers." Finally, "pour a lil vegetable oil, or butter, or even drippings, over the pieces, and place them in a large baking pan."[51]

While visiting his mother for two months "at her suburban home in Mount Laurel, New Jersey," Clarke cooks "African Chicken." The fact that this is a dish she has never had, let alone cooked, does not keep her from telling Clarke "how much peanut butter to use... how much 'seasning' to rub into the chicken parts."[52] Irritated with his mother's culinary directions about a dish introduced to him as a symbol of rediscovering Africa, he stops just short of deflecting her guidance, stating:

> And I remember just in time, before I disrespected her rigid marking out of the boundary of mother and child, that she is my mother, and that perhaps she does not really have to know about Africa or Africanization or black Amurcan nationalism or soul food to know that a chicken needs the proper "seasning" to make the ingresasements palatable and sweet when they are cooked. And I listen. I have to listen.[53]

What Clarke remembers that he *has to listen to* is a way of knowing that goes beyond political and ideological discourses. He *has* to listen in order to remember that a culinary gene that has been passed on through secretion and absorption of bodily salt from one generation to the next guides his mother's instructions. He has to listen and be guided by her own belief in " 'feeling-up' her meats [with] her fingers to mix in the ingreasements, or what she calls the 'in-goodness.' "[54]

The cause for not listening to the knowledge carried in a culinary gene, which is transmitted by "feeling-up" food, is the loss of an incorporated way of knowing. There are a number of consequences for failing to recognize this form of embodied knowing. At a personal and cultural level, for example, it makes it possible for someone like Esteban Montejo, a Black Cuban ex-slave, to reminisce about his life as both a slave and a free man and simultaneously claim that "there are no Africans in Cuba," while naming numerous foods Cubans eat that have African origins.[55] At the socio-historical and racial level, as Twitty argues in *The Cooking Gene*, this kind of forgetting reinforces power structures by which certain people's culinary practices (what he refers to as their "culinary gene") are either marginalized, appropriated, or completely ignored in the writings of culinary histories.[56] At a Western philosophical level, when the transmission of bodily knowing from one person to the next is dismissed, this simultaneously reinforces as the dismissal of a maternal-based source of knowing.[57] Yet, Twitty asserts the primacy of just this sort of maternal-based knowing when he writes, "The little hearth—located under heaven or a thatch structure or building used during the rainy season—was itself a ritual space, an altar, a face of spirits, usually a female entity representing motherhood and nurture, the pot itself a kind of womb."[58] For Clarke's mother, it is about feeling the "in-goodness." To prevent the loss of an embodied way of knowing, therefore, we must remember that what "allows for the flavors of all other ingredients to swing wide open" is *salt*, an ingredient to "be considered and carefully weighted like all others."[59] "Feeling-up" the "ingreasements" adds a bodily salt that when carefully considered and weighed for its historical and cultural significance is what makes a sauce *worth its salt*.

Feeling-Up the Recipe: Black Pudding and Souse

Early in his memoir, Clarke admits to a seeming contradiction in writing about his life, culture, and history of his place of birth through the lens of food. As he notes: "It is ironical to be suggesting a book about food cooked in Barbados, because in every self-respecting Barbadian household the women…would not be caught dead with a cookbook. To read a cookbook would suggest that she has not retained what her mother taught her."[60] While in this specific passage Clarke speaks of that which is passed on from mother to daughter, the entirety of his book shows that such bodily knowing is also passed on from mother to son. Clarke resolves the seeming contradiction and maintains self-respect by not offering recipes following conventional cookbook formulas: no lists of ingredients, no exact measurements, no step-by-step instructions. What gets transmitted is a practice that began in passing from one generation to the next, adding a "pinch of this and a pinch of that…to a pot, at first by trial and error, and then perfected through history and constant usage," and never without the added bodily salt.[61] Therefore, Clarke invites his readers to recreate the descriptions-as-recipes he offers to guide their cooking process in a way that he inherited them: by "feeling-up" the ingredients and measurements. Imagining that most of his readers who might be interested in recreating the recipes would be other Barbadians, he encourages them to trust their incorporated knowing in recognizing flavors, textures, and aromas of the foods they too grew up eating. Clarke's memoir thus gives recipes in a manner that encourages his readers to *feel* the "ingreasements," to *feel* the cooking process, and to *feel* the moment of consumption.

Of the many recipes Clarke suggests, "Black pudding and souse have to be the ultimate in slave food."[62] He arrives at such a conclusion because the dish is made "from the parts of the pig that nobody else wanted or had the heart to eat. But regardless, pudding and souse is the sweetest thing handed down by our ancestors, African slaves, to each and every one of us present-day Wessindians."[63] To impart the *feel* of Clarke's instructions for making black pudding and souse, his recipe is quoted at length, but without the discussion of killing, gutting, and preserving some blood of the pig, or the process of making the black pudding, since Clarke concludes by stating: "I wouldn't advise you to try your hand in making it, though. It's tummuch work. And too risky."[64] Nonetheless, here is his description on how to make souse:

> It's made from the pig's feet, from the ham hocks, from parts o' the pig head, like the snout and the ears, and from some of the leaner parts of the pig, near the belly. These parts, or "features," are boiled until they are soft. They are either left to cool off in the water in which they were cooked, or are taken out and placed on the counter to cool....
>
> While these pig features cooling off, it's time to make the prickle. The prickle for the souse is the mixture in which the features are put to soak and get "soused-up." Hence the name of the dish, souse.
>
> Cut up onions, green onions, cucumber and fresh thyme in large bowl. Don't slice the cucumber; dice it.
>
> Add salt and pepper to suit your taste. Fresh hot pepper is always better than black pepper shaken from a shaker. Don't forget a touch o' white vinegar, to help the pork draw.
>
> Stir up these ingreasements in a bowl, and taste the prickle to make sure it reach the hotness you like. Expert souse-makers does argue that you *must* pour a lil water in which the features was cooked into the prickle, to give it some body and that nice taste o' pork....
>
> When the pork features cool off, clean them using a lot o' lemon. Rub and rub lemon peth all over them. The cleaning of the features at this stage is the most important part of the preparation of souse.

> Cut up the features in bite-size pieces and throw them in the prickle. Stir them round, and cover them down for at least one hour. . . . Souse, the real Barbadian souse, *have* to be served and eaten one way only: cold. . . .
>
> When you ready to serve . . . [g]et a sharp knife and cut off pieces o' black pudding, about two inches in length. Put a couple of pieces on a plate with a few pieces o' souse, consisting of a pig foot, a piece o' the ear, the snout, and a nice piece from the ham hock. Pour a lil prickle all over the souse, and sprinkle a few pieces of fresh parsley or watercress on the black pudding. You could add some fresh parsley to the souse to make it look pretty, or as North Amurcans would say, to "garnish" it.[65]

After providing the recipe for what he describes as a national dish of Barbados, Clarke does suggest that "to understand and appreciate it" one more ingreasement much be added. This ingreasement comes in the form of a palate recognition that occurs by having been "born in the particular culture that prepares it" and consumes it every Sunday.[66] So next Sunday, try your hand at making Barbados souse by *feeling* your way through Clarke's narrative description on how to make this recipe.

But if you're not from Barbados and have never eaten souse, perhaps a more conventional recipe is an easier place to start. A second edition of Clarke's memoir, published in 2004 under the title *Love and Sweet Food*, includes an appendix with a list of traditionally written recipes. Possibly the publishers felt that readers of a different cultural background, or those not so at ease trusting their ability to *feel* their way in the kitchen, would enjoy expanding their inscribed knowledge of cooking experiences. It is from this edition that this recipe is offered.[67]

Souse (but No Black Pudding)
Austin Clarke, *Love and Sweet Food*, 2004

Ingredients:

4 fresh pig's trotters
2 fresh ham hocks
Fresh pieces of pig's snout and pig's ear (if you can stomach them! Or lean parts near the belly)
3 lemons
3 limes

2 bunches of green onions
2 bunches of fresh parsley
1 bunch of fresh thyme
1 bunch of watercress
2 fair-sized onions
1 large cucumber
White vinegar (a couple of dashes)
Hot fresh red peppers (Scotch Bonnet, with yellow ones mixed in; 1, or more, depending on taste)

Method:

1. Put the trotters, hocks, and pieces of pork in a pot of salted water to boil; bring to a boil slowly. Ladle off the skim regularly.
2. While the pork is boiling, prepare the relish. Dice cucumber and onions, chop the green onions, fresh hot peppers to tastes, and parsley (use only the leaves). Take a half-cup of water from the pot with pork, and leave it to cool. Mix these ingredients in a bowl with a couple of dashes of white vinegar and the cooled pork-water. Pour the relish into a terrine or deep Pyrex dish.
3. Remove the trotters, hocks, and pork from the pot. Clean them thoroughly, and chop them into bite-size pieces, discarding the bones if you want. Place them in the relish, and garnish with a few chopped pieces of watercress and parsley.
4. Leave the terrine on the counter, unrefrigerated, for two hours to "souse up."

Notes

1. Michael Symons, *A History of Cooks and Cooking* (Chicago: University of Illinois Press, 2004), 115.
2. Ibid., 116.
3. Austin Clarke, *Pig Tails 'n' Breadfruit: A Culinary Memoir* (New York: New Press, 2000).
4. Ibid., 2.
5. Ibid., 17.
6. Ibid., 24.
7. In her study of culinary memoirs, Vivian Nun Halloran offers an insightful perspective as to the impact that being a "scholarship boy" had on Austin Clarke's reflections about his growing up in Barbados. See Halloran, *The Immigrant Kitchen: Food, Ethnicity, and Diaspora* (Columbus: Ohio State University Press, 2016), 21–40.

8. Clarke, *Pig Tails 'n' Breadfruit*, 1.
9. Ibid., 212.
10. Teresa Brennan, *The Transmission of Affect* (Ithaca, NY: Cornell University Press, 2003), 147.
11. Gregory J. Seigworth and Melissa Gregg, "An Inventory of Shimmers," in *The Affect Theory Reader*, ed. Melissa Gregg and Gregory J. Seigworth (Durham, NC: Duke University Press, 2010), 1–27.
12. Brennan, *The Transmission of Affect*, 251.
13. Clarke, *Pig Tails 'n' Breadfruit*, 40–41.
14. Ibid., 175.
15. Ibid., 177.
16. Ibid., 183.
17. Ibid.
18. Ibid., 190.
19. Diana Taylor, *The Archive and the Repertoire: Performing Cultural Memory in the Americas* (Durham, NC: Duke University Press, 2003), 82.
20. Paul Connerton, *The Spirit of Mourning: History, Memory, and the Body* (Cambridge: Cambridge University Press, 2011), ix, 60–64.
21. Meredith E. Abarca and Nieves Pascual Soler, "Introduction," in *Rethinking Chicana/o Literature Through Food: Postnational Appetites*, ed. Nieves Pascual Soler and Meredith E. Abarca (New York: Palgrave, 2013), 2.
22. Paul Connerton, *How Societies Remember* (Cambridge: Cambridge University Press, 1989), 7.
23. Clarke, *Pig Tails 'n' Breadfruit*, 113.
24. Ibid., 24.
25. Vivian Nun Halloran, *The Immigrant Kitchen: Food, Ethnicity, and Diaspora* (Columbus: Ohio State University Press, 2016), 14.
26. Elizabeth Rozin and Paul Rozin, "Culinary Themes and Variations," in *The Taste Culture Reader: Experiencing Food and Drink*, ed. Carolyn Korsmeyer (New York: Berg, 2005), 35.
27. Gordon Shepherd, *Neurogastronomy: How the Brain Creates Flavor and Why It Matters* (New York: Columbia University Press, 2011), 233.
28. Ibid., 234.
29. Cruz Miguel Ortíz Cuadra, *Eating Puerto Rico: A History of Food, Culture, and Identity*, trans. Russ Davison (Chapel Hill: University of North Carolina Press, 2013), 2.
30. Michael W. Twitty, *The Cooking Gene: A Journey Through African American Culinary History in the Old South* (New York: Amistad, 2017), 14.
31. Ibid., 11–12.
32. Ortíz Cuadra, *Eating Puerto Rico*, 2.
33. Clarke, *Pig Tails 'n' Breadfruit*, 1–2.
34. Ibid., 2.

35. Ibid., 3.
36. Ibid.
37. Ibid., 65.
38. Ibid., 66.
39. Ibid., 54–55.
40. Ibid., 59.
41. Ibid., 60.
42. Ibid., 229–230.
43. Clarke's memoir offers a challenge to the notion that we can only understand the social significance of food flavors by the way our brains create what neuroscientists refer to as "emotional flavor images." He places this emotional connection as one identified through his belly.
44. Ibid., 64.
45. Ibid., 62.
46. Ibid.
47. Ibid., 63.
48. Ibid., 226.
49. Ibid., 219.
50. Ibid., 220.
51. Ibid., 221.
52. Ibid., 246.
53. Ibid., 247.
54. Ibid., 217.
55. Miguel Barnet, *Biography of a Runaway Slave*, trans. W. Nick Hill (Willimantic: Curbstone Press, 1994), 129.
56. Twitty, *The Cooking Gene*.
57. Brennan, *The Transmission of Affect*.
58. Twitty, *The Cooking Gene*, 13.
59. Monique Truong, *The Book of Salt* (New York: Houghton Mifflin, 2003), 212.
60. Clarke, *Pig Tails 'n' Breadfruit*, 3.
61. Ibid., 2.
62. Ibid., 162.
63. Ibid.
64. Ibid., 158.
65. Ibid., 159–161.
66. Ibid., 162.
67. Austin Clarke, *Love and Sweet Food: A Culinary Memoir* (Toronto: Thomas Allen, 2004), 321–322.

Selected Bibliography

Barnet, Miguel. *Biography of a Runaway Slave*. Translated by W. Nick Hill. Willimantic, CT: Curbstone Press, 1994.

Brennan, Teresa. *The Transmission of Affect*. Ithaca, NY: Cornell University Press, 2003.

Clarke, Austin. *Pig Tails 'n' Breadfruit: A Culinary Memoir*. New York: New Press, 2000.

Clarke, Austin. *Love and Sweet Food: A Culinary Memoir*, 2nd ed. Toronto: Thomas Allen, 2004.

Shepherd, Gordon. *Neurogastronomy: How the Brain Creates Flavor and Why It Matters*. New York: Columbia University Press, 2011.

Taylor, Diana. *The Archive and the Repertoire: Performing Cultural Memory in the Americas*. Durham, NC: Duke University Press, 2003.

Truong, Monique. *The Book of Salt*. New York: Houghton Mifflin, 2003.

Twitty, Michael W. *The Cooking Gene: A Journey Through African American Culinary History in the Old South*. New York: Amistad, 2017.

Meredith E. Abarca, *"Feeling-Up" the "Ingreasements" as Foundations of Sauces: The Culinary Gene in Austin Clarke's* Pig Tails 'n' Breadfruit In: *From Garum to Mole: Sauces and Identity in the Western World*. Edited by: Andrew Donnelly, Beth M. Forrest, and Deirdre Murphy, Oxford University Press. © Oxford University Press 2026. DOI: 10.1093/9780190622138.003.0013

14

Mole Poblano

PROFILE OF TASTE AND CULTURE IN MEXICO THROUGH DIGITAL HISTORY ANALYSIS

Jeffrey M. Pilcher

MOLE POBLANO, A deeply colored sauce of chiles and spices, is widely acknowledged as Mexico's national dish. Eaten on festive occasions throughout the country, this "mestizo" combination of flavorings from the New World and the Old exemplifies the race mixture at the center of Mexican nationalist ideology. The fiery dish is also considered to be a test for foreign visitors; the first taste of mole reportedly brought tears to the eyes of the French-imposed Emperor Maximilian and his consort Carlota in the 1860s. Nevertheless, the couple demonstrated their local affiliation by celebrating the national holiday of the Virgin of Guadalupe with mole for brunch.[1]

While mole is an icon of Mexican cuisine and identity, its own identity, the sauce itself, has changed over time—expanded with regional varieties and growing complexity—and its meaning has adapted, revealing historical and political tensions. This chapter employs digital methods of social network analysis to construct a historical taste profile of mole and, through this, Mexican history and culture. It opens by answering the seemingly simple question: What is mole? It may help to begin with a preliminary contour sketch, while recognizing mole's endless variations. Chile pepper, the foundation of indigenous cuisines, is the lowest common denominator of mole, and recipes often include multiple types of chiles ground together. Mole recipes also generally call for a variety of spices, which were central to elite Spanish cookery at the time of the conquest, although they declined in European usage during the early modern era. Poultry, meat, or occasionally seafood, cooked separately as a broth, distinguished mole as a special dish for peasant communities that subsisted for most of the year on a basically vegetarian diet of corn tortillas and beans. Aromatic vegetables and fruits such as New World tomatoes and tomatillos, as well as Old World onion and garlic, further enhance the dish. Finally, mole is thickened with some combination of ground nuts, seeds, bread, or tortillas, a technique common to indigenous and medieval cookery, though this was superseded in early modern Europe by a roux of flour and butter. Another distinctive Mexican cooking technique is toasting or frying the ingredients separately to heighten their flavor before grinding them together.

From a cook's perspective, the term "profile" refers to the balance of flavors, which vary historically over time and across cultures. The most notorious stereotype of mole—*it's too hot!*—illustrates the cultural embeddedness of flavor. The human body develops a tolerance to capsaicin over time, and higher doses are required to taste the same flavor. Whereas piquancy may overwhelm the chile novice, experienced tasters perceive a more complex range of flavors such as the vegetal notes of green chiles or the latent sweetness of ripened, red peppers. Another foreign stereotype of mole—*it's chocolate sauce!*—reflects a similar discordance of flavor profiles. Early modern European cooks banished sweet flavors (and spices) from main dishes to a separate course, dessert, that often featured chocolate. Although some mole recipes do contain a small amount of Mexican cacao (but not sweetened chocolate), its absence is notable in historical recipes. A well-rounded mole will have an element of sweetness, but this comes primarily from dried chiles, not bitter cacao. The balance of meat to mole also differs from European sensibilities, which usually consider sauce as an accompaniment to the main ingredient rather than as the centerpiece of a dish, which is to be scooped up with tortillas or soaked into rice like curry.

For a flavor profile to be useful historically, recipes must be situated in social context. The historiography of mole comprises three basic interpretations, which might be called the indigenous, the baroque, and the conquistador. The belief that mole was a pre-Hispanic relic went largely unquestioned by Mexican authors and foreign travelers and anthropologists alike until the 1930s. The baroque interpretation, an invention of nationalist ideologues following the Revolution of 1910, considered mole to be the artistic product of seventeenth-century nuns, who combined elaborate mixtures of ingredients as a culinary incarnation of *mestizaje*. The conquistador interpretation, which held that mole was an essentially European dish disguised by an indigenous name, emerged in the 1960s as part of a revisionist attack on the ideological foundations of an authoritarian, one-party state.[2] With the recent rise of food history as a critical field of research, scholars have situated these interpretations within the social contexts of the colonial and revolutionary eras while also raising new historical questions. Scholar of history of science and technology José Luis Curiel Monteagudo conducted the first systematic review of colonial recipes for mole, refuting much of the popular mythology around the dish and providing a more nuanced understanding of culinary *mestizaje* and the precise mechanisms whereby some ingredients were incorporated into the dish and others were not.[3] José Luis Juárez López proposed an innovative periodization of nineteenth-century Mexican cuisine, or at least culinary literature, as largely a continuation of late-colonial trends. According to this view, dramatic change came not with the growth of a male-dominated publishing industry following independence in 1821, but rather with the emergence of female-authored, community cookbooks during the age of Porfirio Díaz (1876–1911).

This chapter was inspired by the research of Curiel Monteagudo and by the literary scholar Franco Moretti, whose book *Graphs, Maps, Trees* called for a quantitative "distant reading" of the changing historical contours of genres and national literatures within larger literary systems.[4] Following this method, it begins by reviewing linguistic evidence in order to outline the basic categories of mole within vernacular usage. The historical appearance of these dishes and the evolution of their constituent ingredients are then charted using data from an opportunistic sample of recipes in three significant periods, the late colonial era (c. 1750–1817), the Porfiriato era (1876–1910), and the contemporary boom in cookbook publishing (1972–2015).[5] Finally, this genealogy of mole is situated within historical contexts of racial and national ideologies. Based on a limited data set of about 450 recipes, it suggests only tentative conclusions that largely confirm the existing historiography, while still advancing a few novel findings. The larger goal is to demonstrate the power of digital methods for culinary history and to encourage more rigorous future research.

The Names of Mole

The state of Oaxaca has been acclaimed "the land of seven moles," but surely there are as many moles as there are cooks, who each bring their own distinctive touches to the dish. Moreover, because cooks generally have more than one recipe, and each preparation is slightly different, the potential number of moles approaches infinity. To reclaim mole from abstract mathematics to quantifiable science, some principle of ordering is needed. This chapter seeks not to impose a taxonomy a priori but rather to look for geographical and cultural patterns of naming and preparation within the vernacular usage of cooks. An individual cook (often accompanied by a circle of *comadres*,[6] because nobody wants to do all that work alone) may declare her dish to be simply mole, but she may also identify it more specifically by color, ingredient, location, or some other denomination. Although linguistic markers are helpful in categorizing the dish, these boundaries tend to dissolve under close examination.

Even the basic name, mole, is far from determinant in historical and modern usage. In Nahuatl, the indigenous lingua franca of central Mexico, *molli* meant simply "stew." It could be modified in multiple ways; for example, *ahuacamolli* comes from the Nahuatl *ahuacatl* or avocado, although most Mexican cooks today would probably not consider guacamole to be a proper mole. Closer to the modern usage would be *clemole* or *tlemole*, a "cooked stew," derived from *tetl*, the Nahuatl word for fire, but this term has largely fallen out of usage. Another version, *chilmole* or *chirmole*, literally meaning "chile stew," is most commonly found in the Yucatán, where it was presumably introduced at some unknown time by Nahuatl-speaking migrants from the central highlands. Spanish has also contributed to the vocabulary of mole, including the fruit-laden dish known as *manchamanteles*, or "tablecloth stainer," because of the persistence of chile oil in fabric. Still another variety, *pipián*, or archaically *pepián*, is thickened with pumpkin or other seeds, *pepitas* in Spanish. Linguistic hybrids also exist, such as the chile and meat broth called *mole de olla* after its rounded, earthenware cooking pot.[7]

Mexican cooks also categorize mole by color across a spectrum ranging from green and yellow to red and black. Green mole invariably calls for fresh chiles, while yellow, red, and black use ripened and dried varieties. This range of colors for chile appeared already in the sixteenth-century *Florentine Codex*, the most important indigenous-language primary source, which was recorded by elite Nahua scribes born shortly before the conquest. Nevertheless, moles are now generally referred to by Spanish names: *rojo*, *verde*, *amarillo*, and *negro*.[8] Black mole has had perhaps the widest range of color names, including *negro*, *mulato*, *moreno*, and *prieto*, which were terms used in the colonial racial hierarchy known as the system of castes. Color names also vary regionally; red mole often goes by *colorado* in the north and by the diminutive *coloradito* in Oaxaca. Indigenous peoples may have assigned symbolic meanings to the color range of chiles, but they reserved the greatest ritual significance to the five colors of maize, their staple grain.

Virtually every small town in Mexico has boosters eager to extol the virtues of the local mole. That Puebla and Oaxaca have the best-known varieties creates a gastronomic and racial polarization: Oaxaca as a center of indigenous civilization and Puebla as a city founded by Spaniards. Yet this dichotomy is misleading, and not only because of race mixture. The state of Puebla contains numerous communities that speak indigenous languages, and the city of Oaxaca was a prominent center of Spanish colonialism. Food cultures also spill across the border between the two states; for example, the *mole de cadera* (spine) eaten during the annual *matanza de chivo* (goat slaughter) in Tehuacán, Puebla, is also prepared on the other side of the Sierra Madre in Huajuapan de León, Oaxaca.

Ingredients such as goat backbone offer another common way of distinguishing the many varieties of mole. The *Florentine Codex* began its *molli* listing with four versions featuring turkey, and *mole de guajolote* remains the most iconic variety, in part because of its local origins.[9] By contrast, Mexico's only other native domesticated animal, the hairless dog, fell off the menu after the conquest. Deer, duck, and the occasional iguana are still used to make mole, usually among rural communities, but the balance of moles is prepared with domesticated animals introduced by the conquistadors. Other modifiers for mole refer to thickeners such as almonds, peanuts, or *guaje*, the seed of a native tree that is used to make *guaxmole*.

Linguistic evidence raises more questions about the nature of mole than it answers. Not everything called mole qualifies; in addition to guacamole, there is a nineteenth-century cookbook with a *mole sin mole* (mole without mole) and an eighteenth-century manuscript recipe for *huevos moles* (egg mole).[10] Dessert mole might seem as alien to Mexican sensibilities as turkey with chocolate sauce is to Europeans, but Francisco Santamaría's authoritative dictionary, first published in 1959, describes a category of *moles dulces* (sweet moles) made with sugar instead of chile.[11] Nor must a dish be called mole to count; the fabled seven moles of Oaxaca include *manchamanteles* and a dish called *chichilo*. Moreover, there are countless boundary cases. Some recipes for Oaxacan *chileajo* (literally, "chile garlic") are chile-pork stews; others resemble a spicy, pickled vegetable appetizer plate. Another ambiguous case is Veracruz's *chilpachole*, a sort of *mole de olla* with crabs. The Yucatecan turkey-chile stew *relleno negro*, made with a distinctive *recado* spice mixture and hardboiled eggs, would likely be rejected in central Mexico, but it might pass under the Nahuatl name *chirmole*. Thus, at times the identity of mole seems more political than linguistic.[12] Language alone cannot police the boundaries of mole; as the Spanish word *moler* (to grind) suggests, mole is in the making.

The Recipes of Mole

Late Colonial (c. 1750–1817)

The early history of mole is as opaque as the dish itself. The primary sources extend little beyond the *Florentine Codex*, which described the "food of the lords" as including *totolin patzcalmolli*, "turkey with a sauce of small chiles, tomatoes, and ground squash seeds"; *nacatlaolli*, "meat stewed with maize, red chile, tomatoes, and ground squash seeds"; *cujatl chilchoio*, "frog with green chiles"; *axoltotl chilcozio*, "newt with yellow chile"; and *chacali patzcalo*, "lobster with red chile, tomatoes, and ground squash seeds."[13] While the basic outlines of meat, chile, and thickener were already present, there is little to suggest the elaborate taste profile of modern mole, which has not stopped imaginative chefs from reconstructing pre-Hispanic menus. Evidence of mole from the early colonial period is virtually nonexistent, present neither in recipes nor even in the names of dishes.

Eight manuscript cookbooks from the late colonial era provide the first documentary evidence of mole. One of these works has been attributed speculatively to the renowned seventeenth-century poet Sor Juana Inés de la Cruz, although it was written on eighteenth-century paper, perhaps copied from an earlier original. Altogether, the manuscripts contain about thirty recipes for mole, *clemole*, *manchamanteles*, and *pipián*. The average number of ingredients in each recipe seems modest, at slightly over ten, with *pipián* distinctly less complex, at about six. A few notable exceptions calling for more than twenty ingredients, together with the small sample size, explain the high standard deviation. Geographical indicators include Puebla, Oaxaca, México, and, somewhat surprisingly, Castille. The latter called for particularly expensive ingredients: mutton, pork, and hen, pine nuts or hazelnuts and small walnuts, and fine bread (bizcocho). Other names also indicated privilege within the orders of early modern society—*colegio* (college) and *monjas* (nuns)—and ingredients, not only *guajolote* but also vinegar mole and cinnamon, walnut, and egg yolk *pipián*. Two outliers appeared only once: *axiaco*, made with hen and fruit, is indistinguishable from *manchamanteles*. *Pichomole* calls for turkey and pork, but the name may derive from *pichón* (pigeon or bird generically) rather than the slang meanings of *picho*: the male member—clearly not a family dinner—and "rotten," perhaps a creolized version of the Spanish *olla podrida* ("rotted pot," a type of stew).

Computation methods for social network analysis showing the relationship between recipes and ingredients offer a methodology for interpreting

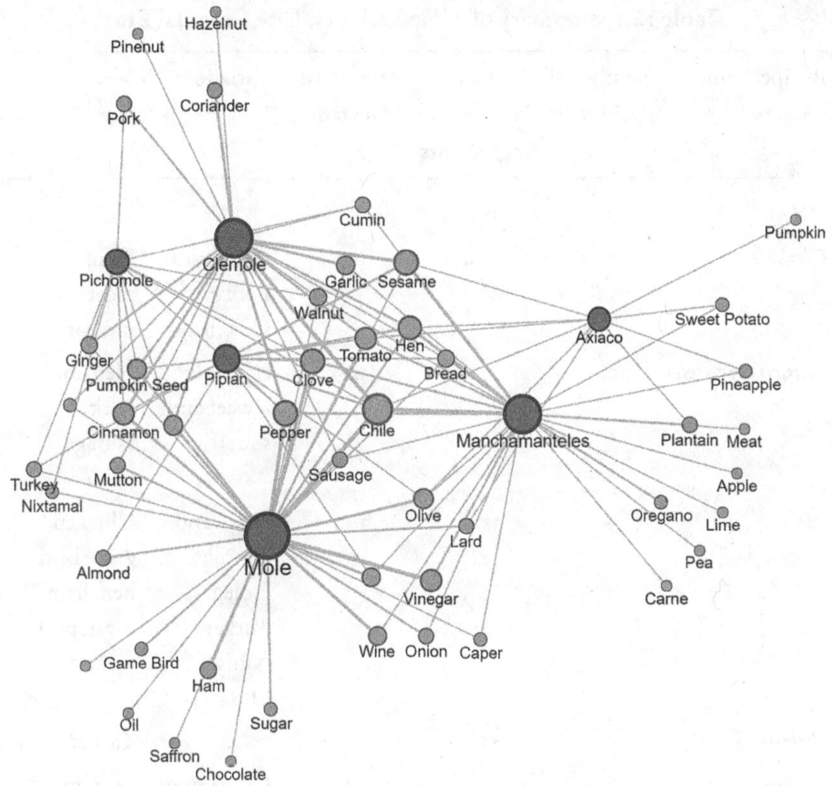

FIGURE 14.1 Historical Mole Network Map. Created by J. Pilcher using Google Fusion Tables.

these recipes. The database for this chapter situates recipe categories (mole, *clemole*, etc.) in one column, with the corresponding ingredients for each recipe (without distinguishing between varieties of chile) in the other. The resulting network map, Figure 14.1, produced by Google Fusion Tables, visualizes the relationship of ingredients to recipes. It should come as no surprise to find chile as the central ingredient connecting all of the recipes. The second most common ingredient, sesame seed, may not be as intuitive, but Santamaría defined mole as "a famous and particular dish that is prepared with sauce of chile and sesame."[14] The other central ingredients are Old World spices and aromatics, cinnamon, clove, pepper, and garlic, excepting only the New World tomato. Spain had a striking presence in the colonial dish. The most common meats were also European in origin, including hen, sausage, pork fat, and mutton; turkey appears surprisingly marginal. Although the average number of ingredients seems relatively low, by comparison with modern versions, many of the colonial recipes included more than one type of meat, and not simply

Table 14.1 Summary of Mole Variants, Late Colonial Era

Recipe Name	Number of Recipes	Average Number of Ingredients	Standard Deviation	Variations	Meat
Axiaco	1	12			Hen
Clemole	5	10.4	1.52	de Oaxaca, Poblano, Castellano	Hen, meat, mutton
Manchamanteles	10	9.8	5.19	*Agridulce* (sweet and sour)	Hen, meat, pork, sausage, none
Mole	9	12.3	3.12	Mexicano, Castilla, Colegio, Turkey, Nuns, Oaxaca	Chicken, game bird, hen, ham, meat, pork, turkey
Pichomole	1	13			Turkey, pork
Pipián	6	6.3	3.14	Cinnamon, nogada (walnut), egg yolk	Hen, meat, turkey, none

as option. Turkey and pork trotters, for example, surely provided a very rich broth as a base for the dish. Other surprising ingredients were olives, capers, wine, and especially vinegar, for example, in the sweet and sour (*agridulce*) *manchamanteles*. By contrast, as Curiel Monteagudo observed, chocolate appeared in only one recipe.[15]

Porfirian (1876–1910)

Porfirian cookbooks encompassed a much wider selection of moles, as Juárez López's research predicted, but notable continuities in geographical scope and the varieties and colors of mole persisted in cookbooks across the nineteenth century. Unlike the colonial data set, which comprised the entire universe of known recipes, the Porfirian data represented a sample of six cookbooks and four published manuscripts from Mexico City, seven Mexican states (Guanajuato, Hidalgo, Jalisco, Michoacán, Puebla, Querétaro, and Zacatecas), and California in the United States.

Puebla and Oaxaca remained the most frequent geographical indicators, but they were joined by references to new places, both where cookbooks were published, *michoacano* and *tapatío* (Jalisco), and to more distant locations, *campechano* and *toluqueño*. Meanwhile, the first avowedly indigenous mole appeared in *tarasco*, a former term for the Purépecha people of Michoacán. Color names became more common, especially green, variants of black, and the occasional yellow, but not red, suggesting it may have been considered the default. *Rojo* and *colorado* appeared only in reference to *pipián*, more commonly a green dish. With the proliferation of recipes came greater variety—exalted, prosaic, and patriotic—ranging from the autocrat's *manchamanteles* to moles of the *aldeano* (village), *corriente* (ordinary), *pobres* (the poor), *en familia* (family-style), and *de la república* (republican). One of the most colorful was the *manchamanteles del arriero*, the muleteer carrying tropical fruit from the *tierra caliente* (coastal plains), a stock character in Christmastime *nacimientos* (crèche scenes). The family of moles even included a late-colonial celebrity chef, Nana Chepa (Granny Josefa), who ran a popular food stand by the Canal de la Viga, where canoes landed produce and flowers for Mexico City markets.[16] Although Castilian mole survived the wars of independence, cookbook authors deported the distinctively named, *manchamantel*-like dish *axiaco* to Havana, where the distinguished scholar Fernando Ortiz later declared it a symbol of Afro-Cuban race mixture.[17]

The names of mole had changed over the nineteenth century, but many colonial-era cooking practices persisted. The average number of ingredients remained about the same as in the colonial era, ten to twelve for mole and *manchamanteles* and seven for *pipián* and *verde*, although once again a few exceptional dishes, such as autocrat's *manchamanteles* with twenty ingredients, formed the long tail of the distribution. The recipes yielded a more elaborate network map, but without displacing the centrality of European ingredients, excepting only chile, tomatillo, peanut, and pumpkin seed. The colonial penchant for combining multiple meats in a single pot was still common. Porfirian cooks were more likely than their grandmothers to use turkey, but they continued to ignore chocolate. Nevertheless, this sample did not portray a completely conservative kitchen; for example, there was far greater variety of seeds and nuts in *pipián*, including almonds, peanuts, dark corn, melon seeds, and even cotton seeds, perhaps a byproduct of the Porfirian

Table 14.2 Summary of Mole Variants, Porfirian Era

Recipe Name	Number of Recipes	Average Number of Ingredients	Standard Deviation	Some Variations	Meat
Chichilo	1	5			Pork
Clemole	20	7.95	2.56	Castellano, de Palacio, Mexicano, Toluqueño	Turkey, mutton, sausage, cecina, hen, pork loin, tripe, veal
Guatzmole	1	7			Pork
Manchamanteles	20	12.4	4.26	Autocratas, de Pobres, del Arriero, en Familia	Hen, chicken, bacon, mutton, pork, sausage, game, turkey
Mole	48	9.1	3.52	Aldeano, Amarillo, Campechano, Corriente, de Nana Chepa, Michoacano, de la Republica, Tapatío, Tarasco	Cecina (dried meat), goat, meat, mutton, pork, tripe, turkey
Mole de Guajolote	13	12.1	1.75		Turkey, pork, rabbit
Mole Oaxaqueno	4	8	1.73		Turkey, hen, sausage, ham
Mole Poblano	9	10	2.73		Turkey, hen, pork, sausage
Mole Prieto	12	11.1	1.36	Moreno, Mulato, Negro	Turkey, hen, meat, suckling pig
Mole Verde	13	7.1	1.55		Turkey, game, hen, chicken, pork, pork loin
Pipián	38	7.1	2.83	Verde, Colorado, Almond, Peanut, Melon Seed, Cotton Seed, with Dark Maize	Duck, game, hen, pork, shrimp, turkey, none

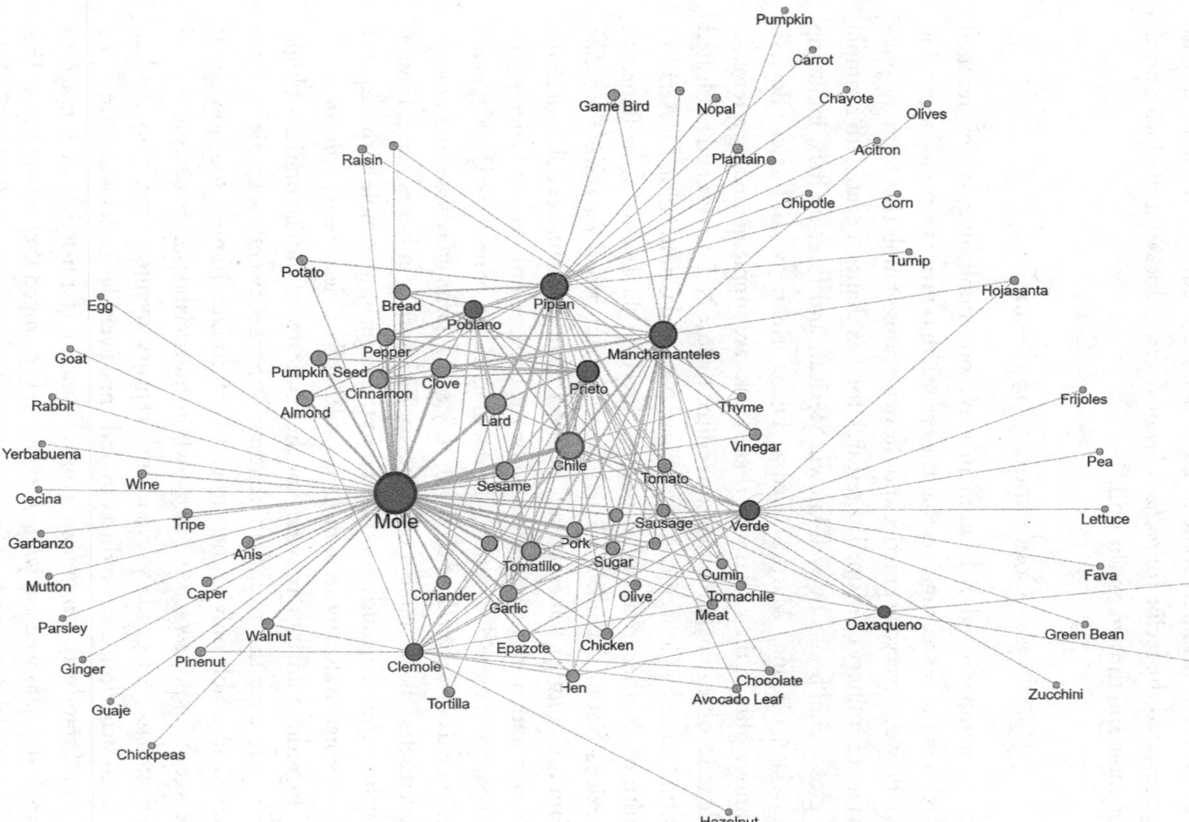

FIGURE 14.2 Porfirian Mole Network Map. Created by J. Pilcher using Google Fusion Tables.

textile industry. Juárez López's review of nineteenth-century cookbooks found the greatest evidence of innovation through the importation of technologies and techniques, and the national dish did not escape this European fascination. It was surely some foreign cookbook rather than common sense that inspired the recipe for *pollos rellenos de mole*, chicken stuffed with pork-loin mole and thrown on the grill.[18]

Contemporary (1972–2015)

The contemporary global boom in cookbook publishing, which reached Mexico in the 1980s, suggests that the twentieth century witnessed a growing split between everyday practice and the depictions of mole that form the public face of culinary tourism. The research for this chapter began with a sample of glossy cookbooks by well-known Mexican and foreign chefs, including Patricia Quintana, Martha Chapa, Diana Kennedy, and Rick Bayless. Ethnographic in their own way, these works are supplemented by a remarkable series of regional investigations edited by José N. Iturriaga and published around 2000 by Conaculta, the Mexican National Commission for Arts and Culture. Another invaluable series, produced in the late 1980s by Banrural, Mexico's National Bank for Rural Development, titled *La comida familiar* (Family Cooking), was essentially a collection of community cookbooks, one for each state, with recipes supplied by the bank's employees and clients. The diversity of their recipes reflects the documentation of neglected local specialties such as *chilatequile*, *chile caldo*, *chileajo*, *chilorio*, *guaxmole*, and *tesmole*. Nevertheless, as the number of recipes for each variety indicates, textualization may have simultaneously contributed to the hegemony of mole at the expense of its former rivals *clemole*, *manchamanteles*, and to a lesser extent *pipián*.

Ingredient inflation provides another indicator of the elaboration of high-end mole over the twentieth century. Whereas twenty ingredients once seemed accessible only to the autocrat Porfirio Díaz himself, it is now about average for mole *poblano* and *negro*, whose more elaborate recipes, such as one dedicated to the legendary seventeenth-century inventor of mole, Sor Andrea de la Encarnación, can top thirty ingredients. Everyday moles with names like *abuela* (grandma), *campirano* (rustic), *granja* (farm-style), and *ranchero* (ranch-style), as well as *pipián*, have scarcely changed their dimensions. This new, bimodal distribution of the ingredient count explains the significantly greater standard deviation in this sample than in its Porfirian counterpart. For a visual representation of *haute mole* and its prosaic counterpart, consider the contemporary network map, with its three concentric circles. The core consists of a mass of more than three dozen common ingredients, enclosed by a belt of moles, and orbited, in turn, by numerous tiny satellite ingredients both elite (salmon, quail, asparagus) and obscure (*quelites*, *flor de chunpancle*, *quiotes de maguey*, meaning wild greens and cactus and maguey blossoms).

The baroque mole enshrined at the heart of Mexican gastronomic nationalism, with its dozens of ingredients, including chiles, spices, turkey, and chocolate, is a product not of colonial convent kitchens but of modern culinary tourism, as the distinctiveness of mole came to rely on the image of mole as a dish with innumerable ingredients. This is not to deny the centrality of culinary *mestizaje* or the ubiquity of mole as a national dish. The data presented here simply confirm the obvious point that Mexican cuisine, like Mexican society, is sharply divided by race, class, and region. To situate mole within these divisions requires a brief foray into Mexican social history.

The Context of Mole

As a marker of status and community, mole's social meanings have evolved over time in response to internal and external pressures. At the risk of historical oversimplification, the focus here falls on four periods: the conquest and Spanish colonialism, Creole nationalism and independence, Porfirian modernization and revolution, and neoliberal globalization. During each period, Mexicans imagined the racial and class connotations of mole with an eye to both outside perceptions and internal social distinctions.

Food denoted privilege within the early modern society of New Spain, where a relatively small number of Europeans ruled over a vast, multiracial empire. In an important study of the embodied experience of Spanish colonialism, historian Rebecca Earle described the conquistadors' fears that a native diet would alter their very physical nature, literally transforming them into Indians.[19] To ensure access to Old World ingredients, settlers introduced a wide range of livestock, staple grains, fruits, vegetables, and the Asian spices cinnamon and ginger. Foods that failed to acclimate, such as pepper and cloves, were imported at great expense. Spices were particularly prized in late medieval Europe, and the combination of cinnamon, pepper, and clove ultimately became the standard spice mixture in colonial moles. The local elite of Creoles, born in the New World of Spanish descent, acquired a taste for some indigenous foods, particularly chiles and chocolate, but sharp racial divisions persisted, at the table as elsewhere. For much of the colonial era, mole was a

Table 14.3 Summary of Mole Variants, Contemporary Recipes

Recipe Name	Number of Recipes	Average Number of Ingredients	Standard Deviation	Some Variations	Meat
Almendrado	3	14.3	3.21		Chicken, hen, pork
Chichilo	3	17.3	5.86		Beef, pork
Chilatequile	1	13			Beef, dried beef, pork
Chile caldo	1	9			Beef, pork
Chileajo	4	12.8	4.35		Chicken, pork, rabbit
Chilorio	1	9			Pork
Chilpachole	1	12			Crab
Chirmole	13	6.25	0.96	also Chilmole	Catfish, crab, duck, pork, shrimp, None
Clemole	4	8.3	1.53		Catfish, turkey, none
Coloradito	7	14.2	4.54		Chicken, hen, pork
Guasmole	5	7	2.82	also Guaxmole, Huasmole	Beef, pork
Manchamanteles	16	14.3	3.86		Chicken, hen, pork, pork loin, sausage
Mole	84	11.8	5.29	Abuela, Campirano, Capitalino, Granja, Ranchero, Pobres, Rosa, Tierra Caliente	chicken, deer, dried beef, duck, goat, iguana, pork, quail, shrimp, tripe, Turkey
Mole Amarillo	10	10.8	4.17		Beef, chicken, deer, pork, none
Mole Colorado	2	6	1.41		Deer
Mole de Olla	11	11.2	3.7		Beef, chicken, pork, none
Mole Negro	20	20.5	5.23	Prieto	Beef tongue, chicken, hen, pork, turkey
Mole Poblano	6	22.8	4.92	Sor Andrea	Turkey

Recipe Name	Number of Recipes	Average Number of Ingredients	Standard Deviation	Some Variations	Meat
Mole Rojo	12	12.5	5.62	Chocomite, Mushrooms	Chicken, pork, tripe, turkey, none
Mole Verde	23	13.9	7.31		Chicken, fish, hen, pork, turkey, none
Pipián	36	7.8	2.53	Sweet Potato, Prune, Quiotes de Maguey, Verde, Rojo, Ranchero	Beef tongue, chicken, deer, duck, hen, iguana, langostino, pork, rabbit, salmon, none
Tesmole	1	8			Hen

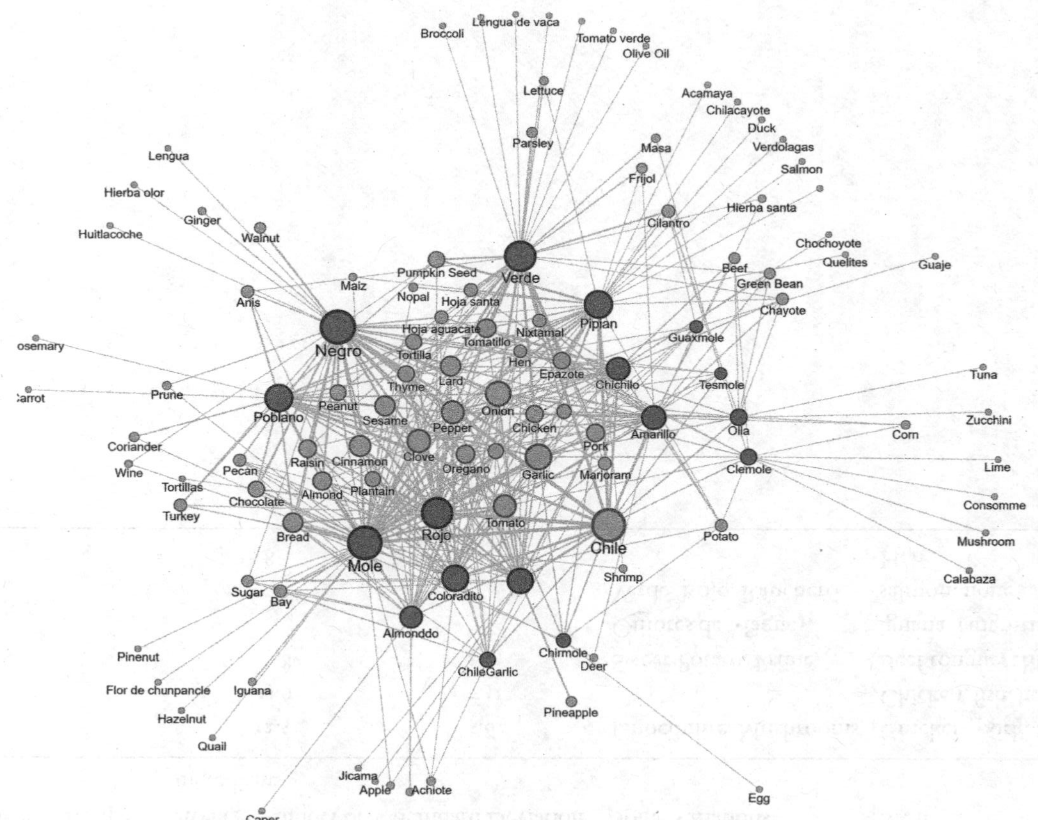

FIGURE 14.3 Contemporary Mole Network Map. Created by J. Pilcher using Google Fusion Tables.

considered a creolized version of medieval Spanish cuisine, and the evidence examined here does nothing to refute those European associations.[20]

The rise of Creole patriotism beginning in the late seventeenth century caused a reappraisal of the indigenous heritage, but elite tastes in food gave a decided preference to French novelties over pre-Hispanic dishes. As the historian Enrique Florescano explained, Creoles sought to claim equality with Spaniards by imagining themselves as heirs to Aztec emperors but had little desire actually to dine with Indians.[21] José Luis Juárez López captured that reluctance in a book entitled *The Slow Emergence of Mexican Cuisine: Creole Ambiguities, 1750–1800*, which described the late-colonial fashion for French *nouvelle cuisine* and the fixation even among sympathetic authors on indigenous ceremonial cannibalism and the consumption of insects and other unmentionable *animalitos*.[22]

With independence, mole's indigenous roots were acknowledged, giving it the status of the national dish, but French cuisine remained the ideal of Mexican elite public dining throughout the nineteenth century. Austrian-born Emperor Maximilian and his Belgian consort Carlota's mole brunches and continental dinners were in keeping with the practices of their aristocratic circle, as well as those of their liberal political rivals. For example, Vicenta Torres de Rubio, author of a landmark 1896 cookbook, wrote that on holidays "the majority of families gather to eat mole poblano or ask for it in rustic *fondas* (restaurants) to finish in private or among family."[23] The novelist Manuel Payno used a dinner of *mole de guajolote* and *mole verde*—"dishes that were served in the fabulous palaces of the Aztec kings"—as a literary device to critique Francophile contemporaries.[24] Nevertheless, satirist José Tomás de Cuéllar revealed a pretentious character's true lack of breeding with the observation that "for lunch he buys mole de guajolote."[25]

The elite Mexican debate over the social status of mole persisted even after the Revolution of 1910, which overthrew the Porfirian oligarchy and installed a regime of populists from the provinces. The revolutionary program of *indigenismo*, which sought to assimilate natives into the national life, had its counterpart in tales of *mole poblano*. In 1926, Hispanophile Carlos de Gante first imagined the invention of mole by colonial nuns in order to redeem "the dirty, stinking" turkey and "make something good and original."[26] Rivals quickly rewrote the mole legend in ways more favorable to the indigenous people, and, as historian Ricardo Pérez Montfort noted, within the context of regional rivalries.[27] Indeed, although I once speculated that Oaxaca's reputation as the "land of seven moles" was invented by restaurant chefs seeking a weekly round of dinner specials, an early reference to the phrase from about

1950, long before the rise of organized culinary tourism in Oaxaca, suggests that local boosters may actually have coined it in response to Puebla's growing fame as the purported cradle of mole.[28]

Oaxaca ultimately triumphed in this rivalry through the indigenization of Mexico's national cuisine in late-twentieth-century global restaurant markets. Mexican culinary professionals embraced the indigenous heritage as a way of distinguishing themselves from industrialized Tex-Mex and Taco Bell versions produced in the United States.[29] An explicit program of gastronomic diplomacy achieved its greatest success in 2010, when UNESCO declared Mexico's peasant cuisines to be an intangible patrimony of humanity. Creolized versions of the dish contributed to this culinary revival, for example, through a romantic mole-grinding scene from the novel and film *Like Water for Chocolate*.[30] But the exoticism of indigenous cooking had the greatest appeal for international culinary tourists. Thus, the interest of outsiders finally convinced Mexican elites to overcome centuries of disdain for the native culture, including mole.

The Genealogy of Mole

The data examined here suggest four trends in the historical development of mole: regional diversification, baroque elaboration, a growing focus on "mole" at the expense of distinctive names, and a hegemony of Oaxaca over its rival Puebla. The growing acknowledgment of regional diversity is largely a product of the sources, particularly ethnographic cookbooks pursuing ever more exotic local recipes. The increasing predominance of the name *mole* over counterparts such as *clemole*, *manchamanteles*, and *pipián* may likewise result from the demands of literary production, as cookbook authors seek out what has become recognized as the national dish. The prominence of Oaxacan moles in recent cookbooks seems to respond to a growing demand for exoticism in Mexican cuisine. Finally, the growing elaboration of mole, indicated by the number of ingredients, also seems to have occurred over the twentieth century, due partly to more efficient supply chains, which made diverse ingredients more readily available to cooks. Nevertheless, the "baroque" interpretation of mole was surely also a self-fulfilling prophecy, driven in part by chefs seeking to claim their own signature dish by adding new ingredients such as blackberries and apricots. The end result of these trends has been a heightened division between mole as a product of domestic and community celebrations and mole as a pursuit of culinary tourism.

This chapter represents only a preliminary approach to the genealogy of mole based on limited, non-random samples of recipes, yet the techniques of network mapping hold promise for future research. Going forward, the lack of early colonial recipes looms as the largest impediment to reconstructing a family tree of the dish. Larger samples of recipes will make it possible to construct a more precise chronology of historical change, at least for the nineteenth and twentieth centuries. There has been no attempt to map the recipes geographically, but this too should be possible using network analysis, at least for the twentieth century. Nonetheless, the potential of digital methods to perceive historical changes in the patterns in mole production, other sauces, and other foods is clear.

Big data holds the potential for constructing a digital flavor profile that could serve as an archive of taste, mapping historical change over time and showing the relationships between particular recipes. Crowd sourcing offers a potentially useful method of constructing the databases needed for such a project. Real-time analysis of the recipes, which could situate the individual user's mole recipe within a graphic depiction of the larger family tree, would serve as an enticement for members of the public to participate. The challenges to producing software for such a project are formidable. Phylogenetic science offers statistical techniques for constructing such family trees, but such methods depend on basic assumptions about the pace of change and the ancestry of members that may not be valid for recipes, which are cultural constructs, not biological organisms. Nevertheless, more sophisticated network analysis on larger data sets could provide striking new insights on the development, not just of mole, but of other dishes such as curry.[31]

The family tree of mole is as complex, colorful, and conflicted as the Mexican nation it represents. With roots in the diverse indigenous cuisines of Mesoamerica, it has grown out along multiple, intertwined trunks. Despite centuries of pruning by culinary authorities, an exuberant, disorderly growth of popular practice surrounds the neat ornamental of nationalist ideology.

Mole de Guajolote (Turkey Mole)

This mole recipe exemplifies the extravagant combinations of Old World meats and spices that distinguished the elite cuisine of New Spain. Nevertheless, a comparison with modern cookbooks still shows a relatively narrow array of spices, demonstrating how the dish continues to evolve. Note that a *real* was one-eighth of a peso. Under the fixed prices of the viceroyalty, quotes were reversed, listing ounces per *real* rather than *reales* per ounce. This helped with the shortage of small change but did little to ease food shortages. The recipe is from the 1831 cookbook *Novísimo arte de cocina* (34–35). Courtesy of Centro de Estudios de la Historia Méxicana, Condumex, Mexico City.

Ingredients and Method:

For a large turkey, use two [ham] shanks [*codillos*] and a *real* of pork loin. [Take] two *reales* of *chile pasilla* and one *real* of *ancho*, de-vein and toast on a *comal* [earthenware griddle] until well browned but without burning. Put a *real* of tomatillos on to boil. Half [a *real*] of clove, half of cinnamon, a few grains of fine pepper, a little toasted coriander, the amount of toasted chile seeds that can be taken with three fingers of a hand, and half of sesame seed, also toasted. Grind together the spices and the chile, sprinkling with water until it is ground, and then remove [from the *metate* or grinding stone] and put in its place tomatoes and grind the seeds well. Season this mole putting a large *cazuela* [cook pot] greased with pork fat on the fire, then when it's hot, add the [divided] turkey in regular pieces [*presas*] and the shank and loin. After [browning], add the chile and soaking water to fry with the meat until it begins to splatter, then add the ground tomatoes and also the soaking water, and add to the meat enough water so that it remains covered and salt. Allow to simmer until the meat softens and thickens the broth. Serve with sesame seeds on top.

Appendix

Colonial

Dominga de Guzmán. *Recetario de doña Dominga de Guzmán, siglo XVIII. Tesoro de la cocina mexicana*. Mexico City: Conaculta, 1996.

Dos manuscritos mexicanos de cocina, siglo XVIII. Mexico City: Conaculta, 2002.

Libro de cocina Convento de San Jerónimo. Selección y transcripción atribuidas a Sor Juana Inés de la Cruz. Mexico City: Instituto de Cultura Mexiquense, 1979.

Libro de cocina de la gesta de independencia. Nueva España, 1817. Mexico City: Conaculta, 2002.

Libro de cocina del hermano fray Gerónimo de San Pelayo. Siglo XVIII. Mexico City: Conaculta, 2002.

Recetario novohispano: México, siglo XVIII. Mexico City: Conaculta, 2000.

Porfirian

Anduiza, Jacinto. *El libro del hogar*. Pachuca, Hidalgo: Ricardo Arquero, 1893.

Cortés, Lorena, Miguel Ferro Herrera, and Cecilia Maciel de Zafrilla. *Cocina queretana de principios de siglo*. Querétaro: Tradición y Cultura de Querétaro, 1997.

del Hoyo Cabrera, Eugenio, ed. *La cocina jerezana en tiempos de López Velarde. Recetas de Carmen Cabrera de Del Hoyo*. Mexico City: Fondo de Cultura Económica, 1972.

Formulario de cocina Mexicana: Puebla, siglo XIX. Mexico City: Conaculta, 2002.

La cocinera poblana y el libro de las familias. Novísimo manual práctico de cocina española, francesa, inglesa, y mexicana. 2 vols. Puebla: Narciso Bassols, 1877.

Maldonado de la Fuente, Celerina. *Recetario tradicional. Celaya, fines del xix*. Mexico City: Conaculta, 1999.

Nuevo cocinero mexicano en forma de diccionario. 1888. Paris: Librería de la Vda. de Ch. Bouret, 1999. Reprint, Mexico City: Miguel Angel Porrúa, 2007.

Pinedo, Encarnación. *El cocinero español*. San Francisco: E. C. Hughes, 1898.

Recetas prácticas para la señora de casa sobre cocina, repostería, pasteles, nevería, etc. Recopilados por algunas socias de la conferencia de la Santísima Trinidad para sostenimiento de su hospital. 2 vols. Guadalajara: Francisco Santoscoy, 1895.

Torres de Rubio, Vicenta. *Manual de cocina michoacana*. Zamora, Michoacán: Imprenta Moderna, 1896. Facsimile edition. Mexico City: Gobrierno del Estado de Michoacán, Fundación Herdez, Universidad Michoacana de San Nicolás de Hidalgo, 2004.

Contemporary

Aparicio Prudente, Francisca. *Recetario popular de Chilpancingo y Tixtla*. Mexico City: Conaculta, 2000.

Bayless, Rick. *Authentic Mexican: Regional Cooking from the Heart of Mexico*. New York: William Morrow, 1987.

Bayless, Rick. *Rick Bayless's Mexican Kitchen: Capturing the Vibrant Flavors of a World-Class Cuisine*. New York: Scribner, 1996.

Botella, Ofelia. *Recetario popular de Campeche*. Mexico City: Conaculta, 2000.

Chapa, Martha. *Cocina oaxaqueña*. León, Spain: Editorial Everest, 2001.

Chapa, Martha. *La república de los moles: El recetario más completo del platillo mexicano por excelencia*. Mexico City: Aguilar, 2005.

Frías Neve, Marcela, and Jesús Vargas Valdez. *Cocina regional de Chihuahua*. Chihuahua: Ediciones Nueva Vizcaya, 1996.

Henestrosa Ríos de Webster, Cibeles. *Recetario zapoteco del Istmo*. Mexico City: Conaculta, 2000.

Kennedy, Diana. *The Art of Mexican Cooking: Traditional Mexican Cooking for Aficionados*. New York: Bantam Books, 1989.

Kennedy, Diana. *The Cuisines of Mexico*. Rev. ed. New York: Harper & Row, 1986.

Kennedy, Diana. *My Mexico: A Culinary Odyssey with More than 300 Recipes*. New York: Clarkson Potter, 1998.

Kennedy, Diana. *Recipes from the Regional Cooks of Mexico*. New York: Harper Collins, 1978.

Levín Kosberg, Larry, ed. *Comida familiar en los estados de la república: Indice general.* Mexico City: Voluntariado Nacional Banrural, 1988.

Martínez, Zarela. *The Food and Life of Oaxaca, Mexico: Traditional Recipes from Mexico's Heart.* New York: Macmillan, 1997.

Olvera, Enrique. *Mexico from the Inside Out.* London: Phaidon Press, 2015.

Ortiz Tirado, Tonantzin. *Cocina tradicional morelense.* Mexico City: Conaculta, 2000.

Quintana, Patricia. *Mulli: El libro de los moles.* Mexico City: Grupo Gráfico Romo, 2004.

Ramos Aguirre, Francisco. *Viejos sabores de Tamaulipas.* Mexico City: Conaculta, 2000.

Trilling, Susana. *My Search for the Seventh Mole.* Oaxaca: Susana Trilling, 1996.

Notes

1. Concepción Lombardo de Miramón, *Memorias* (México, DF: Editorial Porrúa, 1980), 473; Instituto Nacional de Antropología e Historia, box 34, 4th series, leg. 109, doc. 16F, "*Almuerzo del 12 de Dic. 1865.*"
2. Jeffrey M. Pilcher, *¡Que vivan los tamales! Food and the Making of Mexican Identity* (Albuquerque: University of New Mexico Press, 1998), 25–27.
3. José Luis Curiel Monteagudo, "Construcción y evolución del mole virreinal," in *El mole en la ruta de los dioses*, Vol. 12 of *Cuadernos de patrimonio cultural y turismo,* ed. Gabriela Olivo de Alba (Mexico City: Conaculta, 2005), 29–53.
4. Franco Moretti, *Graphs, Maps, Trees: Abstract Models for Literary History* (London: Verso, 2005), 9–10.
5. Opportunistic sampling involves a non-random selection and may well introduce biases. In the future I hope to accumulate enough recipe data to make more robust sampling methods possible.
6. Literally, the godmother of one's child. On the mole-cooking version of the sewing circle, see Maria Elisa Christie, *Kitchenspace: Women, Fiestas, and Everyday Life in Central Mexico* (Austin: University of Texas Press, 2008), 71–74.
7. Francisco Santamaria, *Diccionario de Mejicanismos*, 5th ed. (Mexico City: Porrúa, 1992), 253, 406, 733, 1309.
8. Bernadino de Sahagún, *The Florentine Codex: General History of the Things of New Spain,* trans. Arthur J. O. Anderson and Charles Dibble, 13 vols. (Santa Fe, NM: School of American Research, 1950–1982), 9:37.
9. Ibid.
10. Vicenta Torres de Rubio, *Manual de cocina michoacana* (Zamora, Michoacán: Imprenta Moderna, 1896); facsimile edition (Mexico City: Gobrierno del Estado de Michoacán, Funcación Herdez, Universidad Michoacana de San Nicholás de Hidalgo, 2004), 200; Dominga de Guzmán, *Recetario de Doña Dominga de Guzmán, siglo xxviii, Tesoro de la cocina* (Mexico City: Conaculta, 1996), 152.
11. Santamaria, *Diccionario de Mejicanismos*, 733.
12. One politically connected author provides a mole for every Mexican state except Yucatán: see Martha Chapa, *La república de los moles: El recetario más completo del platillo mexicano por excelencia* (Mexico City: Aguilar, 2005).

13. Sahugún, *The Florentine Codex*, 9:37–38.
14. Santamaria, *Diccionario de Mejicanismos*, 733.
15. Curiel Monteagudo, "Construcción y evolución del mole virreinal," 33–34.
16. José Joaquin Fernánde de Lizardi, *The Mangy Parrot: The Life and Times of Periquillo Sarniento, Written by Himself for His Children*, trans. David Frye (Indianapolis: Hackett, 2004), 408–409.
17. Fernando Ortiz, "Los factores humanos de la cubanidad," in *Etnia y Sociedad*, ed. Isaac Barreal (Havana: Editorial de Ciencias Sociales, 1993), 1–20.
18. Jacinto Anduiza, *El libro del hogar* (Pachucaa, Hidalgo: Ricardo Arquero, 1893), 105.
19. Rebecca Earle, *The Body of the Conquistador: Food, Race, and the Colonial Experience in Latin America, 1492–1700* (Cambridge: Cambridge University Press, 2012).
20. Pilcher, *¡Que vivan los tamales!*, 42–43.
21. Enrique Florescano, *Memory, Myth, and Time in Mexico: From the Aztecs to Independence*, trans. Albert G. Bork and Kathryn R. Bork (Austin: University of Texas Press, 1994), 186.
22. José Luis Juárez López, *La Lenta emergencia de la comida mexicana: Ambigüedades criollas, 1750–1800* (Mexico City: Porrúa, 2000), 124–133.
23. Rubio, *Manual de cocina michoacana*, 94.
24. Manuel Payno, *Los bandidos del Rio Frio*, 24th ed. (Mexico City: Editorial Porrúa, 2004), 31.
25. José Tomás de Cuéllar, *The Magic Lantern*, ed. Margo Glantz, trans. Margaret Carson (New York: Oxford University Press, 2000), 84.
26. Carlos de Gante, "Santa Rosa de Lima y el Mole de Guajolote." *Excelsior*, December 12, 1926, n.p.
27. Ricardo Pérez Montfort, "El mole como símbolo de la mexicanidad," in *El mole en la ruta de los dioses*, Vol. 12 of *Cuadernos de patrimonio cultural y turismo*, ed. Gabriela Olivo de Alba (Mexico City: Conaculta, 2005), 71–85.
28. Josefina Velázquez de León, *Cocina Oaxaqueña* (Mexico City: Editorial Diana, 1991), 16.
29. Jeffrey M. Pilcher, *Planet Taco: A Global History of Mexican Food* (New York: Oxford University Press, 2012).
30. Laura Esquivel, *Como agua para chocolate* (Mexico City: Planeta, 1989), 74.
31. Moretti, *Graphs, Maps, Trees*, 110.

Selected Bibliography

Christie, Maria Elisa. *Kitchenspace: Women, Fiestas, and Everyday Life in Central Mexico*. Austin: University of Texas Press, 2008.

Curiel Monteagudo, José Luis. "Construcción y evolución del mole virreinal." In *El mole en la ruta de los dioses*. Vol. 12 of *Cuadernos de patrimonio cultural y turismo*, edited by G. Olivo de Alba, 29–53. Mexico City: Conaculta, 2005.

Earle, Rebecca. *The Body of the Conquistador: Food, Race, and the Colonial Experience in Latin America, 1492–1700*. Cambridge: Cambridge University Press, 2012.

Florescano, Enrique. *Memory, Myth, and Time in Mexico: From the Aztecs to Independence*. Translated by Albert G. Bork and Kathryn R. Bork. Austin: University of Texas Press, 1994.

Juárez López, Jose Luis. *La Lenta emergencia de la comida mexicana: Ambigüedades criollas, 1750–1800*. Mexico City: Porrúa, 2000.

Juárez López, Jose Luis. *Engranaje culinario: La cocina mexicana en el siglo XIX*. Mexico City: Conaculta, 2012.

Moretti, Franco. *Graphs, Maps, Trees: Abstract Models for Literary History*. London: Verso, 2005.

Ortiz, Fernando. "Los factores humanos de la cubanidad." In *Etnia y sociedad*, edited by Isaac Barreal, 1–20. Havana: Editorial de Ciencias Sociales, 1993.

Pérez Montfort, Ricardo. "El mole como símbolo de la mexicanidad." In *El mole en la ruta de los dioses*. Vol. 12 of *Cuadernos de patrimonio cultural y turismo*, edited by Gabriela Olivo de Alba, 71–85. Mexico City: Conaculta, 2005.

Pilcher, Jeffrey M. *¡Que vivan los tamales! Food and the Making of Mexican Identity*. Albuquerque: University of New Mexico Press, 1998.

de Sahagún, Bernadino. *The Florentine Codex: General History of the Things of New Spain*. Translated by Arthur J. O. Anderson and Charles Dibble, 13 vols. Santa Fe, NM: School of American Research, 1950–82.

Velázquez de León, Josefina. *Cocina Oaxaqueña*. Mexico City: Editorial Diana, 1991.

Jeffrey M. Pilcher, *Mole Poblano: Profile of Taste and Culture in Mexico Through Digital History Analysis*
In: *From Garum to Mole: Sauces and Identity in the Western World*. Edited by: Andrew Donnelly, Beth M. Forrest, and Deirdre Murphy, Oxford University Press.
DOI: 10.1093/9780190622138.003.0014

15

Mother of Whom, Exactly?

TOWARD A SCIENCE-INFORMED SAUCE CURRICULUM

Jonathan Deutsch

ONE OF THE first chefs discussed in Western culinary education is Georges Auguste Escoffier (1846–1935), often dubbed "the King of Chefs,"[1] or, with only some hyperbole, "the Patron Saint of Chefs."[2] Escoffier's journey to iconic chef was not unlike the career trajectory of many other boys at the time: He apprenticed at an uncle's restaurant in Nice, France, starting from the age of thirteen, from which he moved into a coveted hotel cook position. He was drafted into the army, serving as a chef there as well (and developing an interest in larger-scale food processing), and upon his return to civilian life opened a restaurant, *Le Faisan d'Or*, in Cannes.[3] Escoffier's rise from regional success to global leader was made possible through his affiliation with legendary hotelier Cesar Ritz (1850–1918), first at the Grand Hotel in Monaco, from 1884, and later at the Savoy Hotel in London, beginning in 1890, where he is credited with professionalizing the culinary workforce and praised for the development of iconic dishes such as Peach Melba.[4] Escoffier and his management colleagues were summarily fired from the Savoy in 1898 due to later substantiated allegations of receiving kickbacks from suppliers and diverting inventory—especially wine—from the Savoy to a new project, the Carlton Hotel.[5]

It is important to note that this last part of the story is not typically taught in culinary schools nor included in textbooks, though the ethics of purchasing and inventory controls are part of most culinary school curricula.[6] In any case, Ritz and Escoffier remained a team and went on to consult on many projects, including the Carlton, a partnership whose eponymous legacy endures.[7] Escoffier is generally credited not so much with being a cuisine innovator as with simplifying, systematizing, updating, and codifying French culinary practice, including much of the grandiose and complex work documented by his celebrity chef predecessor Marie-Antoine Carême.[8] In doing so, he produced a seminal book in culinary arts, *Le Guide culinaire* (2011/1903), translated in English as *The Complete Guide to the Art of Modern Cookery* (and similar titles in translation). In providing such a guide, Escoffier's work laid out the basic curriculum of formal culinary education that can be traced both to the major textbooks and course catalogs of secondary and postsecondary culinary programs in the United States and, indeed, throughout much of the West.[9] *Le Guide* is often referred to as the "culinary bible"[10] or, among cooks, simply as "the bible."

The three leading comprehensive culinary textbooks—*The New Professional Chef*;[11] *On Cooking*;[12] and *Professional Cooking*[13]—give credit where it is due. *The New Professional Chef*:

> When the Savoy Hotel opened in London in 1898 (under the direction of Cesar Ritz and Auguste Escoffier), *grande cuisine* was still the exception. These two gentlemen waged a successful campaign to assure that their *a la carte* offerings were of the finest, that their service was the best, and that it was all delivered on the finest china and crystal. As a result, ladies and gentlemen of good standing finally could be found in the dining rooms of restaurants in England, France and elsewhere.... Georges Auguste Escoffier (1847–1935) was a renowned chef and teacher. He was the author of *Le Guide culinaire*, a major work codifying classic cuisines that is still widely used by professional chefs. His other significant contributions include simplifying the classic menu in accordance with the principles advocated by Carême, and initiating the brigade system. *Escoffier's influence on the foodservice industry cannot be overemphasized.*[14]

On Cooking:

> One of the finest restaurants outside France was the dining room at London's Savoy Hotel, opened in 1889 under the directions of Cesar Ritz... and Auguste Escoffier. Escoffier is generally credited with refining the *grande cuisine* of Carême to create *cuisine Classique*.... By doing so, he brought French cuisine into the 20th century.... Called the "emperor of the world's kitchens," he is perhaps best known for defining French cuisine and dining during La Belle Époque.... Crediting Carême with providing the foundation for great—that is, French—cooking, Escoffier simplified the profusion of flavors, dishes and

> garnishes typifying Carême's work. He also streamlined some of Carême's overly elaborate and fussy procedures and classifications. *For example, he reduced Carême's elaborate system of classifying sauces into the five families of sauces still recognized today.*[15]

Professional Cooking:

> Georges-Auguste Escoffier (1847–1935), the greatest chef of his time, is still *revered* by chefs and gourmets as the father of twentieth-century cookery. His two main contributions were (1) the simplification of classical cuisine and the classical menu, and (2) the reorganization of the kitchen.... *Escoffier's books and recipes are still important reference works for professional chefs. The basic cooking methods and preparations we study today are based on Escoffier's work.* His book *Le Guide Culinaire*, which is still widely used, arranges recipes in a simple system based on main ingredient and cooking method, greatly simplifying the more complex system handed down from Carême.[16]

This chapter argues that the chef/hero worship of Escoffier's *Guide* belies its author's very intent. Escoffier would be disheartened to see so many direct parallels between his *fin de siècle* kitchen and ours. He would be especially troubled by the stagnant pedagogy as it relates to the work of the *saucier* and the retention of his own clean, but not very logical, classification of sauce types. A close read of Escoffier's writing, something that few of my fellow chef instructors admit to having done—though the editors note that it is now required reading in gastronomy courses at the Culinary Institute of America—reveals a much more tentative and evolving understanding than the dogmatic presentation of mother and small sauces common to culinary schools might suggest.[17] Indeed, chef-scholars Sarah Labensky, Alan Hause, and Priscilla Martel write in *On Cooking: A Textbook of Culinary Fundamentals*, "In this way, we follow the trail blazed by Escoffier, who wrote in the introduction to *Le Guide Culinaire* that his book is not intended to be a compendium of recipes slavishly followed, but rather a tool that leaves his colleagues, 'free to develop their own methods and follow their own inspiration... the art of cooking... will evolve as a society evolves... only basic rules remain unalterable.'"[18]

The points made in this chapter come from sources including the writing of *Escoffier* himself, the three leading culinary texts, which together comprise the "big three":[19] The Culinary Institute of America's *The New Professional*

Chef (for the purposes of this chapter, abbreviated as *ProChef*); Labensky, Hause, and Martel's *On Cooking: A Textbook of Culinary Fundamentals* (abbreviated as *OnCooking*); and Gisslen's *Professional Cooking* (abbreviated as *ProCook*), and my experience over the past decades in culinary education as a student and an instructor, and through countless discussions with colleagues.

Mother Sauces in Textbooks

Before *ProChef*, culinary curriculum was a hodgepodge of materials and approaches.[20] Some instructors taught from *Le Guide*, while others cobbled together their own recipes gathered from apprenticeships,[21] cookbooks designed for home cooks such as *The Joy of Cooking*,[22] and/or job training or military instructional manuals focused on large-scale feeding. The Culinary Institute of America (CIA) changed this practice when in 1962 they published *The Professional Chef*, now in its 11th edition (Folson 1962). *ProChef* was important in systematically and comprehensively presenting recipes for the U.S. professional kitchen; taken cover to cover, it served as a foundational curriculum for culinary students, covering cooking techniques as well as topics like professionalism, sanitation, cost controls, and service. The book, also referred to as "the bible," is used to this day at the CIA as well as other culinary schools. Two decades later, Wayne Gisslen (1983) published *Professional Cooking*, known for its exhaustive recipe testing and a different recipe-writing format, but it largely followed *ProChef*'s organization. With the explosion of food media (*The Food Network* first aired in 1993) and the proliferation of culinary schools in the 1990s, other competitors followed, notably Sarah Labensky and Alan Hause's *On Cooking* in 1995. Because these three books are comprehensive in scope, most culinary programs adopt only one of the three and use them across multiple courses, sometimes as a required or primary text, and other times as a reference book or supplemental source for recipes.

ProChef references Escoffier three times: in the chapter detailing the history of the profession, in discussing the origins of the toque, and in the chapter on stocks and sauces. Nearly every culinary program in the Western world emphasizes the mother sauces, as outlined by Escoffier. Using these three main culinary texts as a lens, let us consider how Escoffier's mother sauces are presented:

ProChef:

> Demi-glace, velouté, béchamel, tomato, and (in at least some instances) hollandaise are often referred to as the "grand sauces" or "mother

sauces." A sauce is considered to be a grand sauce if it met some basic criteria: It can be prepared in large batches, and then flavored, finished, and garnished in great variety, producing the hundreds and thousands of so-called "small sauces." This principle was still considered revolutionary in Carême's time. Escoffier's codification of sauces was considered a major advance.[23]

OnCooking:

> Classic hot sauces are divided into two groups: mother or leading sauces (Fr. *sauce mere*) and small or compound sauces. The five classic mother sauces are béchamel, velouté, espagnole (brown), tomato, and hollandaise. Except for hollandaise, leading sauces are rarely served as is; more often they are used to create the many small sauces.[24]

ProCook:

> Most classic sauces are built on one of five liquids or bases. The resulting sauces are called the leading sauces or mother sauces: white stock… for velouté sauces, brown stock for brown sauce or espagnole, milk for béchamel, tomato plus stock for tomato sauce, clarified butter for hollandaise.[25]

A close read reveals inconsistency and illogic in the way these sauces are presented. First, whither hollandaise? Hollandaise stretches the definition of a mother sauce, as these authors note. It is notoriously finicky, does not hold well (so should not be prepared in large batches), and is often served as a sauce as is. While it does have a number of classic derivatives, flavored derivatives are often made directly in modifying the mother sauce from the outset, rather than small additions later added to the mother sauce, due to the difficulty in safely holding for more than a few hours. Second, *ProChef* identifies *demi-glace* as a mother sauce (also served mainly as is), while *ProCook* and *OnCooking* classify it as a derivative sauce made from its mother, espagnole. Tomato is further challenging. While some recipes call for roux and also stock, it is easily thickened with the puréed flesh of the tomato and reduction, as is common in Italian cooking.

The three starch-thickened *grand* sauces work beautifully as a classic cuisine lesson in leading and derivative (or mother and small) sauces, as shown in Table 15.1. As the liquid becomes increasingly dark, from milk through

Table 15.1 Starch-Thickened Grand Sauces. Created by J. Deutsch.

Sauce	Liquid	Thickener	Small Sauce Examples
Béchamel	Milk	White roux	Cream (add cream)
			Mornay (add Gruyère)
			Soubise (sautéed onions)
Velouté	Chicken, white veal, or fish stock	Blond roux	Suprême (cream)
			Mushroom (sautéed mushrooms)
			Hungarian (sautéed onions and paprika)
Espagnole	Brown veal stock	Brown roux	Robert (dry mustard)
			Chasseur (mushrooms, shallots, and tomatoes)
			Bordelaise (red wine, shallots, and herbs)

brown veal stock, the color of the roux also deepens—and its thickening power lessens, teaching additional lessons about starch gelatinization. Each of these *grand* sauces boasts an expansive family tree of derivatives, many of which are named for important characters or for characteristic regional flavors; the etymology is a lesson in itself. Sauces like soubise and bordelaise appear on the finest menus today without irony. Other classic small sauce flavor combinations can be mined for contemporary interpretations. A further lesson is the continuum of thickness—the thickest béchamel becomes the glue that binds the croquette; a thinner version is the secret to good lasagna or macaroni and cheese. A thick velouté is a sauce, a thin one a cream soup base. There is a logic and order to the table for which Escoffier received his rightful praise.

But how do the rest of the mother sauces fit?

As seen in Table 15.2, the neat logic of the initial table breaks down. Tomato is not a liquid but rather a fruit that cooks into a liquid. Puréeing it, along with reducing, provides the necessary thickness by allowing the starches and pectin occurring in the tomato to gel, even without roux, as necessary to the other sauces which, if reduced without added thickener, turn to *glace* or syrup (in the case of stock) or burn and/or boil over (in the case of milk), rather than sauce. Clarified butter is not an aqueous liquid but rather a liquefied fat; the egg is used to emulsify in an entirely different process to starch gelatinization as in a roux-thickened sauce.[26] The tomato sauce derivatives have never endured in the canon; the hollandaise derivatives are more often flavored hollandaise sauces, and typically made into small sauces from the

Table 15.2 The Five Grand Sauces. Created by J. Deutsch.

Sauce	Liquid	Thickener	Small Sauce Examples
Béchamel	Milk	White roux	Cream (add cream) Mornay (add Gruyère) Soubise (sautéed onions)
Velouté	Chicken, white veal or fish stock	Blond roux	Suprême (cream) Mushroom (sautéed mushrooms) Hungarian (sautéed onion and paprika)
Espagnole	Brown veal stock	Brown roux	Robert (dry mustard) Chasseur (mushroom, shallots, and tomato) Bordelaise (red wine, shallots, and herbs)
Tomato	Tomatoes, white chicken, veal or pork stock	Optional roux	Spanish (sautéed onion, bell pepper, garlic and mushrooms) Creole (sautéed onion, celery, green bell pepper, garlic, and cayenne)
Hollandaise	Clarified butter	Egg	Béarnaise (tarragon) Mousseline (cream) Choron (Béarnaise plus tomato paste)

outset. We have kept the five mother sauces of Escoffier intact to the point where we teach them by caveat.

Escoffier would have hoped these books—and the instructors who teach from them—would have surpassed his classification published in 1903. He begins that book, "If the art of cookery in all its branches were not undergoing a process of evolution, and if its canons could be once and forever fixed, as are those of certain scientific operations and mathematical procedures, the present work would have no *raison d'être*."[27] He continues, later in the preface:

> I had at first contemplated the possibility of including only new recipes in this formulary. But it should be bore [*sic*] in mind that the changes that have transformed kitchen procedure during the last twenty-five years [approx. 1878–1903] could not all be classed under the head of new recipes; for, apart from the fundamental principles of

> the science, which we owe to Carême, and which will last as long as Cooking itself, scarcely one old-fashioned method has escaped the necessary new moulding required by modern demands. For fear of giving my work an incomplete appearance, therefore, I had to refer to these old-fashioned practices and to include among my new recipes those of the former which most deserved to survive. But it should not be forgotten that in a few years, judging from the rate at which things are going, the publication of a fresh selection of recipes may become necessary; I hope to live long enough to see this accomplished, in order that I may follow the evolution, started in my time, and add a few more original creations to those I have already had the pleasure of seeing adopted; despite the fact that this discovery of new dishes grows daily more difficult.[28]

If Escoffier anticipated a new volume a few years later, one can only imagine how he would feel to see his *Guide* as the foundational curriculum over a century later, likely a combination of chef ego gratification and disappointment in our glacial evolution.

Le Guide became the canonical work it is through a series of factors. First, Escoffier himself knew the significance and import of his work. He was the best-known chef of his time in Europe and even its title, *Le Guide*, underscores its definitiveness. His grandiose preface both marks the culmination of the publication of this seminal work and encourages readers (cooks and aspiring chefs) to surpass him in continuing their work. Second, until relatively recently, Escoffier's book was the only professional Western cooking training manual of its type. Third, the big three culinary textbooks, while updating and surpassing Escoffier in many ways, continue to be patterned after its topics and flow, allowing it to withstand many of the shifts in our culinary landscape and taste preferences over the past century.

Hollandaise as a Case

To reinforce our need for evolution beyond Escoffier's categorization, consider *sauce hollandaise* as currently taught by our big three textbooks and in most culinary schools.[29] Here is an excerpt from Escoffier's (1907) recipe:

> Move the saucepan to a corner of the fire or into a bain-marie [double boiler], and add a spoonful of fresh water and the yolks. Work the whole with a whisk until the yolks thicken and have the consistence of

> cream. Then remove the saucepan to a tepid place and gradually pour the butter on the yolks while briskly stirring the sauce. When the butter is absorbed, the sauce ought to be thick and firm.[30]

With only minor variations, our big three culinary texts reproduce Escoffier's recipe.

Gisslen acknowledges the difficulty of the technique, "Students tend to be afraid of hollandaise because it has a reputation for being difficult to make. True, precautions are necessary to avoid overcooking the eggs and to get the right consistency. But if you follow the instructions in the recipe carefully and keep in mind these guidelines, you should have no trouble."[31] In fact, my experience and that of my colleagues reveals quite a bit of trouble with teaching hollandaise in this way. First, it is as much an exercise in coordination (not without value in the professional kitchen, to be sure) as understanding. Hollandaise using Escoffier's method is best performed by a five-handed chef. One hand is needed to secure the pot and another the bowl atop the double boiler or bain-marie. Another is needed for whisking, another for pouring the butter, and a fifth to regulate the heat and mop the cook's brow. Students get the joke and do wish for their extra hands, especially as towels stabilizing the bowls ignite from the gas flame, eggs curdle, or arms tire. The technology of 1903 is simply inconvenient for making emulsified sauces. A proper hollandaise in the model of Escoffier has, along with perfecting the other mother sauces, become a rite of passage for foundational culinary education. Consider, however, Escoffier's fine print remark that follows his hollandaise recipe: "Experience alone—the fruit of long practice—can teach the various devices which enable the skilled worker to obtain different results from the same kind and quality of material."[32] Even without knowing what it would be, Escoffier knew that there is surely a better way than the method we still teach today.

While none of the three textbooks include blender or food processor instructions in their hollandaise recipe, many chefs find the higher shirr these machines provide to be a more reliable way to maintain a stable emulsion. While there is value to hand-whisking hollandaise in understanding the process, living history, and building coordination, to ignore technological advances that could simplify the method seems both technophobic and counter to the ethos of the *Guide*. Further, there are alternative methods entirely that are easier, more reliable, and eschewed by the texts and most instructors. In 1992, writer Harold McGee published a foolproof recipe for hollandaise. Seeing that a hollandaise is, essentially, an emulsified *beurre blanc*, he advocates combining cubed butter, egg yolk, and lemon juice in a small sauce pan and heating it over a low flame, stirring occasionally. It works! No vinegar and peppercorn reduction, no cumbersome double boiler, no coordination test, and no arm-fatiguing whisking. When I presented this idea at a conference, a self-assured culinary instructor claimed that McGee's recipe was not, in fact, a true hollandaise, since a classic hollandaise uses clarified butter.[33] That is because many chefs claim that clarified butter, with its moisture and milk solids removed, is more reliable in stabilizing the fickle emulsion that Escoffier's method yields. Whole butter is much more flavorful and more cost effective (since the milk solids removed in clarifying butter are typically discarded) and the advantage of clarification (namely, separating and removing the milk solids that burn at low heat) is moot in this application where the eggs curdle well below the temperature at which butter would burn.

Escoffier was indeed a culinary master. His vision and intelligence led him to understand that, when it comes to hollandaise—it bears repeating, "Experience alone—the fruit of long practice—can teach the various devices which enable the skilled worker to obtain different results from the same kind and quality of material."[34] He predicted that advances in food chemistry and the kitchen technology would supersede his method.

Toward a Science-Based Sauce Curriculum

While I do want my students to know and appreciate Escoffier, I do not want them to take his words as gospel but rather to see them as a key step forward in the codification of French classic cuisine. I do not want them to value French sauces more than Italian, Ethiopian, or Japanese simply because Escoffier dubbed them *grand* and the Western press agreed. I want them to understand that the key aspect of an emulsion is the science of an emulsion, not the coordination required to make it by hand. I want them to understand that an emulsion can be as weak as a vinaigrette stirred with a spoon and as strong as a permanent suspension made with an ultrasonic emulsifier, and all points on the continuum between, from rotary beater through high shirr blender. I want them to use these tools to achieve the desired outcome. The goal is not to push the boundary for its own sake—as 1970s chefs did by proving one could roast a chicken in a microwave or 2000s chefs did when they foamed anything that could possibly be foamed. But I do want them to know that a foam can be a sauce and how to make one. I want them to know that *mole* is a systematic sister to *romesco,* the latter of which can be traced to bread-thickened sauces of Persia, made popular in the Western world in the

Middle Ages. With that context, I want them to know that a reliable way to both thicken a sauce on the fly and reduce food waste is to keep some stale bread on hand—and I want them to remember the allergen implications of doing so. Restaurants have evolved, restaurant guests have evolved, and culinary education must do so as well.

Culinary schools have taken to *Le Guide* because its genius is in its organization. We crave simplicity and order. However illogical, there is a convenient neatness to the simplicity of *Le Guide* and particularly with regard to stocks, soups, and sauces. While Escoffier is somewhat less clear, imagine an instructor presenting a lesson on chicken, as ordered in Table 15.3. It's logical, neat, and tidy, at least until the exceptions—jus, pan gravy, coulis, poaching liquid, and so on—must be explained.

Joseph Hegarty, former head of the school of Culinary Arts and Food Technology at the Dublin Institute of Science and Technology (now called Technological University Dublin), ascribes our current reliance on these convenient but illogical frameworks to the lack of a strong research foundation in culinary arts.[35] He identifies four paradigms that chef-instructors use to justify their practices: (1) tradition (the way we do things); (2) prejudice (how I like it done); (3) dogma (this is the only way); and (4) ideology (this is what is done by the current orthodoxy). Being reliant on these practices keeps our field from reaching its potential, discourages exploration and innovation among students who would otherwise be at the height of their creativity (think of a fine-arts or performing-arts school and its students by analogy), and limits the generation of new knowledge.[36]

Of course, to abandon Hegarty's paradigms and shift the meaning-making to the students also shifts the power dynamic of the instructional kitchen—from "*Oui, chef*!" to "Why, chef?"[37] In response, chef-educators need to be secure enough to say, "I don't know," knowledgeable enough to explain the reasons, and skilled enough to motivate students to investigate. Traditional

Table 15.3 Culinary Building Blocks. Created by J. Deutsch.

Bones + Water	Stock
Bones + Meat + Water	Broth
Stock or Broth + Other Ingredients + Thickener	Soup
Stock or Broth + Thickener	Sauce

culinary educators would argue that this dynamic is sufficiently far-removed from industry reality to be inadvisable. Progressive educators would argue that our hierarchical industry environment is in concomitant need of reform.

It is time to leave the mother sauces, complete with the misfit purée and emulsified sauce, as a culinary history lesson, and move on to a science-informed sauce curriculum such as one stemming from Allen's codification of sauces based on their physical properties.[38] Sauces can be categorized not by mother and small or based on Escoffier's nineteenth-century simplification of the work of his eighteenth-century predecessor, Carême, but by their chemical and physical properties, as seen in Table 15.4.

Of course, this curriculum would benefit from more work and nuance, as well as comprehensiveness and the collaborative effort of colleagues. We could address, among other issues: How do we categorize packaged sauces like fish sauce or Worcestershire and their applications? Done properly, this approach to sauce curriculum would be cuisine agnostic, celebrating examples including but by no means limited to classic French sauces. Perhaps techniques made possible through advancing technologies, newly available ingredients, or new understandings of traditional foods will more quickly become part of the canon. For how many centuries has chickpea liquid (aquafaba) been part of the human diet? At what point do we see vegan "mayonnaise" (aquafaba emulsion) introduced as an essential sauce that every cook should know? As a cook, I certainly find it more useful than *chaud-froid sauce* (literally hot-cold sauce, a velouté usually with gelatin, served cold), which I made once in culinary school and never again.

Further, modernist or molecular gastronomy approaches would be normalized. In his chapter on sauces, Gisslen writes, "One category of new techniques is the use of nontraditional thickeners or binding agents for sauces [hydrocolloids].... To give you a taste of these techniques, the end of the chapter features several unusual sauces and other condiments employing these ingredients."[39] While ingredients like carrageenan, xanthan gum, and maltodextrin may be "unusual" in the classical kitchen, they are ubiquitous in packaged food and a logical/natural extension of our understanding of sauces. They are higher performing than the all-purpose flour, gelatin sheets, and yellow box of cornstarch that our colleagues have been relying on to teach the classical range of sauces. As our fetish for molecular cuisine fades into culinary history, even as its techniques and contributions are remembered, and applied, spheres become not an "unusual sauce," as Gisslen considers it, but rather a technique that the chef can employ as desired or needed.

Table 15.4 Toward a Science-Informed Sauce Curriculum. Created by J. Deutsch.

Base	Thickener	Example	Variation
Stock/Broth	Roux	Classic "mother" sauce: velouté or espagnole; gravy	Milk rather than stock yields béchamel; thinner for soup
Stock/Broth	Slurry	*Jus lié*, stir-fry, braising liquid; gravy	
Fat	Egg	Hollandaise (warm), mayonnaise (cold)	Gums can form a permanent emulsion
Fruit/Vegetable	Purée via natural starch/pectin or reduction	Tomato sauce, apple sauce, bean purées, coulis, pesto, barbecue sauce	Dips if thicker, starchy vegetable or additional pectin added if needed
Fruit/Vegetable	Chopped	Salsa, pesto, *pico de gallo*, relish, chutney, raita, curry paste, peanut sauce, cocktail sauce	
Oil	None	Flavored oil, *chimichurri*	Oil powders with maltodextrin
Sweetened liquid (juice, cheap balsamic, wine)	Reduction	Reduced balsamic, syrup, glaze	Can add hydrocolloid to enhance gel
Nearly any with potential structure	Air	Vegan mayo, foams	
Butter	None or emulsion	Brown butter, *beurre blanc*, *beurre noir*, *beurre rouge*, compound butter	
Cream	Reduction	Cream sauce, alfredo, infused cream	

My further hope is that such a curriculum can make culinary schools places of reflection, challenge, and innovation, rather than quasi-military academies that produce compliant and complacent workers for the industry. The recipe-based approach to sauce-making is transactional, literally *le guide*: follow these steps to get the desired result. A science-informed approach is transformative: these are ways we know sauces can be formed; try it. Further, a science-based approach allows sauce-making to remain cuisine agnostic, celebrating sauces wherever and however they may be made, in whatever flavor combinations make sense within the bounds of culture and creativity, rather than ascribing *grand-mère* status to French sauces and considering if one first needs others, lesser and secondary in importance. In our shrinking, multicultural world, the distinctions many culinary schools maintain between "classic" and "ethnic" cuisine is an ethnocentric anachronism.

As a start, read—really read—Escoffier. In 1903 he was bemoaning that:

> the number of alimentary substances is comparatively small, the number of their combinations is not infinite, and the amount of raw material placed either by art or by nature at the disposal of a cook does not grow in proportion to the whims of the public.... Personally, I have ceased counting the nights spent in the attempt to discover new combinations, when, completely broken with the fatigue of a heavy day, my body ought to have been at rest.[40]

In 1903, Escoffier thought culinary creativity was at the point of diminishing returns. How I would love to take Escoffier to dinner to see what chefs in 2023 are doing. And to see how he would rethink his sauce typology if he were as well traveled and well tasted as we can be today.

Variation of McGee's Science-Informed Hollandaise Recipe

Jonathan Deutsch, 2022
Yields one cup.

Ingredients:

2 egg yolks
4 ounces cold butter
1 tablespoon water
½ lemon, juiced
Salt and cayenne pepper to taste

Method:

1. In a small saucepan over low heat, whisk yolks, butter, and water together constantly until butter is completely melted.
2. If too thin, turn up heat slightly and whisk vigorously until nappe (coating the back of a spoon) texture is achieved.
3. Remove from heat and add freshly squeezed lemon juice, salt, and cayenne to taste. Strain through cheesecloth and serve immediately.

Thanks to Chefs Robynne Maii, James Feustel, and Edward Bottone for their work with foundational pieces that led to the development of this manuscript.

Notes

1. Kenneth James, *Escoffier: The King of Chefs* (London: Bloomsbury, 2003).
2. Paul Levy, "The Master Chef Who Cooked the Books," *The Telegraph*, June 2, 2012, http://www.telegraph.co.uk/foodanddrink/9320918/The-master-chef-who-cooked-the-books.html/.
3. Georges Auguste Escoffier, *Auguste Escoffier: Memories of My Life* (New York: John Wiley and Sons, 1996).
4. Levy, "The Master Chef Who Cooked the Books."
5. Ibid.
6. Jeffrey P. Miller and Jonathan Deutsch, "Culinary Arts: A Guide to the Literature," *Choice* 53, no. 8 (2016): 1115–1127.
7. Levy, "The Master Chef Who Cooked the Books."
8. Michael Symons, *A History of Cooks and Cooking* (Champaign: University of Illinois Press, 2000).
9. Jonathan Deutsch, "Revolutionizing Culinary Education: Can Cooking Save Our Food System?" *Dublin Gastronomy Symposium*, 2016, https://arrow.tudublin.ie/cgi/viewcontent.cgi?article=1098&context=dgs/.
10. Georges Auguste Escoffier, *Le Guide culinaire* (New York: John Wiley and Sons, [1903] 2011).
11. The Culinary Institute of America, *The New Professional Chef* (New York: Van Nostrand Reinhold, 1996).
12. Sarah Labensky, Alan House, and Priscilla Martel, *On Cooking: A Textbook of Culinary Fundamentals* (Englewood Cliffs, NJ: Pearson, 2011).
13. Wayne Gisslen, *Professional Cooking* (New York: John Wiley and Sons, 2015); Miller and Deutsch, "Culinary Arts: A Guide to the Literature."
14. The Culinary Institute of America, *The New Professional Chef*, 5, emphasis added.
15. Labensky, Hause, and Martel, *On Cooking*, 6, emphasis added.
16. Gisslen, *Professional Cooking*, 3, emphasis added.

17. Michael Ruhlman, *The Making of a Chef: Mastering Heat at the Culinary Institute of America* (New York: Henry Holt, 1997); Deutsch, "Revolutionizing Culinary Education."
18. Labensky, Hause, and Martel, *On Cooking*, 4.
19. Miller and Deutsch, "Culinary Arts: A Guide to the Literature."
20. Joseph Hegarty, *Standing the Heat: Assuring Curriculum Quality in Culinary Arts and Gastronomy* (London: Routledge, 2004).
21. Jacques Pépin, *The Apprentice: My Life in the Kitchen* (New York: Houghton Mifflin, 2003).
22. Irma Rombauer, *The Joy of Cooking* (St. Louis, MO: AC Clayton, 1931).
23. The Culinary Institute of America, *The New Professional Chef*, 276–277.
24. Labensky, Hause, and Martel, *On Cooking*, 195.
25. Gisslen, *Professional Cooking*, 160.
26. Gary Allen, *Sauces Reconsidered: Après Escoffier* (Lanham, MD: Rowman and Littlefield, 2019).
27. Georges Auguste Escoffier, *A Guide to Modern Cookery* (London: William Heinemann Ltd., 1907), i.
28. Escoffier, *A Guide to Modern Cookery*, ii.
29. Deutsch, "Revolutionizing Culinary Education."
30. Escoffier, *A Guide to Modern Cookery*, 22–23.
31. Gisslen, *Professional Cooking*, 194.
32. Escoffier, *A Guide to Modern Cookery*, 30.
33. Deutsch, "Revolutionizing Culinary Education."
34. Escoffier, *A Guide to Modern Cookery*, 30.
35. Deutsch, "Revolutionizing Culinary Education."
36. Hegarty, *Standing in the Heat.*
37. Deutsch, "Revolutionizing Culinary Education."
38. Allen, *Sauces Reconsidered.*
39. Gisslen, *Professional Cooking*, 202.
40. Escoffier, *A Guide to Modern Cookery*, iii.

Selected Bibliography

Allen, Gary. *Sauces Reconsidered: Après Escoffier*. Lanham, MD: Rowman and Littlefield, 2019.

The Culinary Institute of America. *The New Professional Chef*. New York: Van Nostrand Reinhold, 1996.

Deutsch, Jonathan. "Revolutionizing Culinary Education: Can Cooking Save Our Food System?" *Dublin Gastronomy Symposium*, 2016, 1–4. https://arrow.tudublin.ie/cgi/viewcontent.cgi?article=1098&context=dgs/.

Deutsch, Jonathan. "Can Improvisation Save Culinary Education?" *Liminalities: A Journal of Performance Studies* 14, no. 1 (2018): 169–184.

Escoffier, Georges Auguste. *A Guide to Modern Cookery*. London: William Heinemann Ltd., 1907.

Gisslen, Wayne. *Professional Cooking*. New York: John Wiley and Sons, 2015.

Hegarty, Joseph. *Standing the Heat: Assuring Curriculum Quality in Culinary Arts and Gastronomy*. London: Routledge, 2004.

Labensky, Sarah, Priscilla Martel, and Alan Hause. *On Cooking: A Textbook of Culinary Fundamentals*. Englewood Cliffs, NJ: Pearson, 2011.

Miller, Jeffrey P., and Jonathan Deutsch. "Culinary Arts: A Guide to the Literature." *Choice* 53, no. 8 (2016): 1115–1127.

Jonathan Deutsch, *Mother of Whom, Exactly?: Toward a Science-Informed Sauce Curriculum* In: *From Garum to Mole: Sauces and Identity in the Western World*. Edited by: Andrew Donnelly, Beth M. Forrest, and Deirdre Murphy, Oxford University Press. DOI: 10.1093/9780190622138.003.0015

Index

Note: Tables and figures are indicated by an italic "*t*" and "*f*", respectively, following the page number.

For the benefit of digital users, indexed terms that span two pages (e.g., 52–53) may, on occasion, appear on only one of those pages.